GENERATIONS PAST

GENERATIONS PAST

Youth in East African History

Edited by

Andrew Burton and

Hélène Charton-Bigot

OHIO UNIVERSITY PRESS
ATHENS

Ohio University Press, Athens, Ohio 45701
www.ohioswallow.com

Printed in the United States of America
Ohio University Press books are printed on acid-free paper ∞ ™

17 16 15 14 13 12 11 10   5 4 3 2 1

Library of Congress Cataloging-in-Publication Data

Generations past : youth in East African history / edited by Andrew Burton and Hélène Charton-Bigot.
p. cm.
Includes bibliographical references and index.
ISBN 978-0-8214-1923-6 (hc : acid-free paper) — ISBN 978-0-8214-1924-3 (pbk. : acid-free paper) — ISBN 978-0-8214-4343-9 (electronic)
1. Ethnology—Africa, Eastern. 2. Social change—Africa, Eastern. 3. Age groups—Africa, Eastern. 4. Intergenerational relations—Africa, Eastern. 5. Young men—Africa, Eastern. 6. Africa, Eastern—Social conditions. I. Burton, Andrew (Andrew Ross) II. Charton-Bigot, Hélène.
GN658.G46 2010
967.6—dc22

2010024450

Contents

Acknowledgments

This book has its origins in a multidisciplinary 2006 conference held in Nyeri, Kenya, titled Youth in Eastern Africa: Past and Present Perspectives. It was organized by the British Institute in Eastern Africa (BIEA) and the Institut Français de Recherche en Afrique (IFRA) (Nairobi). We thank both institutions and the French Ministry of Foreign Affairs for their financial support for the conference, and we thank the presenters and participants who attended the conference. Although not all the conference papers were suitable for inclusion in a book on the history of youth, the presentations and the debates they provoked have nevertheless shaped this volume. We are most grateful to Benson Kimeu of the British Institute in Eastern Africa for providing the map that appears at the front of this volume; to Gillian Berchowitz of Ohio University Press, for making the production of the book such a painless experience; and to Centre d'études de l'Afrique noire and l'Institut d'études politiques de Bordeaux. Finally, as ever, thanks go to our spouses, Paulette Jones and Vincent Bigot, for their patience, encouragement, and support.

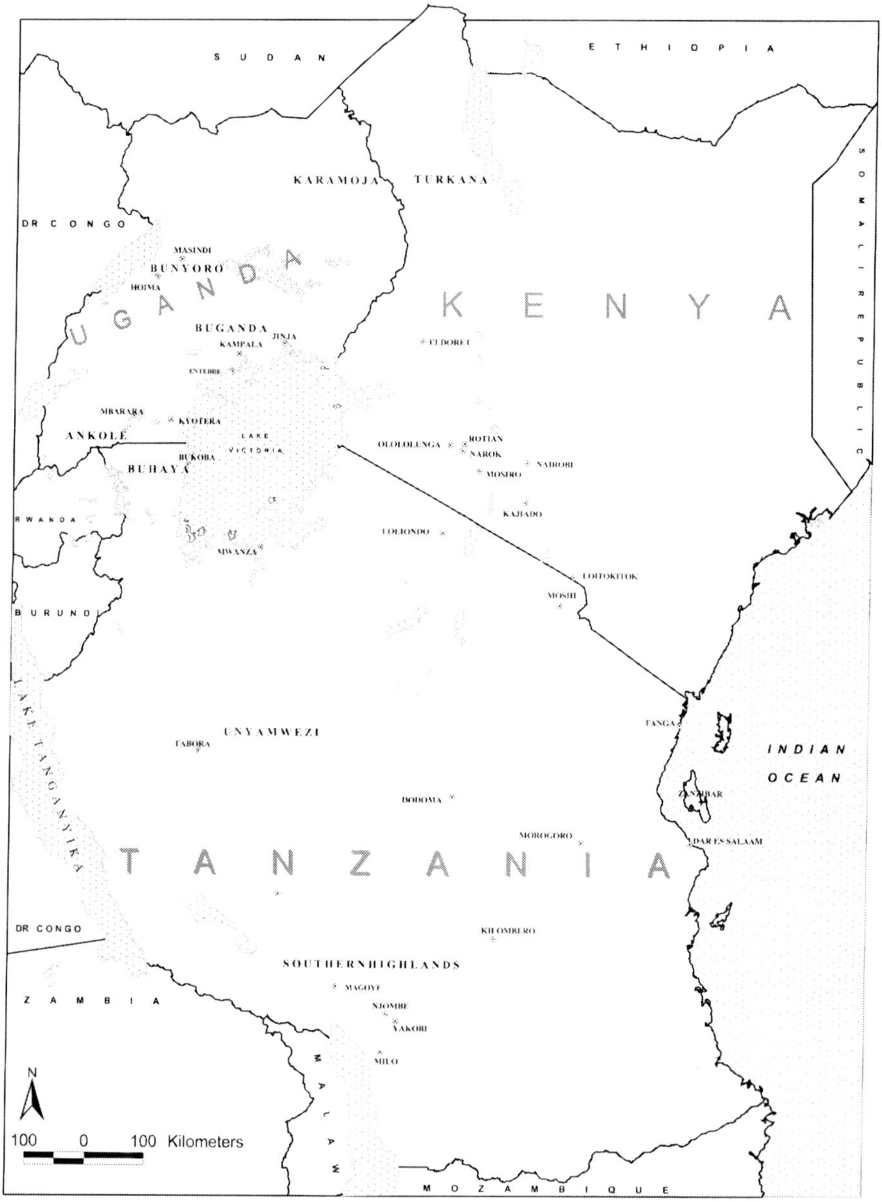

East Africa with places mentioned in the text marked

Introduction

G. THOMAS BURGESS AND ANDREW BURTON

GENERATION HAS LONG formed a key theme of Africanist scholarship. For much of the twentieth century anthropologists produced classic monographs on age-grades and age-sets in rural societies, frequently observing how formal rituals such as initiation and marriage mark the passages of the life cycle and endow Africans with status, control over resources, wisdom, and civic virtue. They characterized gerontocracy and patriarchy as systems of order and/or dynamic tension, and correctly observed that, at least in male society, no concept or social category surpassed generation both in terms of its importance in governing relations and as a source of values and sensibilities. In no way fixed or immune to internal or external pressures, patriarchal discourse and ritual served as references and anchoring principles that were inherited, contested, and reinvented over time.

Although anthropologists developed a series of well-rehearsed understandings and explanatory terms such as age grades and age sets, their ethnographies did not always examine how, particularly in the colonial era, the common understandings and institutions that had long governed relations between generations—and which constituted a key means by which Africans maintained social order—were experiencing profound and often irreversible change. The major exceptions were studies animated by colonial worries over the perceived decline of "tribal" discipline. What is perhaps more obvious now is that, as young people in Africa migrated in greater numbers to towns and cities, their immersion in a new world of urban tastes, sounds, and stimuli, and new encounters with diverse peoples and conditions led to relative anonymity and often a process of personal reinvention and the embrace of new identities. Generation lost its fixed currency and was often reduced to the status of a secondary or tertiary category—and for most scholars a conceptual afterthought. And as the village and clan in Africa lost integrity—at least in the eyes of many observers—as reportedly timeless and self-enclosed entities, so also in Africanist literature did the concept of youth lose its once seemingly immutable aspect. While some anthropologists and others sought to understand and chart the endurance or demise of gerontocratic values and control over the young, most scholars by the 1970s chose, if anything, to simply note the youthfulness of their actors, to recognize youth as a transitional category, while paying little attention to the label as a discrete social—or analytical—group.[1] Most anthropologists no longer considered generation fashionable or compelling and turned toward the study of other categories such as gender, class, and ethnicity. Historians were particularly uninterested in generation as a conceptual tool.

Of late, however, this has begun to change. After absorbing some of the recent advances made in African studies, scholars now find themselves better placed to reexamine categories such as generation that once had, and continue to have, descriptive power. And as historians begin to assume the same confidence regarding the examination of postcolonial Africa as they have long possessed in their analyses of colonialism, they will likely find the endurance of generation as an ordering principle and means by which Africans explain the world as a promising field of research. In the first decade of the twentieth century scholars have, fortunately, revisited youth, and a number of major, interdisciplinary conferences have taken place with generation as the organizing theme. An important literature on the subject is emerging.[2] As an academic topic, it appears that youth has—so to speak—come of age. This is equally true of East Africa as of other parts of the continent.[3]

Some publications chart the emergence of a "youth bulge" in African populations.[4] However, youthful predominance has in fact been characteristic of African societies for at least half a century now. Taking mainland Tanzania as an example of continent-wide trends, the first reliable national census in 1948 discovered 45 percent of the population was under sixteen and almost 90 percent under forty-five. In the 1957 census the percentages of those under sixteen and forty-five were broadly similar. Breaking the age groups down further one discovers a full 70 percent of the population was 29 or under. Children remained the dominant group; those from birth to age fourteen constituted 42 percent of the overall population. By contrast, that section of the population which might be characterized in the African setting as having reached full maturity—those over forty who as elders would have achieved positions of seniority and power in local societies—represented a mere 17 percent of the total population. The main features of this lopsided age distribution continued throughout the remainder of the twentieth century. In the most recent 2002 census those aged twenty-nine or under constituted 76 percent of the total population; those forty and older, 17 percent.[5] Given the numerical preponderance of the young in Africa, the recent scholarly interest is hardly surprising. Indeed, when children and youth have formed a demographic majority from at least the middle of the last century, one may ask why youth has not attracted more attention and, in particular, why generation has not been at the heart of historiographical analysis.

Population statistics suggest that the young matter, but they don't explain why or how. Probably the greatest proportion of recent interest in youth derives, unsurprisingly, from the questions raised by Africa's demographic imbalance, which is often blamed for a series of social, economic, and political problems. Many now embrace the term "youth crisis," the general contours of which include accelerating urbanization, chronic underemployment, delinquency, violence, and the spread of HIV/AIDS. This crisis appeared more obvious in the late twentieth century, when many states in Africa were no longer able to maintain patrimonial ties and networks sustained over previous decades, and underwent a process of contraction and at least partial collapse. In the 1980s and 1990s hundreds of millions of young people were less able to look to the state to provide a minimum of security, employment, or education. Failures on the macro political level worsened an already intense competition over scarce land, work, and schooling. Michelle Gavin observed that "[m]any of Africa's youth are [now] caught in a Peter Pan scenario gone terribly wrong. Try as they might, they cannot seem to become adults."[6]

While observers disagree over the precise relationships between demography, underdevelopment, weakening social ties, and political crises, it is hard not to see a broad correlation among all of these, or that youth may serve as both victims and unwitting agents of general crises. Jon Abbink noted that although young people are often victims of a "faulty modernization," and that to be young in Africa has come "to mean being disadvantaged, vulnerable, and marginal," it is also true that "[b]y their sheer numbers, their availability, and their eagerness to take up anything that may relieve them of conditions of poverty, idleness or ennui, youth are easily recruited by political parties, armed groups or criminal networks."[7] The title of Abbink and van Kessel's edited collection, *Vanguards or Vandals,* illustrates the ambiguous position in which many youth find themselves today. The phenomenon of the child soldier, of a boy or girl at the same time vulnerable and ultra-empowered, speaks tragically of the limits to which young people in Africa could be pushed at the end of the twentieth century by poverty and hopelessness. Exploited by thugs and warlords who force them to perform ritualized acts of inhuman violence—in a modern-day perversion of what in precolonial times was a fairly common warrior ethic—gun-toting youth have played an obvious role in state collapse from Somalia to Sierra Leone. In this instance global media images do not necessarily deceive; they suggest the capacity of youth—in limited and specific locations—to both resist and reproduce systems of violence and exploitation, to both desire and destroy a social order that provides a minimum of security and opportunity.[8] According to Frederick Cooper, the "blockages of generation" in the late-twentieth century produced an "apocalyptic destructiveness" among young people.[9] The crisis of the postcolonial state is at least partly a crisis of the process of maturation, particularly for males.

Few would disagree with the term "youth crisis." Discerning the extent to which the crisis has contributed to—or been the consequence of—the weakening of Africa's social fabric and the decline of the state remains, however, one of the more challenging research agendas in African studies. Gavin observed that "[i]t is easy to develop a generalized sense that "youth bulge" is code for marauding, angry young men,"[10] even though such violence has become a way of life for only a relative unfortunate few. Another continual temptation is to assume that generational conflict and the youth "crisis" are only about as old in Africa as the millions the term is intended to represent, when in fact it is much older. Nor is youth involvement in crime and violence anything new; the service rendered by child and youth soldiers to latter-day warlords has its precolonial analogue, when during the slave trade youth in Africa performed a similarly destructive role for equally exploitative elders.

Another temptation is to consider youth violence a problem unique to Africa—an example of African exceptionalism—or to be certain that there is something in youth that is inherently violent. It's also easy to ignore the social, economic, and political contexts of violence. No one has perhaps drawn more attention outside the academic community to Africa's youth crisis than Robert Kaplan, for whom—in his travels through West Africa in the 1990s—young men were "out of school, unemployed, loose molecules in an unstable social fluid that threatened to ignite." Visiting a slum in Cote d'Ivoire, Kaplan observed, "Geology, like the birthrate . . . appeared to be unduly accelerating. Here, young unemployed men passed the time drinking beer, palm wine, and medicinally strengthened gin while gambling on pinball games. . . . These are the same youths who rob houses at night in more prosperous Ivorian neighborhoods. . . . The decaying, vegetal odor . . . was intense. Nature appeared far too prolific in this heat, and much of what she created spoiled quickly."[11] Kaplan's remarkable claim that crowds of unemployed men in West Africa constituted a serious potential threat to the security and stability of Western societies became, after September 11, 2001, more or less accepted wisdom in the sphere of American policymaking, as fears of terrorism spawned by poverty and injustice overlaid worries about the capacity of the West in an era of globalization to quarantine itself from Third World crises.

Most scholars working in Africa would probably disagree with such an assessment; moreover, we consider it our duty to understand, with some degree of sympathy, the social origins of such violence, and to resist the slur of "senseless" violence often imputed to African societies. Yet the character of youth violence in Africa is not always clear. What is it that strikes the observer most immediately or remains after long reflection—the strategic and rational aspects of violence or instead its lumpen and whimsical cruelty? Donald Donham reminds us that "one of the crucial properties of violence" is "the inherent potential to 'unmake' the social world, to create murk and uncertainty. Sometimes analysts will not be able to rise above this murkiness, and pretending to do so may be one of the most serious kinds of misrepresentations of violence."[12] The difficulties of rising above such uncertainty may explain why sometimes we, like Kaplan, depend on literary evocations of the "youth crisis" and employ similarly apocalyptic and totalizing terms to describe its violence. For example, youth in the 1990s, due to lack of education and employment, were "a smoldering fire ready to burn African urban areas."[13] Youth are often the "mutant citizens of the modern nation, purveyors of its violent undersides."[14] "Illegality has become the norm for young people and their territory for affronting the permanent counter-violence of the state."[15]

The uncertainties inherent in understanding the origins of youth violence extend also to any assessment of the global or continent-wide conditions faced by contemporary African youth; in some treatments "youth" becomes a catchall existential category that encompasses all the subaltern despairs—and desires—of the postcolonial condition. Such youth are also sometimes hard to pin down. They are at the center and the periphery; they are at the forefront and at the margins; they are empowered agents, and they are hapless victims; they are everywhere and nowhere, everything and nothing. Yet not entirely so: they do overwhelmingly tend to be urban, hypercosmopolitan in their consumer tastes and cultural repertoires, and utterly precocious in their rejection of their elders and the social imaginary of the postcolonial state. In the memorable words of Mamadou Diouf, youth in Africa are engaged in "the radical questioning of the nationalist discourse, of its imaginary and the totality of its texts." They have "embraced irregular ways and adopted dissident and unconventional practices that transport them towards worlds where Africa is either absent or ignored."[16] Youth are seeking "the constitution of individuality on the margins of the ethnic group, citizenry, and the state." They reject "the past of ancestors, traditions, and the state."[17]

There is no denying the distance between pre- and postcolonial Africa, or that patriarchal and nationalist narratives have in some settings been eclipsed. Yet such an exclusive emphasis on precocious resistance and the "logic of rupture"[18] invites a corrective response. The same applies to a more general fixation shared by journalists and academics alike on youth violence. Both Frederick Cooper and Jay Straker have recently and separately called for more attention to the "invisible" and "inaudible"[19] cousins of the hyperhip left out of such accounts. "Before African youth becomes intellectually recast as a protean social collective that operates mysteriously beyond the nation-state and the entire postcolonial epoch," Straker writes, "one should check in with the local youths to find out precisely what is on their mind at the millennial turn." He asserts, based on his research among secondary school students of Guinea's forest belt, that the world evoked by some scholars would appear "strange to the great majority of African youth struggling to forge optimal lives in settings where, for the foreseeable future, matters of nationhood, state authority and local socio-cultural customs still impinge powerfully on everyday life." Straker's young informants "eschew rather than embrace or embody socio-historical rupture." They "seek improved possibilities for productive citizenship within the structures of community, nation and epoch they already know, love, and hate."[20]

Generation *does* help to explicate contemporary crises, both as an idiom for ordering social and political relations and as a language of values and attitudes centered, for example, on such questions as how a boy becomes a man. The quest for masculine respectability, which animates young political actors, officers, and child soldiers to wage war or make peace, seems at the very heart of the matter. Yet it is a mistake to assume that all the study of generation can possibly yield are further insights into war and conflict in African history. Generation speaks to the core of social sensibilities in Africa and how they are reproduced and reinvented over time.

As the study of generation continues to develop, we will likely see more works that seek to gender our understandings of "youth." While both males and females are included in the language of generation, its emphasis was and is masculine. In precolonial patriarchal societies, men were the leading antagonists in contests over access to public power, women, and ritual authority. John Iliffe observes that "[c]ompetition for wives in polygynous societies made conflict between male generations one of the most dynamic and enduring forces in African history, whereas the ample availability of land minimized other forms of social conflict."[21] Richard Waller notes that in colonial times, "youth" had more relevance to the experience of males; adolescence was largely a male category.[22] For girls and women, the lines of conflict were more commonly drawn along lines of gender than generation. In light of the complex and fluid ways in which individuals have sought through the maturation process to become men or women, it is likely that separate studies of male and female and generations will continue to emerge. The pursuit of both masculine and feminine success and dignity have been key animating principles of historic change, in Africa as on other continents; the most violent crises of maturation have been predominantly male crises, hence the male bias in the scholarly literature.[23] With the recent rise of violence as a specific category of research, the male bias to youth studies will likely continue.[24]

In general, generation embodies a rich and shifting language of rights, duties, and expectations that in the past and until now helps explain what Africans perceive to be the bases for both social order and chaos. To what extent gerontocratic values have endured or deteriorated and how these processes relate to images of past order and present chaos seem to make up a promising research agenda. Certainly the decline of village institutions, secret societies and rituals dedicated to reproducing knowledge, respect, and discipline, and the incapacity of the postcolonial state to sustain modern institutions of comparable pedagogical power appear relevant to the questions asked by a growing assortment of observers of Africa's contemporary "youth crisis." How did children and youth in precolonial times learn the duties and rights of membership and belonging? And how do they arrive at such notions today? Generation seems important enough for scholars to be willing to engage with rather than walk away from the category's subjective meanings, especially when they remember that such contingency, when compared with that of other identities, is in no way exceptional. This collection aims to address some of the existing absences in the study of youth and generation, offering exploratory accounts of the position of youth in East African societies over the past two centuries.

Youth in East African History

Scholarly reluctance to study youth in part derives from doubts about the label's utility as an analytical category. What usefulness does a term have if it refers to a possible majority of the population, or does not seem to be discrete, homogeneous, or possess any constant boundaries in terms of class origins, interests, worldviews, gender, or even age? Definitions of "youth" emerge out of local idioms and circumstances and are constantly shifting, located somewhere between ten and as much as forty-nine years of age.[25] It's easier to simply note the youthfulness of historical actors, or that youth play a key role, both positive and negative, in the continent's history and current conditions, than to work toward a set of common understandings about youth that are neither banal nor easily assailable. How can youth be defined? How is the category constructed? Is youth a primary or secondary identity? Are young people to be known as "youth" or by some other name? Do youth share distinct characteristics as a stage in the life cycle? With the intelligibility of youth agency in doubt, generation has frequently served as an ambiguous and obscure reference point on historiographical maps.

It's helpful to remember that in twentieth-century East Africa, generation constituted both a hard and a soft conceptual category, both an "ancient" and a temporary cultural label. Youth appeared as a recognized phase in the life cycle, carefully framed and enshrined by a continuous cycle of public rituals, and possessing a host of well-established understandings regarding its characteristics and functions. Young males were often cast as warriors, servants, or tolerated delinquents. In such communities a high value was placed on age, reproduction, continuity, and security. Where discontinuity was more decisive, however, youth emerged less as a phase in the life cycle than as a historical cohort. Youth were defined less by a set of inherited discursive constructs than by unique historical circumstances and narratives that set their generation apart from others before or after, and which allowed a greater degree of negotiation, flux, and invention.

A vast anthropological literature has emphasized youth as an "ancient" category and has asserted that generation in East Africa to varying extents determined men's access to authority, status, women, and ritual power. The reverse was also true: distinctions in male society between autonomy and dependency were expressed locally through generation. In some groups, pastoralist societies in particular, generation embodied a series of precise and highly articulated rankings, each rank or age grade possessing a considerable degree of affinity and connectedness, and with its own codes of discipline. Although women sometimes employed their own age rankings, the tensions embedded in relations between female generations did not as often provide the substance of village ritual, since public authority remained largely a masculine preserve, in protest of which the women often organized. Eisei Kurimoto and Simon Simonse note that women did not overlook "the opportunity the system offered them: to unite in opposition to the men."[26]

Male initiation rites, meanwhile, celebrated seniority and provided instruction that reinforced age deference as a principle necessary for communal cohesion. They institutionalized stratification, promised eventual advance, and gave generational antagonisms an acceptable and controlled public expression. They were "as much arenas for power games" as "a mechanism for dealing with corporate tasks or a ceremonial façade for gerontocratic power."[27] In most agrarian societies, meanwhile, social promotion was achieved through the institution of marriage. A "youth" was typically a bachelor without the resources, as yet, to marry and to exercise authority over the labor of his wife or wives and children. Marriage wasn't just an initiation that ended an age of reputed irresponsibility; it signaled a man's promotion, however contested, to the rank of overseer. Thus if Marx defined classes according to their access to modes of production, anthropologists have repeatedly described how, despite endless local variations, access to women and reproduction determined men's generational status.[28] The manner in which juniors in Africa have historically been cast as clients in relation to their elders has been as real as class divisions between workers and capitalists in Europe.

Such systems were characterized by conflict as much as cooperation. Female agency, for example, often complicated conflicts between junior and senior males over women, cattle, and land. All-male generational disputes were sometimes forgotten when women sought to renegotiate their rights as wives and daughters. Junior and senior men formed alliances when their control over wives and daughters was threatened.[29] Or not. Justin Willis writes that in precolonial East Africa junior-senior male relations were characterized by constant strain, hostility, insubordination, and the potential for violence. Young men posed serious challenges through their indiscriminate cattle raiding or when they seduced the wives of their elders. "Men's collective power was threatened by the sexual power of women and the sexual weakness of men. . . . The seductive power of women regularly breached the imagined solidarity of elder men, creating disputes amongst those who claimed to control society."[30]

Youth referred not only to a system of ranks but also to a world of social expectations, of ideas of duty, honor, and virtue. While Meru youth in precolonial Kenya were supposed to abstain from alcohol and sex, and display their bravery and cunning through cattle theft and combat, their elders were exempt from such expectations.[31] Such social mores were most sustainable during periods of security and social stability; in conditions of natural catastrophe or social crisis, youth rebelled against such standards. When youth in large numbers were unable within the village or clan to marry and assume adult status, the patriarchal principles that served as the bases for village ethics lost meaning and force. Age corresponded less and less with generation, inheritances were postponed or lost completely, and junior status extended indefinitely. Such delays undermined the capacity of the old "to manipulate knowledge and re-invent tradition"[32] and encouraged juniors to look for exit options from dependence on their seniors. When young men were no longer convinced they could realize respectability through their patience, conformity, and best efforts, they looked for alternative ways of advancing their status outside the community. Through migration, long-distance trade, or slave raiding they could escape a system that failed to offer promotion, or only did so after what young men regarded as intolerable delays. Warlords able to acquire guns and ranks of young followers threatened lineage systems that awarded power and privilege according to ancestry and seniority.[33] Young men turned to violence as an opportunity, then and now, to seize and usurp power, women, and status, especially in conditions of deteriorating patrimonial ties.

While gerontocratic practices and discourses endured throughout the twentieth century, changing political and economic conditions forced revision and adaptation. Colonialism introduced unprecedented tensions between youth and elders, in part through the contradictory ramifications of policies pursued. On the one hand, as they erected early structures of colonial governance the British sought to access legitimacy in East Africa by identifying and associating colonial rule with established indigenous, mostly gerontocratic, sources of authority. Under indirect rule officials invariably turned to elders in their attempts to understand, and to order, local societies; in doing so they fossilized relations between young and old at a time of unprecedented change. Indeed, Christianity, capitalism, and urbanization infinitely complicated generational relations. "Two aspects of [colonial] subjection most offended men of honour [i.e., elders]," observes John Iliffe, " . . . loss of authority over the women and young people of their homesteads."[34] From the early colonial period elders voiced perennial complaints bemoaning the degenerative impact of foreign influences on youth behavior.[35] As in other parts of the world, such complaints had cyclical characteristics as one generation contrasted nostalgic, idealized versions of their youth with the behavior of their successors.[36] The pattern extended into the postcolonial period as familiar concerns continued to be voiced.[37]

For many Africans, their colonial journeys compelled an encounter with at least selected elements of the modernist package. They went to school, migrated long distances, worked for wages, and became responsible for their own bridewealth payments. They adopted new religious identities and became "self-made" men and women of the towns. Colonial conditions undermined the categorical stability of generation as young people reevaluated their roles, rights, and duties in society, in reference to accepted wisdom and the texture of public rituals, as well as a new set of social and economic relationships of unique colonial provenance. In such circumstances young people gained the analytical distance to question the validity of gerontocratic discourse and the assumption that superior age should automatically endow their elders with specialized knowledge, wealth, or ritual power. Their distance from patriarchal expectations only increased when colonial policy began to shift around 1940. During World War II and its immediate aftermath officials abandoned elders as conservative relics of an outmoded African past—though they often retained a certain administrative and rhetorical utility—in favor of a younger generation exposed to colonialism's more progressive aspects.[38]

By the postwar years, seniority was in many respects no longer celebrated so much as youthfulness—both by the colonial state and younger educated Africans who increasingly came to share a developmental rhetoric in their analysis of African problems. The experience of young people in a range of colonial institutions produced new knowledge, skills, and attitudes. As they distanced themselves from networks that defined juniors as subjects of their seniors, young people came to support and to elaborate a discourse of rights that came to challenge both patriarchy and the colonial state. Juniors possessed more exit options from years of servitude to their seniors, or at least the choice between different forms of servitude. Young people in one way or another sought to redefine their rights and obligations as both subjects and citizens. Jean-François Bayart claimed that "the period of the whites became one of insolence, where 'children' 'with fire in their belly' broke their silence."[39] Among the Giriama of Kenya, "youth" became synonymous with money and social independence.[40] Young Gusii women eloped with their male lovers and fought over the nature of marriage with both their fathers and husbands.[41] Makonde elders in Tanganyika lamented in the 1950s that young migrant laborers had "lost all their manners. They are too proud."[42]

Mission Christianity fed off generational tensions. The new faith promised young Meru of Mt. Kenya redemption not only from sin, but freedom from the blessings and curses of the ancestors and older generations.[43] The missions reshaped the process of maturation, particularly for girls, whose initiations they considered obscene. They had new things to say about sexuality, work, play, courtship, and marriage, and structured opportunities for advancement according to observed obedience to Christian norms.[44] Mission schools taught new notions of masculinity and femininity and forms of duty and discipline that separated juniors and seniors, Christian and non-Christian youth. Seeking to become men and women, youth negotiated the conflicting pressures and influences of patriarchs and missionaries.[45] As Richard Waller has recently pointed out, the erasure of rites for both young women and men left them often uncertain of their status.[46] Warrior bands were abolished, and village ceremonies and festivals died out. Education, Christianity, and capitalism combined to end, or at least dramatically modify, the formation of formal age-sets and the intense group solidarities that such rankings aroused.[47] In Meru, local elders, in alliance with the colonial state, sought to end the initiation through excision of girls into womanhood.[48] Youth left their home societies and sought inclusion in colonial towns, where the means to achieve social promotion were often improvised rather than inherited.[49] Immediately influential was the ideal of "productive masculinity, tamed by work and made responsible through the obligations of marriage and citizenship, and of modern wifehood that taught girls the disciplines of a new but still subordinate domesticity."[50]

It is, however, easy to overstate the revolutionary dimensions of social change in the colonial era. The new ideas and opportunities were in no way equally extended to all. Waller writes that elders "continued to hold most of the cards throughout the colonial period. They controlled marriage, access to land and livestock, education, employment, and also the social knowledge that the young would need to survive and prosper. . . . Only the most alienated youth were beyond their reach."[51] Though references in oral histories and colonial archives to the new autonomies of young men and women are legion, most youth, especially in rural areas, remained dependent on their seniors. And if the cultural and economic currents of colonial rule did help to produce educated, commercial, and working "classes" that embraced the progressive rhetoric of late-colonial developmentalism, the flip side was a growing class of young Africans whose contact with modernity was rather more ambiguous and who, colonial officials believed, had a solvent effect on traditional social order. The colonial state, despite its progressive rhetoric, was still largely reliant on "tradition," the health and vitality of which it viewed with as much concern as African elders solicitous of social stability and customary order.

Thus the new kinds of youth autonomy drew considerable comment among British officials who, deeply concerned with "detribalization," discovered idleness and delinquency, though they had been there all along. They defined the moral order of the towns as inferior to that of the villages and worried over the potential emergence of an urban crowd of materialistic youth with little respect for their seniors or the laws of the land. The very presence of underemployed young African men, no longer considered "tribal" but not yet worthy of urban respectability, was seen as a contamination of the disciplined and ordered municipal environment the colonials sought to create. Officials and some African elders separated youth into two categories, depending on their perceived success in embracing modernity: useful youth and their disorderly, loafing, and criminal counterparts. These two categories formed a dialectic in East Africa during the 1950s and embodied the hopes and anxieties of officials attempting to control the process of modernization and to either resolve or ignore its contradictions.[52] For female youth, behaving badly was defined not so much in terms of their labor as their sexuality.[53]

To counter the perceived ill effects of urbanization on "detribalized" young men, the British expelled them from townships, and encouraged "rational recreation" through youth associations such as football teams and the Boy Scouts. The Boy Scouts were meant to instill lessons in service and fraternity,[54] whereas team sports would promote a sense of fair play, time discipline, and obedience to authority. Football teams and their clubs of fans did in fact provide some of the most formative influences on young men in colonial times, producing friendships, reputations, and memories lasting lifetimes. They provided new forums for masculine display, as well as anticolonial agitation.[55] Colonial schools, meanwhile, were meant to cultivate discipline and a sense of citizenship in a world empire and provided novel ways for young men to assert their masculinity that were intellectual and careerist; for young women, the emphasis was on how to become "modern" wives and mothers, not to mention independent wage earners.

Despite the proliferation of schools, Scouts, and sports, the British still worried. It became common for officials to correlate youth, the city, and nationalism, and to construe willingness to question the authority of seniors with a challenge to the legitimacy of colonialism. This was actually no fantasy: nationalist movements were quick to invoke generational categories and to call into official existence youth as one of several privileged agents. They did not hesitate to employ labels arranged by their own imagination and subjective reading of history, and which resonated with local understandings. They sought to mobilize coalitions in either support or rejection of "natural" principles of patriarchy and clientelism. At times nationalists appropriated historical memories of generational deference in order to cement party unity and to distribute institutional power and responsibilities. Youth served in nationalist associations in order to earn merit through which to obtain patronage from their seniors. At other times nationalists put (relatively) young men firmly in charge, prepared to challenge the authority of the elders. Young educated Zanzibaris, for example, regarded themselves a vanguard generation, endowed by history to perform, in their island's revolution, the role of agents of progress as defined in their own universal, cosmopolitan terms.[56] East African students who went abroad and then returned were representative of an increasingly assertive urban culture and often at the forefront of what Cooper refers to as the new "politics of citizenship" of the 1940s through the 1960s.[57] Youth in the nationalist era thus assumed roles of either vanguards or clients, in reference either to an imagined transnational generation of "modern youth" or enduring forms of patriarchy.

The role of young men in nationalist mobilization can also be seen as part of their ongoing struggle to make claims on adulthood and as an assertion of their masculinity. Waller writes about crowds of young people "looking for confrontation, reputation, and self-esteem."[58] They mixed protest with the search for fun, display, and distraction. Bruce Berman and John Lonsdale have argued that youth seeking manhood took to the forests to become Mau Mau fighters more readily than their elders as a form of resistance to an alien power that most inhibited their social mobility. The male Kikuyu search for land, autonomy, virtue, and manhood was at the heart of the "moral and intellectual" context of Mau Mau.[59] The Mau Mau insurgency may in fact be taken as a case study of the late-colonial crisis of maturity in East Africa and the violence it sometimes engendered.

Nationalists after independence also upheld patriarchal values. They sought to "immunize themselves from a politics of citizenship and stake their futures on a more personalistic, clientalistic form of politics."[60] They employed modern techniques of mass mobilization to get youth to fulfill their allegedly ancient obligations. They awarded the state a pedagogical mandate and asserted themselves as great elders or teachers. If the primary metaphor for President Julius Nyerere's version of socialism in Tanzania was the family, then youth were theoretically obligated to serve their nationalist elders as readily as their parents or village elders. In this context young people were obliged to consider whether or not their displays of commitment would be sincere or purely instrumental, and to what extent the prosperous nationalist elite could legitimately and appropriately clothe themselves in the sacred mantle of the ancestors. The politics of generation after independence were at the same time inclusive and exclusive: the state recruited, celebrated, and foregrounded the vitality of youth on the public stage. And yet the state also excluded images of youth that appeared to conflict with the nationalist imperative of building the nation and its selective invocation of African traditions.[61] Imagining the postcolonial state as a precolonial family inevitably provoked quarrels. Youth were supposed to serve as the indebted servants of a new order but stood accused of some of its most flagrant transgressions. When they wore bell bottoms and miniskirts during a time of "cultural revolution" in Zanzibar, they were rounded up, beaten, and detained.[62] When, in 1966, Tanzanian university students protested against compulsory National Service, they were collectively rusticated as punishment for their ingratitude toward the state.[63] While such incidents lack the spectacular quality of, say, a decade of insurgency in Sierra Leone, in which young subalterns in the 1990s produced a bloody and "grotesque caricature of revolution,"[64] they do reveal profound tensions in East Africa between the competing notions of patrimonialism and democratic citizenship.

Thus independence from colonial rule did not resolve debates and questions about the status of young people in East Africa as either subjects or citizens. Is citizenship founded upon an ethic of contractual rights or a sense of obligation, submission, and sacrifice? Does citizenship imply a voice in community debates or participation in the implementation of the decisions of one's seniors? Is authority exercised in reference to democratic or gerontocratic principles? Are citizens sovereigns or instead juniors whose status derives from their familial bond with the supreme elder of the nation? Does the state assume merely a regulatory function or a parenting role? Is citizenship based on a neutral and secular balancing of competing individual interests or integration in a national/familial effort toward an objective considered by all to be good?

These were questions asked in East Africa at least through the 1970s. By the end of the century some of these debates had receded in correspondence with the contraction of the postcolonial state and its demonstrated inability to assert itself as a parent or patriarch, particularly in an international environment increasingly hostile to such displays. In the context of the passing of the first generation of nationalist elders, bankruptcy, civil war, or the demise of statist strategies of economic development, the links between ruling elites and the ancestors have been severed or at least seriously disturbed. Family metaphors no longer suffice; ruling factions are forced to seek new avenues toward popular legitimacy. This is especially true for postcolonial cities, where a new generation has emerged for whom nationalist claims have little potency. In East African cities a social imaginary founded on the myth of consensus has collapsed.

Chapter Overview

The opening two chapters examine links between generational relations, youth, and conflict in nineteenth- and twentieth-century East Africa. The impact of contemporary African wars on youth has inspired an important and burgeoning literature in recent years in which internal conflict is seen to have had a notable impact on local youth, which has in turn exacerbated a spiral of social breakdown and violence. From Sierra Leone to South Africa, political tension and diminished life chances have led to the resort to violence with momentous consequences for the social order.[65] In his chapter on war and youth in nineteenth-century East Africa, Richard Reid provides a historical context to this debate. Dramatic socioeconomic change resulting from increased contact with an expanding global economy exacerbated tensions both within and between East African societies at this time. In certain areas, notably what is now central Tanzania, a dramatic breakdown of order occurred in which youth were both victims and perpetrators. The rapacious impact of Mirambo's *ruga-ruga* betrays a distinct similarity to what has become the depressingly familiar phenomenon of child soldiery in contemporary African conflicts. According to Reid, the apparent increase in violence in nineteenth-century East Africa was associated with mounting tensions between generations. External influences in many cases proved solvent of the social structures through which historically adulthood had been negotiated. With the restriction in opportunities to attain adulthood, young Africans were more frequently led to adopt violence to achieve maturity. Negotiation of adulthood also lies at the heart of the second chapter by Dave Eaton on generational relations in pastoralist communities in the northern Rift Valley. Much of the academic literature and political commentary on this area describes a breakdown of social bonds occurring in the recent past between the young and old associated with commoditization and the proliferation of modern weaponry. The situation is viewed by many as critical, with diminishing paths to adulthood leading, as in Reid's discussion of nineteenth-century East Africa, to the spiraling incidence of cattle raiding and violence. Taking a rather longer view than most previous commentators, and utilizing evidence stretching back to the early colonial period, Eaton instead demonstrates the durability of local age systems in the negotiation of power between generations. The pessimism of much commentary on the position is in part associated with judgmental assumptions by one generation about preceding ones, arising from unwelcome and seemingly uncontrollable external influences. Pokot elders, for example, link the proliferation of modern arms with a degeneration in the behavior of Pokot youth. However, while superficially the claim may appear persuasive, Eaton demonstrates that neither changing behavior among young Pokot men nor the increase in guns has necessarily led to an increase in violence that many assume. As we shall see, commonsense assumptions associating external influences, social change, and the perceived degeneration of youth have formed an abiding concern among those in positions of power in East African societies up to the present.

The next three chapters explore the experience of three generations who, for contrasting reasons, matured at pivotal moments in their countries' history. In his chapter on a generation coming of age in early colonial Ubena, James Giblin explores its position in what John Iliffe coined the "age of improvement," when young Tanzanians abandoned armed resistance against the colonizer and instead pursued the more developmental goals of education and economic advance. Although this was clearly a time of massive social, cultural, and economic change, Giblin highlights important continuities in Bena society. Although Bena youth may have adopted novel means to attain adulthood—notably through association with colonial institutions, in this case missions—the pursuit of maturity was a timeworn social process. Moreover, even the novel means adopted by young Bena—although in many respects alien and subversive of a moral order that shaped precolonial society and which remained normative for Bena elders and others in Bena society—appear to have had less impact on intergenerational relations than one might first assume. These remained negotiated rather than conflictual, with a "culture of mutual obligation and responsibility to kin remain[ing] robust" both within and between generations. In Hélène Charton-Bigot's chapter a cadre of the educated African elite in post–Second World War Kenya is described as pursuing its own determined path to improvement via university attendance, despite the manifold obstacles provided by a discriminatory education system. Independent and ambitious, these Kenyan youth exceeded the expectations of earlier generations and of a colonial system intent on limiting their development: a system that generally associated Africans with immaturity. Through determination and ingenuity they gained access to higher education abroad, which provided opportunities in adulthood that far exceeded those envisaged by more conservative British officials and settlers. In turn they contributed to the wider national maturity associated with emancipation from colonial rule, before going on to play a central political role in post-independence Kenya. This was a key generation in the region's political history, and this chapter provides important insights into the political context of its maturation as well as the role of education in the attainment of adulthood. The context facing our third "generation of change," that of educated and less-educated youth in late-colonial urban Tanganyika, as discussed by Andrew Burton in the next chapter, proved far less propitious for achieving the expectations of advance generated by dramatic socioeconomic change starting in the early 1900s and accelerating substantially after the Second World War. Exposed to the cash economy and to the commodities of consumerist society to a greater extent than previous generations, being products of a substantially expanded postwar colonial education system, and imbibing a heady atmosphere of economic and political advance associated with late-colonial developmentalism and with the inexorable nationalist march to independence—members of this generation had high hopes of their progress to adulthood. This was reflected by an accelerating wave of migration to urban centers, where—seemingly—youthful ambitions had the best chance of being realized. Cruelly, however, by the mid-1950s an enduring problem of unemployment was emerging in urban economies throughout the region that had previously been characterized by labor scarcity, a problem fed in large part by the heady aspirations of these youthful migrants. As it turned out, a shortage of urban opportunities to achieve social and economic independence was to prove a substantial obstacle for young urbanites that has persisted—if not intensified—up to the present.

Chapters 6 and 7 examine shifting conceptions of youth and generation in colonial East Africa. While colonialism had significant repercussions for intergenerational relations, and for ways of thinking about these, both chapters in the end emphasize the fundamental resilience of indigenous modes of thought and social organization. Richard Waller describes the tensions surrounding the Maasai warrior age-grade of *murran* in twentieth-century Kenya. With the imposition of pax Britannica, murran's precolonial role as community defenders and livestock gatherers was considered obsolete. Instead, lacking any positive role, murran were viewed by Maasai elders and British officials as idle and unruly, and efforts were made to control them, including an unsuccessful attempt to abolish murranhood altogether. However, as Waller observes, murranhood was an integral part of the larger social organization of age and an important stage in the process of "becoming Maasai," and murran resisted such initiatives. For them murranhood continued to provide more effective models of masculinity and citizenship than any alternative institutions introduced under colonialism. In the next chapter, Carol Summers considers youth as a metaphor in Ganda social and political thought. She describes three ways of thinking about youth. The first is a developmentalist rhetoric in which Uganda and Ugandans are portrayed as being in their adolescence, first enunciated by colonials but adopted by Ganda activists in the postwar period as a narrative that implied a natural passage to self-determination and maturity. Summers then discusses contrasting Ganda conceptions of youth. The first, associated with the Bataka movement of 1940s/50s Buganda, emphasizes the complementary relationship between elders and their grandsons as heirs of an uncorrupted inheritance, bypassing an intervening generation contaminated by colonialism. The second examines ideas surrounding the cathartic aspects of succession between generations particularly associated with the appearance of a new kabaka. Such diffuse conceptions of youth, cautions Summers, severely complicate any straightforward interpretation of youth as an analytical category.

The political role of youth is the focus of the next chapters on mainland Tanzania and revolutionary Zanzibar. James Brennan and Thomas Burgess both examine efforts to control the political threat posed by youth and, through institutional discipline, to channel youthful energy in a state-sanctioned manner. Chapter 8 is primarily concerned with Dar es Salaam, where, like Summers, through his analysis of the political history of youth in the town Brennan highlights the relational aspects of local understandings of youth. An educated elite, dismissed as impudent youth by established groups within the urban population in the interwar years, grows into power following World War II as the Tanganyika African National Union (TANU) and in turn identifies a succeeding generation as a threat to the sociopolitical order. The organization of a party youth league enables the political class to exert control over a rapidly expanding class of urban youth, both through patronage in the provision of employment and through the policing role of the league itself. Like the TANU youth league on the mainland, Zanzibar's revolutionary Afro-Shirazi Party in the 1960s/70s also devised institutions aimed at the control of this potentially destabilizing section of the population. These included its own youth league, however, Burgess in chapter 9 focuses instead on a network of camps aimed at inculcating nationalist spirit and discipline among postsecondary island youth. These were supposed to act as a kind of revolutionary finishing school, exerting a model influence in particular over what was perceived as a class of dissolute youth emerging in urban centers and instilling the developmentalist habits appropriate to this nation-building generation. Like other youth-centered institutions such as Zanzibar's Young Pioneers and Youth League (and TANU's mainland equivalent), the camps were a product of the high nationalist period following independence. With the economic and political position of the government in serious decline by the 1980s support for such institutions was substantially reduced or withdrawn entirely. Moreover, as Brennan observes in mainland Tanzania, the spiraling numbers of urban youth at a time of rapid urbanization severely undermined the capacity of party and state "to manage and act as patrons for young, employment-hungry men." Nevertheless, as Burgess observes, in Zanzibar the youth camps actually "lingered on and continue to this day as one of the few relics of what in the islands is regarded universally as a more disciplined time."

Chapters 10 and 11 examine youth in connection with sexuality and gender. Both chapters provide insights into the HIV/AIDS pandemic and youth in contemporary East Africa. In his chapter on patterns of early sexual behavior among young Africans in interlacustrine societies in twentieth-century Uganda and Tanzania, Shane Doyle provides important historical background to the contemporary debate surrounding sexuality and HIV/AIDS. He identifies shifts in youthful sexuality occurring in particular from the late colonial period, when accelerating socioeconomic, cultural, and even legal change was associated with an increase in premarital sex. Evidence of change dating to this period belies assumptions later made by elders at the time of the emergence of HIV/AIDS, attributing the rise of the disease to increasing promiscuity among the generation reaching maturity from the 1970s. Here once again we note the tendency of elders to not only assume the worst of succeeding generations but also to idealize the experience and behavior of their own. Doyle observes that HIV/AIDS has in fact resulted in significant risk-reducing changes in the sexual behavior of young people but that this has "not yet altered the perception of most elders in Great Lakes societies that youthful sexual morality is in terminal decline." In the penultimate chapter, Joyce Nyairo and Eunice Kamaara's analysis of two recent Kenyan texts connected to HIV/AIDS sheds light on not only the potency of the pandemic in the popular imagination but also on enduring aspects of gender relations among youth. The furor surrounding a text purportedly written by an HIV/AIDS victim at Moi University in particular provides fascinating insights into sexual politics of a student body in contemporary Kenya. In contrast to Doyle's observations in Uganda, Nyairo and Kamaara find among their cohort of youth little evidence of changes in sexual behavior arising from the presence of HIV/AIDS. They ascribe this to inappropriate official approaches to tackling the pandemic that offer little hope and tend to reinforce a gender imbalance among youth that in part is responsible for its spread.

Justin Willis's closing chapter, while also focused primarily on contemporary Kenya, provides another example of enduring concerns that have been perennially reiterated from the colonial period, at least, up to the present. In his discussion of the 2005 moral panic surrounding the impact of foreign alcoholic drinks on Kenyan youth Willis provides a recent illustration of anxieties over the contamination of youth by alien influences. The Kenyan government provided a token response to public concern by banning the advertisement of such drinks. "The ban," Willis observes, "was the consequence not of clear evidence of a youth drinking crisis, but of wider anxiety about youth, through which this lobbying became drawn into discursive efforts to create an authentic morality." Willis's chapter demonstrates the enduring strength of narratives of degeneration that have featured prominently in many earlier chapters.

Indeed, in varying forms the theme of youth's degeneration features in most of the chapters herein. From an increased propensity to violence among young warriors in Reid's account of nineteenth-century conflict to the purported collapse of sexual morality of young Ugandans and Kenyans in the late twentieth and early twenty-first century, as described by Doyle and Nyairo and Kamaara. Continuities are likewise evident in perceptions of behavioral decline in Waller's and Eaton's depictions of Kenyan pastoral societies in colonial and postcolonial Kenya. Even in those chapters where concern over supposed degeneration isn't foregrounded, such as Burton's and Brennan's discussion of urban politics in Tanzania or Burgess's account of Zanzibar youth camps, youth's perceived susceptibility to indiscipline arising from socioeconomic change often prompts action on the part of the state and/or elders. This tendency to view youth in terms of crisis can be explained largely by the unprecedented sociocultural, political, and economic forces shaping East African societies from the nineteenth century. This was a time of dramatic change and the reshaping of local cultures of authority, honor, and exchange often had significant repercussions for generational relations. Elders and/or those in positions of authority perennially identified foreign influences, which they had a restricted ability to control, as exerting a malign influence on youth. The rose-tinted spectacles invariably adopted by elders in viewing their own youthful past in comparison to the conduct of contemporary youth reinforced pessimism over declining behavior. Moreover, in a context where intergenerational tensions were frequently the product of competition over resources it was often in the interests of elders to denigrate their juniors.

The vigor of young males has a long history of being harnessed by men in power to advance their own cause, and the preoccupation with controlling youth over the *longue durée* forms another theme at the heart of the collection. Exertion of greater control over youth was generally motivated by material or political self-interest, a perceived need for discipline, or a combination of the two. In Eaton's and Waller's discussion of the Pokot and Maasai, for example, the need for order is invoked, though the material benefits of elders' control are clearly evident. Likewise, the imposition of discipline among Tanzanian urban youth as described by Burton and Brennan, although characterized as a social necessity, had clear political benefits for those exercising power. Charton and Burgess, meanwhile, examine institutional efforts to channel youth in colonial and postcolonial Kenya and Zanzibar aimed at producing cooperative subjects at a time of rapid social change. Shifts in social mores, authority, and economic organization promoted deep anxiety among officials and elders that was often ameliorated by initiatives aimed at molding youth. However, the limited impact of those institutional initiatives described by Charton and Burgess indicate how wider social forces usually overwhelmed state attempts to moderate change, as is borne out too, by Willis's account of the moral panic surrounding youth and alcohol in twenty-first-century Kenya.

Generational tensions were in part a product of shifting expectations among youth regarding their obligations and responsibilities, which also figure prominently in many chapters. What was expected by and of youth changed dramatically over the century and a half covered by this collection. Although, as we have seen, this could often result in conflict between generations, Giblin describes how a time of great change, in which young people's expectations and outlook fundamentally shifted, was successfully negotiated in part through the adaptation of old social mores. Idioms of kinship in early colonial Ubena are shown to have had a resilience and suppleness that made them key relational tools at a time of socioeconomic transformation. This is further exemplified by their later use by nationalists in the shaping of youth as a political category, as discussed by Summers, Brennan, and Burgess. Moderating—and/or placating—the expectations of youth and establishing its responsibilities to the new nation was a key project in early postcolonial East Africa, in which invocation of kinship idioms played a useful part. Postcolonial politicians were no doubt aware that changing expectations among youth had already had profound long-term consequences for East African societies. They were, after all, products, of a late-colonial generation located at the cutting edge of political and demographic transformations in mid-twentieth-century Kenya and Tanzania, as described by Charton-Bigot and Burton. Initiatives arising from the rising aspirations of late-colonial youth in these countries had by independence transformed their political and urban landscapes.

THIS BOOK represents the first extended collection of essays examining African youth in historical context. It forms an important contribution to a burgeoning literature on contemporary youth that has emerged in African studies in recent years. Given both the long demographic predominance of youth in the region and the often central role of generation in African social order and understanding, it is perhaps surprising that such a collection has taken so long to appear. Above all, youth as a category should matter to scholars because it matters to Africans. When it does not matter to Africans, when they do not understand their own circumstances and relations at least partially through the language of generation, then such labels need not concern scholars. Generation, however, does matter; indeed it's hard to understand culture and history in Africa, either ancient or contemporary, without grasping how Africans employ this category as a means by which to order the world, explain social differences, and to determine manners, social customs, and aspirations. The language of generations speaks to how boys and girls become men and women, helps define notions of masculinity and femininity, and informs local ideas of what is right and what is wrong.

Notes

1. Africa is not unusual in this regard. In Western societies too the concept of "youth" as a discrete social category is a relatively recent one, arising in the course of the twentieth century. For an old, though useful, overview, see John R. Gillis, *Youth and History: Tradition and Change in European Age Relations 1770–Present* (New York: Academic Press, 1974).

2. For instance, conferences were organized by the University of Edinburgh (2002), University of Leiden (2003), Northwestern University (2003), Amherst College, and the African Studies Association (2003). For examples of the growing literature, see the collections edited by Barbara Trudell, Kenneth King, Simon McGrath, and Paul Nugent, *Africa's Young Majority* (Centre for African Studies, University of Edinburgh, 2002); Jon Abbink and Ineke van Kessel, *Vanguard or Vandals: Youth, Politics and Conflict in Africa* (Leiden/Boston: Brill, 2005); Alcinda Honwina and Filip de Boeck, *Makers and Breakers: Children and Youth in Postcolonial Africa* (Oxford: James Currey, 2005); and the special issue of the *African Studies Review* 46, no. 1 (2003).

3. As illustrated by a spate of recent PhD research on youth in East Africa: see, e.g., for Zanzibar. G. Thomas Burgess, "Youth and the Revolution: Mobility and Discipline in Zanzibar, 1950–80," Indiana University, 2001; for mainland Tanzania, Eileen Moyer, "In the Shadow of the Sheraton: Imagining Localities in Global Spaces in Dar es Salaam, Tanzania," University of Amsterdam, 2004; for Uganda, Kirstin E. Cheney, "The Pillars of the Nation: Child Citizens and Ugandan National Development," University of California, Santa Cruz, 2004, and for Kenya, Paul Ocobock's forthcoming thesis at Princeton on youth in colonial Nairobi. Themed issues on East African youth (*Africa Today* 51, no. 3 [2005], and the *Journal of African History* [*JAH*] 47, no. 1 [2006]) are also representative of this trend.

4. E.g., Michelle Gavin, "Africa's Restless Youth," in *Beyond Humanitarianism,* ed. Princeton Lyman and Patricia Dorff (New York: Council on Foreign Relations, 2007); Robert Kaplan, *The Ends of the Earth: A Journey to the Frontiers of Anarchy* (New York: Vintage, 1996).

5. In 1967 those aged between birth and 29 represented 69 percent of the population, those over 40, 20 percent; and in 1978, respectively, 71 percent and 18 percent. Census data comes from Government of Tanganyika, *African Census Report 1957* (Dar es Salaam, 1963), 25–31; Government of Tanzania, *1967 Population Census Vol. 4: Economic Statistics* (Dar es Salaam, 1971), Table 301; Government of Tanzania, *1978 Population Census Vol. 5* (Dar es Salaam, 1982), Table 6; http://www.tanzania.go.tz/census/pdf/Evaluation%20and%20Analysis%20of%20the%20Age%20Structure.pdf.

6. Gavin, "Africa's Restless Youth," 71–72.

7. Jon Abbink, "Being Young in Africa: The Politics of Despair and Renewal," in *Vanguard or Vandals,* ed. Abbink and van Kessel, 3, 5, 7.

8. Less well known, yet perhaps more ambiguous, has been the phenomenon of youth vigilantism, the Nigerian manifestation of which has drawn considerable scholarly interest. See the essays by David Pratten, Murray Last, Laurent Fourchard, and Fatima Adamu in *Africa* 78, no. 1 (2008); Johannes Harnischfeger, "The Bakassi Boys: Fighting Crime in Nigeria," *Journal of Modern African Studies* (*JMAS*) 41, no. 1 (2003): 23–49; Insa Nolte, "Identity and Violence: the Politics of Youth in Ijebu-Remo, Nigeria," *JMAS* 42, no. 1 (2004): 61–89; Wale Adebanwi, "The Carpenter's Revolt: Youth, Violence and the Reinvention of Culture in Nigeria," *JMAS* 43, no. 3 (2005): 339–65; Kate Meagher, "Hijacking Civil Society: The Inside Story of the Bakassi Boys Vigilante Group of South-eastern Nigeria," *JMAS* 45, no. 1 (2007): 89–115; Daniel Jordan Smith, "Violent Vigilantism and the State in Nigeria: The Case of the Bakassi Boys," in *States of Violence: Politics, Youth, and Memory in Contemporary Africa,* ed. Edna Bay and Donald Donham (Charlottesville: University of Virginia Press, 2006), 127–47. For Kenya, see David Anderson, "Vigilantes, Violence, and the Politics of Public Order in Kenya," *African Affairs* 101 (2002): 531–55.

9. Frederick Cooper, "Possibility and Constraint: African Independence in Historical Perspective," *JAH* 49, no. 2 (2008): 189, 194.

10. Gavin, "Africa's Restless Youth," 74.

11. Kaplan, *Ends of the Earth*, 16, 19.

12. Donald Donham, "Staring at Suffering: Violence as a Subject," in *States of Violence*, ed. Bay and Donham, 28.

13. Edna Bay, Introduction to *States of Violence*, ed. Bay and Donham, 10.

14. Jean Comaroff and John Comaroff, "Reflections on Youth: From the Past to the Postcolony," in *Makers and Breakers: Children and Youth in Postcolonial Africa*, ed. Alcinda Honwana and Filip de Boeck (Trenton, NJ: Africa World Press, 2005), 20.

15. Tshikala Biaya, "Youth and Street Culture in Urban Africa," in *Makers and Breakers*, ed. Honwana and de Boeck, 222.

16. Mamadou Diouf, Afterword to *Makers and Breakers*, ed. Honwana and de Boeck, 229, 231, 232.

17. Mamadou Diouf, "Engaging Postcolonial Cultures: African Youth and Public Space," *African Studies Review* 46, no. 1 (2003): 7.

18. Biaya, "Youth and Street Culture in Urban Africa," 217.

19. Jay Straker, "Youth, Globalization, and Millennial Reflection in a Guinean Forest Town," *JMAS* 45, no. 2 (2007): 302; Cooper, "Possibility and Constraint," 194.

20. Straker, "Youth", 302, 314–15.

21. John Iliffe, *Africans: The History of a Continent* (Cambridge: Cambridge University Press, 1995), 95.

22. Richard Waller, "Rebellious Youth in Colonial Africa," *JAH* 47, no. 1 (2005): 82, 83.

23. The reconstruction of the crises of female maturation has also recently been undertaken. See, for example, Lynn Thomas, "'Ngaitana (I Will Circumcise Myself)': The Gender and Generational Politics of the 1956 Ban on Clitoridectomy in Meru, Kenya," in *Gendered Colonialisms in African History*, ed. N. R. Hunt, T. Liu, and J. Quataert (Oxford: Blackwell, 1997), 16–41; Tabitha Kanogo, *African Womanhood in Colonial Kenya* (Oxford: James Currey, 2005); Brett Shadle, *Girl Cases: Marriage and Colonialism in Gusiiland, Kenya, 1890–1970* (Portsmouth, NH: Heinemann, 2006).

24. For a review of literature on violence in Africa, produced mostly by anthropologists, see Donham, "Staring at Suffering," 16–33.

25. Youth's problematic nature as an analytical category is highlighted by the fact that in many sub-Saharan countries life expectancy barely exceeded broader definitions of youth. A recent survey of statistics on youth put life expectancy in sub-Saharan Africa for those aged fifteen at just forty-three. Serguey Ivanov, "Existing Youth Development Indicators and Data on Youth," copy at http://www.un.org/esa/socdev/unyin/documents/ydiSergueyIvanov_Demographicindicators.pdf.

26. Kurimoto and Simonse further claim, "Women's age-sets do not form a coherent system in themselves. They do not have the neatly balanced pairs that can unite people and split them according to a mechanism of complementary opposition. Their principal reference is the male system," Eisei Kurimoto and Simon Simonse, Introduction, to *Conflict, Age and Power in North East Africa: Age Systems in Transition*, ed. Kurimoto and Simonse (Oxford: James Currey, 1998), 19. In the same volume, Kaori Kawai asserts, "Women's age categories serve as a compromise between sociocultural constructivism and biological determinism. . . . [A]lthough age categories are determined by systems and rules, they also take the natural facts of fertility and birth

into account" ("Women's Age Categories in a Male-Dominated Society: The Case of the Chamus of Kenya," 165).

27. Kurimoto and Simonse, *Conflict, Age and Power in North East Africa*, 6–7.

28. Peter Geschiere, *Village Communities and the State: Changing Relations among the Maka of South-Eastern Cameroon since the Colonial Conquest* (London: Kegan Paul, 1982).

29. See the doctoral dissertation of Margot Lovett, "Elders, Migrants, and Wives: Labor Migration and the Renegotiation of Intergenerational Patronage and Gender Relations in Highland Buha, Western Tanzania, 1921–1962," (Columbia University, 1996).

30. Justin Willis, *Potent Brews: A Social History of Alcohol in East Africa, 1850–1999* (Oxford: James Currey, 2002), 55.

31. Jeffrey Fadiman, *When We Began, There Were Witchmen: An Oral History from Mount Kenya* (Berkeley: University of California Press, 1993).

32. Mario Aguilar, "Gerontocratic, Aesthetic and Political Models of Age," in *The Politics of Age and Gerontocracy in Africa*, ed. Mario Aguilar (Trenton, NJ: Africa World Press, 1998), 24.

33. See Richard Reid, *War in Pre-colonial Eastern Africa: The Patterns and Meanings of State-Level Conflict in the 19th Century* (Oxford: James Currey, 2007).

34. John Iliffe, *Honour in African History* (Cambridge: Cambridge University Press, 2005), 203.

35. See, e.g., ibid.; Joanna Lewis, *Empire State Building: War and Welfare in Kenya, 1925–52* (Oxford: James Currey, 2000), 135; Andrew Burton, *African Underclass: Urbanisation, Crime and Colonial Order in Dar es Salaam* (Oxford: James Currey, 2005), 74.

36. For the cyclical, generational anxieties surrounding youth delinquency in nineteenth- and twentieth-century Britain, see Geoffrey Pearson, *Hooligan: A History of Respectable Fears* (London: Macmillan, 1983).

37. See, e.g., for the "undesirable percentage of children [who] have acquired rotten behaviour" in contemporary Uganda, the book of manners and parenting by Henry F. Mirima, *Shaping Modern Behaviour*, 3d ed. (Fort Portal, 1997), 2; and for Maasai elders bemoaning lack of respect and the individualistic ways of postcolonial youth, Dorothy L. Hodgson, *Once Intrepid Warriors: Gender, Ethnicity and the Cultural Politics of Maasai Development* (Bloomington: Indiana University Press, 2001), 257, 273.

38. For a useful introduction to shifting colonial policy in the 1940s, see R. D. Pearce, *Turning Point in Africa* (London: Frank Cass, 1982).

39. Jean-François Bayart, *The State in Africa: The Politics of the Belly* (London: Addison Wesley Longman, 1993), 113–14.

40. David Parkin, *Palms, Wine, and Witnesses: Public Spirit and Private Gain in an African Farming Community* (London: Intertext, 1972).

41. Shadle, *Girl Cases.*

42. J. Gus Liebenow, *Colonial Rule and Political Development in Tanzania: The Case of the Makonde* (Evanston, Ill.: Northwestern University Press, 1971), 231.

43. Fadiman, *When We Began, There Were Witchmen*, 175–254.

44. Waller, "Rebellious Youth in Colonial Africa."

45. The impact of Islamic knowledge, belief, and custom on youth and generation has received less attention, especially in East Africa. For West Africa see Louis Brenner, *Controlling Knowledge: Religion, Power and Schooling in a West African Muslim Society* (Bloomington: Indiana University Press, 2001); Lamin Sanneh, *The Crown*

and the Turban: Muslims and West African Pluralism (Boulder, CO: Westview Press, 1997). Young men constituted a core element of Sufi converts and likely gravitated toward Sufi orders in part out of a general desire to access a more universalistic system of belief than village pantheism.

46. Waller, "Rebellious Youth in Colonial Africa," 81.

47. Sometimes the rise of ethnic politics, such as when smaller entities like the Kipsigis merged into a larger identity like the Kalenjin as a defense against powerful ethnic rivals, was responsible for the summary reform of existing age-systems. See Toru Komma, "Peacemakers, Prophets, Chiefs, and Warriors: Age-Set Antagonism as a Factor of Political Change among the Kipsigis of Kenya," in *Conflict, Age and Power in North East Africa,* ed. Kurimoto and Simonse, 186–205.

48. Thomas, "'Ngaitana.'" For the process in East Africa of female maturation in Western schools in the colonial and postcolonial periods, see Corrie Decker, "Fathers, Daughters, and Institutions: Coming of Age in Mombasa's Colonial Schools," in *Girlhood: A Global History,* ed. Jennifer Helgren and Colleen Vasconcellos (New Brunswick, NJ: Rutgers University Press, 2010); Mary Ann Porter, "Resisting Uniformity at Mwana Kupona Girls' School: Culture in an Educational Setting," *Signs* 23, no. 3 (Spring 1998): 619–43; Amy Stambach, *Lessons from Mount Kilimanjaro: Schooling, Community, and Gender in East Africa* (New York: Routledge, 2000); Lynn Thomas, "Schoolgirl Pregnancies, Letter-Writing, and 'Modern' Persons in Late Colonial East Africa," in *African Hidden Histories: Everyday Literacy and Making the Self,* ed. Karin Barber (Bloomington: Indiana University Press, 2006), 180–208. For female youth culture more generally, see Zubeida Tumbo-Masabo and Rita Liljestrom, eds., *Chelewa, Chelewa: The Dilemma of Teenage Girls* (Uppsala: Scandinavian Institute of African Studies, 1994); Minou Fuglesang, *Veils and Videos: Female Youth Culture on the Kenyan Coast* (Stockholm: Stockholm University Press, 1994).

49. For excellent studies of changing constructions of modern masculinity in Africa, see Stephan Miescher, *Making Men in Ghana* (Bloomington: Indiana University Press, 2005); Lisa Lindsay and Stephan Miescher, eds., *Men and Masculinities in Modern Africa* (Portsmouth, NH: Heinemann, 2003).

50. Waller, "Rebellious Youth in Colonial Africa," 78.

51. Ibid., 87.

52. Thomas Burgess, "Mobility and Discipline: Colonial Age Discourse in Tanzania," in *Rethinking Age in Africa: Colonial, Post-colonial and Contemporary Interpretations of Cultural Representations,* ed. Mario Aguilar (Trenton, NJ: Africa World Press, 2006), 50–51; Paul Ocobock, "'Joy Rides for Juveniles': Vagrant Youth and Colonial Control in Nairobi, Kenya, 1901–52," *Social History* 31, no. 1 (2006), 39–59; Burton, *African Underclass.*

53. Waller, "Rebellious Youth in Colonial Africa," 83. For the younger generation of Haya youth making their way in colonial Kenya, see Luise White, *The Comforts of Home: Prostitution in Colonial Nairobi* (Chicago: University of Chicago Press, 1990).

54. See, e.g., Timothy Parsons, *Race, Resistance, and the Boy Scout Movement in British Colonial Africa* (Athens: Ohio University Press, 2004).

55. See, e.g., Laura Fair, *Pastimes and Politics: Culture, Community, and Identity in Post-Abolition Urban Zanzibar, 1890–1945* (Athens: Ohio University Press, 2001), chap. 5; Tadasu Tsuruta, "Simba or Yanga: Football and Urbanization in Dar es Salaam," in *Dar es Salaam: Histories from an Emerging African Metropolis,* ed. James R. Brennan, Andrew Burton, and Yusuf Lawi (Dar es Salaam: Mkuki na Nyota, 2007), 198–212.

56. G. Thomas Burgess, "An Imagined Generation: Umma Youth in Nationalist Zanzibar," in *In Search of a Nation: Histories of Authority and Dissidence from Tanzania: Essays in Honor of I. M. Kimambo,* ed. Gregory Maddox, James Giblin, and Y. Q. Lawi (London: James Currey, 2005).

57. Cooper, "Possibility and Constraint," 172.

58. Waller, "Rebellious Youth in Colonial Africa," 89.

59. Bruce Berman and John Lonsdale, *Unhappy Valley 2: Violence and Ethnicity* (London: James Currey, 1991).

60. Cooper, "Possibility and Constraint," 179.

61. See, e.g., Diouf, "Engaging Postcolonial Cultures"; Andrew M. Ivaska, "Negotiating 'Culture' in a Cosmopolitan Capital: Urban Style and the Tanzanian State in Colonial and Post-colonial Dar es Salaam," PhD thesis, University of Michigan, 2003; and Ivaska's forthcoming monograph, *Cultured States: Youth, Gender and Modern Style in 1960s Dar es Salaam* (Durham, NC: Duke University Press).

62. Thomas Burgess, "Cinema, Bell Bottoms, and Miniskirts: Struggles over Youth and Citizenship in Revolutionary Zanzibar," *International Journal of African Historical Studies* 35, no. 2 (2002): 309–11.

63. Andrew Ivaska, "Of Students, 'Nizers,' and the Struggle over Youth: Tanzania's 1966 National Service Crisis," *Africa Today* 51, no. 3 (2005): 83–107. For a history of university student protest in Kenya, see Maurice Amutabi, "Crisis and Student Protest in Universities in Kenya: Examining the Role of Students in National Leadership and the Democratization Process," *African Studies Review* 45, no. 2 (2002): 157–78.

64. Ibrahim Abdullah, "I Am a Rebel: Youth Culture and Violence in Sierra Leone," in *Makers and Breakers,* ed. Honwina and de Boeck, 186.

65. See, e.g., Paul Richards, *Fighting for the Rain Forest: War, Youth and Resources in Sierra Leone* (Oxford: James Currey, 1996); Clive Glaser, *Bo-Tsotsi: The Youth Gangs of Soweto, 1935–1976* (Portsmouth, NH: Heinemann, 2000).

1 Arms and Adolescence

Male Youth, Warfare, and Statehood in Nineteenth-Century Eastern Africa

RICHARD REID

IN THIS ESSAY I explore the impact of warfare on eastern African male youth, as well as their involvement in various forms of conflict, during the nineteenth century. A selective approach has been adopted in defining "eastern Africa": the paper is focused largely on lacustrine central eastern Africa, encompassing present-day central and southern Uganda and northern and western Tanzania. This zone constitutes a "corridor of conflict," in which, during the eighteenth and nineteenth centuries, warfare and violence were especially intense and markedly cyclical.[1] The essay is also concerned primarily with state-level conflict, although some attention is paid to non-, extra- and antistate violence; the analysis is concerned, too, with (normally) densely populated areas, characterized by high agricultural yields. The lacustrine "corridor" discussed here was caught up in the forces of global commerce, which seems to suggest the importance of an "external dynamic"; the states used in this study, moreover, in addition to exemplifying particular phenomena in terms of the triangular relationship of age, polity, and violence also represent convenient units for study from the sources available (the fact that the European sources are most dense for these areas in itself reflects the global connection). It should also be noted that occasional reference is made to the Ethiopian region which—while geographically beyond the scope of this volume—offers much in the way of thematic congruity and both comparison and contrast with central East Africa. The region of the Ethiopian highlands in the eighteenth and nineteenth centuries shares with the lacustrine zone the experience of dramatic political and economic change, and of war as an instrument of such change.

It is no straightforward matter to define "youth" in the nineteenth century, as age is clearly interpreted differently across cultures and according to circumstances. This is further complicated by the fact that active participation in war itself often indicated a passage to adulthood or at least the beginnings of a transition to seniority. At this juncture it should be reiterated that the focus of this paper is on *male* youth: the sources are regrettably uninformative on the role of women in war, and I recognize that this is an unfortunate but unavoidable omission from the discussion that ensues. As will be seen, when young women are discussed, it is usually as victims of violence, notably in terms of the eastern African slave trade. Although defining "youth" is not a straightforward matter, it is true that a careful reading of the evidence allows us to distinguish "childhood" from "adolescence," and both from full adulthood, in a range of scenarios and according to various exigencies, and to examine the ways in which children and youth were caught up in conflict. The sources also permit us to draw certain conclusions about the relevance of their experiences in a broader social and political context. It is possible to consider the subject from several angles, and in some respects this essay merely serves to indicate potential areas of research. For example, children were clearly one of the key targets of military campaigns, or at least their capture was an important by-product of conflict: to a very real extent the trade in slaves was the trade in children and young women. The source material unfortunately affords few glimpses into the lives of these children, but there is plentiful anecdotal evidence to suggest that the movement of captured children across the areas under examination constitutes one of the most important socioeconomic phenomena of the nineteenth century. This essay therefore seeks, albeit briefly, to understand the impact of war and militarism on children within particular communities—from patterns of play using toy weapons, to the apparent recruitment of children to fight—and on teenagers traumatized by violence, for example in the form of the so-called *ruga ruga* (young warriors) of central and northern Tanzania. This needs to be examined alongside the representation of youngsters in eastern African history as candidates for kingship and/or as soldiers achieving political greatness through battlefield exploits. Violence, moreover, often becomes culturally significant, representing not simply a "rite of passage" but in fact a way of life in certain circumstances.

In this way, male youth and violence were indelibly intertwined in terms of underpinning sociopolitical order and generating loyalty to the extant system; yet armed youth could also represent a challenge to the existing order, facilitating disloyalty, rebellion, and sociopolitical breakdown. In the case of the latter, the destruction or at least radical reformulation of family units and notions of kinship was clearly crucial; the role of armed youth must be understood vis-à-vis older members of the politico-military establishment, in terms of violent generational conflict. It is suggested here that only by examining the experience of young men in war and in other forms of low-level violence in the nineteenth century can we begin to understand perceptions of and attitudes toward European invasion and the colonial state itself. There is a great deal more work to be done in this respect, and this essay can only signpost the issue, at this juncture and in the conclusion to the piece; but it is hoped that examples from precolonial eastern Africa can contribute to an appreciation of how experiences of violence in the nineteenth century influenced responses to colonialism in the twentieth.

Intergenerational Conflict

War and socioeconomic change in the nineteenth century opened up considerable gulfs between generations, setting young against old in terms of modes of behavior, experience, and political and material aspiration. It may be assumed that to some extent it was ever thus; but with rapid commercial change in the nineteenth century, particularly in the states and societies of central East Africa, came new pressures and new sources of conflict between generations. Indeed there is evidence of intergenerational conflict in much of the warfare of the late precolonial region, exemplified in Urambo, Mirambo's state, which was built on the violence of young men who had been ripped from the familial compound, many of the values of which were in turn aggressively eschewed. In what must have been a familiar scene across the region, Ebenezer Southon observed among the Gogo posturing, belligerent young men, making "a great parade of immense bows & arrows," while the older men "simply carry a long stick."[2] Political and economic power increasingly rested with this generation, whose adventures and sacrifices had led them to a position whereby they might expect to inherit their fathers' power and indeed construct new forms of it.

Yet even Mirambo, young revolutionary though he was once, was wary of wholesale rejection of the values and structures of the preceding generation: he struggled with continuity and discontinuity, and with the historical meaning of his own violence. In so many ways, as is well documented, Urambo was a novel creation, a polity of the young; Mirambo himself had begun to lay its foundations when he was a young man, and it owed its success to youthful sacrifice. He was also self-conscious in his articulation of a "new order," which would rise from destruction and discontinuity: across Mirambo's domain, old chiefs were deposed, to be replaced by new political lineages, and relatives of the former were "retired," according to Philippe Broyon, and took the title "*Muanangua-Waniamalonga*," or "prince of ruins." This was because "each new chief destroys the village of his predecessor . . . and builds himself a new one."[3] The image of "ruins," of destruction and breakage from the past, is striking; yet Mirambo also claimed that he was seeking to re-create the supposed ancient domain of Usagali, a great kingdom of large cities and a teeming population, and stressed the restorative aspect of his violence. He even named his eldest son Mshimba, after the last (and the greatest) ruler of that long-defunct realm. This was a young state seeking antiquity, celebrating and elevating youth even as it was trying to tie them to a deeper past, as though they were reclaiming status in a much older political order.

Urambo represented youthful rebellion against an older sociopolitical order and was the product of a unique set of circumstances in nineteenth-century Tanzania, namely the intrusion of global commerce and its representatives in the form of coastal Arab merchants, and the political and commercial upheaval that resulted from the slave trade and the opportunities (and grave dangers) thus presented. Yet intergenerational conflict within states is a common enough theme across precolonial Africa, from assassinations with a view to capturing kingship[4] to outright armed rebellion. Mirambo's "boys" participated in the creation of a new order; but in Buganda, the young sought to inherit the existing order, and monarchs sometimes found themselves warily eyeing their own sons. One such was Semakokiro, in the late eighteenth century, who on learning that a number of his offspring was plotting a revolt had them arrested and the majority burned alive. A pardon of sorts was granted to Kakungulu, who was auspiciously the father of twins, but even he was banished to Bunyoro, where he then proceeded to organize armed expeditions into Ganda territory. These Nyoro-backed incursions troubled his father for a number of years.[5] Another would-be rebel, Kamanya, was also pardoned and eventually succeeded his father as kabaka, but he too had difficulties with his progeny. His son Nakibinge had the precocity to question Kamanya's wisdom in executing a rival to the throne, Kamanya's brother Mutebi, and thereafter Kamanya "nursed a grievance against his son. As the latter grew up, his father's fears and suspicions also grew. He even used to consult the witch doctors and to complain that his son Nakibinge was plotting to overthrow him." At length Kamanya had his son executed, only to be tortured by the latter's ghost, a torment that eventually resulted in paralysis on one side of the kabaka's body.[6] Children could be troublesome indeed, and youth was a constant threat in the paranoid enclosures of the royal capital.

Ambiguous attitudes toward youth are in evidence in the northern lacustrine kingdoms, where celebrations of youthful physical prowess sat uncomfortably alongside misgivings about the violence that such physicality frequently engendered. In the early 1860s J. H. Speke's descriptions of the young Mutesa—he had succeeded his father when perhaps sixteen or seventeen years of age, and in 1862 was therefore twenty-one or twenty-two—are dense with references to the kabaka's celebrated physicality, and to his immaturity. Described as a mere "stripling," Mutesa's juvenility figures prominently in these early representations of him, both explicitly, in the form of his caprice and childish nature, and implicitly, in the depictions of his physicality.[7] According to A. Kagwa, he excelled at the sport of spearing cattle and also outclassed his chiefs in archery and swimming.[8] Mutesa was youthful, vigorous, and physical to the point of brutality. He enjoyed watching men fighting with sticks and patronized wrestling in the royal enclosure, in which chiefs too were expected to participate; Mutesa had the decency to excuse older members of the political establishment from this, but no doubt it offered younger chiefs an opportunity to impress the young kabaka who was clearly moved by physical prowess.[9] Speke described Mutesa as "a good-looking, well-figured, tall young man of twenty-five," in the prime of life and indulged to the point of absurdity.[10] His youthful vigor was recalled years later, when debilitating illness set his earlier physicality in tragic juxtaposition. One missionary recalled in the late 1870s how "[b]efore his illness, Mtesa was a very energetic man, and was in the habit of making long hunting excursions."[11]

From the point of view of the young, naturally, it was the elders who were the problem, and youthful impatience, angst, and insecurity not infrequently led to precipitous action. In the late 1850s, Kabaka Mutesa had owed his accession very largely to the sponsorship and protection of his chief minister, Kayira; however, convinced by several prominent persons that Kayira had become dangerously powerful, Mutesa plundered and imprisoned the erstwhile kingmaker—an action, notably, that Mutesa later came to regret. "When Mutesa grew up and became a mature man," Kagwa tells us, "he deeply regretted his treatment of Kayira, and confessed that he did wrong to dismiss him." According to Kagwa, it later struck Mutesa as tragic that Kayira should have suffered such a fate, considering all that the latter had done to help the young prince. Thus is youth presented as violent, volatile, and unstable in Kagwa's account, with Mutesa later offering chieftainships to Kayira's sons as compensation.[12] There is no record of similar reparations being offered to the kin of several other senior chiefs, whom the insecure young Mutesa had burned alive shortly after becoming kabaka.[13] We are led to believe that Mutesa was at this time "immature," incapable of making rational decisions; later, through the beneficence of time, he acquired sufficient maturity to ponder the cruelty of his actions and, perhaps, indeed, the pathos of the human condition. And in due course Mutesa's own son, Mwanga, behaved in much the same way, though this time with a European audience on hand to make disapproving remarks. One source described Mwanga as "a young man with a hard heart and warped mind." Worse, the new kabaka had "made it his study to destroy the little good that his father had done. The first thing he did was to reject the counsels of the old ministers, and to place foolish and badly disposed men in the chief offices."[14] A missionary declared that Mwanga "had not the political astuteness of his father Mutesa, nor the military prowess of his grandfather Suna."[15] For Europeans, of course, Mwanga was the embodiment of the childlike savage potentate: foolish, headstrong, childish—"weak and invertebrate," as a British officer described him in 1893[16]—he carried the burden of late Victorian prejudice on his young shoulders.

Male youth was an emphatically physical state, with robustness and even cruelty the essential characteristics of the young who would inherit the kingdom; but youth was also warlike, a metaphor for the exercise of legitimate violence. The new kabaka might have no military experience whatsoever—Mutesa certainly did not, and by the middle of the nineteenth century it was rare in any case—but it was vital that he was bathed in militaristic imagery. One European observer noted of Mutesa how "[i]n his younger days he proved himself brave and warlike, and, in spite of his many cruelties, seems to have a strong hold on the affections of the lower classes."[17] Another later felt moved to write that Mutesa was "the greatest and wisest of all the kings in his methods of carrying on war; he reduced the surrounding tribes to order."[18] The young Mwanga was likewise depicted in glorious colors. Toward the end of his reign, Mutesa took his son under his protection and began to promote him as his successor. According to Zimbe, Mutesa asked his chiefs, "'Can't he lead an army successfully?' The chiefs answered, 'Yes, Your Lord, he certainly can do so.'"[19] The chiefs, of course, had as little clue as Mutesa himself about Mwanga's military capabilities, but this was hardly relevant. This was a metaphor for what it was to rule the kingdom of Buganda.

In Bunyoro, a king who reigned peacefully and died in old age was only remembered *precisely because* he had reigned peacefully and died in old age. Young, violent monarchs who lived and quickly died by the sword (or spear), however, were the subject of much detailed analysis by posterity, whether they be judged "good" or "bad," though it was very often the latter: only the bad die young, as it were. In late nineteenth-century Buganda, the young were often to be feared, even despised, owing to their violent propensities. For the nineteenth-century Ganda, the mythical founding father Kintu was the purest image of themselves, the representation of a time before the kingship became steeped in blood and violence. H. M. Stanley's 1875 account of Kintu's ghostly reappearance during the reign of an eighteenth-century king was doubtless based on a Ganda informant, Sabadu, who appears to have had a particular message to transmit: here, Kintu was "a mild, humane, and blameless man" with a great aversion to the shedding of blood. His children, however, were a different matter, growing up to be violent, debauched and rebellious; and this, according to the version given to Stanley, was what prompted the old man to disappear: "See, my sons whom I brought into this world have become wicked. . . . They shed the blood of their brothers daily, and there is nothing but killing and bloodshed now, until I am sick of blood. It is time for us to get away and depart elsewhere."[20]

Many years later, however, Kintu made a brief, ghostly return to Buganda during the reign of Kabaka Mawanda, and Kintu reminds Mawanda why he left: Buganda had become a land "unfit for him to live in," because his children "loved to shed blood"; the kingdom "became red and filthy with the blood of innocent men and women and children, it became hateful to Kintu, and he departed from the horrid, cruel land."[21] Whether, as has been argued, this was a coded criticism of Mutesa, it is certainly clear that offspring could be destabilizing, ungrateful, reckless; the elderly had sagacity and loved peace. It is, of course, common across Africa, and indeed wherever there has been human society, for elders to view the past as more peaceful and orderly than the present; for our purposes, however, the Kintu story illustrates the point very well.

Buganda also offers a good example of intergenerational conflict more broadly, notably within the ranks of the army, which had emerged quite dramatically by the 1880s. At the Ganda capital there appeared a class of young chiefs, armed pages, and royal bodyguards, developing in part out of the new military *batongole*[22] created by Suna in the mid-nineteenth century. The increasing preoccupation with the signs and symbols of military and political power, and the lavish favor poured upon these ambitious youngsters, meant that there was growing rivalry between them and the older, more professional war chiefs. It was an antagonism that contributed to Buganda's military decline in the last years of the nineteenth century. In his twilight years, Mutesa was increasingly uneasy about what appeared to be growing pockets of hostility and resistance to his rule: in promoting youth to positions of power, he had created a class characterized by hubris and insolence. He attempted to keep them busy by launching a series of military campaigns in the early 1880s.[23] It did not work. They had enough time on their hands to flirt with imported faiths and consider themselves free from inhibiting tradition through their access to guns and the accoutrements of power. The rivalry between the favored young men and the older representatives of the "military establishment" grew as the former were accorded greater political and military responsibility. One Ganda source recorded that "[w]hen after a war the old chiefs came back defeated, the bitongole of the young men jeered them very much. The Kabaka always appointed young men to distribute what booty the old chiefs had brought back and he always gave them power to jeer them."[24] Moreover, these arrogant youth increasingly disregarded the tenets of Ganda military tradition, of personal courage and hard-won reputations; they owed their positions largely to court intrigue, royal patronage, and access to commerce rather than real military skill or experience.

The Ganda kingship was buoyed by the language of military greatness, even if such achievement was largely imaginary, as it certainly was when Mutesa was kabaka; nonetheless, into his relative old age—after all Mutesa was only in his mid-forties when he died—he was accorded the kind of respect due to one who had supposedly been a magnificent warrior in his youth. Mirambo, for much more tangible reasons, likewise retained the adoration of his young followers until the very end. Although the physical well-being of commanders was often important, it was not always necessary so long as the accomplishments of one's formative years retained their allure and currency, as demonstrated by the Ethiopian example of Ras Welde Selassie, ruler of Tigray and, in the following passage, a frail old man: "It is scarcely possible to imagine a more striking instance of the superiority which intrepid spirit and mental ability confer in a barbarous country, than that which was exhibited on the present occasion; for though the Ras was so feeble, that he could scarcely walk unsupported, and Liban . . . possessed all the strength and energy of youthful vigour, yet, on the approach of the old man, he was evidently awed."[25] Welde Selassie's reputation was assured, "having been successfully engaged in upwards of forty battles, and having evinced on these occasions even too great a disregard of his own personal safety in action."[26]

Inheritance and Renewal

Inevitably, young men came to inherit that which their fathers had in their turn inherited. In some areas, acquaintance with weaponry and the uses of violence came early. Children played games in which they emulated their elders. As Wylde observed in Ethiopia: "One of their favourite amusements is playing at soldiers. . . . They arm themselves with sham swords made of wood, lances from some long reed and a shield of wicker-work made out of rushes. I have often watched these sham battles quite closely. . . . They show a great deal of intelligence and strategy when they scout."[27]

Even more remarkably, the young boys of Unyanyembe described by David Livingstone in 1872 "make play guns of reed, which go off with a trigger and spring, with a cloud of ashes for smoke. Sometimes they make double-barrelled guns of clay, and have cotton-fluff as smoke."[28] But in the traumatized communities of Tanzania, it was not all proverbial fun and games, as the toy guns carried by Nyamwezi children attest. Young Ngoni boys in the area of southern Lake Tanganyika carried heavy knobsticks,[29] and, according to Burton the "only education" received by Nyamwezi boys was "in the use of the bow and arrow." From the age of four, "the boy begins to learn archery with diminutive weapons, which are gradually increased in strength,"[30] doubtless in anticipation of the violence with which they became so quickly familiar. The young were groomed, and image-making was all important. Children born to great military families were exposed to the accoutrements and culture of violence at an early age. Mirambo's younger son, Mtengegna, about eighteen years old in early 1884, presented a fine picture: with the looks and "fervour" of his father, reputedly brave in combat, he strutted around like "a schoolboy on holiday," according to one source, and had caused troubled by killing a donkey belonging to an Arab, an act for which Mirambo sent the latter ivory in compensation.[31] In 1868, the twelve-year-old son of Sebhat, head of the Sebagadis family of Tigray, carried a double-barreled shotgun.[32] As noted above, the children of Ganda chiefs often became pages at the royal court; the practice of "privileged enslavement" or "indentureship" was of some antiquity, but in the late nineteenth century the boys among them (for there were girls, too) began to emerge as a distinct "class" with access to firearms and the signs and symbols of military power.[33] They constituted a privileged adolescent elite borne aloft on the currents of political intrigue but, despite the fact that they were increasingly used in battle, with little of the military prowess of their illustrious forebears. An interesting comparison, again, is with Ethiopia, where the children of army officers by the 1880s and 1890s were part of a burgeoning military aristocracy. A. Bulatovich mentioned the *elfin ashkers,* servants of the inner chambers at the imperial court, most of whom were "children of former chief officers of the army. . . . From childhood they are raised at court as pages, and then become *elfin ashkers.*"[34] More broadly, however, intergenerational rivalry may have been institutionalized; it was expected, even desirable, and was an integral part of the process by which states and societies were sustained.

The formalization of violent youthful inheritance is perhaps most clearly demonstrated in the use of civil war to resolve succession disputes. Some European observers undoubtedly adopted a rather deterministic and formulaic approach to these matters, and John Roscoe is typical in his quest for ritual, but what he has to say about Bunyoro is nonetheless worthy of note: "When the king ended his life, the question arose who should be his successor; this decided by the princes taking arms, each securing what following he could, and fighting with his brothers, until all the princes were killed but one, and he claimed the throne. In these wars only the peasants were allowed to take an active part by bearing arms and fighting under the princes, while the chiefs were neutral."[35]

Civil war also served to underpin the importance of military order, and the sanctioned chaos was the direct opposite of the armed order provided by the state. Territorial hegemony disintegrated; no one had a monopoly on the use of force; the state had effectively collapsed. "[N]o property was safe," wrote Roscoe, as "princes" robbed and plundered with impunity: "the king being dead, there was no government."[36] Succession disputes resolved by arms, moreover, ensured that "the best man won," at least according to whoever did actually win. In a conversation with Speke, Kamurasi proudly (and somewhat transparently) extolled the virtues of the Nyoro system in comparison to that of Buganda: "'Was the king of Unyoro chosen, as in Uganda, haphazard by the chief men—or did the eldest son sit by succession on the throne?' [Speke enquired.] The reply was, 'The brothers fought for it, and the best man gained the crown.'"[37] This ethos was apparently present in Karagwe, too, where "the civil wars which broke out at [the king's] death ensured that he should be succeeded by the strongest among his sons," according to J. Ford and R. de Z. Hall.[38] In mid-eighteenth-century Buganda, Kabaka Kyabaggu encouraged a group of young princes to fight for the kingdom, and watched the proceedings from his marginalized camp on the banks of the Nile.[39] Above all, such generational conflict and change in the states around Lake Victoria was seen to bring about renewal, a cleansing and reinvigorating of the polity through violence, out of which a newly empowered generation would emerge.[40]

Such renewal could come about *during* a particular reign, too. In Buganda there was a stark contrast between the celebration of those who had come to greatness through humble origins and the late nineteenth-century reality of a hubristic politico-military class. Indigenous histories told tales of individual derring-do on the part of men who achieved prominence through military endeavor; often possessed of phenomenal physical strength, they appeared most commonly at times of military crisis and, notably, were used to shame the extant political establishment. The story told by Stanley of Kasindula, a young subchief with "neither pride of birth nor riches to boast of," demonstrates the theme admirably. Defeating the Soga during the reign of Suna, Kasindula—clearly emblematic of the rejuvenating power of youth—then traveled to Suna's court where he delivered a stirring oration:

> My dear Lord, Namujurilwa and Setuba are great chiefs, and stand in your presence daily, but I am only a Mtongoleh under Sekebobo. I have neither farm nor house, wife nor child, and my only wealth consists of my spear and my shield, and my only cloth is this rotten mbugu [bark-cloth]. Namujurilwa and Setuba brought slaves and cattle by hundreds, but the kopi [peasant] Kasindula brings his thousands to Suna. Behold where they stand! Kasindula gives them all to Suna.[41]

He was well rewarded for his patriotic efforts, and certainly military repute could clearly bring rapid promotion and heightened social status. Stanley describes the new haughtiness in his friend Sambuzi, recently promoted: "I am not a child, I am a man, and . . . the Wanyoro and Wasongora have felt the sharpness of my spear. . . . I stand in the place of *Kabaka* now, for I represent him here, and the army is under my command. Sambuzi, your friend at Uvuma, is changed now to Sambuzi the general. You understand me?"[42] Again, we have seen, the situation changed by the 1880s, when political intrigue and patronage was more likely to ensure elevation at the royal court.

It is possible to discern a historical pattern whereby the transition from youth to adulthood was a political and military process that involved the institutionalization of violence. Here, it is instructive to draw on examples from Ethiopia as well as Tanzania to illustrate the point. Three key figures across the region between the mid-eighteenth and the mid-nineteenth centuries—the future ras Michael and the future emperor Tewodros in Ethiopia, and Mirambo in Tanzania—began their "careers" as bandits (in the Ethiopian context, *shifta*) when in their adolescence. Michael had been a "rebel" in the 1750s and 1760s, in defiance of the crumbling state in the mountains around Adwa in Tigray; likewise, Tewodros—then known as Kassa—had operated as a shifta on the edges of the Gondarine state when barely out of boyhood in the mid- and late 1830s. Mirambo, of course, suffered the indignity of being referred to by some European observers as a "mere bandit" even at the height of his success. Yet what distinguished each of these men was their ability to institutionalize war: state-building in this context was often the institutionalization of violence, and it was this that marked their passage from youth to manhood. Their passage to maturity was accompanied—indeed was facilitated by—the exercise of violence on a large scale: the capture or rejuvenation of extant states or the creation of new ones. When a youth, Michael was a troublesome northern bandit; as a man, he became kingmaker at Gondar at the outset of the *zemene mesafint*.[43] When a youth, Tewodros was an angry outcast, delighting in audacious raids and in irritating regional potentates; as a man, he had himself crowned king of kings and, according to received wisdom, reunited the ancient Ethiopian empire. When a youth, Mirambo was the upstart in a minor chiefly lineage, the product of Ngoni violence; as a man, he built the largest polity witnessed in the region during the nineteenth century and dominated the interior.

In other words, nothing succeeds like success, and scale was all-important: the exercise of real power over a wide area was enough, in the eyes of many, to distinguish "legitimate" from "illegitimate" violence, however implicitly. In this context we can see how youthful violence was so often interpreted as illegitimate, but also how such violence might become legitimate through successful expansion of scale: maturity and seniority was a state brought about through sheer force of arms. At the same time, of course, legitimacy could seep from one leader to another, usually from one generation to the next, and thus the former was drained of both real power—for legitimacy was often rooted in actual military might—and moral cause. The description of the escalating conflict between the young Menelik and the aging Tewodros by the beginning of 1866 demonstrates this very well. As one contemporary chronicler explained:

> Minilik, the son of the king of Shewa . . . has deserted the king and gone to Shewa. The king's governor, Bezzabih, fought against him. Minilik was victorious. All the people of Shewa received him with joy. . . . He has grown very powerful. Because of this, King Tewodros had twenty-eight imprisoned Galla noblemen pushed . . . over the cliff. . . . The king's only domain is Begemdir. All his soldiers have deserted. The king has grown weak.[44]

Tewodros's loss of legitimacy is almost tangible and is underpinned by his resort to acts of extreme violence.[45]

Youth and the Bearing of Arms

The privileged inheritors of an extant order may be contrasted with the ruga ruga of Tanzania, wild young men who were seen as symptomatic of sociopolitical disorder, and to whom we return below. Yet more broadly the existence of aggressive youth with ambitions beyond their presumed roles as passive recipients of the extant order was a sign of the health of the body politic, and of the vibrancy and political fecundity of society. In the interlacustrine region, the states of Buganda, Bunyoro, and Ankole each experienced military reforms in the nineteenth century which saw the arming of youth in response to the challenges of the age. Buganda underwent dramatic expansion in the late eighteenth and early nineteenth centuries, and then sought to consolidate its gains while attempting to seize the burgeoning commercial opportunities stemming from long-distance trade. Bunyoro, in the second half of the nineteenth century, was resurgent in terms of expansion and ambition, largely at the expense of the Ganda. Although less is known about Ankole, it can be assumed that here too challenges on and beyond the frontiers of the kingdom prompted the military mobilization of the young. The creation of increasingly military offices in Buganda in the mid-nineteenth century under Kabaka Suna may be interpreted in this way; similar chieftaincies were created in Ankole.[46] Arguably the most successful transformation in the northern lacustrine region took place in Bunyoro, where Kabarega's formation of the *barusura* in the 1870s represented not only a military revolution of sorts but also a political one. This was, in Nyakatura's words, a "national army," organized into a number of "divisions."[47] With the creation of the barusura, Uzoigwe argued, "Kabalega struck a serious blow at the socio-economic and political influence of the chiefs and military aristocracy: the new standing army now saw Kabalega as its sole and ultimate authority."[48] No other state in the region under examination, with the possible and somewhat anomalous exception of Urambo, could be said to have experienced quite the same thing in this period.

War was so often a young man's game, notably in the turbulent region of northern Tanzania in the second half of the nineteenth century. Male youth constituted the bulk of eastern African soldiery to such a degree that it is impossible to consider warfare without acknowledging the contribution of the young in making it possible. Mirambo was deliberate in selecting youths as his assault troops, recruiting among an age-group which he could mold, and indeed sacrifice, for his own ends. Mirambo's youths were lads barely past puberty, laying down their lives for the nascent state of Urambo, or for Mirambo himself, depending on one's interpretation of late nineteenth-century Tanzania. He told Stanley that:

> He preferred boys or young men to accompany him to war; he never took middle-aged or old men, as they were sure to be troubled with wives

or children, and did not fight half so well as young fellows who listened to his words. Said he, "They have sharper eyes, and their young limbs enable them to move with the ease of serpents or the rapidity of zebras, and a few words will give them the hearts of lions. In all my wars with the Arabs, it was an army of youths that gave me victory, boys without beards. Fifteen of my young men died one day because I said I must have a certain red cloth that was thrown down as a challenge. No, no, give me youths for war in the open field, and men for the stockaded village.[49]

Mirambo's apparent disregard for the loss of young life, indeed his seeming to revel in it, is striking, although other evidence suggests that he groomed his charges with rather greater concern than Stanley's account suggests; indeed in many respects this passage tells us more about Mirambo's military revolution than any number of graphic descriptions of the organization of his army and polity. Mirambo's army was composed of young men "who had formerly been victims of [the slave trade]";[50] he also systematically recruited among newly conquered districts, and the latter were expected to contribute "a number of youths to be trained as warriors," and on these he "bestowed considerable care & attention; he armed them with guns & taught them how to use them; he conspicuously rewarded the brave & loyal; he rigorously punished the cowardly & unfaithful."[51]

These were the ubiquitous ruga ruga, the term used to describe Mirambo's soldiers as well as any group of bandits or miscreants haunting the forests of northern Tanzania in the second half of the nineteenth century. While there is little doubt that petty violence and relatively low-level robbery did indeed take place, the problem is that this frequently looks very similar to the kind of guerrilla tactic which Mirambo had come to employ against Arabs by the end of the 1870s and early 1880s. Mirambo doubtless did not invent this mode of low-level harassment: more likely, he harnessed extant insecurity—of which he himself was both product and perpetrator—and took advantage of earlier forms of highway banditry, formalizing these into extensions of his tactical armor. Much of this depends on how we interpret the term *ruga ruga.* As Shorter observed, *ruga ruga,* or *valuga luga* in Nyamwezi, meant "young, unmarried, professional soldiers"; yet "[t]hese wild young men were a heterogeneous collection of war captives, deserters from caravans, runaway slaves and others," which suggests something other than military professionalism.[52] The term was frequently used indiscriminately: the French missionary Lourdel inserted the word *soldats* (soldiers) after describing the ruga ruga, but more often it was applied to any young man with a gun and a drug habit.[53] Mirambo's men were described as such; and so were various categories of the rootless, the displaced, the thuggish. Contemporaries were frequently—and understandably—unable to distinguish between highway robbers searching for a quick profit, and armed columns deliberately dispatched by Mirambo to do much the same kind of work.

Across the region, armed male youth either emulated Mirambo's ruga ruga or appeared spontaneously as products of the same circumstances. Stanley's disdainful description of the soldiers belonging to the king of Uvinza that he encountered is worth quoting at length in this context:

> These warriors, perceiving that the word Ruga-Ruga, or bandits, influences weak minds, call themselves by that name, and endeavour to distinguish themselves by arresting all native travellers suspected of hostility or property. . . .
>
> ZEGI, swarming with a reckless number of lawless men, was not a comfortable place to dwell in. . . . Here were a number of youths suffering under that strange disease peculiar to vain youth in all lands which Mirambo had called "big head." The manner in which they strutted about, their big looks and bold staring, their enormous feathered head-dresses and martial stride, were most offensive. Having adopted, from bravado, the name of Ruga-Ruga, they were compelled in honour to imitate the bandits' custom of smoking banghi (wild hemp).[54]

This seems to be testimony to the social and cultural changes which had come about through prolonged conflict, with a new generation of disaffected, aggressive young men staring boldly at the world. Stanley, notably, regarded them as arrogant imitations of ruga ruga, but they were as genuine a product of the age as Mirambo's hemp-smoking heroes, and certainly just as important in terms of the region's future. In fact, the arrogant young chiefs of the Ganda royal court were in some respects cut from the same cloth, taking advantage of the commercial and political change at the capital and exhibiting criminal tendencies in the process. A missionary recorded how two youths at the kabaka's court were condemned to death for selling a young slave belonging to the *katikiro* (chief minister) to the Arabs. This kind of behavior, it was suggested, was not uncommon.[55]

The impression given of contemporary assessments of Mirambo's recruitment strategy is that it was relatively unusual to systematically target boys quite so young, and that this was both symptom and cause of the social breakdown across the region.[56] In Ethiopia in the second half of the nineteenth century, a period of violent state-building, a similar phenomenon can be discerned. One observer concluded in the late 1860s that "incessant wars have encouraged the growth of a great body of worthless soldiers of fortune, who are the curse of the country,"[57] and in the mid-1880s another source lamented that "every young man of good physique prefers to enrich himself by plunder rather than by toil."[58] Elsewhere, the conscription of the very young was often symptomatic of crisis, or of especially vigorous military expansionism, as in early nineteenth-century Buganda during the reign of the ambitious Kabaka Kamanya. Kamanya's reign was remembered for what is described in one source as "restless warfare," during which "the men were not permitted to rest and even children of fourteen were required to carry each his two spears and shield to war."[59] This was clearly exceptional, for ordinarily mere children were hardly expected to participate in the business of expanding the kingdom; they were, nonetheless, a resource to be utilized, if necessary. It is notable that in the Ethiopian region, where military service clearly offered opportunities to the young, age was no particular barrier, other than that soldiers should have "attained some degree of manhood, but also who are not yet decrepit."[60]

It is also the case that there were societies for whom the bearing of arms and indeed killing itself was a rite of passage, through which manhood might be achieved and a wife obtained. This was the case in eastern Ethiopia, for example, where "when a young man wishes to marry he must bring a trophy to his young woman to show his gallantry." A. Wylde considered that this was straightforward in times of war, but during peace, raids had to be organized for the purpose, often into the Danakil area.[61] Thus was violence a specifically masculine, youthful activity. Closer to our region, twentieth-century anthropology has shed much light on the ways in which violence and courage in the face of pain was associated with the passage to manhood. Suzette Heald, notably, demonstrates that among the Gisu of Uganda, to be a "man" is measured in terms of the capacity for violence, which is a crucial part of male self-conception: there is manliness in violence, just as women are "kind-hearted." "Violence and killing," she writes, "did not happen by default but were an expression of male purpose."[62]

Victims

Children and adolescents were the victims of violence across the region, and traumatized children must have abounded in central East Africa, for example, during the second half of the nineteenth century. Children were, of course, a key target of slaving violence, and tens of thousands must have been caught up in conflict and absorbed into new communities in Tanzania between the 1850s and the 1880s. The Ngoni, for example, engaged in the seizure of children as slaves: according to one report, they attacked Bukune in mid-1884 and took their captives—women and children—to Unyanyembe to be sold.[63] The seizure of children was common in and around Buganda. By the second half of the nineteenth century, the Buvuma islanders were periodically raiding the Ganda shore, mostly seizing women and children.[64] Children were frequently among captives brought to the Ganda capital for sale. One missionary described a group of around thirty boys recently brought in from Busoga, "not more than four years of age, lean, lank, & hungry looking, some mere skeletons."[65] In the Ethiopian region, too, children were caught up in conflict as captives, often being seized wholesale during campaigns that might be fought for other reasons; a proportion of these would have been retained for domestic use, while the rest were presumably sold on to slave traders with commercial concerns on the Red Sea coast and the Arabian peninsula. And as in central East Africa, so in the Ethiopian region: in Hamasien in the 1870s, Ras Weldemichael took advantage of the insecurity of the frontier and raided extensively for slaves, mostly women and children, many of whom were destined for Arabia.[66]

The case noted in the White Fathers' diary for May 1884 is surely indicative of a wider phenomenon. The mission had purchased a Nyamwezi boy, whom they baptized Adolphe, and discovered that he had been seized by the Ngoni when younger. His ears had been scarified in the manner of the latter, but his teeth were filed according to Nyamwezi fashion. He told his "liberators" that he had been born in Msalala to Nyamwezi parents, and then he had been taken during an Ngoni raid when a mere infant. The mission diarist noted how it was clear that the boy had "grown up among the ferocious hordes of the forests. He has their bold and belligerent temper." He tried continually to get hold of a gun. He responded violently to those Nyamwezi children who mocked him, presumably on account of his being somewhat "different," sneering to them with unnerving maturity and world-weariness, "Why do you have a fear of dying? . . . It must be confronted sooner or later." When the Ngoni attacked near the mission, setting buildings alight before withdrawing, Adolphe apparently climbed a tree and screamed delightedly, "I am the fire!," in the midst of the general chaos. The mission diary notes sadly that the sight of the fire obviously pleased this traumatized child, who clearly "regrets no longer being with his former companions."[67] Adolphe's story must have been a common one. While there is no evidence that children as young as this were actual combatants, it is clear that children in this age-group were witnesses to extreme violence, and it is probably the case that youths not much older than Adolphe—as soon as physical growth permitted—were able to take up arms. They would join the ranks of the ruga ruga, who were as much victims of violence as they were practitioners of it.

Violence was also committed directly against children. Speke heard that among the Nyamwezi, children were "sacrificed" to ensure victory in battle, but I have encountered no direct evidence of this.[68] However, children were both killed and mutilated in the course of fighting. Notably, the Ngoni had set new precedents in the standards of violence, and in conduct toward enemy populations. It is certainly clear that there *had been* conventions, limits beyond which one had not been able to go without incurring general disgust. But once precedent was set, new levels of violence became "normal." The missionary Lourdel recorded a conversation with Mirambo's right-hand man Kirunga in June 1884, in which the latter told him that:

> The Watutas and Kapera's people have committed horrors as befitted real savages at the Bakandis' place (allies of Mirambo). They severed feet and hands, noses and lips of women and children, leaving them there in order to strike terror into the hearts of everyone; even the children . . . have not been spared. The eldest son of the mtemi of the Bakandis has been killed and burnt. . . . The Wanyamouezis here . . . are enraged.[69]

They were so enraged, indeed, that they responded in kind. According to Kirunga's report, his men captured a number of enemy chiefs and "cooked them," in response to the burning of one of theirs; moreover, "[t]heir women and children suffered the same treatment as ours had been made to suffer. It was they who started this, they cannot complain if we do the same to them."[70] Such cumulative brutality may well have been characteristic of the age. It is notable that restraint was not considered an option in this context, but rather true vengeance—the infliction of that which had been inflicted—was the only appropriate response. This was true despite the initial outrage at the behavior of Kapera's men. Women and children were clearly not normally targeted in this way, but once it had begun, new forms of violence aimed at the noncombatant community were no longer considered out of bounds. In a vicious war such as that between Mirambo and Kapera—the last of Mirambo's life—the desired end clearly justified the means. Mutilation had become part of total war, aimed at the destruction of entire communities.

In Ethiopia, notably, children were also regarded by some as a legitimate target in war. In Rassam's opinion, Tewodros' Magdala stronghold could not be captured because the Oromo "preferred their own detestable way of revenge by hiding themselves behind trees and rocks and killing helpless boys, or women. They fought well enough in defence, but on the attack were 'contemptible'";[71] Rassam's disgust recalls Clausewitz's view of the Cossacks on the retreat of Napoleon's army from Moscow. The fact that military activity was frequently attended by massacres of women and children raised moral concerns for many; and there appears to have been ambiguity in attitudes toward mass killing. For some, doubtless, there was in fact no such thing as a "non-combatant," and women and children were legitimate targets. But others were morally uncomfortable with the notion. When in 1832 Wube's soldiers "butchered nearly three hundred women and children," he was said to have "expressed his disapprobation of it."[72]

Victimhood and inheritance were often part of the same process; the young who were the victims of particular circumstances would then come to inherit the very systems that had grown out of these circumstances. Indeed, much of the intergenerational conflict described above was clearly an essential part of the process by which youth came to inherit the proverbial earth, as we have seen. Moreover, inheritance was depicted in many different ways, while the actual process of inheritance—the roles which legatees performed, the imagery surrounding them, the experiences that the young had to undergo—also varied considerably across time and space. The dispossessed and rootless, described at some length by everyone from Richard Burton in the 1850s onward, were almost certainly often youngsters, brutalized young men who had become a law unto themselves. This is perhaps one of the clearest manifestations of trauma across the region. Many of these young men were themselves the victims of the slave trade—many were either in the employ of renegade coastal merchants, or represented the human debris of slaving violence by which communities were torn apart in the 1860s and 1870s—and then served to perpetuate that same mode of violence. The victims would have victims of their own.[73] This was lawlessness on the back of commercial, political and military upheaval, violence as spasm rather than policy. There was a grey area between Mirambo's soldiery and small-scale petty criminality. Low-level violence was endemic, according to Cameron, by *ruga ruga* who "infested the country," and generally plundered small caravans, or snatched "one or two people out of the fields"; at their most ambitious, they went for larger caravans or villages.[74] They were the rootless and the displaced, both the products and the perpetuators of violence; they were the clearest manifestation of social collapse, and yet, on a certain level, no more so than many of Mirambo's own recruits. They were doubtless often the same people; many may well have claimed to be acting on Mirambo's behalf. But Verney Lovatt Cameron suggested that "[m]any of the atrocities ascribed to Mirambo should properly be placed to the account of these ruffians, who, bound by no laws human or divine, placed no limits upon the brutalities in which they indulged."[75] Certainly, distinctions were made at the local level: at Uyui, for example, individuals who fell into a life of crime by preying on passing caravans might face execution if caught, as in the case described by the missionary A. W. Copplestone in 1881. He noted: "I knew the men well and often thought they had much of the 'Warugaruga' about them."[76] Social breakdown or at least turmoil resulted from heightened military activity, and boisterous youth became one of the key agencies of social change in certain areas. In Uguha, on northern Lake Tanganyika, in July 1882, it was reported that preparations for war had been going on for a month, and that it was increasingly difficult to keep control of armed, drunk, and violent youth, with quarrels and robbery frequent.[77] Cultures of violence and armed adventurism clearly took their toll on communities on the eve of colonial invasion.[78]

Assessing Youth, War, and Statehood in Precolonial Eastern Africa

Defining male "youth" in the nineteenth century can be problematic, especially when dealing with societies in which there were shifting notions of what constituted "childhood," or "juvenility," usually in times of upheaval and social crisis. War, indeed, frequently prompted redefinitions of minority and certainly provided the young with new roles and opportunities, as well as making victims of them. It is clear that war was often a young man's game, sometimes even the business of children; but generalizations are dangerous. Mirambo might want boys, not men, to do his fighting; but the Ethiopian region offers a useful contrast, for here war was sometimes considered much too important to be left to the young. Active participation in conflict often represented a passage to manhood, but although culturally important, this kind of violent transition from juvenility to seniority is historically significant too, with changes in the balance of power within states, and even the creation of new states altogether, taking place as a result. Ganda "traditions" tell of boys becoming men in heroic and violent circumstances; but as the intellectual property of the aged, they also offer salutary lessons in terms of boys whose innocence is tragically lost through their attempts to gain the world too fast, too soon. Nonetheless, cultures of heroism, chivalry, courage, and ambition—alternately righteous and dangerous—grew up around the young. Older generations needed their power, yet feared them, too, often with very good reason. And this is not solely about boys: girls too, notwithstanding the shortcomings of the sources noted earlier, discovered various routes to maturity in the midst of conflict, though only occasionally as soldiers themselves, more often as captives, wives, mothers, and daughters, statuses which all involved the exercise of varying degrees of political guile in an ostensibly violent male world. Boys needed to be brave, to display courage and valor (differently interpreted from society to society), to spill blood in some cause public or otherwise, and to see blood spilled; and young male captives, too, found themselves exposed to a world of bloody conflict. Although their lives are almost impossible to reconstruct in any detail, it can be suggested that young female slaves likewise had to develop networks of knowledge and resistance, which were indelibly intertwined; young wives and mothers might use their positions to influence political-military events.

Many nineteenth-century eastern African societies were traumatized communities, and at the root of social crisis was traumatized childhood. Children learned to play with toy weapons, but it was not long before some were handling the real thing. Yet even in traumatized communities, there were often conventions that governed and defined "childhood," and a recognition that when children were thus caught up in violence, there were major disturbances in the natural order. In any case the young—whether traumatized or merely ambitious—were prone to challenging the state, and bringing about political and social change through violence. Afterwards this might be legitimated, remembered in itself as being natural and inevitable: this is what young heroes did, continually rejuvenating old states through violent intercession, or destroying societies and building new ones in their stead. This is the scenario in which we see violence initiated by youth victimizing the middle-aged and the elderly; but it is not the only one. We also find situations in which violence initiated by the middle-aged victimizes the young; yet this unleashed forces that older generations might find difficult to control. So often, violence offered the young opportunities to bring about change, and they were thus given the wherewithal to challenge and capture the very system that sought to harness their physical power. In this context, when we think about youth and war, it is important to consider both continuity and discontinuity in the lives of states and societies, inheritance alongside rebellion, independence and self-reliance, in explaining the actions of the young. It is clear that the young often started their own wars, but just as often they inherited the wars of their fathers. War was an institution, through which one generation after another must pass; and seen from a certain perspective, wars were never owned, but merely passed from one generation to the next.

Finally, war pushed forward social change in different ways, as the African youth of the colonial era created new norms and values in "postconflict" society. Jim Giblin has recently written of how the people of Njombe in southern Tanzania remember having to flee during the Maji Maji war, which was itself seen as just another episode in a series of violent irruptions. As they dispersed, and especially as young people moved to urban centers, they could no longer recognize their own kin, making it vital that they consulted their elders, especially when it came to marriage. Family had been broken up by war in the late nineteenth and early twentieth centuries; and as a result, Giblin writes, "[T]he range of stories about wartime flight . . . constitute an elaborate commentary on both the moral imperatives of family living and the failure of individuals to meet those imperatives."[79]

The implications of the breakdown of kinship and a sense of belonging across swathes of northern Tanzania,[80] and elsewhere, must have been just as profound; and so too were the implications of the emergence of a politically astute young elite in Buganda significant for political stability in the early years of colonial rule. It must be assumed that among younger members of communities traumatized by violence, perceptions of European invasion and colonial rule were colored by the experiences of the late nineteenth century. To what extent, and in what ways, is a matter for further research. Perhaps one consequence was the emergence of youth as a potentially more strident, militarized (in the loosest sense of the word) sociopolitical group, more willing than even in the nineteenth century to challenge older generations and engage in new patterns of intergenerational conflict.[81] Moreover, while nineteenth-century violence perhaps weakened states and societies, Ethiopia being a notable exception, on eve of the "scramble" for Africa—many were in the process of reforming themselves and engaged in sociopolitical reconstruction—it might also be suggested that the generation that came of age in the years immediately before and after 1900 had developed a resilience that enabled it to recover from the traumas of the period more quickly than might otherwise have been the case. At the same time, however, denial of the assumed right to violent self-expression, and the experience of violent defeat itself at the hands of European armies, may have stored up trouble for the future; the violence of the postcolonial era may be seen as unfinished business, the inevitable, if delayed, response to violent emasculation at the outset of colonial rule.

Notes

1. Sections of this chapter are derived from my recent monograph, *War in Precolonial Eastern Africa: The Patterns and Meanings of State-Level Conflict in the Nineteenth Century* (Oxford: James Currey, 2007), which appeared subsequent to the conference upon which the present volume is based.

2. Ebenezer Southon to Whitehouse, 6 August 1879, SOAS, London Missionary Society (hereafter LMS) Central Africa, Incoming, Box 2.

3. Philippe Broyon-Mirambo, "Description of Unyamwesi, the Territory of King Mirambo, and the Best Route Thither from the East Coast," *Proceedings of the Royal Geographical Society* 22, no. 1 (1877–78): 33.

4. It is a recurrent theme in the "traditions" of Buganda. An early kabaka, Tembo, for example, came to power having assassinated his grandfather, Kimera, according to traditions compiled by Kagwa. A. Kagwa, *The Kings of Buganda*, trans. M. S. M. Kiwanuka (Nairobi: East African Publishing House, 1971), 18. See also Carol Summers, "Youth, Elders, and Metaphors of Political Change in Late Colonial Buganda," chapter 7 in this volume.

5. Kagwa, *Kings of Buganda*, 96–98.

6. Ibid., 110.

7. J. H. Speke, *Journal of the Discovery of the Source of the Nile* (Edinburgh: William Blackwood and Sons, 1863), 252, 295, 312, 443.

8. Kagwa, *Kings of Buganda*, 140–41.

9. Ibid., 141.

10. Speke, *Journal of the Discovery of the Source of the Nile*, 290–91.

11. C. T. Wilson and R. W. Felkin, *Uganda and the Egyptian Soudan* (London: Sampson Low, Marston, Searle and Rivington, 1882), 2:23. It is interesting to consider this alongside more recent representations of President Idi Amin of Uganda as the embodiment of the masculine warrior tradition in Africa, and the degree to which he was seen as a reassertion of the precolonial in the "postcolony." Though by no means a young man when he seized power, Amin nonetheless attracted much comment vis-à-vis his physical stature and his youthful accomplishments, notably in boxing. See M. Leopold, *Inside West Nile: Violence, History and Representation on an African Frontier* (Oxford: James Currey, 2005), 57 ff.

12. Kagwa, *Kings of Buganda*, 151–52.

13. Ibid., 145–46.

14. G. Casati, *Ten Years in Equatoria* (London: Frederick Warne, 1891), 2:16.

15. A. R. Cook, *Uganda Memories, 1897–1940* (Kampala: Uganda Society, 1945), 43.

16. G. Portal, *The British Mission to Uganda in 1893* (London: E. Arnold, 1894), 189.

17. Wilson and Felkin, *Uganda and the Egyptian Soudan*, 1:199.

18. J. Roscoe, *The Baganda: An Account of Their Native Customs and Beliefs* (1911; London: Frank Cass, 1965), 229.

19. B. M. Zimbe, "Buganda ne Kabaka," trans. F. Kamoga, c. 1939, 83. MS in Makerere University Library, Kampala.

20. H. M. Stanley, *Through the Dark Continent* (London: George Newnes, 1899), 1:272–73.

21. Ibid., 280.

22. *Batongole* were chieftainships appointed directly by the kabaka. The batongole were the main agents of government between the sixteenth and the nineteenth centuries. They were not normally of a military character but became increasingly so in the course of the nineteenth century.

23. Zimbe, "Buganda ne Kabaka," 82.

24. Ibid., 174.

25. H. Salt, *A Voyage to Abyssinia and Travels into the Interior of That Country* (1814; London: Frank Cass, 1958), 298.

26. Ibid., 325.

27. A. Wylde, *Modern Abyssinia* (Westport, CN: Negro Universities Press, 1970), 251.

28. H. Waller, ed., *The Last Journals of David Livingstone in Central Africa* (London: Murray, 1874), 2:227.

29. V. L. Cameron, *Across Africa* (London: Daldy, Isbister and Co., 1877), 1:285.

30. R. F. Burton, *The Lake Regions of Central Africa* (New York: Harper and Brothers, 1995), 295.

31. Diary for Bukune (Djiwe la Singa), 13 April 1884, White Fathers Archive (hereafter WF), Rome.

32. C. R. Markham, *A History of the Abyssinian Expedition* (London: Macmillan, 1869), 200.

33. R. J. Reid, *Political Power in Pre-colonial Buganda: Economy, Society and Warfare in the Nineteenth Century* (Oxford: James Currey, 2002), 129.

34. A. Bulatovich, *Ethiopia through Russian Eyes: Country in Transition, 1896–1898* (Lawrenceville, NJ: Red Sea Press, 2000), 121.

35. J. Roscoe, *Twenty-five Years in East Africa* (Cambridge: Cambridge University Press, 1921), 254.

36. J. Roscoe, *The Bakitara or Banyoro* (Cambridge: Cambridge University Press, 1923), 314.

37. Speke, *Journal of the Discovery of the Source of the Nile,* 547.

38. J. Ford and R. de Z. Hall, "The History of Karagwe (Bukoba District)," *Tanganyika Notes and Records* (Dar es Salaam) 24 (1947): 9.

39. Kagwa, *Kings of Buganda,* 85–86.

40. Again, see also Summers's chapter in this volume.

41. Stanley, *Through the Dark Continent,* 1:294.

42. Ibid., 333.

43. Amharic for "age of the princes," conventionally held to have lasted between c. 1770 and 1855.

44. Asseggahen to Antoine d'Abbadie, 14 January 1866, in *Tewodros and His Contemporaries 1855–1868,* trans. and ed. S. Rubenson et al. (Addis Ababa: Addis Ababa University Press, 1994).

45. See also D. Crummey, "Tewodros as Reformer and Moderniser," *Journal of African History* 10, no. 3 (1969): 457–69; D. Crummey, "The Violence of Tewodros," in *War and Society in Africa,* ed. B. A. Ogot (London: Frank Cass, 1972), 65–84.

46. Kagwa, *Kings of Buganda,* 124; J. Roscoe, *The Banyankole* (Cambridge: Cambridge University Press, 1923), 15.

47. J. Nyakatura, *Anatomy of an African Kingdom: A History of Bunyoro-Kitara,* ed. G. N. Uzoigwe (Garden City, NY: Anchor Press, 1973), 31–33.

48. G. N. Uzoigwe, "Pre-colonial Military Studies in Africa," *Journal of Modern African Studies* 13, no. 3 (1975): 473.

49. Ibid., 386–87.

50. Edward Hutchinson, in Broyon-Mirambo, "Description of Unyamwesi," 37.

51. Southon to Whitehouse, 28 March 1880, encl. "History, Country and People of Unyamwezi," LMS Central Africa, Incoming, Box 3.

52. A. Shorter, "Nyungu-ya-Mawe and the Empire of the Ruga-Rugas," *Journal of African History* 9, no. 2 (1968): 240–41.

53. Diary of the Journey of Père Lourdel. De Kipalapala au Bukune, 3 April 1885, WF.

54. Stanley, *Through the Dark Continent,* 1;397.

55. Lourdel to Directeur, 1 June 1888, WF C14/185. See also Richard Waller, "Bad Boys in the Bush? Disciplining Murran in Colonial Maasailand," chapter 6 in this volume.

56. See also for example A. D. Roberts, "The Nyamwezi," in *Tanzania before 1900,* ed. A. D. Roberts (Nairobi: East African Publishing House, 1968); and J. Koponen, *People and Production in Late Precolonial Tanzania: History and Structures* (Helsinki: Finnish Society for Development Studies, 1988).

57. Markham, *Abyssinian Expedition,* 45.

58. Gleichen, "The Abyssinian Army," 28 December 1887, Public Record Office, London (hereafter PRO), FO 881/5530X, 2.

59. A. Kagwa, *The Customs of the Baganda,* trans. E. B. Kalibala, ed. M. M. Edel (New York: Columbia University Press, 1934), 43.

60. Bulatovich, *Ethiopia through Russian Eyes,* 105.

61. Wylde, *Modern Abyssinia,* 358.

62. S. Heald, *Controlling Anger: The Anthropology of Gisu Violence* (Oxford: James Currey, 1998), 57–58; see also S. Heald, *Manhood and Morality: Sex, Violence and Ritual in Gisu Society* (London: Routledge, 1999).

63. Diary for Bukune (Djiwe la Singa), 23 May 1884, WF.

64. Stanley, *Through the Dark Continent*, 1:238; J. R. L. Macdonald, *Soldiering and Surveying in British East Africa* (London: Edward Arnold, 1897), 149, 159.

65. Pearson to Wright, 29 September 1879, University of Birmingham, Church Missionary Society Archive (hereafter CMS), CA6/019/13.

66. Wylde, *Modern Abyssinia*, 125.

67. Diary for Bukune (Djiwe la Singa), 1–9 and 22 May 1884, WF.

68. Speke, *Journal of the Discovery of the Source of the Nile*, 500.

69. Diary of Père Lourdel, 10 June 1884, WF St-Marie Bukune.

70. Ibid.

71. Rassam to Stanley, 1 September 1868, PRO, FO 881/1609, 1.

72. S. Gobat, *Journal of Three Years' Residence in Abyssinia* (New York: Negro Universities Press, 1969), 426.

73. Livingstone to Stanley, 15 November 1870, PRO, FO 881/2060; Smith to Wright, 2 November 1877, CMS C/A6/M/1; Cameron, *Across Africa*, 1:201.

74. Cameron to Derby, 4th March 1874, PRO, FO 881/4189.

75. Cameron, *Across Africa*, 1:212.

76. Copplestone to Hutchinson, 22 March 1881, CMS G3/A6/0/1881.

77. Griffith to Thompson, 1 July 1882, LMS Central Africa, Incoming, Box 4.

78. Again, see Waller's chapter in this volume for a discussion of these issues into the colonial era.

79. J. Giblin, *A History of the Excluded: Making Family a Refuge from State in Twentieth-Century Tanzania* (Oxford: James Currey, 2005), 39, 49.

80. For example, A. Shorter, *Chiefship in Western Tanzania: A Political History of the Kimbu* (Oxford: Clarendon Press, 1972), 276.

81. There is a growing body of literature on this topic in colonial and postcolonial settings. See, for example, J. Abbink and I. van Kessel, eds., *Vanguard or Vandals: Youth, Politics and Conflict in Africa* (Leiden: Brill, 2004); E. G. Bay and D. L. Donham, eds., *States of Violence: Politics, Youth and Memory in Contemporary Africa* (Charlottesville: University of Virginia Press, 2006); B. Carton, *Blood from Your Children: The Colonial Origins of Generational Conflict in South Africa* (Pietermaritzburg: University of Natal Press, 2000). For the region under examination here, see E. Kurimoto and S. Simonse, eds., *Conflict, Age and Power in North East Africa: Age Systems in Transition* (Oxford: James Currey, 1998).

2

Youth, Cattle Raiding, and Generational Conflict along the Kenya-Uganda Border

DAVE EATON

> A cartel of traders, politicians and administrators is raking in millions of shillings through cattle rustling in Pokot, Turkana, Marakwet and Samburu Districts. The cartel hires youths, and, sometimes, even members of the disciplined forces on leave, to carry out their dirty work. Others are profiting from supplying the raiders with guns. Guns cost about 30,000/–, or 2 cows. Said one intelligence officer, "My friend, these are very powerful people with equally powerful friends. We've filed this information and nothing has been done. It's an issue which requires action from the very top."
>
> "Cartel Funds Stock Raids," *Daily Nation*, 20 July 1999

MOST DESCRIPTIONS OF modern cattle raids mention the involvement of young men. Writers suggest that "the possession of guns has enabled some people to draft the lumpenized youth into their private armies for cattle-raiding expeditions."[1] The youth, it is assumed, have been empowered by the arrival of modern weapons, integration into the market economy, and the state's undermining of the authority of the elders. Better able to take advantage of these "emerging changes" in pastoral areas, young men, led by a new generation of cattle warlords, are challenging cultural norms and disobeying their elders.[2] The relationship between pastoral youth and their elders is alleged to have been transformed.

The arguments made to explain the transformation in the relationship between young and old in pastoral societies owe a great deal to those used to explain general changes in conflict during the past twenty years. The end of the Cold War and the generalized breakdown of order in sub-Saharan Africa dramatically changed the way the relationship between youth and violence was studied. The wars of the future no longer seemed likely to be nuclear exchanges between major powers; instead, theorists postulated that they would be about "communal survival, aggravated or in many cases, caused by environmental scarcity. These wars will be subnational, meaning that it will be hard for states and local governments to protect their own citizens."[3] Several authors believe this breakdown of gerontological authority has also taken place in the impoverished Horn of Africa.[4]

The results of this profound change, it is argued, manifest themselves in what Chris Allen considers the five main characteristics of modern African violence: the targeting of civilians as opposed to combatants, extreme brutality in the conduct of the wars, state sponsorship of the violence, the commercialization of warfare, and the emergence of warlords in conflict zones.[5] Some authors contend that guns have given young men the confidence to challenge their elders, whom they suppose would otherwise restrain extreme acts of violence. Others note that the structures of the Kenyan and Ugandan states continue to undermine the traditional authority of the elders.[6] In virtually all analyses, however, it is presumed that the elders would exert their authority in order to restrain the acts of violent young raiders.[7] Commercialization is also presumed to have profoundly changed cattle raids; young men adept at exploiting commercial opportunities now have a new motivation to seek conflict. This desire is also fueled by changes to the institution of bride-price. It is suggested that the cattle required has risen while the per capita livestock population has almost certainly entered a steep decline. This creates a situation where many young men's primary ambition, to get married, is almost impossible to fulfill before they enter their thirties or forties. Cattle raids represent a method for youths to independently acquire the cattle needed to make an earlier marriage possible, and as such have become more common.

From a historical perspective, however, it is clear that young men have bitterly contested the authority of their elders for centuries in the North Rift (Northeastern Uganda and Northwestern Kenya) and that modern manifestations of this are hardly proof that the pastoral youth are out of control or that cattle raids have become increasingly violent. As Justin Willis points out in chapter 12 on alcohol sales in contemporary Kenya, this "wide anxiety about youth" is a discourse with a long history in East Africa, one that may have more to do with "moral panic" among officials and older African men than with an accurate representation of the situation. It is far from clear that the pastoral youth are out of control or that the elders as a corporate unit have a real desire for peace. As I argue elsewhere, what they seek would be better termed security, and this does not require an end to raiding.[8] Finally, this essay will use bride-price as a case study to examine changes in the relationship between young men and the elders in the North Rift. While pessimistic theorists argue that "lumpenized" youth are a significant threat to pastoral societies and that the authority of the elders is disintegrating, a historical perspective gives grounds for hope.

Small Arms and Cattle Raiding

Cattle raiding has a long history in conflict literature, but mainly as an example of primitive war. Authors were primarily interested in the many social restraints placed on cattle raids, and they even suggest that it represents the antithesis of the total wars of the twentieth century.[9] However, viewing cattle raids as essentially different from other forms of conflict has become increasingly rare, and it is argued that raiding has been transformed.[10] The new cattle raids are said to be a product of two main agents of change. The first is the increasing penetration of the market economy into pastoral areas. There is little doubt that a combination of colonial and postcolonial development projects has brought pastoral regions into the ambit of the global economy. Perhaps the most obvious manifestation of this is the proliferation of small arms throughout East Africa. Initially made possible by civil wars in south Sudan and Ethiopia, these weapons have become much more common owing to the war between Tanzania and Uganda from 1978 to 1979, as well as the collapse of the Soviet Union.[11] These events are alleged to have undermined the traditional restraints that regulated earlier cattle raids. Thus, contemporary raids are described as predatory and benefit only a small, criminal element predominantly composed of young men, far different from the "redistributive raiding" that marked the precolonial and colonial period.[12] Since this is taking place against a backdrop of extreme resource scarcity and a fast-growing population, some scholars have suggested that predatory raiding will lead to the end of pastoralism as a viable way of life.[13]

Young men factor into this discourse in a number of ways. First, they are presumed to have benefited disproportionately from the arrival of automatic weapons in the region during the 1970s. One study on small arms found that "culturally the possession of guns by young people encourages them to engage in cattle rustling. . . . This in effect increases the number of attacks and the reasons to organize for the same."[14] The AK-47 also transformed social norms within pastoral society, namely by "favouring the emergence of warlords and the decline of elders."[15] Young men, it is argued, have been better positioned to take advantage of the arrival of firearms, and "armed militias and the income available through banditry [have] further eroded the position of elders."[16] Before the arrival of numerous automatic weapons, the relationship between youths and their elders was usually described as respectful; after the arrival of the gun, most authors believe this relationship was completely transformed. Karimojong warlords, some as young as thirty-five, were able to emerge in a society that had previously been strictly stratified by age. Raids became much more frequent and were marked by increasing examples of shocking brutality.[17]

Although the argument described above is quite popular and makes a great deal of sense, it is far from clear that pastoral communities led by elders are helpless in the face of younger men equipped with modern weapons. The limited strength of the new warlords in the region can best be illustrated by the story of Lotem. Lotem was a young Kasauria Pokot man who rebelled against his family, killed a number of people during a series of violent raids, and then fled to the hills around Mount Moroto. From here he commanded an army of young bandits drawn from not only the Kasauria Pokot but also the Matheniko Karimojong, and he himself took a Matheniko Karimojong wife.[18] By 2005 he was such a problem that both the Kasauria Pokot and Matheniko Karimojong had exiled him from their kraals, and vowed to cooperate in order to defeat him. By July 2006 he had been killed by a force of Matheniko Karimojong.

Bandits such as Lotem are simply not able to gather sufficient strength to carve themselves a place in the deeply divided North Rift. Without the support of at least one territorial section, a warlord is rarely strong enough to create an independent power base. That said, it is difficult to be considered part of a territorial section without demonstrating one's obedience to the elders of that group.[19] Firearms did not give Lotem any edge in combat since every community in the area was already armed to the teeth. In fact, guns are so noisy they may inhibit young bandits since it has become much more difficult to raid with the stealth numerical inferiority requires.[20] This combination of factors makes it difficult to imagine the region being overrun by young warlords or bandits in the near future, and suggests that the proliferation of firearms may not have had such a transformative impact on relations between young and old as is sometimes assumed.

The Commercialization of Cattle Raiding

It is also argued that young warriors have been dramatically affected by the increasing penetration of the market economy into the remote pastoral locations along the border of Kenya. One study attributes this change to the colonial government and notes that as early as 1931 the British recognized that raiders had organized themselves into multiethnic gangs "that operated across a vast area . . . pasturing [herds] in secluded valleys while awaiting opportunities to market them, moving cattle effortlessly back and forth across a porous Tanganyika-Kenya border in response to regional price fluctuations"[21] With opportunities to sell cattle on the rise, the postcolonial era was marked by a period of unparalleled commercial raiding. These raids were led and organized by cattle warlords who then sold the loot at distant markets in Bungoma or Dagoretti.[22] Raiders were alleged to have started selling stolen cattle for money, and there are numerous reports suggesting that young raiders themselves were available for hire as mercenaries.[23] One researcher observed in nearby Baringo District that the youth "are being manipulated by certain local elders, regional traders and politicians, who make use of the communities' armed youth . . . to enrich themselves."[24] The commercialization of raiding led to dramatic changes in the practice, with the youth providing the muscle for powerful "cattle warlords."

It is curious to note that young men are just as likely to be described as the victims of commercialization. Most researchers based in the North Rift are keenly aware of the economic strength of the elders, and they often suggest that this power has increased dramatically. Blame for this lies with the penetration of the market economy and with it increasing inequalities within pastoral society. These inequalities, it is presumed, have worked to undermine the traditional responsibilities of the elders and have led them to act in a much more selfish manner.[25] Young men are faced with a difficult situation where they are dependent on their elders for bride-price cattle, but the elders are often unwilling to fulfill their responsibilities when it comes time to give their sons the livestock they need to marry.

It is still unclear exactly why young warriors would go to fight for a warlord, putting their lives at risk, in exchange for a gun and a pittance of a salary. The most common argument is that a shrinking resource base has increased conflict.[26] The poorest youths end up living on the margins of the few towns in the region, and they form a ready army for those willing or able to arm them.[27] These youths then take part in the commercialized raids, which provide them with badly needed resources that can then be sold for cash.

This is a very popular theory, but it suffers from a number of flaws. First, the most recent research in Karamoja suggests that the poorest of the poor do not commonly take part in raids; they lack connections with kraal leaders who have access to firearms and more experienced raiders. It is likely that the impoverished youth living in the towns simply make poor fighters because they lack experience in the bush.[28] Second, it is increasingly difficult to suggest that scarcity encourages people to raid. A growing number of authors have changed their views on this issue and now suggest that scarcity is in fact of only limited importance.[29] Finally, this theory provides young men with very little agency. In the words of Thandika Mkandawire, "The view that the manipulations of rebel leaders can move an otherwise inert mass to do what they command suggests, on the one hand, a view of human conduct which credits leaders with more instrumental rationalism than they deserve while, on the other hand, failing to account for the irrationality of the followers."[30] Indeed, some writers doubt that cattle warlords have ever existed, particularly in Karamoja, something that casts into doubt many of the other changes listed above.[31] It is unlikely that the "lumpenized" youth are as easily manipulated as some authors would like to suggest.

Bride-Price and Modern Raiding

Despite the many grounds for doubt about a transformation of conflict, the literature on youth in Africa has undergone its own transformation to account for the impact of small arms and commercialization. One major compilation on youth and conflict noted that pastoral societies "have great difficulty in absorbing the challenges and problems of 'modernity.' [These societies] are faced with processes of economic exclusion, unmediated commercialization, wrong-headed state policies and so-called development schemes that do not enhance interaction, cooperation or well-being, but rather the reverse. These societies also face intensified armed conflict. . . . The wide availability of arms (particularly automatic rifles) has enhanced this."[32] The main explanation put forth for young men's participation in cattle raids is their desire to accumulate bride-price. While this has a long history in the North Rift, it is argued that recent changes have made the institution unsustainable, something that has contributed to increasing violence. The recent changes being referred to are none other than commercialization and the proliferation of small arms. Given that there are so many reasons to be skeptical of this narrative, it seems possible that changes in the relationship between youth and conflict have been similarly overstated.

The argument connecting commercialization, bride-price, and youth suggests that a combination of declining livestock numbers and the extremely high level of contemporary bride-price is making the practice unsustainable. This view is still given particular prominence by the Kenyan and Ugandan administrations.[33] They tend to see bride-price in a straightforward manner, arguing that it is too high for the vast majority of young men to afford. These warriors therefore must raid to try and pay the exorbitant cost of marriage. This is then put forth as the root cause of many cattle raids, especially against agricultural peoples on the fringes of the North Rift. This is a view shared by many farmers who have been targeted by raiders. One group of Bukwa Sebei men told me, "The girl who wants to be married whereby they want one hundred head of cows, that thing should be banned."[34] Even in Karamoja this view is not uncommon; one faith-based peace group noted that a key cause of raids was the extremely high bride-price in the region, which ranged from fifty to three hundred head of cattle.[35] It is quite common in the literature to see statements such as this: "Nowadays, male youth from increasing[ly] poor families have to raise bride-price by themselves, sometimes through armed cattle raids."[36] Reducing bride-price or eliminating it altogether remains a popular suggestion at focus group discussions arranged by nongovernmental organizations.

This view has a long history in the region and was first systematically analyzed in the literature as a cause of conflict during the colonial period. The British bandied about the idea of reducing bride-price in the North Rift in an effort to curb thieving and pastoralism in general, but in West Pokot District this never came to fruition.[37] One early Kenyan government report suggested that doing so would be "an excellent thing, allowing young men to obtain wives, and removing a fruitful cause of cattle theft."[38] In Tanganyika, they were more ambitious and made a concerted effort to restrict bride-price payments to a mere three head of cattle, plus one additional head that could be slaughtered at the wedding feast. As Michael Fleisher argues, "Before long, the British colonial administration had become persuaded that a crucial, causal link existed between high bridewealth and the upwardly spiraling incidence of cattle raiding."[39] By the 1960s, this was evident in most official writing on the subject. The Bataringaya Report, published in 1961, argued that a dramatic rise in bride-price in Karamoja was a direct cause of raiding.[40] This sort of straightforward linking of cattle raids and high bride-price was characteristic of the colonial administrations in East Africa.

There is considerable evidence that bride-price has varied dramatically among the pastoral peoples of the North Rift and is heavily dependent on local conditions. In 1906, C. W. Hobley found that Turkana bridewealth could be as high as one hundred head of cattle and any number of small stock. This contrasted sharply with the pastoral Pokot sections, then a recently created community of herders, where bride-price rarely exceeded twenty head of cattle. This average was hardly applicable among those Pokot who made a living through agriculture; in their communities bride-price was often much lower, in some cases as low as three to four cows and a number of small stock.[41] Bride-price was highly variable even within the Pokot ethnic group, and men from the pastoral areas were highly valued as husbands by daughters (and fathers) from the hills, since they paid dowry in cattle. The gap became even more pronounced during the colonial period as Kasauria Pokot herders took advantage of new grazing areas assigned to them by the British. In the Kanyangareng, where the wealthiest herders lived, bride-price was as high as sixty to seventy head of cattle by 1935. In areas to the south bride-price dropped dramatically, and in the hills, where it was impossible to keep cattle, bride-price dropped even further, down to as low as ten goats for a poor man's daughter in Mwino. Cases even existed of women being paid a goat or two to accept a poor man in marriage.[42] Bride-price varied considerably during the colonial period based on the livestock population of a region; during times when cattle populations grew, bride-price grew right along with it.[43]

Despite the imposing costs, during the precolonial and colonial periods there were still a number of strategies for a poor man to marry. The first involved payment in installments, which was generally acceptable, and while this reduced a husband's immediate claims to his children, it provided a valuable avenue for an enterprising man to arrange a marriage.[44] A second was that bride-price varied enormously based on a number of independent factors beyond the general wealth of the region as a whole. One observer felt this was so prevalent there was no reason to even provide a range of values for Pokot bride-price, and indicated that factors that had to be taken into account were the wealth of the groom, the locality, the kindness of the girl's father, and the depth of feeling involved. Girls seem to have generally had the last word on whom they would marry, and if a match was obviously heart-felt it was not unusual for the family to accept a lesser amount of bride-price.[45] Finally, if it was not possible to marry a woman locally, there were always other areas where the demands of relatives were not so prohibitive.

For similar reasons, it is difficult to accept that high bride-price is a direct cause of cattle raiding. The relatively large numbers of cattle paid as dowry are used to establish ties with a wide range of people, and the cattle themselves come from numerous relatives and friends as well as the groom. In one example taken from Jieland in the 1950s, the family of the groom provided twenty-one animals from a total of fifty; twenty-two came from brothers, cousins, uncles and half-cousins, and the rest from clansmen or friends.[46] Bride-price was an important way for a fortunate father to obtain wealth, but it was also a key method of cementing clan and kin relations. The institution of bride-price was also extremely flexible; values tended to decline during periods of scarcity, which cushioned the impact of epizootics and droughts on the ability of a young man to marry. During periods of extreme disaster, bride-price can often be arranged simply by promising to pay later. One elderly man described the crisis of 1979–84 in the following terms:

> R1: Now, girls were given to lease because there were not enough livestock to give as bride-price . . .

R2: Providing you seemed to be hard-working in finding the bride-price, you were given.

Q: So [they] were given off for free?

R1: What would you do as parents if the girls were also serious about getting married? So was not free. You would pay later.[47]

A similar practice can be found in Karamoja, where raiders indicated that women can be married "on credit."[48] It is rare for the raiders themselves to ever mention bride-price as a reason they go raiding.[49]

The prominence of high bride-price as an explanation for raiding may have political origins. In Kenya, the Moi government in particular has used traditional raiding, allegedly inspired by young men's insatiable desire for bride-price cattle, as an explanation for violence. But much of the allegedly traditional raiding was in fact politically motivated and actively encouraged by the government.[50] One prominent newspaper saw through this, and made the following comment on the situation:

> Government officials here will say rustling is a traditional pastime for communities in this vast land. The young men steal the animals to pay bride-price, they say, or for food, or to replenish stocks decimated by drought and disease. Do not be fooled. True, animals are being stolen for these reasons. But by far the most significant factor in the rustling, which has killed, maimed or displaced thousands—men, women and children—is pure commercial criminal greed.[51]

Straightforward explanations of raids through high bride-price oversimplify a complex reality. They tend to be encouraged by those who wish to apportion blame for raids on pastoral culture and have served as an alibi for both political repression and inadequate state security. Bride-price has a long history in the North Rift, and a number of the methods used by poor men in the early twentieth century to get married are still in use today. Bride-price creates a large expense for young men, but it obviously also creates an alternate source of income for a family with a number of daughters. Several pastoralists mentioned bridewealth as a method for poor families to become rich.[52] The fact that bride-price is higher than a young man can afford alone does not necessarily make him increasingly prone to violence.

Bride-Price and the "New" Raiding

Most studies of modern cattle raids suggest that bride-price has become unsustainable owing to recent changes linked to guns and the pressures of predatory capitalism.

They suggest that traditional responsibilities and restraints on bridewealth have been undermined by the greed of both the elders and youths in the region. In general, this discourse suggests that the elders and the young raiders have been pitted against each other through the commercialization of the pastoral economy. This new competition has led to abuses of power, particularly by the elders, and this has created desperation and frustration on the part of the youth. Faced with the bitter reality that the elders wish to maximize their own gains through a refusal to pay their sons' bride-price, young men turn to raiding as the only alternative.

One of the earliest examples of this writing comes from Charles Ocan. He argues that precolonial raids were a community venture aimed at ensuring optimal herd sizes; in this way, they represented a means to ensure community survival. However, from 1970 to 1990 cattle raids developed what he terms "self-acquisition motives." Instead of being inspired by declines in livestock numbers, raiders aimed to sell livestock for individual gain. As he points out, "While the first kind of raids hinge on community interest and are controlled by the community through elders' councils, the latter hinge on private interest and [are] controlled by armed kraal leaders."[53] Increasing violence and raiding "promotes personal reputation and vitalizes the military organization, but it also strengthens the development of unequal levels of wealth . . . captured cattle have an inflationary effect on the size of bridewealth."[54] This led to unprecedented inequalities in herd sizes, causing major changes in the fabric of Karimojong society. As elders acquired more and more animals, they began "to represent private or individual property as opposed to community interests."[55]

The competition between elders and raiders focused on the issue of marriage. This was crucial in the North Rift, especially during periods of extreme violence and declining livestock populations. A wife was a source of children; sons became additional herders and provided protection for the family herd, and daughters would be invaluable owing to the bride-price they would eventually generate. But when wealthy kraal leaders and young men are both trying to obtain the hand of a young woman, the father of the bride will often choose the highest bidder; normally, this means the older of the two suitors.[56] A consequence of this is that competition over women between wealthy kraal leaders and younger herders during times of conflict drives bride-price ever higher.[57] It also leads some fathers to refuse to pay their son's bride-price, and some authors have even suggested that the extended family no longer helps its young sons who are seeking to get married. Elders may deliberately inflate bride-price to give themselves an advantage over the younger men.[58] The young men thus have to raid much more frequently to have a chance to marry. It has even been reported that some kraal leaders recruit young men for raiding parties by promising to assist them in paying their bride-price, a promise that is fulfilled only after considerable time has passed.[59] Under these circumstances, young men will rarely be able to compete for a wife until they are quite old. Recent observations have confirmed this and suggest that many raiders do not marry until they are in their thirties.[60] Given the situation, it is easy to understand why young men raid; in order to create their own independent herd, from which they can then negotiate dowry.

This was occasionally mentioned in the North Rift. One renowned cattle raider in the village of Alakas told us that "if you don't have the money, you will never marry, and for a long time, you will go, the woman will look at others, but you have an alternative if your father is poor, you must raid to get the cows, in order to get the woman."[61] This particular raider himself comes from a very wealthy family, but as the fifth son he does not always have access to his father's herds. When my research assistant asked him why he went for raids, he bitterly noted that his father would not give him the cattle he needed to pay bride-price: "The animals are there, but you must beg for three days. The first day, he says come back tomorrow, the second day, he says come back tomorrow, and on the third day, he finally gives you maybe one cow."[62] His problematic relationship with his father had forced him to take a wife who was half Bukusu and half Sebei; the bride-price he had negotiated with her family was several times smaller than that typically given to a Pokot family. In this case, a younger son's ambitions combined with an obstinate father led him to a career as a raider.[63] However, an opposite example can be found in Ruben de Koning's recent study on Jie raiders. Here, the well-known raider Lokui successfully obtained twenty head of cattle during a raid on the Bokora. He gave fifteen of these to his father, who in appreciation gave ten animals to the father of Lokui's future wife as a first bride-price payment. Three of the leftover cattle were also used for a form of bride-price, in this case to pay the father of Lokui's eventual second wife compensation for her first child, which had been born out of wedlock.[64] This was very fortunate for Lokui, since he was not a first son, and thus his father was under no obligation to assist him before assisting his elder brother. It clearly demonstrates the importance of the father-son relationship and the nature of raiding. Fleisher has argued that in northern Tanzania it is more likely for families with more sons than daughters to produce cattle raiders, a phenomenon that seems present in the North Rift as well.[65]

Marriage has always been a crucial event in a young man's life, and, especially among the Turkana and Karimojong, it represents the transition from childhood to full manhood.[66] For this reason one can imagine how dramatic an impact a lengthy delay can have. However, this was a common problem even at beginning of the twentieth century. Most observers agreed that women in the North Rift married at a much younger age than men. Among the Elgeyo, this seems to have meant that women of sixteen or seventeen married warriors of twenty-five to thirty.[67] This was also true in Kotido District in the 1950s; here P. H. Gulliver surveyed 140 men from ages eighteen to thirty, and found only six were married.[68] Polygyny was practiced, but it was extremely rare for a man to have more than three wives.[69] Old men could compete for wives, but in certain regions this was either frowned upon or forbidden; in most cases, women preferred to marry an unmarried man, since this enhanced their prestige through becoming a first wife.[70] Recent commentators have suggested that delayed marriage may be a cause of the current insecurity in Karamoja.[71] This seems unlikely; young men have married during their late twenties and early thirties throughout the history of the North Rift, and as such this does not represent a recent change to the institution of bride-price.

The tensions created by late marriage and the elders' economic power have long been managed through age systems.[72] Age systems did this through both spiritual and economic sanctions.[73] The latter generally centered on the issue of marriage; since cattle were owned by the family patriarchs, they wielded tremendous power over their juniors through the withholding of the cattle needed to pay bridewealth. Among the Jie, this seems to have encouraged young men to "play out a role entailing group solidarity, communal brotherhood, and obedient deference until such time as they enter a new role where individual acquisitiveness and differentiation are the norm."[74] Age systems helped shoulder "the strain of youthful resentment," which might otherwise be aimed at the family itself.[75] In a pastoral region where raids were a constant fact of life, age systems used the economic control that elders possessed to restrain the young men, whose ferocity and combat ability was vital to ensuring the survival of the community.

Most elders in the region will argue that these systems of control have broken down. Elders repeatedly complain that their sons do not respect them and that they even threaten them with modern weapons. One Pokot elder ruefully reminisced about the good old days during one interview:

> R: They [youths] are the worst lot today. They are the ones who have spoiled good relations among the Pokots and other peoples. They even kill their own mothers for quarrelling with his wife or the father and elders like us for stopping them from going for raids. They are very bad people in the community.
>
> Q: Who is to blame? Is it the youths for indiscipline or the elders for treating them too gently?
>
> R: We are the ones who let the situation go. During our time, we were beaten up in case of a mistake by any elders, not necessarily our parents. But today, if I caned your son, he will shoot me and you.[76]

This is a very common complaint among the elders, who will routinely produce the names of any number of old men allegedly shot by youths; as one group at Nauyapong told me, "We old men are tired of these killings, of being killed by our sons."[77] The key factor causing problems remained bridewealth. One elder told us, along with a group of intent young men, "Your generation, they are rude; when they see that the old man cannot give him cows to pay dowry, they shoot him. They target the old men and first-born boy who respect their fathers."[78] It was impossible for me to investigate the allegations made by the elders, and in a number of instances they were obvious fabrications, but it is indicative of the fear that currently pervades age relations in the North Rift.

There is considerable evidence that age relations are in a state of turmoil in the North Rift. Young men can be denied cattle by their fathers and thus have their hopes of an early marriage threatened. But it is important to note how problematic relationships between young and old have been throughout history. Karimojong tradition suggests that the Jie were "young men" who split with their fathers by taking the cattle to the dry-season cattle camps and then refusing to return. When the elders ordered them to come back, the youths resisted with spears, thus rejecting their authority and creating their own community, named Ngijie, or "the fighting people."[79] Although it is difficult to pinpoint other disruptions in normal age-set relations with similar accuracy, it is clear that breakdowns in traditional restraints were possible, particularly during periods of extreme scarcity.[80] There is no doubt that tensions exist between the generations in Karamoja, Turkana, and West Pokot, but this needs to be put into context. Bitterness, frustration, and anger have been common between warriors and elders since the 1700s, and the mere presence of these tensions today is not necessarily indicative of any dramatic changes.

Commercialization and Bride-Price

Some argue that bride-price itself has been commercialized, a change that would have a significant impact on age relationships. In the place of cattle, they suggest bridewealth is now more widely paid in cash. These cash payments are easier for elders to monopolize than cattle, and this has allowed them to benefit a great deal more than was customary.[81] It has also become much easier to spend money than cattle, and elders are now spending much of the bride-price they receive on their daughters without saving any to help their sons pay for marriage.[82]

This would certainly represent a dramatic change, but this simply does not seem to have happened in the North Rift. In 1935, for example, one observer was told that "payment of a bride-price, except in small part, by Shillings is refused as having, to the native taste, too crude a flavour of prostitution. The silver has to be on the hoof before it is acceptable as the price of beauty."[83] Thirteen years later in neighboring Baringo District, dowry was still considered unacceptable unless it took the form of cattle. One missionary who stayed in the region during the late 1970s found an identical situation: cattle were still necessary when it came to paying bride-price.[84] More recently, Vigdis Broch-Due found that "livestock are the prime mediators of the Turkana world, between production and exchange, between representation, between memory and morality." Money could be used to purchase animals, but even purchased cattle are unable to serve certain functions, such as being presented as bride-price.[85] It is difficult to pinpoint the exact reason for the limited importance of cash in bride-price payments in the region. There can be no doubt, however, that it is related to the influence of the pastoral lifestyle. The most detailed study of bride-price payments in the region was that done by Walter Goldschmidt among the Sebei. He found that cash had entered bride-price earlier than 1915, and among farming communities had gone from representing 13.3 percent (1910–20) of the total payment to 31.8 percent (1956–60), a substantial increase. Among the pastoral community of Kapsirika, the comparable statistics were much less dramatic, with a rise from 8.4 percent to 20 percent during the same time period. Significantly, the importance of livestock in bride-price payments at Kapsirika actually increased over the same period as well, revealing that cash was not replacing cattle in bride-price payments.[86] Bride-price does not operate in a vacuum, and there have certainly been changes. However, it is possible that the continuities throughout the twentieth century are more important. It is crucial to note that bride-price has not been brought into the money economy; payment still requires cattle, and in some cases these cattle cannot even have been purchased.

Wealth in cattle can obviously be manipulated as well, and the case has been made that elders have intentionally driven bride-prices up in order to maximize their own gains. B. A. Rwezaura argued that Kuria elders felt that their control over traditional society was slipping during the 1920s and 1930s owing to the fact that the young men were better positioned to use new income-generating activities in the cash economy to purchase cattle, and with these cattle, pay bride-price independent of their elders. The elders began to lose faith in the social networks that bridewealth provided and began insisting on large lump sums in order to maximize their own individual accumulation. There was some debate as to whether increased bride-price was indeed due to the factors described by Rwezaura or whether it was inspired by a more general increase in the size of Kuria herds, but it is quite likely that in the North Rift elders are making every effort to maximize their own profits from bride-price.[87] Certainly Pokot elders believe it is an easy way to become rich.[88]

Youth are thus portrayed in two extremely different ways. In the first instance, as expounded by the elders and many conflict theorists, they are seen as a violent rabble that represents a significant threat to public order. Motivated by little more than a simplistic desire for wealth, these youths provide the muscle for powerful warlords, who agree to assist the youths in exchange for their support. Other authors and many young warriors, however, paint a different picture. The youth, far from being a problem, actually are seen as the victims of the insecurity in the North Rift. The superior economic clout of the elders is emphasized, and it is suggested that they are using their power to prevent their own sons from marrying. It is not clear why it is in the interests of the elders to do this, but this narrative has acquired a great deal of authority, and it is repeated in most publications on the region. In both cases, however, the issue of bride-price remains front and center, and changes in the practice are used to help explain the violence of the youth.

Youth Relations throughout History

At this point, it makes sense to examine these changes from a historical perspective. First, it should be clear that the high bride-price that so alarms both the administration and some academics is hardly unprecedented. Mkutu was incredulous when he noted that Jie women receive a bride price of 60 to 160 animals, but this does not seem particularly out of the ordinary in comparison with amounts observed before or during the colonial occupation.[89] It also does not seem to have been linked causally with raids at any point in the past; increases in bride-price tend to take place during times of prosperity. Thus, the increases in bride-price observed recently in Karamoja may well be linked to the massive numbers of animals they raided from the Teso and Lango—one survey suggested that the Jie and Dodoso alone have increased the livestock population of Kotido District by 374,000 cattle.[90] It seems likely that high bride-price is really just a manifestation of a large livestock population; it is hardly a cause of raids in and of itself.

In the same way, there are numerous examples of conflict between elders and young men that are seen as indicative of enormous changes in the region. One such example of this is the issue of elders' withholding bride-price from the warriors, as a result of which young men are forced to seek their bride-price on their own through predatory raiding. It is argued that this is due to the commercialization of the economy in the region, something that has led the elders to become protowarlords, maximizing their own accumulation and abrogating their responsibilities to the youth. That said, there is considerable evidence to suggest that many of these "new" conflicts existed in the early colonial and even the precolonial periods. Warriors currently marry in their thirties, a fact viewed with alarm by many observers.[91] The implication is that late marriage is indicative of the tension between elders and warriors, and indeed this may well be the case. But it must be kept in mind that even during the colonial period men in the North Rift married late, and Gulliver's survey cited above indicates there are perhaps more similarities with the present than is generally understood. The same is true with regard to half-marriage, a practice which allows young men to pay only a small portion of bride-price at any one time. Since the woman remains living with her parents, a half-marriage can dissolve quickly if there are payment problems or a wealthier rival makes a more substantial offer. However, this practice has been around for over a century, and it is hard to prove that it is any more prevalent now than it was in the past. While it is tempting to suggest that half-marriage represents an aspect of the breakdown of traditional society in the face of impoverishment and modernity, this seems unlikely. In reality, mechanisms that allow young men to marry have a long history in the North Rift.

It seems that many authors have crafted their arguments to fit a wider discourse on youth and conflict in Africa. These have tended to portray the youth as not responsible for their actions, suggesting that they are the pawns of powerful cattle warlords, or driven to violence by extreme poverty.[92] In the North Rift, this is simply not true. There is considerable evidence that the young warriors who participate in raids are in fact among the wealthiest in the region, whereas the poorest tend to take advantage of alternative economic opportunities available in the towns. And the powerful kraal leaders do not represent a new wave of authority based on the penetration of the market economy. I have met and interviewed two major kraal leaders in the region, Aramtori at Achorichor and Emunongole at Nabilatuk, and in both cases they were old men in their sixties at the very least.[93] Their control over young men lay not so much in their access to markets or their ability to supply firearms, but rather in the more mundane fact that they organized the security of the kraals, and thus could give disobedient youths a series of miserable or lengthy tasks. A group of elders from Aramtori's kraal told me that the youth were out of control and creating chaos, but not twenty minutes later described an incident where they had forced a group of Pokot youths from Achorichor to return some stolen cattle to the Matheniko, with whom they had a truce.[94] The elders are often keen to point out that they cannot control the youth. In reality this seems to be due to a desire to avoid the consequences of admitting collaboration; when questioned closely, most elders and warriors admit that they cooperate during raids.[95]

AGE RELATIONS have always been incredibly tense in the North Rift. This was the case even in the precolonial period, where the fracturing of the Jie from the wider Karimojong polity provided ample warning to elders against the flagrant abuse of their powers. Thus, the relationship between the young warriors and the old men has long been the site of conflict, particularly as it relates to bride-price. It seems possible that this relationship has been misconstrued in light of other literature on cattle raiding and conflict in Africa, which suggests that the practice has been recently transformed. In reality, practices such as "half marriage," struggling with an elder to get him to release bride-price cattle, and waiting until one is at least in his thirties before marriage have a long history, and if these strategies seem insufficient at times of great stress, this was also true in the past.[96] Indeed, it seems possible that the violence of modern cattle raiding has been greatly overstated; in Marsabit, it seems that violent deaths during raiding have actually been in decline since the 1940s.[97] If this is the case, the quest to explain the origins of increasing youth violence in the region may well be of little value.

Impoverished young men can play a key role in initiating a series of raids by committing small thefts of unattended livestock. These small thefts can eventually escalate into major raids, and cycles of violence are continually born in the North Rift. This potential connection between poverty, youth, and raiding is quite intriguing. However, in the aftermath of a small theft a rational decision must be made by the victims and their friends and family as to whether the incident is worthy of retaliation. This decision-making process is absolutely crucial to determining whether raiding begins in earnest and deserves far greater analysis than it has heretofore been accorded. Recent studies have shown that these decisions are heavily informed by local interpretations of the origins of the thieves as well as a pragmatic assessment of the current security situation.[98] In the North Rift, the elders still retain considerable influence over this decision-making process and are not nearly as powerless as they often pretend to be.[99]

It seems more important to note that the youth and their elders operate within a common framework. There is a great deal of conflict over the issue of when the resources of the elders should be made available to the younger generation, and there is no doubt that a small but significant number of youths find this relationship very frustrating. But this frustration has been part of age relations in the region long before many analysts suggest, and its presence in and of itself does not indicate that raiding or violence has profoundly changed. As one can see from the example of bride-price, it is truly remarkable how capable these institutions have been at adapting to things like the market economy. These adaptations have successfully limited the potential impact of commercialization in a society situated on the extreme fringes of the global economy. Modern raiding is supposed to be the result of dramatic changes wrought by the commercialization of the pastoral economy; in the absence of the latter, however, it seems likely that the damage attributed to the former is less dramatic than often claimed. As one raider told me and my research assistant, "There are powers in the youth and also in the old."[100] This seems a fair assessment of the situation. The relationship between the elders and the young warriors in the North Rift has not been transformed recently; the conflicts seen in the present are simply new manifestations of issues that have existed for over one hundred years.

Notes

I thank the Killam Trust, the Social Sciences and Humanities Research Council (SSHRC) of Canada, and Dalhousie University for their generous support during the writing of this chapter.

1. C. Ocan, "Pastoral Crisis in North-Eastern Uganda: The Changing Significance of Cattle Raids" (Kampala: CBR Working Paper #21, 1992), 7.

2. J. Abbink, "Being Young in Africa: The Politics of Despair and Renewal," in *Vanguard or Vandals: Youth Politics and Conflict in Africa,* ed. J. Abbink and I. van Kessel (Boston: Brill, 2005), 5.

3. R. Kaplan, "The Coming Anarchy," *Atlantic Monthly* 273, no. 2 (1994): 75.

4. M. Fleisher, *Kuria Cattle Raiders* (Ann Arbor: University of Michigan Press, 2000), 2–3.

5. For the targeting of civilians such as women and children see M. Turshen and C. Twagiramariya, eds., *What Women Do in Wartime: Gender and Conflict* (London: Zed Books, 1998); A. de Waal, *Famine Crimes* (Bloomington: Indiana University Press, 1997), 106–132. On the issue of brutality, see S. Ellis, *The Mask of Anarchy* (New York: New York University Press, 2001). For state sponsorship of violence, see J. Bayart, S. Ellis, and B. Hibou, *The Criminalization of the State in Africa* (Bloomington: Indiana University Press, 1999), 1–31. For the commercialization of warfare, see P. Collier and A. Hoeffler, *Greed and Grievance in Civil War* (Washington, DC: World Bank—Development Research Group, 2001); D. Keen, *The Economic Functions of Violence in Civil Wars* (London: Oxford University Press, 1998). Regarding the emergence of warlords, see W. Reno, *Warlord Politics and African States* (Boulder, CO: Lynne Rienner, 1999).

6. M. Duffield, "Ethnic War and International Humanitarian Intervention: A Broad Perspective," in *War and Ethnicity: Global Connections and Local Violence,* ed. D. Turton (Rochester: University of Rochester Press, 1997), 206.

7. A good treatment of an exception can be found in S. Kratli and J. Swift, *Understanding and Managing Pastoral Conflict in Kenya* (Sussex: Institute of Development Studies, 1999), 31–33.

8. D. Eaton, "Violence, Revenge and the History of Cattle Raiding along the Kenya-Uganda Border, c. 1830–2008" (PhD thesis, Dalhousie University, 2008), 279.

9. See J. Keegan, *A History of Warfare* (New York: Vintage, 1993), 29; K. Fukui and D. Turton, Introduction to *Warfare among East African Herders*, ed. K. Fukui and D. Turton (Osaka: National Museum of Ethnography, 1979), 1–14.

10. D. Turton, "Mursi Political Identity and Warfare: The Survival of an Idea," in *Ethnicity and Conflict in the Horn of Africa*, ed. K. Fukui and J. Markakis (Athens: Ohio University Press, 1994), 25.

11. M. Quam, "Creating Peace in an Armed Society: Karamoja, Uganda, 1996," *African Studies Quarterly* 1, no. 1 (1997): 6; Ugandan Human Rights Commission (UHRC), *Karamoja: Searching for Peace and Human Rights* (Kampala: UHRC, 2004), 28; "Why Disarming the Karimojong Has Not Been an Easy Choice," *East African*, 17–23 March 1997; Interview #154, Amukuriat, West Pokot District, Kenya, 17 February 2006.

12. Ocan, "Pastoral Crisis in North-Eastern Uganda."

13. J. Markakis, *Conflict and the Decline of Pastoralism in the Horn of Africa* (London: Macmillan, 1993), 12–15.

14. Security and Research Information Centre (SRIC), *Terrorized Citizens* (Nairobi: SRIC, 2003), 76.

15. M. Mirzeler and C. Young, "Pastoral Politics in the Northeast Periphery in Uganda: AK-47 as Change Agent," *Journal of Modern African Studies* 38, no. 3 (2000): 419; B. Okudi, "Causes and Effects of the 1980 Famine in Karamoja" (Kampala: CBR Working Paper #23, 1992), 42.

16. Duffield, "Ethnic War and International Humanitarian Intervention," 206.

17. S. Gray, "A Memory of Loss: Ecological Politics, Local History, and the Evolution of Karimojong Violence," *Human Organization* 59, no. 4 (2000): 401–7, 413–14; D. Hendrickson, R. Mearns, and J. Armon, "The Changing Nature of Conflict and Famine Vulnerability: The Case of Livestock Raiding in Turkana District, Kenya," *Disasters* 22, no. 3 (1998): 190–92.

18. Interview #160, Achorichor, Moroto District, Uganda, 19 February 2006; Interview #153, Lokitalauyan, West Pokot District, Kenya, 17 February 2006; Interview #163, Amudat, Nakapiripirit District, Uganda, 20 February 2006; Interview #152, Lengorok, West Pokot District, Kenya, 17 February 2006.

19. B. Knighton, *The Vitality of Karimojong Religion* (London: Ashgate, 2005), 189.

20. See Interview #007, Akorkeya, Nakapiripirit District, Uganda, 15 October 2005.

21. Fleisher, *Kuria Cattle Raiders*, 51.

22. S. Simonse, "Warriors, Hooligans and Mercenaries: Failed Statehood and the Violence of Young Male Pastoralists in the Horn of Africa," in *Vanguard or Vandals: Youth Politics and Conflict in Africa*, ed. J. Abbink and I. van Kessel (Boston: Brill, 2005), 252; NCCK and SNV Kenya, *Pacifying the Valley: An Analysis on the Kerio Valley Conflict* (Nairobi: SNV Kenya, 2002), 8–9.

23. S. Kratli and J. Swift, *Understanding and Managing Pastoral Conflict in Kenya* (Sussex: Institute of Development Studies, 1999), 8.

24. J. Cappon, *Why Do Communities Want Arms?* (Utrecht: Pax Christi, 2003).

25. K. Mkutu, *Armed Pastoralist Conflicts and Peace Building in Karamoja: The Role of Gender* (Kampala: SNV Uganda, 2005), 26.

26. See for example Duffield, "Ethnic War and International Humanitarian Intervention," 206; T. Dietz, *Pastoralists in Dire Straits* (Amsterdam: Instituut voor Sociale Geografie, 1987), 290.

27. See J. O. Osamba, "The Sociology of Insecurity: Cattle Rustling and Banditry in North-Western Kenya," *African Journal on Conflict Resolution* 1, no. 2 (2000): 24–25; Ocan, "Pastoral Crisis in North-Eastern Uganda," 17. Neither author mentions specific towns, but it seems likely both believe impoverished and aggrieved youth live on the margins of most urban centers and villages in the region.

28. R. de Koning, *What Warriors Want* (Utrecht: Pax Christi, 2004), 49–50.

29. J. T. McCabe, *Cattle Bring Us to Our Enemies* (Ann Arbor: University of Michigan Press, 2004), 238; K. Hussein, J. Sumberg, and D. Seddon, "Increasing Violent Conflict between Herders and Farmers in Africa: Claims and Evidence," *Development Policy Review* 17 (1999): 413–14; T. Dietz, W. Adano, and K. Witsenburg, "Natural Resources and Conflicts: Theoretical Flaws and Empirical Evidence in Northern Kenya" (unpublished paper prepared for a keynote address at the Moi University First Annual Conference, 14 and 16 February 2005, Eldoret), 1. It is important to note that both Ton Dietz and J. T. McCabe used to be prominent advocates of resource scarcity as a cause of cattle raiding. See Dietz, *Pastoralists in Dire Straits*, 126; V. R. Dyson-Hudson and J. T. McCabe, *South Turkana Nomadism* (New Haven, CT: HRAF Press, 1985).

30. T. Mkandawire, "The Terrible Toll of Post-Colonial 'Rebel Movements' in Africa: Towards an Explanation of the Violence against the Peasantry," *Journal of Modern African Studies* 40, no. 2 (2002): 189.

31. B. Knighton, "The State as Raider among the Karamojong: 'Where There Are No Guns, They Use the Threat of Guns,'" *Africa* 73, no. 3 (2003): 431–32; Simonse, "Warriors, Hooligans and Mercenaries," 252.

32. Abbink, "Being Young in Africa," 12.

33. Amani Forum-Uganda, "Fact-finding Mission on the Sabiny-Pokot Conflict" (Kampala: Report Produced by the Amani Forum-Uganda, 2003), 9–12; "DO Links Dowry with Rustling," *Daily Nation*, 10 January 1998.

34. Interview #056, Cheminy, Kapchorwa District, Uganda, 17 November 2005; Interview #038, Suam, Kapchorwa District, Uganda, 6 November 2005.

35. L. M. Rose, *Peace Together* (Moroto: Karamoja Agro-pastoral Development Program [KADP] Report, 1999), 24–25; see also M. Quam, "Cattle Marketing and Pastoral Conservatism: Karamoja District, Uganda, 1948–1970," *African Studies Review* 21, no. 1 (1978): 52, for examples of high bride-price.

36. Mkutu, *Armed Pastoralist Conflicts*, 26.

37. "A Partial Survey of the Agricultural Resources," by Colin Maher, Agricultural Officer, no. 40; January–June, 14 February 1935, Kenya National Archives, Nairobi (KNA), DC/WP/8/6; see also A. J. Docherty, "The Karamojong and the Suk," *Uganda Journal* 21, no. 1 (1957): 39–40.

38. Cited in M. Ruel, "The Social Organization of the Kuria: A Field Work Report" (Nairobi: Institute of African Studies, University of Nairobi, 1959), 175. See Fleisher, *Kuria*, 58. It is interesting to note that in a publication on stock theft at a similar time, the issue of bride price as a cause of raiding never was discussed. This was likely due to the fact that theft in white areas and raiding elsewhere were dealt with in very different manners. See *Report of the Stock and Produce Theft Committee* (Nairobi: Swift Press, 1925).

39. Fleisher, *Kuria Cattle Raiders*, 58.

40. Government of Uganda, Report of the Karamoja (Bataringama) Committee (Entebbe: Government Press, 1961), Public Records Office, London (PRO), CO 822/2788 and CO 822/3050.

41. C. W. Hobley, "Notes on the Geography and People of the Baringo District of the East Africa Protectorate," *Geographical Journal* 28, no. 5 (1906): 478; K. R. Dundas, "Notes on the Tribes Inhabiting the Baringo District, East Africa Protectorate," *Journal of the Royal Anthropological Institute of Great Britain and Ireland* 40 (January–June 1910): 63.

42. "A Partial Survey of the Agricultural Resources," by Colin Maher, Agricultural Officer, 14 February 1935, KNA DC/WP/8/6.

43. H. K. Schneider, *Economic Man: The Anthropology of Economics* (New York: Free Press, 1974), 83–84.

44. Dundas, "Notes on the Tribes Inhabiting the Baringo District," 68.

45. "Appendix to January 1931 Safari Diary," January 1931, KNA DC/WP/3/42; Interview #015, Lokitalauyan, West Pokot District, Kenya, 18 October 2005.

46. H. Gulliver, *The Family Herds* (London: Routledge and Kegan Paul, 1955), 231, 239.

47. Interview #015, Lokitalauyan, West Pokot District, Kenya, 18 October 2005.

48. Interview #088, Namalu, Nakapiripirit District, Uganda, 21 December 2005.

49. Out of a sample of about sixty interviews with raiders, only one mentioned bride-price as a motive for raiding. This was interview #061, Alakas, Nakapiripirit District, Uganda, 28 November 2005, and it will be discussed in more detail below. That said, the vast majority did cite "poverty" or "hunger" as a reason for raiding, which in some cases may well involve bride-price.

50. This was the conclusion reached by Human Rights Watch (HRW), *Playing with Fire: Weapons Proliferation, Political Violence, and Human Rights in Kenya* (New York: HRW, 2002), 2–3.

51. "Rustling Brings Life to Standstill," *Daily Nation,* 20 July 1999.

52. Interview #118, Kasei, West Pokot District, Kenya, 19 January 2006.

53. Ocan, "Pastoral Crisis in North-Eastern Uganda," 3.

54. V. Broch-Due, "Remembered Cattle, Forgotten People: The Morality of Exchange and the Exclusion of the Turkana Poor," in *The Poor Are Not Us,* ed. David M. Anderson and Broch-Due (Athens: Ohio University Press, 1999), 85.

55. Ocan, "Pastoral Crisis in North-Eastern Uganda," 28.

56. R. B. Edgerton and F. Conant, "Kilapat: the 'Shaming Party' among the Pokot of East Africa," *Southwestern Journal of Anthropology* 20, no. 4 (1964): 412–13.

57. Ocan, "Pastoral Crisis in North-Eastern Uganda," 31–32.

58. Mkutu, *Armed Pastoralist Conflicts,* 26.

59. Action for Development of Local Communities (ADOL), "Karamoja Response to Disarmament: Six Months Later" (Kampala: ADOL, 2002).

60. S. Gray, M. Sundal, B. Wiebusch, M. Little, P. Leslie, and I. Pike, "Cattle Raiding, Cultural Survival, and Adaptability of East African Pastoralists," *Current Anthropology,* 44 supplement (2003): S3–S30.

61. Interview #061, Alakas, Nakapiripirit District, Uganda, 28 November 2005.

62. Ibid.

63. Ibid. This man had previously served a brief stint with the Ugandan government's Local Defence Units (LDU); LDUs were ex-raiders who were given a salary and allowed to keep their weapons in exchange for a loose affiliation with the Ugandan army.

64. De Koning, *What Warriors Want,* 27.

65. Fleisher, *Kuria Cattle Raiders,* 126; Interview #140, Kiwawa, West Pokot District, Kenya, 13 February 2006.

66. "Political History of the Turkana," May 1, 1926, KNA, PRB/211, TURK/59.

67. J. Massam, *The Cliff Dwellers of Kenya* (London: Frank Cass, 1927), 161.

68. Gulliver, *Family Herds,* 242.

69. "Appendix to January 1931 Safari Diary," January 1931, KNA DC/WP/3/42.

70. Massam, *Cliff Dwellers of Kenya,* 56–57.

71. Mkutu, *Armed Pastoralist Conflicts,* 25–28.

72. See P. Baxter and U. Almagor, Introduction to *Age, Generation and Time,* ed. P. Baxter and U. Almagor (New York: St. Martin's Press, 1978), 10–11.

73. For good examples of the power of spiritual sanctions, see R. Abrahams, "Aspects of Labwor Age and Generation Grouping and Related Systems," in *Age, Generation and Time,* ed. Baxter and Almagor, 53–54; Knighton, *Vitality of Karimojong Religion,* 106, 187–89.

74. J. Lamphear, "Brothers in Arms: Military Aspects of East African Age-Class Systems," in *Conflict, Age and Power in North East Africa,* ed. E. Kurimoto and S. Simonse (Athens: Ohio University Press, 1998), 81.

75. P. Spenser, "Opposing Streams and the Gerontocratic Ladder: Two Models of Age Organization in East Africa," *Man* 11, no. 2 (1976): 155.

76. Interview #139, Kiwawa, West Pokot District, Kenya, 13 February 2006.

77. Interview #012, Nauyapong, West Pokot District, Kenya, 17 October 2005.

78. Interview #151, Kalapata, West Pokot District, Kenya, 16 February 2006; Interview #145, Mbaru, West Pokot District, Kenya, 15 February 2006; Interview #149, Kases, West Pokot District, Kenya, 16 February 2006.

79. See Gulliver, *Family Herds,* 5; J. Lamphear, *A Traditional History of the Jie of Uganda* (Oxford: Clarendon Press, 1976), 106–7, expresses skepticism at this version of events, arguing that in reality a combination of factors, but particularly ecological factors, were to blame. No doubt there is truth in this, but the tradition remains common in Karamoja as a ceremonial warning to young men before leaving for the cattle camps. See Knighton, *Vitality of Karimojong Religion,* 60–61, 193.

80. Knighton, *Vitality of Karimojong Religion,* 203–5.

81. For a customary example, see Dundas, "Notes on the Tribes Inhabiting the Baringo District," 68. He writes that "the marriage price [among the Turkana] is very high and consists nominally of twenty head of cattle and thirty donkeys to the mother of the bride; this is due before the marriage takes place; next thirty head of cattle and a large number of camels, donkeys, sheep and goats to the father, five head of cattle to each of his remaining wives and finally two head of cattle to each of the brides brothers and sisters." Obviously bridewealth cattle were widely distributed.

82. P. Geschiere, "Applications of the Lineage Mode of Production in African Studies," *Canadian Journal of African Studies* 19, no. 1 (1985): 82.

83. "A Partial Survey of Agricultural Resources," by Colin Maher, Agricultural Officer, 14 February 1935, KNA DC/WP/8/6.

84. J. J. Visser, *Pokoot Religion* (Oegstgeest, the Netherlands: Hendrik Kramer Instituut, 1989), 239–40.

85. Broch-Due, "Remembered Cattle, Forgotten People," 84–85. Exceptions obviously exist, primarily over goats, but they remain rare.

86. W. Goldschmidt, "The Economics of Brideprice among the Sebei and in East Africa," *Ethnology* 13, no. 4 (1974): 317. The rise in the value of livestock as a proportion of bride-price over the same period was from 55 percent to 68.8 percent.

87. See Fleisher, *Kuria Cattle Raiders,* 58.

88. Interview #118, Kasei, West Pokot District, Kenya, 19 January 2006.

89. P. Gulliver and H. Gulliver, *The Central Nilo-Hamites* (London: International African Institute, 1953), 40–41; Mkutu, *Armed Pastoralist Conflicts,* 26. Gulliver argues that the average was about fifty head of cattle in the 1950s, but says that more than seventy head was not unusual. In the 1930s, he notes that more than two hundred head of small stock was added to this, but due to disease this practice was in decline.

90. Ocan, "Pastoral Crisis in North-Eastern Uganda," 23–24.

91. De Koning, *What Warriors Want,* 28; Gray et al., "Cattle Raiding," S18.

92. NCCK and SNV Kenya, *Pacifying the Valley,* 11; Osamba, "Sociology of Insecurity," 24–25.

93. Interview #074, Loro, Moroto District, Uganda, 2 December 2005; Interview #082, Nabilatuk, Nakapiripirit District, Uganda, 20 December 2005. It should also be noted that a great deal of Aramtori's authority derives from the fact that it is widely rumored he is a *kapolok,* or powerful seer.

94. Interview #153, Lokitalauyan, West Pokot District, Kenya, 17 February 2006.

95. Interview #140, Kiwawa, West Pokot District, Kenya, 13 February 2006; Interview #005, Amudat, Nakapiripirit District, Uganda, 14 October 2005; Interview #109, Losam, West Pokot District, Kenya, 18 January 2006; Interview #004, Alakas, Nakapiripirit District, Uganda, 14 October 2005; Interview #012, Nauyapong, West Pokot District, Kenya, 17 October 2005; Interview #048, Karita, Nakapiripirit District, Uganda, 15 November 2005.

96. Knighton, *Vitality of Karimojong Religion,* 203–5.

97. Dietz, Adano, and Witsenburg, "Natural Resources and Conflicts," 15–16; KADP, 7–8.

98. D. Eaton, "Revenge, Ethnicity and the Causes of Cattle Raiding in North-Western Kenya," in *Conflicts of Identity, Interests, and Territory in Kenya,* ed. K. Witsenburg and J. Akonga (forthcoming).

99. Interview #153, Lokitalauyan, West Pokot District, Kenya, 17 February 2006.

100. Interview #163, Amudat, Nakapiripirit District, Uganda, 20 February 2006.

3

Setting a Moral Economy in Motion

Youth in Tanzania's "Age of Improvement"

JAMES L. GIBLIN

THE CONCEPT OF moral economy has never been far from the view of historians of Tanzania.[1] Yet, the most prominent approach to moral economy in Tanzanian studies has been neglected over the past two decades. After generating intense debate in the first half of the 1980s, Goren Hyden's concept of the "economy of affection" gradually faded from view.[2] It disappeared as the object of Hyden's critique, Tanzania socialism, gave way to economic liberalization and capitalism. Recently, however, debate over the "economy of affection" has revived through the collaboration of Tanzanian and Japanese scholars.[3]

In a contribution to the renewed debate, Hyden writes that "the easiest way of describing the economy of affection is to suggest that it is constituted by personal investments in reciprocal relations with other individuals as ways of achieving goals that are seen as otherwise impossible to attain."[4] Its basis in rural Africa comprises "the affective ties based on common descent, common residence, etc."[5] Just as it did in the 1980s, the renewed debate asks how moral economy affects rural development. In his seminal *Beyond Ujamaa in Tanzania* (1980), Hyden argued that the vigor of the "economy of affection" explained why rural Tanzanians successfully resisted both a colonial market economy and a postcolonial socialist economy. In his view, agrarian societies managed to remain "uncaptured" by using their "affective ties" to maintain an alternative economy. The recent debate has reconsidered these issues. Rather than insisting that rural populations have remained "uncaptured," it asks whether the "economy of affection" facilitates the integration of agrarian communities into market economies.[6]

For scholars who wish to consider whether economies of affection stimulate change, one difficulty is their static appearance. Although Hyden has warned that adherence to affective ties should not be understood as a "traditionalism,"[7] the importance of kinship, family, and "small-scale, face-to-face contexts"[8] in descriptions of economies of affection encourages an understanding of them as deeply embedded African culture stubbornly resisting modern outside influences. Historians are partly to blame. They have not used their stock-in-trade—sensitivity to change through time—to set economies of affection in motion by studying them during moments of transition. Indeed, in my own writing about family and kinship as sources of transformation in twentieth-century rural Tanzania, I, too, have neglected the concept of economy of affection.[9] However, new perspectives that consider kinship as sites of dynamic relationships and creative discourses can help us ask whether Hyden's "affective ties" caused change in the past. In particular, they lead us to ask whether the particular "affective ties" that define "youth"—relations between the young and their elders—have catalyzed rural transformation. For this reason, the concept of economy of affection provides a way of attacking two problems that have arisen throughout the conference and subsequent rounds of revision that led to this book. One problem is the tendency to see youth as acted upon and even victimized, rather than as significant social actors in their own right. The second problem is the tendency to see youth in negative contexts, as the cause of problems and consequence of crisis. Here I seek an approach that allows us to perceive the agency of youth in processes of social improvement.

The role of youth in agrarian change is the issue addressed by this essay. I address this by considering youth during a period that many historians consider a moment of fundamental transition. This was the transition after the Maji Maji war of 1905–7 to what John Iliffe called "The Age of Improvement."[10] Iliffe and other historians who wrote in the early postindependence period believed that this transition began when Africans, having suffered defeat, humiliation, and famine in war, abandoned hope of successful armed rebellion against colonialism. According to this interpretation, which is still widely taught in Tanzania, they turned toward the new opportunities created by colonialism for literate education, vocational training, and wage-earning employment. These opportunities, holds the interpretation of the 1960s and 1970s, would provide the resources and skills needed to challenge colonialism through political mobilization.

Recent reconsideration of the "Age of Improvement" resembles debate over the "economy of affection" in an important respect. Like the debate inspired by Hyden, it considers whether rural transformation is caused by dynamics inside agrarian societies or by pressures exerted from the outside by governments and markets. Historians such as Iliffe saw the growth of colonial markets, schooling, and wage employment as the results of initiatives by agrarian communities. More recent work has suggested that the notion of "improvement" underestimates the unrelenting pressure on rural societies from colonial government and economy to enter exploitative markets and relations of production.[11]

Whether they were exercising initiative or acceding to pressure, there can be no doubt that youth played a leading role in the process of transformation. Youth largely determined whether the "economy of affection" became a catalyst or an obstacle to change. It was mainly young people who entered schools, joined churches and mosque communities, and increased the ranks of wage earners after Maji Maji. Throughout the portion of southern Tanzania where Maji Maji had been fought, communities integrated themselves into the colonial economy through long-distance labor migration. While the shift toward labor migration involved whole communities, it was the youth, mostly young men, who established the patterns of migration to the plantations of northeastern Tanzania that dominated the regional economy through the remainder of the colonial period. The prominence of the young in this movement shows that we need to pay them special attention if we are to understand better the role of the economy of affection in the transition toward "improvement."

Although it draws on extensive study of twentieth-century family life and agrarian change in the extreme western portion of the Maji Maji region, the Southern Highlands, this essay discusses a quite limited number of sources. They offer a rare glimpse of social change in the Southern Highlands during the German colonial period yet appear never to have been used by historians. They are particularly helpful in revealing the combination of constraint and opportunity through which affective ties defined the experience of youth. For although the years after Maji Maji may be seen as a time of innovation, the young in this period were engaged in a struggle that surely has reoccurred in all generations. Through their interaction with elders they sought ways of escaping their condition of dependent minority. For this reason, revisiting the turn toward "improvement" allows us to see how transformation was driven forward by the very sphere of everyday social activity in which Hyden locates the economy of affection.

For the period discussed in this essay we have few recorded examples either of action by youth or of specific cross-generational interaction. In the absence of a record of action, this essay focuses primarily on the language in which such action was discussed and understood. This focus on language informs the understanding of generation adopted in this essay. My experience with both written and oral accounts suggests that while talk about family articulated conceptions of youth, seniority, and the existence of the different cohorts that we call generations, a generation was unlikely to be described as a collective actor. Certainly speakers recognized differences in the perceptions of older and younger people, and understood them to be the result of different kinds and amounts of life experience. Yet, elders and youth were not often described as engaging in generation-based collective action. Although speakers might refer to the actions of "elders" or to "youth," they were most likely to do so with reference to small numbers of individuals, such as the older members of a particular group of kin. Moreover, features of language such as terms of address blurred distinctions between younger and older people, particularly by loosening connections between age and seniority. It would not have been at all uncommon, for example, to hear a younger man addressed by an older relative as "uncle," or a younger woman as "aunt" or "mother." The relationships that we describe as intergenerational were animated and sustained through interaction and negotiation among individuals. The net result of this approach is a departure from the view of intergenerational relations taken by some historians of late nineteenth- and early twentieth-century East Africa. Rather than emphasizing increasing tension and distance between generations, as does, for example, Richard Reid in this volume, this essay stresses that the sources of tension between generations changed relatively little, and that older and younger people remained in intense engagement with each other. We see the persistence of these continuities even though changing historical circumstances, including the increasing influence of Christianity in particular, provided both youth and their elders with new discursive weapons that they used in launching arguments and appeals across the boundary of generation.

The sources discussed in the following pages are brief publications written by German Lutheran evangelists of the Berlin Mission Society (BMS) who worked in the Southern Highlands. These accounts provide a glimpse of social conditions in a period for which there is no substantial ethnographic reportage. Brief as they are, they provide a foundation for considering how youth and the economy of affection shaped the transition toward "improvement."

The Texts

The three texts discussed here are *Amelye: Ein Lebensbild aus dem Benavolk in Deutsch-Ost-Afrika* ("Amelye: A Life-Story from the Bena People of German East Africa") (1911) by Paul Gröschel; *Asajile Kyabwe: Ein Helfer in Magoje, Deutsch Ostafrika* ("Asajile Kyabwe: An Assistant in Magoye, German East Africa") (1913) by E. Källner; and *Lutengamaso in Milow oder, Was Gottes Gnade aus einem Heiden Machen kann'* ("Lutengamaso in Milo, or What God's Grace Can Do Among the Heathen") (1920) by Wilhelm Neuberg. All three were published as booklets by the Buchhandlung der Berliner Evangelischen Missionsgesellschaft, the publishing arm of the BMS.[12] Each of the three texts relates the life story of a young man who became a Christian convert and employee in a Lutheran mission.

In their own generation these three men were not typical. They were forerunners, for as Christians and employees of Europeans they shared experiences that would become common across their region only later, in their children's generation. In their day, before and just after Maji Maji, Christian communities were few and very small in the Southern Highlands, and only a handful of people worked in European employment. Only in the 1920s would membership in Christian congregations and working for Europeans become common. Nevertheless, while the young men featured in these texts were forerunners, their innovation came from an old form of youthful activity—striving to achieve maturity. They found new ways of achieving maturity which would be taken up by increasing numbers of youths in later decades.

Although the lives of these young men were atypical in their own generation, the missionary authors presented them as representative of African youth. The authors interwove incidents in the lives of their young protagonists with background discussion of situations and problems common among the young. The missionaries' reconstructions of the lives of these young men were based only partially on their autobiographical accounts. Equally important in the creation of these texts were the missionaries' observations of children and youth. Also important were oral accounts of events that had preceded the arrival of the missionaries in the Southern Highlands. They used them to imagine the childhoods of the young men. In numerous passages, particularly those describing events that the young men themselves would have been too young to remember, one finds conventions and tropes common to oral narratives still told in the Southern Highlands. While the missionaries may have encountered these clichéd images of the past in the autobiographical stories of the young men, they also found them in the stories of war, famine, and other events of the past that circulated among their employees, neighbors, and congregations.

By emphasizing the representative nature of these life stories, the missionaries made them vehicles for presenting ethnographies of youth. Theirs was an applied ethnography. In the guise of individual life stories, the missionaries sought to provide a picture of African youth which would explain how the young might be led to accept Christian faith. The ethnographic character of the texts enhances their usefulness. For rather than concentrating exclusively on individuals who were exceptional in this period by virtue of their Christianity, literacy, and close association with Germans, the texts situate the young men within the circumstances shared by most youth, including those who experienced Maji Maji as defeat. Thus they provide insight into the situation of youth at the beginning of the "Age of Improvement."

Amelye

The ethnographic character of these texts is most explicit in Paul Gröschel's account of Amelye, a young man baptized at the Yakobi mission in Njombe in 1903. Gröschel opens his story by saying that Amelye's life provides an opportunity to describe the culture of the "isolated" Bena people. Much of the account consists of descriptions of boyhood (boys tending cattle and making bird-traps, for example), which were surely drawn from his own observations, together with ethnographic comment (accurate when he notes the shallowness of genealogical knowledge, misleading when he exaggerates lack of interest in the past). As did his fellow authors, Gröschel fleshed out his story with imagined accounts of how Amelye had presumably experienced incidents that occurred before Gröschel's arrival in the region in 1898. He must have heard about earlier episodes of war and famine from stories told by his Bena neighbors.

Gröschel organized his narrative of Amelye's childhood and youth so that it would explain his decision to become a Christian. In so doing he played heavily on two themes. The first was the nature of Bena political authority. Gröschel believed that the marginalization of his family by political leaders had made Amelye exceptionally receptive to Christian evangelization. Here a bit of background helps us understand the highly critical view that Gröschel takes in *Amelye* of Bena chiefs, particularly Mbeyela Mkongwa. In earlier writings, Gröschel had described Mbeyela much more favorably as a personal friend and sponsor of the Yakobi mission. At the outset of Maji Maji, however, Mbeyela suddenly turned against the mission. He attacked it, forced its residents to flee, and later permitted his warriors to destroy it. Gröschel's writings after Maji Maji reflected his feeling that he had been betrayed by a friend turned mortal enemy.

In *Amelye,* Gröschel portrayed Mbeyela as a usurper who, in the course of imposing his rule over southern Njombe, had forced Amelye's father to flee his home. Amelye's father later became involved in a war with the Hehe in which he perished. This war forced Amelye's mother to flee attackers. According to Gröschel, as an infant Amelye was carried into hiding in uninhabited woodland on the back of his mother. Here Gröschel was certainly drawing on commonly told oral narratives, for tales of wartime flight by mothers carrying babies are one of the most common stories told about the precolonial past in Njombe. The greater tragedy of Amelye's childhood came later, however, when his mother died during a community witch-hunt conducted by Mbeyela. Gröschel estimates that Amelye was then about eight or ten years old. Gröschel leads us to wonder whether the discovery of the witchcraft of Amelye's mother was related to her prior ostracism by Mbeyela as the widow of his enemy.

Gröschel founded the Yakobi mission in 1899. Not long afterward Amelye, who lived in a nearby settlement, decided to seek employment at the mission to obtain bridewealth. Gröschel suggests that Amelye's alienation from the regime of Mbeyela explains why he was willing to defy his prohibition on his subjects working for the missionary. Initially Amelye tended mission cattle and participated in construction projects in the mission. His involvement in the mission deepened after he began catechism studies. In 1903 he was among the first small group of converts who received baptism at Yakobi.

If Gröschel's first theme was the tendency of chiefly rule to generate enmity, alienate youthful subjects, and increase their receptiveness to Christianity, his second theme concerned Bena culture and the problems it posed for Christian evangelism. Gröschel was generally a sympathetic observer of Bena culture. He described Bena boyhood in favorable terms, contrasting carefree Bena boys with stressed-out German schoolchildren. He pointed out that, despite the relatively unstructured nature of Bena boys' lives, they were continually engaged in learning cattle-keeping, farming, hunting, and crafts. His account shows that Amelye's boyhood provided him with skills that proved useful in mission employment.

Gröschel was also sympathetic when discussing the defining characteristic of childhood and youth: their subordination to elders. Intergenerational relations imposed responsibilities on the young, he showed, but at the same time provided them opportunities to negotiate with their elders. Thus when Amelye decided to seek employment at the mission, he had to overcome the reluctance of his elders and their warnings that he might face trouble from Mbeyela. He did so by assuring them that by working for Gröschel he would be able to provide them with a prized commodity, cloth. This is perhaps the earliest recorded example of the negotiation that generations of young Bena men would undertake when seeking the assent of their elders to travel far from home for long periods as migrant laborers.[13]

Marriage was another crucial moment of negotiation between the young and their elders. Here again, Gröschel provides a sympathetic account of Bena custom. Unlike many later observers, Gröschel does not describe bridewealth as an opportunity for elders to exploit young men. To the contrary, he consciously addresses such a view when pointing out that fathers of brides "are not monsters" (22) but are willing to allow young men to complete the payment of bridewealth in installments. Gröschel goes on to describe the benefits of bridewealth, saying that it improves the status of married women, assures that the paternity of children will be recognized, and serves usefully as a "barrier" (24) to regulate interaction between unmarried young men and women.

In his discussion of marriage as elsewhere in *Amelye,* Gröschel is concerned about relations between young Christian converts such as Amelye and their elders. He takes a pragmatic approach, realizing that separating the newly married members of his Christian flock from their non-Christian relatives would be neither possible nor desirable. He argues that African Christians must continue to practice customs such as bridewealth which provide moral benefit.

Yet, despite the sympathy which marks his discussion of Bena culture, from the point where Amelye marries onward, Gröschel's account is dominated by the struggle of young Christians to avoid being pulled off the path of Christian salvation by their "heathen" kin. For Amelye, the struggle began during his wedding celebration and appears to have been prompted by Gröschel himself. During Amelye's wedding feast, Gröschel warned some of the bride's non-Christian relatives against forcing the young couple back into "heathen ways" (26). The relatives left the wedding "dissatisfied and grumbling," wrote Gröschel. The next morning, Amelye told Gröschel that during the night they had taken his bride back to her parents' home. Gröschel immediately mounted his donkey and rode to their settlement, where he persuaded the bride's reluctant relatives to allow her to return to her husband. After this incident, reported Gröschel, Amelye's relatives continued to urge him not to distance himself from their lifeways. Sometimes they appealed to him by using the language of Christianity, as when they urged him to join in drinking the favorite Bena intoxicant, *ulanzi* or bamboo wine. Because it was a "gift of God" (27), they said, Christians had no reason to abstain from it.

Here we find a tantalizingly brief hint that, rather than effacing indigenous culture, Christianity instead expanded the discursive options employed by the young and their elders in negotiating their relationships. Elsewhere I have pointed out that in later decades the young found in Christianity a new language in which they articulated individual preferences and desires, particularly when claiming the right to choose spouses.[14] Nevertheless, young Christians sometimes chose not to use the language of Christianity when speaking with their non-Christian elders, opting instead to appeal to them with more familiar conceptions of moral behavior. Here, Gröschel suggests that Amelye's relatives performed a reciprocal discursive operation, learning some of the language of Christianity so that they might use it to persuade their Christian young.

In Gröschel's view, another form of baleful heathen temptation for young converts such as Amelye was the attempts of their relatives to persuade them to exploit their position in the mission community for political advantage. Gröschel wrote that some of Amelye's relatives tried to persuade him to use his missionary connections to make himself a chief. Sometimes Amelye appeared disposed to use his position for material benefit. Gröschel describes one instance in which he employed intimidation to seize the livestock of a neighbor, claiming that he was merely seeking the final installment of a thirty-year-old bridewealth debt owed originally to his father. In another instance, while traveling with Gröschel he exercised the customary prerogative of chiefs' retinues, seizing food and drink from a homestead on their route. Apparently the elderly women from whom Amelye took the food managed to spoil it before handing it over, for after eating it Gröschel's cook died and Amelye himself suffered near-fatal poisoning.

The ultimate crisis in relations between the young Christians and their non-Christian relatives and neighbors was the Maji Maji war. Amelye remained loyal to Gröschel, helping to defend the mission when Mbeyela besieged it in September 1905. Yet, with the end of war Amelye appeared to recognize the need to avoid remaining estranged from his relatives and neighbors. Gröschel praised him for assisting his non-Christian relatives, including some who had joined in Mbeyela's attack on the mission, during the terrible hunger that followed the war. Amelye himself became a victim of postwar hardship, for he contracted an illness that killed him in 1907.

Asajile Knabwe

One of Gröschel's colleagues, E. Källner, provided an account of the life of a young employee at another Berlin Mission Society (BMS) station, the Magoye mission in Uwanji, which Källner founded in 1900. In themes and methods, Källner's account is similar to Gröschel's *Amelye.* For Källner as for Gröschel, stories of precolonial warfare provide vital background for his discussion of Asajile's childhood. Källner explains that, as a two-year-old, Asajile was saved dramatically from Hehe raiders who killed his mother. As with some of the passages in Amelye, this passage bears close resemblance to a genre of storytelling about precolonial warfare which is still common in the Southern Highlands. Källner built his station very near the settlement in which the young Asajile lived. Initially the local chief discouraged contact with the Europeans, but after two years one of his subordinates, a settlement leader at Magoye, decided to seek friendship with Källner by sending some of the village's youth to school. The village head instructed Asajile's father to select one of his sons for schooling. He chose Asajile, Källner explains, as the easiest way out of a situation in which meeting the demand of his chief threatened to provoke quarrels with his wives. His father knew that the mothers of his sons would object strenuously to sending them to the European school. He chose the fourteen-year-old Asajile because he was the only one of his sons whose mother was dead.

Asajile was baptized in 1906 at the age of eighteen, married a young, non-Christian woman very soon afterward, and went off with her to begin a two-year course of training as an evangelist at the BMS station at Manow in Unyakyusa.

The tension between Asajile's Christian faith and his wife's lack of interest in Christianity soon brought the marriage to an end. Quite possibly an additional source of tension was his father, because many men objected to Christian marriage of their sons, knowing that it would prevent them from marrying multiple wives. Nevertheless, Asajile completed his studies and returned to Magoye, where, up to the time of Källner's writing in 1913, he remained in missionary service as a teacher in Magoye's small satellite "bush schools."

Like Gröschel, Källner took a favorable view of numerous aspects of local culture in Uwanji. He, too, described the variety of practical skills learned in boyhood. He went well beyond Gröschel in describing the moral education of children, taking as one example the stories and punishments that adults used to teach children not to steal. Källner used the occasion of Asajile's first marriage to describe, again in favorable terms, the instruction given by elders to young men and women at the time of marriage. Asajile was taught that he must not "grumble" should his wife make mistakes in her cooking and housekeeping; his wife was counseled to tolerate his impatience and keep him well fed (18).

Also like Gröschel, Källner used his life story of Asajile to illustrate the persistent struggle of young Christian converts against "heathen" influence. The most vivid incident in his struggle came when Asajile dreamed that his non-Christian wife had dragged him off a ladder that Asajile was climbing toward heaven. This dream led Asajile to end his marriage, though later he married a Christian girl who, most, unusually for a woman of her generation in the Southern Highlands, spoke Kiswahili. Although Asajile, like Amelye at Yakobi, worked at negotiating his relationship with his non-Christian kin, he, too, ran into trouble during his wedding celebration. Although he provided beer for the feast, his refusal to share in its drinking provoked much criticism. Another source of criticism was his lack of a house of his own because he lived at the mission station. Thus his wife's family had no proper place to deliver the bride in completion of the marriage ceremony. The primary source of dissatisfaction among Asajile's relatives, however, was probably the fact that as a Christian he was obliged to remain monogamous. Källner mentions repeatedly that the missionaries' opposition to polygamy was the primary objection to Christianity in Uwanji.

Lutengamaso

By comparison with *Amelye* and *Asajile,* Wilhelm Neuberg's sketch of his assistant, Lutengamaso, was much briefer. It shares some of their themes nevertheless. It, too, speaks of the impact on children of the regional wars of the last precolonial decades. Lutengamaso was born into the family of a minor chief who lived in the Uzungwa Mountains of eastern Iringa. Neuberg met Lutengamaso's father and learned that he had served in the Hehe force that, under the leadership of Mkwawa, annihilated a German column at Lugalo in 1891. During the subsequent German guerrilla campaign, Lutengamaso's family was forced to move as the Germans tried to drain the Iringa countryside of supporters of the fugitive Mkwawa. They moved to a village in present-day Mufindi where his older brother was a village chief. After Neuberg established a mission nearby in 1899, Lutengamaso took employment in the mission and soon afterward began religious instruction. When Neuberg decided to establish a new mission at Milo in Upangwa (present-day Ludewa District), Lutengamaso became his primary assistant.

Neuberg lavished praise on Lutengamaso's ability to master all aspects of the construction process, from the felling of timber to the finer work of masonry. Indeed, a major theme of Neuberg throughout the account concerned Lutengamaso's hardworking diligence. Neuberg praised his quickness and aptitude for all sorts of learning, from acquiring literacy and a variety of languages to mastering a range of practical skills. Although Neuberg did not say this explicitly, readers who were familiar with *Amelye* and *Asajile* might well have concluded that Lutengamaso's upbringing had equipped him with curiosity and love of learning.

Lutengamaso was baptized in late 1903. Shortly afterward he married the missionary's nanny. Neuberg relied very heavily on him, leaving the Milo station in his hands for a year in 1904–5 while he returned to Germany for surgery. Despite Lutengamaso's status as an outsider in Upangwa, both German military authorities and Neuberg himself praised him for keeping the mission in good order. When the Maji Maji war erupted in 1905, Lutengamaso remained loyal to the mission despite losing his personal property. From the end of Maji Maji through 1916, when Neuberg was interned by the British during the First World War, Lutengamaso remained in the service of the Milo mission, making himself invaluable to Neuberg as a teacher.

Youth, Talk about Family and Transformation in an Economy of Affection

The stories of youth told by the BMS accounts help us understand the potential for change in an economy of affection. They do so by revealing a neglected dimension of these economies—the discursive nature of "affective ties." For one issue rarely addressed by studies of these economies is the manner in which individuals use language to define, negotiate, and enforce their responsibilities and obligations.

In the historical examples that we are considering here, "affective ties" were defined through a language of family and kinship. While talk about familial obligation obviously included intergenerational relations, men and women extended it to define political relations as well. They used the language of kinship to articulate concepts of chiefly authority and responsibilities toward clients. They likened the chief's role as leader and patron to that of a family head, and the position of his subjects to his children.[15] Not infrequently, their complicated ties of kinship and affinity allowed them to address a relative appropriately in more than one way (for example, a male might be both one's "brother" and "brother-in-law"). For youth, a particularly important form of complication was that talk about family could blur generational lines, loosening the connection between age and seniority (one might be addressed by a relative who, despite being younger in age, was considered one's senior by virtue of status as "aunt" or "uncle," for example). Choosing which term to prefer in daily interaction presented them with an opportunity to craft a relationship by attaching to it a particular weight of obligation and respect.[16] They also used the idiom of familial obligation—particularly "classificatory" terminology, which permitted terms such as "brother" and "sister" to be extended far beyond the children of one's biological mother and father—to create relationships with "fictive" kin. Indeed, it was this heritage of creativity and flexibility in the use of idioms of kinship which nationalists drew upon in the later twentieth century to make "youth" a political category (a development discussed in several chapters of this volume, including those by Brennan, Burgess, and Summers).[17]

Whereas relations of production and redistribution may be considered the foundation of economies of affection, it was the creative use of language that gave them great adaptability and flexibility. Talk of kinship facilitated cooperation by extending networks of patronage, dependence, and reciprocal obligation. By using this language with facility, individuals widened their opportunities for making "personal investments in reciprocal relations with other individuals."[18] Indeed, if the societies of the early twentieth-century Southern Highlands can be considered an economy of affection, this talk was its very heart. The rich heritage of family idiom gave the economy of affection its dynamism and adaptability.

The BMS ethnographies document some of the discursive creativity in an economy of affection by showing its use by youth and elders in intergenerational relationships. They also reveal the crucial role played by youth in adapting an economy of affection to changing historical circumstances. The three young men discussed by the missionaries experienced youth at a time when it was just beginning to be reshaped by schooling and by the need to prepare the young for the colonial economy. They adapted to these changing times through negotiation for new opportunities. They conducted their negotiations through talk of intergenerational responsibilities, doing so not only with family members, but also with political leaders whose authority they likened to that of family heads.

It was through such negotiation that the young men gained permission to enter the mission communities. Gröschel shows that for Amelye it involved negotiation to overcome the objections of older kin. Neuberg and Källner say that their young men sought employment and schooling in the missions only when ordered to do so by chiefs. Yet, Källner hints at a process of negotiation between youth and chiefs. He says that during the first two years of the Magoye mission before Asajile arrived, young people were poised between their youthful curiosity about the mission and their fear of provoking the wrath of the chiefs who wished to isolate the missionaries.

The impulse to such negotiation was the desire of the young for greater autonomy in determining the course of their lives. Writing in the 1930s about the Unyakyusa portion of the Southern Highlands, the region's most influential pre–Second World War ethnographers, Monica and Godfrey Wilson, concluded that this youthful desire for personal autonomy was stirred into existence by the revolutionary impact of Christian teaching.[19] By contrast, the BMS accounts suggest that robust, youthful individuality predated the arrival of Christianity. For analysts of economies of affection who believe that they function through individual choices about "investing" personal resources, this sign of deeply embedded individuality is quite important.

One sign of individuality among the young were names. As the BMS essays show, names of the young reflected personal character and circumstances of their birth and childhood. They changed their names, moreover, at moments of personal transition and achievement. Gröschel first knew Amelye by the fearsome martial praise name "Ngembejamahindza" [better rendered as "Ngewmbejamahindza"] or "The Butcher's Shield." Before his baptism, said Neuberg, Lutengamaso was known by a name that celebrated his skill with cattle, "Deninombe" [better as Denying'ombe] or "Tamer of Bulls." Perhaps more interestingly, his brother was "Muhavimugendwa" or "One Who Is Used by a Witch." Baptism provided Christian youth with a new occasion for taking names of their own choosing. After his baptism, Ngewmbejamahindza renamed himself Amelye, meaning "He [God] Has Given Me a Gift." Denying'ombe became Lutengamaso, or "Peaceful," and chose "Luhuvilo," or "Hope," as the baptismal name of his wife. "Asajile" was a Kinyakyusa name meaning "God Has Blessed Me."[20] Taking new personal names was not merely a Christian practice, as is shown by later generations of young men who took new names to express the individuality of their experience as migrant laborers.[21]

The strength of youthful individuality, I would argue, stemmed from the nature of family life in which individuals, including the young, struggled continuously to widen their networks of support (this was the very same activity that proponents of the economy of affection might call "personal investments in reciprocal relations").[22] As Gröschel noted, although children inherited from fathers their *mulumbo*, or clan names, they were not members of strong patrilineages. A sign of this noted not only by Gröschel but also by later ethnographers was that genealogical knowledge was shallow and, for most people, incomplete and uncertain. As observant ethnographers would find in the 1930s, families consisted of maternal as well as paternal kin.[23] The ethnographers saw that families were highly "egocentric" in the sense that, rather than being formed merely through descent, they were continually constructed and reformed as individuals labored from childhood to create and widen their own supportive networks. I believe that this kind of family life encouraged both strong individuality among the young and also the intergenerational negotiation observed by Gröschel.

The primary change in childhood and youth during the "Age of Improvement" was not that intergenerational negotiation became important for the first time, but rather that older forms of negotiation changed their premises and widened their discursive contexts. Gröschel provides an early example of the widening of the conceptual range of intergeneration negotiation. He showed that Amelye's non-Christian relatives turned Christian ideas against him in urging him not to forget his cultural roots. In later generations such negotiation would be practiced with great discursive flexibility as the young drew on concepts learned in Christian teaching as well as ideas more familiar to non-Christian elders. A young man inspired by Christian teaching to remain monogamous, for example, might choose to explain his position to his non-Christian father by speaking of the danger of jealousy and witchcraft that a second wife would introduce into his household.[24] The young might defend their passion for schooling by reminding their elders of the more traditional forms of learning in childhood that gave young men such as Lutengamaso a broad base of skills and aptitude for learning.

Although its discursive and conceptual field widened, intergenerational negotiation remained focused on the mutual obligations of the young and their elders. However, now the young argued for new ways of meeting their responsibilities. The fathers and grandfathers of Amelye, Asajile, and Lutengamaso had striven to meet their obligations by increasing the size of their circles of kin. In their generations, wider networks of support offered security, greater agrarian productivity, and more diverse sources of assistance. Their primary means of widening networks lay through marriage to multiple wives and child rearing. It was this conception of polygamy as responsibility to which Källner referred when saying that chiefs in Uwanji opposed Christianity because they feared (and here again the chiefs quite likely expressed themselves to the missionaries in talk about family responsibility) that it would encourage monogamy and reduce the number of their subjects (22).

Amelye, Lutengamaso, and Asajile were pioneers in seeing new ways of living morally responsible lives. Their new way of meeting familial obligations lay in schooling and participation in the colonial economy, particularly through wage labor. (In this respect, the Southern Highlands societies provided a most vivid contrast with societies such as the Maasai, where school life, as Richard Waller tells us in this volume, was in the minds of the young no substitute for more familiar forms of youthful experience. In the farming villages of the Southern Highlands, however, young people found schools to be new ways of achieving the maturity and independence that had long been the aspiration of youth.) In his own generation, a young man such as Amelye, who promised cloth to his elders in return for permission to work in the European mission, was a rare exception. Only in the 1920s and 1930s would wage employment become common among youth. The burden of the young, beginning in Amelye's generation and continuing through subsequent decades, was to persuade their elders that the new ways of Christianity and labor migration would not lead them into irresponsible neglect of their obligations.

In the context of modernization and colonialism, intergenerational relations have usually been seen in negative terms. Often they have been described as a constraint, or even as a source of exploitation (particularly in relation to inflated demands by elders for bridewealth). The young have frequently been seen as having reacted against their elders by seeking greater autonomy in the colonial economy. Sometimes historians speak of "struggle" between youth and elders. Novelists such as Chinua Achebe in *Things Fall Apart* (1958) enjoy more leeway than historians in imagining the psychological complexity of such relationships. They have pictured them as a cause of alienation to which the young reacted by embracing Christianity and Western modernization.

From the standpoint of economies of affection, this negative view might be taken to demonstrate that such economies change only when they are penetrated by outside forces that prompt youth to flee to modern economies. However, I suggest that relations between young and elders should be seen in more subtle and balanced terms. If youth can be seen as "struggling," it was not as a corporate group. Instead, their tactic was individual persuasion. Among their many intergenerational relationships, each of which expressed a different calibration of obligation, respect, and subordination, they sought ties with older persons willing to provide support and assistance. For their part, elders practiced child rearing that provided the young with aptitude for learning, taught them to become self-reliant individuals, and instructed them in moral obligations of kinship. These practices and relationships inspired as much innovation as conformity.

There is some reason to suggest that the old kinship-based order collapsed with the defeat in Maji Maji. After the war, one German missionary wrote that "old chiefly authority and prestige were smashed, and family and kinship circles were torn apart."[25] Many village heads and chiefs met their end during Maji Maji, perishing in war, suffering execution, or simply being deposed. They were quickly replaced by new chiefs whose appointment by the Germans permitted them to rule in a draconian manner, but provided little popular legitimacy. Thus there is some basis to the claim that agrarian transformation occurred during the "Age of Improvement" because rural societies already shattered by war finally crumbled under the pressure of colonial government and authority.

Nevertheless, the preponderance of evidence indicates that the culture of mutual obligation and responsibility to kin remained robust despite defeat. It continued to provide the primary idiom in which chiefly authority was debated, even though the debate turned to increasingly aggressive questioning of chiefly legitimacy as the colonial period advanced.[26] Evidence of the continuing vitality of an older moral order suggests that the increased participation in the colonial economy that characterized the "Age of Improvement" was the result of dynamic adaptability generated inside rural communities.

The movement toward schooling and wage labor after 1920 likely took place in much the same moral and political environment in which these innovations had been pioneered by forerunners such as Amelye, Asajile, and Lutengamaso. With the introduction of Native Administration after 1926, participation in the colonial economy would become more strongly motivated by a desire to evade conservative authoritarianism. By the 1950s, youthful resentment of chiefs and desire to find new opportunity in the colonial economy would feed into the growing nationalist movement. Part of nationalist mobilization involved harnessing the grievances and ambitions of youth through the attempts of organizations such as the TANU (Tanganyika African National Union) Youth League to give "youth" a conscious political identity and agenda.

By looking at youth during the "Age of Improvement," we find strong reason to agree with John Iliffe and other historians of the 1960s and 1970s that agrarian transformation in this period was both a product of rural initiative and one of the developments that led to the nationalist movement. We also find strong reason to continue working with ideas of the economy of affection, particularly in their newer formulations. We do not find that economies of affection resisted market economies and remained "uncaptured." Instead, we see that the moral foundation of "affective ties" inspired youth to seek new opportunities in the colonial and national economies to meet their responsibilities.

Between the social history of intergenerational relations and analysis of economies of affection there is considerable convergence. For analysts of economies of affection, fine-grained studies of change through time by social historians test their understanding of how such economies function. Conversely, the analysis of economies of affection provide social historians, and in particular those who are interested in youth and intergenerational relations, new ways of interpreting their evidence. It allows social historians to remain faithful to their evidence, facilitates comparison, and orients them toward questions about change and development that remain crucially important in agrarian societies.

Notes

1. In particular Thomas Spear, *Mountain Farmers: Moral Economies of Land and Agricultural Development in Arusha and Meru* (Oxford: James Currey, 1997).

2. Goren Hyden, *Beyond Ujamaa in Tanzania: Underdevelopment and an Uncaptured Peasantry* (Berkeley: University of California Press, 1980).

3. Papers from a conference held in Morogoro, Tanzania, in August 2004 were published in the *Tanzanian Journal of Population Studies and Development* (Special Issue: "African Economy of Affection," 11, no. 2 [2004], hereafter *TJPSD*, "Special Issue"). Papers from a second conference in August 2005 are forthcoming in the same journal. A third conference on African economies of affection was held in Japan in 2006.

4. Goren Hyden, "Informal Institutions, Economy of Affection and Rural Development in Africa," *TJPSD*, "Special Issue," 6.

5. Hyden, *Beyond Ujamaa in Tanzania*, 18.

6. Discussing the potential for transformation within economies of affection are Tomomi Tokuori, "The Role of Networks in the Construction Industry: Case Study of Burkina Faso"; Koichi Ikegami, "Fair Trade and Moral Economy: The Japanese Experience"; Tadasu Tsuruta, "Changing Values in Reciprocity: A Case Study of Commercialized Thai Farmers"; and Kumiko Sakamoto, "Moral Economy and Endogenous Development: People's Diverse Perspectives of Culture and Development in Lindi Region," in *TJPSD*, "Special Issue," 69–130. In the same issue, heavy doubt is cast on their potential for change by S. Maghimbi, "Small Is a Curse: The Stagnation of Peasant Economy and Moral Economy in Tanzania since *Ujamaa*," 55–68.

7. Hyden, "Informal Institutions," 17.

8. Ibid., 9.

9. James L. Giblin, *A History of the Excluded: Making Family and Memory a Refuge from State in Twentieth-Century Tanzania* (Oxford: James Currey, 2005).

10. The presentation of this argument that is still widely read in Tanzania is John Iliffe, "The Age of Improvement and Differentiation (1907–45)," in *A History of Tanzania*, ed. I. N. Kimambo and A. J. Temu (Nairobi: EAP, 1969; reprinted 1997), 123–60. The argument is summarized on page 124.

11. Thaddeus Sunseri, "Reinterpreting a Colonial Rebellion: Forestry and Social Control in German East Africa, 1874–1915," *Environmental History* 8, no. 3 (2003): 430–51.

12. These pamphlets were found at the Archive of the Berlin Mission Society in Berlin.

13. Giblin, *History of the Excluded*, 116–17, 123–24.

14. Ibid., chap. 3.

15. Although this use of language is not brought out fully in the BMS accounts, it emerges more clearly from other sources (ibid., 56–60).

16. Ibid., 80–84.

17. See also Thomas Burgess, "Introduction to Youth and Citizenship in East Africa" and "The Young Pioneers and the Rituals of Citizenship in Revolutionary Zanzibar"; Andrew M. Ivaska, "Of Students, 'Nizers,' and a Struggle over Youth: Tanzania's 1966 National Service Crisis"; and Carol Summers, "Young Buganda and Old Boys: Youth, Generational Transition, and Ideas of Leadership in Buganda, 1920–1949," *Africa Today* 51, no. 3 (2005): vii–xxiv, 3–29, 83–128.

18. Hyden, "Informal Institutions," 6.

19. Godfrey Wilson and Monica Wilson, *The Analysis of Social Change* (Cambridge: Cambridge University Press, 1945); Monica Wilson, *Communal Rituals of the Nyakyusa* (London: Oxford University Press, 1959), *For Men and Elders: Change in the Relations of Generations and of Men and Women among the Nyakyusa-Ngonde People, 1875–1971* (London: Oxford University Press, 1977), *Religion and the Transformation of Society: A Study in Social Change in Africa* (Cambridge: Cambridge University Press, 1971).

20. Several of these names were translated by the authors. Translations of other names were provided by Blandina Kaduma Giblin.

21. Giblin, *History of the Excluded*, 111–15.

22. Hyden, "Informal Institutions," 6.

23. Elizabeth Fisher Brown, "Hehe Grandmothers," *Journal of the Royal Anthropological Institute of Great Britain and Ireland* 65 (July–December 1935): 83–96; G. Gordon Brown, "Bride-Wealth among the Hehe," *Africa* 5, no. 2 (1932): 145–57; G. Gordon Brown, "Hehe Cross-Cousin Marriage," in *Essays Presented to C. G. Seligman*, ed. E. E. Evans-Pritchard, Raymond Firth, Bronislaw Malinowski, and Isaac Schapera (London: Kegan Paul, 1934), 27–39; G. Gordon Brown and A. Mcd. Bruce Hutt, *Anthropology in Action: An Experiment in the Iringa District of the Iringa Province, Tanganyika Territory* (London: Oxford University Press, 1935); A. T. and G. M. Culwick, "The Functions of Bride-Wealth in Ubena of the Rivers," *Africa* 7, no. 2 (1934): 140–59; A. T. and G. M. Culwick, *Ubena of the Rivers* (London: George Allen and Unwin, 1935); W. Bryant Mumford, "The Hehe-Bena-Sangu Peoples of East Africa," *American Anthropologist* 36, no. 2 (1934): 203–22.

24. Giblin, *History of the Excluded*, 152–55.

25. F. Büttner, *Der Aufstand in Deutsch-Ostafrika und Seine Folgen* (Berlin, n.d. but 1911?), 28.

26. Giblin, *History of the Excluded*, 209–72.

4 Colonial Youth at the Crossroads

Fifteen Alliance "Boys"

HÉLÈNE CHARTON-BIGOT

> He seemed to me like a young god with his smart clothes, and shoes, his watch and beautiful bicycle. I worshipped in particular his bicycle that day and I decided that I must somehow get one for myself. As he talked with us it seemed to me that the secret of his riches came from his education, his knowledge of reading and writing and that it was essential to me to obtain this power.
>
> J. M. Kariuki, *Mau-Mau Detainee*

JEAN AND JOHN Comaroff define youth as a sociocultural category constructed in the context of modernity.[1] As Foucault had earlier observed, it is in fact in modern nation-states that the gap between childhood and adulthood is most emphasized and where youth can be addressed as an autonomous category. Colonial polities brought their own processes of modernity. It is mainly in those places directly produced by colonial modernity that youth started to appear as a specific category of self-conscious actors. Towns were one such place, and it is unsurprising that the issue of urban youth is addressed in several chapters in this collection. As far as Kenya is concerned, it is interesting to underline the political economy of the emergence of this category. In 1921, a new political association was founded in Nairobi by Harry Thuku: the Young Kikuyu Association (YCA). This choice of name directly refers to the Kikuyu Association (KA), which was engaged in a traditional struggle against colonial authority mainly on land issues. YCA members were young people who had migrated to Nairobi, where their conditions of working and living were awful, in opposition to which they started to challenge the colonial power. This led to the first insurrection in Nairobi in 1921 and the killing of twenty-one people by the police. The short history of the Young Kikuyu Association embodies an emerging social category: urban youth directly produced by the colonial situation, in which the youth identify themselves as products of a new modernity, different from the traditional order embodied by KA leaders. The development of colonial schools also contributed to the emergence of youth as a specific social category. During the time of their studies, African students were disengaged from the productive system. Schools created the conditions of existence of a new category of actors between childhood and adulthood. In most studies on colonial education, the "educated" appear as a distinct category. But education can also be seen as the link, the common language, of a specific social category produced by colonial schools. This is precisely the question raised by this essay.

As in many African countries, World War II brought significant change to Kenya, a new phase in the modernization of the colony. The development of secondary and higher education was one of the touchstones of the new colonial policy initiated in the British Empire in the 1940s through the Colonial Development and Welfare Schemes. However, progressive policies along these lines were resisted by sections of colonial society, notably the settlers, and at the other end of the continuum were too insubstantial for the great majority of the African population. At this time there were growing demands for major change (economic, social, and political) in colonial society, and although such demands were partially fulfilled, changes proceeded too slowly and on too small a scale. In 1945 there was no university in the colony, and only two schools provided a complete secondary cycle for the African population. In 1945, Alliance High School, Kenya's oldest and most famous African school, was the only place where students could take the Cambridge School Certificate (the highest diploma available in the colony);[2] and only fifteen Africans completed their secondary education by passing this examination. This chapter focuses on this group of fifteen school boys later known as the class of "notables," because of the role they played in Kenyan politics after independence.[3] Of the group of fifteen, eight pursued a public career mainly in politics. They were not only influential as individuals, but their power also derived from the strong links they had established both at school and when studying abroad.

The absence of females in this cohort is notable. At this stage, few girls reached this level of education in Kenya; just two were in junior secondary school in Kenya in 1945. Through its education system colonialism did create new paths for female emancipation; however, this was more evident in the 1950s.[4] This study will therefore not address the issue of women's empowerment through education as it occurred after men had opened these new alleys.

The colonial turning point of the 1940s is well exemplified by a school such as Alliance. In fact, the contradictions of the modernization process within the colonial frame are embodied by the management of Alliance's new headmaster, Edward Carey Francis, appointed in 1940. This type of school attempted to achieve two contradictory goals. On one hand, the education provided was aimed at helping the students become responsible adults. On the other, an institution such as Alliance High School embodied the colonial spirit, and its very nature was to preserve and maintain the colonial order as long as possible. Although education might offer opportunities to enhance one's social or economical status, real opportunities were in fact few and far between in the colony. These contradictions were very much felt by Alliance students who started to express their social and political frustration. It is in this context that this group can be seen as the pioneer of a new social category sharing a common language and a common set of social representations and expectations, not only driven by their educational background but also nurtured by their intermediate place in society as youth.

As a category, youth appears as a liminal stage in the life process. By essence, youth is basically in-between: not a child anymore but not yet an adult. It is precisely the emancipating process leading from one stage to another that characterizes best what youth is: a journey toward autonomy. Education, and more specifically Western education, can be part of this process but appears quite limited in the colonial context. In a colony such as Kenya, native people were considered socially and politically dependent. Under colonial rule Africans were children who needed to be guided by their European guardians through the "long civilizing mission." Early schools in Kenya, such as Alliance High School, were places where this paternalistic spirit of imperialism was strongly felt. Paradoxically, it is at Alliance High School, which was supposed to shape obedient servants, that the colonial model and its underlying principles were most effectively challenged. But in this kind of school the emancipating process could never be totally completed; it was limited by European social and political domination.

Colonial schools played a critical role in shaping an African educated youth, which was at the same time the product and the promoter of Western modernity and found its self-consciousness in the fight against a paternalist colonial system that denied African students full access to social and political adulthood. I first examine the conditions under which this new category of African educated youth emerged in Kenya and then try to understand what connected this "imagined community" that enabled them as individuals to play their part in the struggle for independence.

Alliance High School and the Making of a Colonial Educated Youth

The development of education in Kenya was one expression of colonial modernity. Secondary schools were spaces where young people could act and be considered an autonomous social category. However, colonial education never aimed at producing responsible adults and citizens; its purpose was to train skilled, obedient servants. For this reason, schools were a place where youth had to fight continuously against a colonial system that inhibited their intellectual, social, and political ambitions. Students' expectations about higher education as a means of emancipation were hampered by a paternalist colonial order embodied by the headmaster, Carey Francis. In addition, one should note that Alliance schoolboys were part of a new community contributing to the erosion of traditional ethnic and social frontiers.

Historical Background of Alliance High School

After World War I, the British administration started to consider the opening of a colonial secondary school operating on the same basis as King's College Budo in Uganda or Tabora in Tanzania. Such schools were specifically dedicated to the sons of the ruling elite; they aimed at training a colonial African elite that would play a role in the British administration. However, this project encountered strong resistance both from the white settler community and from missionaries. On the one hand, the settlers who needed skilled workmen to sustain their farms' development were asking for a professional school that could fulfill their needs. On the other hand, some missionaries opposed the secondary school project on the ground that the general level of education was too low in the colony and that this kind of school would only widen the gap within African society;[5] though the real reason was probably that they wanted control over the molding of an African elite. An agreement was finally reached among the government, the missionaries, through the Reverend John William Arthur, and the settlers, through Hugh Cholmondeley, 3rd Baron Delamere. Alliance High School was opened in Kikuyu near Nairobi in January 1926 with twenty-six pupils. However, as Benjamin Kipkorir points out, the initial controversy about the role of secondary education in colonial Kenya affected the very nature of the school: "It was agreed that higher education had to be given to Africans provided that literary education was seen as a means to building up character and not as an end in itself."[6]

Initial vocational courses provided by Alliance were progressively dropped. In 1938 a first batch of students was able to sit for the Cambridge School Certificate after four years of secondary education. At this time Alliance was the only secondary school in the colony. In 1940, Carey Francis, previously the head of Maseno School in western Kenya, became the new principal of Alliance, where he remained up to 1962.[7] Carey Francis ran the school for more than twenty years over a period of tremendous change in Kenya. In many ways he tried to model the school in his own image. Former students would recall Carey Francis's strong personality and high standards. His contribution was critical for the development of the school. When he arrived in 1940, nine students were sitting for the Cambridge School Certificate, but only five passed.[8] Five years later, in 1945, all fifteen boys were successful. Although Alliance enrolled the best students of the colony, completing the course of study was very difficult: out of the fifty-six boys in form 1 in 1942, just fifteen managed to complete form 4.[9] This small group emerged as the pioneers of an African modern educated youth in Kenya; it is therefore interesting to focus on their social and geographical origins.

Genesis of the First African Educated Youth

Alliance's students came from throughout Kenya. After World War II it seems that the social background of the students was more diverse than in its earlier years, when it was merely training sons of Kikuyu chiefs.[10] In 1945, nearly half the Form 4 students were Kikuyu (seven out of fifteen) and a quarter were Kamba (four); other students came from western Kenya (two Luo and one Luyha), and one student originated from the Coast. Alliance High School is located in the Kikuyu heartland, twenty kilometers from Nairobi. This could partly explain its attractiveness for people from the neighboring areas. However, student composition also reflects the uneven distribution of school facilities in the colony. In Central Province as well as in western Kenya (Western and Nyanza Provinces) Western education spread quickly through missionary work. After World War I, the colonial government started to build its own network of schools in places where the missionaries were not well represented (Masaïland, Ukambani, Coast); students from the new schools eventually diversified Alliance's student body. This diversity contributed to the development in the student body of the feeling of belonging to a wide community. In fact, for most of the students, it was the first time that they had met and lived with people from other provinces and ethnic groups. This experience certainly built up a communal feeling that overrode ethnic difference, a fact underlined in most interviews conducted with former students.[11] Kyale Mwendwa captured the essence of this process with the observation, "I became a Kenyan at Alliance and an East African at Makerere."[12]

Social diversity was also evident among the student body. In 1945 Alliance students came from a range of backgrounds. Julius Gecau, for example, was the son of a squatter, and Njoroge Mungai's father was a cook for the Presbyterian Church in Kikuyu. Julius Kiano's father was a domestic servant before starting his own business in Nairobi at the time his son started his higher studies. Henry Mulli's father was an independent cultivator and an elder in the Native courts. Kyale Mwendwa and Munyua Waiyaki were sons of chiefs. In spite of the diversity of their social origins, all shared some connection to the colonial system, either directly for the chiefs' sons or more indirectly for church-related men and the squatters. This enlargement of the social basis of the school reflects the development of education in Kenya through the involvement of Local Native Councils (LNC). LNCs contributed to the secondary education of their students. In 1941, only 5 percent of Alliance pupils lacked LNC sponsorship.[13] Kyale Mwendwa, who came from a rich family, was one exception, though the LNC sent a truck for the transportation of the students from Eastern Province.[14] But the head of the school, Carey Francis was actually opposed to these scholarships, which he thought were spoiling the students. His educational philosophy, deeply rooted in paternalistic colonial principles, was based on a sense of sacrifice and discipline.

Carey Francis, Alliance High School, and the Colonial Spirit

Carey Francis took over from Georges A. Grieve as school head in 1940.[15] Born in 1897, he was educated at Cambridge and became a lecturer in math at Peterhouse College, Cambridge. Of his call to serve in Africa, he observed: "I thought educating Africans would be something like running Christian scouts, for, to me, education and Christianity both had to embrace the whole of life."[16] In 1928, he arrived at Maseno in western Kenya, where he was the principal until 1940. Ironically, during his years at Maseno, Carey Francis blamed Alliance High School for the lack of discipline that would spoil "his best boys": "Our best boys go on to Alliance. In work they do very well indeed, but in all the ways I care most about they do badly. They seem to me to become insufferably conceited, unctuously pious; selfish, slack at everything except books and examinations. Year by year the best boys go; the rot sets in and they disintegrate. They lose all love of Maseno, which stands for different things."[17]

As we can see from this quotation, Carey Francis's principles of education embraced far more than just academic schoolwork. His primary mission was to build up the character of the pupils through two main principles: discipline and obedience. According to him, education was by no means aimed solely at satisfying personal aspirations but was supposed to serve the whole community. When he arrived at Alliance, he was ready to make what he thought were necessary changes:

> When the AHS was started, a secondary boy was a phenomenon. He was given rather wonderful food, rather wonderful clothes, and generally felt like an undergraduate. He cost accordingly. . . . Much of this attitude still persisted, and I was ready to do anything to see that it didn't take root here. In laying this down I knew that I should have most of the boys against me: grandness, my great enemy, is singularly attractive to them.[18]

In order to build up the sense of responsibility among his pupils, Carey Francis developed the prefect system at Alliance. He also introduced annual reports, which were sent to the student's family and to chiefs and education officers. Colonial education was from his point of view one aspect of the "civilising mission": its first purpose was to serve the people and the community as a whole, not individuals. From the very beginning, Carey Francis managed to develop a kind of anti-elitist attitude, which totally contradicted the students' expectations. In fact this echoed the initial debate about Alliance High School. For Carey Francis, like many other Europeans in the colony, there was no space for an African elite, and the role of schools like Alliance was to prepare obedient servants.

Carey Francis was remembered by his former students as a very difficult person. Most ex-students interviewed acknowledged the high educational standards of the school. Carey Francis was a fantastic math teacher according to them. But they also deplored and criticized his personality and authoritarianism. Julius Gecau, for instance, didn't much like Carey Francis: "He was a good Christian but a colonial minded man . . . a misguided man, victim of his time."[19] Henry Mulli expressed the same opinion. "It was a very good school but at this time we did not like it," he observed. This was, according to Mulli, mainly due to Carey Francis's attitude toward Africans, an attitude that differed little from that of colonial district officers.[20] Julius Kiano remembered Carey Francis as a "very, very difficult man." About the school he said: "We had a good time, as good as it can be under Carey Francis."[21]

The views expressed by former students epitomize the paradoxical nature of education provided in this kind of school. The paternalist attitude of Carey Francis compromised the whole process of emancipation and autonomy. Having been treated as children, this generation of educated young men found it difficult to become fully responsible adults. The frustration generated by the colonial system among the youth was actually rooted in this kind of education. Whereas education was supposed to lead children toward adulthood, the colonial context in Kenya erected invisible barriers preventing youth from becoming full adult citizens.

The Fight for Adulthood and Social Recognition

After World War II, many students were prepared to challenge the colonial social order. Their strong desire for recognition took various forms, extending beyond the school boundaries and being transformed into a set of social and political grievances. It was during their studies at Alliance High School that this cohort forged its own identity. If education was their lingua franca, they need to be socially identified as a new category (through their clothes, for instance). Their faith in education, which propelled most of this group into a worldwide academic pilgrimage to gain academic degrees, was also part of this new identity. A determination to challenge colonial rules that hampered their move toward adulthood turned their quest into a political issue.

Shorts versus Long Trousers: The Clothing Controversy at the AHS

The school's dress code is symptomatic of the different meanings and expectations raised by secondary education at this time. Alliance students wore short-sleeved shirts and khaki shorts (the school uniform), and most went barefoot. The issue of what could and what could not be worn had considerable significance in the school's history. During Alliance's first decade the students were given two pairs of khaki shirts and shorts, one striped shirt, two pairs of long trousers, two blue ties, two jackets, and one khaki coat. They also received a red fez, which became the symbol of the school.[22] Soon after he arrived Carey Francis decided to change certain items. The striped shirt was replaced by a white shirt, and the long trousers and the fez were banned.[23] As Kipkorir has noted, these changes had deep consequences; the change in uniform was interpreted by "the boys not as a measure of economy in the war years but as direct challenge to the dignity of the educated African youth."[24]

Carey Francis also decided to completely ban shoes from the school (students were allowed to wear shoes only for medical reasons). Actually before 1940, very few students wore shoes at school. But they were slowly introduced by the richest students as a symbol of wealth. To avoid this kind of discrimination, Carey Francis decided to forbid them. He considered shoes and long trousers "extravagances" that were betraying the "African way of life."[25] Africans usually went barefoot, and he saw little reason for them to behave differently at school. For Carey Francis education was valuable for itself, and it should not cut the people from their culture and environment. Of course Carey Francis was blind to the social and symbolic value of education viewed by many Africans as a means toward responsibility and emancipation. A clash occurred soon after he arrived when he tried to force the African staff to wear shorts instead of trousers. The ruling was symptomatic of his deep misunderstanding. For many Africans in the colony, whether one wore shorts or trousers really made a difference in status.

In many ways, shorts epitomize Kenyan colonial culture. The African staff of a prestigious school such as Alliance High School, as well as the advanced students from this same school, found it humiliating to have to wear them. They were grown up, and they wanted to dress like adults, not like kids. Charles Njonjo, for instance, went to King's College Budo, in Uganda, where students were allowed to wear trousers and blazers, as he recalled fifty years later; the issue was that of being treated as a man.[26] For most students, education implied a degree of social recognition that was denied by Carey Francis. By contrast, Bernard de Busen, the principal of Makerere in 1945, perfectly understood the social meaning of education. In his memoirs he wrote the following about the desire of students to wear British-style gowns:

> Friends at home tell me that academic dresses such as ours were irrational and so it is. The students wanted it, felt the better for it, and perhaps many needed all the boosts they could get to their self-confidence. They needed recognition. Some of course enjoyed the social climb and had not the experience or sensitivity to hide it. Many more found themselves uncomfortably but unavoidably on social pedestals, not so much of their own erection, but placed there by society, their parents, and extended families, their home neighbours, their tribes, who may all have been involved in getting them through the narrow gate into secondary school and the yet smaller aperture of Makerere entrance.[27]

In fact what was behind the superficial issue of shoes, trousers, or fez was the critical question of social recognition. In banning trousers from school, Carey Francis expressed his strong paternalist feelings and ignored the symbolic value of education. The African staff and students of Alliance were conscious of the new social status education was supposed to bring them. The determination expressed by this group of students to get university degrees after World War II is another expression of this critical desire for recognition.

Thirst for Higher Education

In 1945, secondary and higher education were still rare in Kenya: there were just 395 African secondary pupils in Kenya (among them two girls), and 52 Kenyan students were studying at Makerere College in Uganda, which was the only post-secondary institution in East Africa.[28] Makerere was established in 1922 as the Native Technical College located on Makerere Hill near Kampala. Its initial aim was to provide technical training and qualifications to promising East African students. In 1938 it became the Higher College of East Africa, offering a two-year general course diploma: the higher sciences and the higher arts and professional courses in education, medical studies, veterinary and agricultural sciences.[29] It was open to all successful students from British East Africa, but since Makerere was not a "real university," some students did not see the point of spending three years in Uganda for a local diploma; they would rather go abroad to read for a degree.

This was Julius Gecau's point of view, and accordingly he refused to take the entrance exam. He did not accept the fact that an African medical student was required to study for seven years to become a medical assistant and not a doctor.[30] Gecau eventually managed to study privately in India. Munyua Wayaiki, the son of a wealthy chief, passed the Makerere entrance examination but opted instead to study medicine in South Africa, where he first enrolled at Fort Hare.[31] Others, like Julius Kiano, entered Makerere but continued to seek a bursary award elsewhere. Kiano left Makerere after one year without even taking his exams. He was offered a scholarship at a small American college.[32] According to Kiano, university education was a kind of necessity for this group of students. In fact ten of the students succeeded in getting a university degree abroad, ranging from BAs to PhDs: "This group of fifteen was very ambitious. I guess that it was because at this time they had had Eliud Mathu as a teacher, the same one who was later appointed at the Legislative Council to represent his fellow Africans. Mbiyu Koinange had also just returned in Kenya. We had the feeling that we needed a university education; all the fifteen of us."[33]

As emphasized by Kiano in his interview, the return of former students from abroad fostered their desire to continue their education abroad. Eliud Mathu had taught at Alliance, and some of the students must have met him before his departure in 1942. Mathu's experience in South Africa and in England seems to have encouraged other young Africans to study abroad. In fact, between 1937 and 1943 six Africans from Kenya studied in South Africa. All but one (Aram Kibue) were former Alliance pupils; most were sons of chiefs.[34]

The return to Kenya in 1938 of Mbiyu Koinange, the first African from Kenya to have graduated from an American university, might have encouraged students to look for scholarships in the United States of America. Peter Mbiyu Koinange was the son of senior Chief Koinange; he studied in the United States for nearly ten years and returned to Kenya with a master's degree. Instead of taking one of the positions he was offered in the administration, Koinange decided to head the independent African Teachers College in Githunguri.[35] The new school was a stone's throw from Alliance High School; he frequently used to meet Alliance students.[36] The stories told by these two men no doubt fostered the desire of many students to study abroad and return to the colony with a university degree.

Carey Francis strongly resisted his students' desire for higher education. He did not see the point of getting costly degrees abroad as there was no room to accommodate African graduates in the colony:

> The best educated Africans in Kenya—those who have passed the school certificate and especially those who have studied at Makerere—are seldom doing real jobs of work. This is to be deplored. The chief reason is that these men, instead of getting down working, go to continual "courses" overseas. When one course is completed they ask for another. Some courses are unsuitable, a waste of time or worse, a very great waste of money; because of them men are kept from, and sometimes

incapacitated for, the planned ordinary jobs which they might have done and which so greatly need to be done. I know of no one who has clearly benefited from an overseas course. Some have clearly been harmed, some ruined. Even those who are unsuccessful in getting overseas are damaged; they long to go and their minds are taken from their work.[37]

According to Carey Francis, the new colonial policy implemented after World War II was much to blame because it emphasized the importance of degrees and diplomas. In fact, the development of education in the colonies was one of the cornerstones of the modernization process that was supposed to lead the colonies to independence. New bursaries schemes (namely the Colonial Development and Welfare schemes and the Government African Overseas Bursaries) allowed a couple of African students to read for degrees in the United Kingdom. In the meantime, Makerere College in Uganda was gradually upgraded to become a full-fledged university college. Most officials were not happy with these events. They were doubtful of the relevance of such courses for the development of the colony. For instance, Norman Larby, the director of Education in Kenya, tried to prevent Kyale Mwendwa from continuing his studies in South Africa on the ground that qualified teachers were immediately needed in the colony. "The shortage of teachers is so acute," he observed, "that if I am unable to post this man to Machakos in 1949, the postponement of development in Ukamba is inevitable."[38] Kyale Mwendwa eventually studied at Fort Hare. When he returned to Kenya in 1952 with a BA degree, he went to see Norman Larby and told him: "Now I am ready." He was posted to the Government African School in Machakos.[39] The general view shared by most officials was that Makerere was enough to fulfill the need for qualified Africans in the colony. In 1949, the selection committee for the overseas bursaries stated that at this stage, general education in Kenya was not sufficiently developed to allow more candidates to study abroad.[40] Whereas these bursary schemes were designed "to enable residents in colonial territories to obtain qualifications necessary for appointments or promotion to the higher grade of the Public Service,"[41] in Kenya, whatever their degree of qualification, Africans occupied subaltern positions. The egalitarian principle underlying university education—with students evaluated according to their own merit—clashed with a colonial system that was in essence discriminating. Bernard de Busen, the principal of Makerere College recalls in his memoirs, for Africans being educated was a matter of adjusting to a changing world, a way to become part of the process that would metaphorically turn children into adults:

> Africa was changing through its young people beginning to wear trousers, to the alarm of many DC's [district commissioners] and Kenya settlers and the sadness of those anthropologists who preferred them naked. It was only certain missionaries and a very few of the most senior of the civil servants willy-nilly handling political affairs, who had some touch and sometimes sympathy with the new generation, however disturbing the results of education might become.[42]

As we have already mentioned, a strong desire for recognition drove the students in their quest for higher education. And it is precisely because this demand was systematically turned down by headmasters such as Carey Francis and other officials that the struggle for education became a political issue in Kenya.

The Struggle for Higher Education: A Political Grievance

After World War II, as in other colonies, Kenya experienced "a second colonial occupation." The number of European residents rose from 30,000 to 50,000 between 1948 and 1952. Most of these newcomers settled in urban areas and worked as employees for international companies or in the colonial administration.[43] With an average level of education they were basically competing for the same jobs as the new African elite. The best way to protect the European labor market was to keep the different populations of the colony separated from one another. The growing demand for higher education for Africans, directly related to the lack of opportunities for Kenyan Africans, was strongly resisted by the administration and in this particular context the struggle for education had political implications. In 1940 one petition addressed by the Kikuyu Central Association[44] already emphasized education as a tool for modernization:

> To bar an African from opportunities of self-help in order to uphold the view of his disqualification is not the solution of the local problem. To close the market for Africans for the same reason of exposing his inadequacy to think as businessmen is not stimulation of Colonial economic development and financial independence. To segregate him from educational facilities is not to increase the number of useful able men needed to manipulate modern machinery for modern man.[45]

In 1945, a member from the Nyanza LNC sent a letter to the colonial secretariat in which he presented the development of education for Africans as a social demand for emancipation.

> Unless Kenya is to be reserved in Africa as a whole, as a quarry for museum specimens of ancient Africa, there cannot be any justification in such overdue controls. . . . Africans ought to be trained not just because one office or institution needs such a one, but for the general welfare of the whole country. . . . If we make future development of Kenya the central theme of our consideration, it is the African students whose backward conditions require them to go for studies overseas, for then assimilation of the western culture would be ensured. It is the Europeans who have little need to go overseas, for they already have the western culture in their homes and in their blood. . . . We are also British heirs and have a right to claim the best that the Empire can afford for the progress of her people.[46]

Carey Francis was one of those people who refused to acknowledge the social and political changes taking place partly as a result of the development of education in the colony. This paternalist attitude contributed to the development of political consciousness among staff and students at Alliance. As previously indicated, Carey Francis believed in a specific African way of life and on these grounds systematically turned down the social demands of the African staff in terms of salaries and work conditions. By 1944, all the African staff had been replaced. James Gichuru and Eliud Mathu, who became key political actors in postwar Kenya, were among the teachers forced to resign. Eliud Mathu was the first African master at Alliance. He was the twentieth student to join the school in 1926. After subsequently completing a teaching course in 1929 he was hired as a master at the school. Between 1932 and 1934 he studied at Fort Hare and passed the South Africa matriculation.[47] He returned to Alliance and taught history while reading for a BA degree through a correspondence course. In 1938 he was admitted to Exeter University, where he earned a diploma in education. He spent one more year in England, reading history at Balliol College in Oxford, to which he had been invited by Margery Perham.[48] He rejoined Alliance in 1940, a few days before the arrival of the new headmaster. In 1942 he left Alliance and opened his own school in Waithaka, his place of birth. Carey Francis had refused to increase his salary, not taking into account the new qualifications he gained in the United Kingdom. James Gichuru was another former Alliance student. He was also one of the first Kenyans to study at Makerere in 1933. When he returned to Kenya in 1935 with a teaching diploma in mathematics he was appointed teacher at Alliance High School. After E. Mathu he was the second African teacher at the school. He resigned in 1941, as he could not get along with Carey Francis. The departure of these two African members of the staff who belonged to the very first African educated elite a couple of months after the arrival of Carey Francis as the head of the school is symptomatic of the gulf between them.

After they left the school, the African staff fired by Carey Francis remained influential through the Old Boys association. The Alliance High School Old Boys association was created in 1931. Eliud Mathu was one of his founders. The organization grew progressively and in 1940 had 125 members. In 1941, soon after he resigned from the school, James Gichuru became the secretary of the association. Gichuru, Mathu, and Joseph Otiende were members of the executive committee of the Alliance Old Boys Association between 1941 and 1948.[49] Over this period they managed to resist Carey Francis's attempts to control the association. But in 1948 Carey Francis succeeded in replacing this group of "politicians" by "well disposed old boys."[50]

By this time, however, these same people were already national political personalities. In 1944, Eliud Mathu was one of the first Africans appointed to the Legislative Council (LegCo). One year later, in 1945, James Gichuru became president of the Kenya African Union (KAU), a national organization aimed at conveying African grievances to the LegCo. In 1946, Otiende was appointed vice president of the KAU. Many former Alliance students were also involved in this organization. The link between education and politics was early established through this first generation of educated men, most of them teachers. The African staff of the school were the first to experience this active rebellion, and in doing so they opened up new opportunities to the students. It is actually during their school years that Alliance's students had to fight for recognition and against restrictive colonial rules. To become fully adults, the "boys" need symbolically to kill the "father." Challenging Carey Francis's views in the field of higher education or politics was part of this process.

Alliance High School was paradoxically a place where this political consciousness could grow. In fact the individual stories of the fifteen boys who finished their studies at Alliance High School in 1945 show the extent to which the struggle for education became a political issue.

A Schoolboy Generation at the Crossroads: Typology of the First Kenyan African Educated Youth

Julius Gecau was still a student at Alliance High School when he first met West and South African soldiers during World War II. He was struck by their ability to speak fluent English, and this meeting made him realize that in other parts of the world black people had access to better standards of education. This was an important factor in his decision to study abroad.[51] In fact after World War II, the growing demand for higher education gained increasing support from various actors within and outside the colony. The group of fifteen Alliance students directly benefited from this new interest in African education. Their individual stories, the places where they studied, and also the careers they pursued after their studies help us understand the meaning of this struggle for education, which was part of a broader struggle for recognition and liberation. In addition, the individual quest of this youth cohort to be fully recognized as active citizens and responsible adults epitomizes the struggle for independence.

Diversification of Actors and Resources

After World War II, new opportunities for higher education were opened through various bursary schemes. Both the Government African Overseas Bursaries and the Colonial Development and Welfare Act bursaries enabled students, who could not afford to study privately abroad, to read for university degrees in the United Kingdom. The aims of these programs were to encourage the Africanization of the colonial administration. The ideal candidate was a graduate from one local secondary school who had usually completed his studies at Makerere and after a couple of years of teaching or service in the colony was recommended for further education. It was a very selective process: each year, only three or four new students would benefit. Between 1946 and 1956 a total of seventy-two African students benefited from these two programs for periods of study between three months and four years; five students from the Alliance group of fifteen were among them.[52]

Some African students also received local financial support. In 1941, the North Kavirondo Local Native Council decided to raise an extra tax to enable five students from the district to study abroad. This initiative was rejected by the colonial government. Only in 1952 were district councils allowed to give bursaries to students.[53] However, unofficial organizations did not wait for government clearance to help local students study abroad. The Akamba Union organized a fundraising drive to send Frederick Mati and Henry Mulli to South Africa. The involvement of such an organization in this area underlines the political dimension of the quest for higher education.

Simultaneous with these local and colonial initiatives, foreign governments or associations were also increasingly receptive to African demand for higher education. In 1947, the government of India started a bursary scheme for colonial students. A couple of Africans from Kenya managed to study in India through this program during the 1950s, although most studied there privately.[54] Between 1947 and 1956 fifty-five Africans from Kenya went to study in India.[55] After he left Alliance High School, Joseph Otiende successfully applied for a Government of India Bursary in 1947. Julius Gecau who refused to go to Makerere also benefited from an Indian bursary in 1949. The colonial government was unhappy with these new programs, which were highly political. For instance, the first selection committee in 1947 was composed of members of the Kenya African Union (KAU) and representatives of the East African Indian National Congress.[56] J. Otiende was the vice-president of the KAU. In 1949, Mbiyu Koinange traveled to India in order to expand the program.[57]

Black American colleges were at this time also offering full scholarships to young Africans, as was the American government through its Fulbright program. Between 1946 and 1956, about thirty Africans from Kenya studied in the United States of America, mostly privately.[58] Julius Kiano left Makerere in 1946 when he received a scholarship from a small private college in Pennsylvania (Pioneer Business College, Philadelphia). Two years later Njoroge Mungai, who was ready to study medicine at St Andrews in Scotland, changed plans when he received a scholarship from Stanford University.[59] As with the Indian bursaries, the main idea was to help the African population in the colonies in their struggle for education. As a result, it of course challenged the colonial educational model.

After 1945 more opportunities were opened to colonial students who wished to study abroad. In fact these new initiatives counterbalanced the narrow colonial schemes. As we will see, most of the students from the "fifteen group" who studied abroad did not follow the usual colonial path but benefited from one of these alternative programs. Studying abroad was no longer the exclusive privilege of the sons of the colonial elite.

The Colonial Model of Education Challenged

The fifteen students who completed their secondary education at Alliance High School in 1945 were expected to go to Makerere; and after a couple of years of service in the colonial administration the luckiest might eventually benefit from

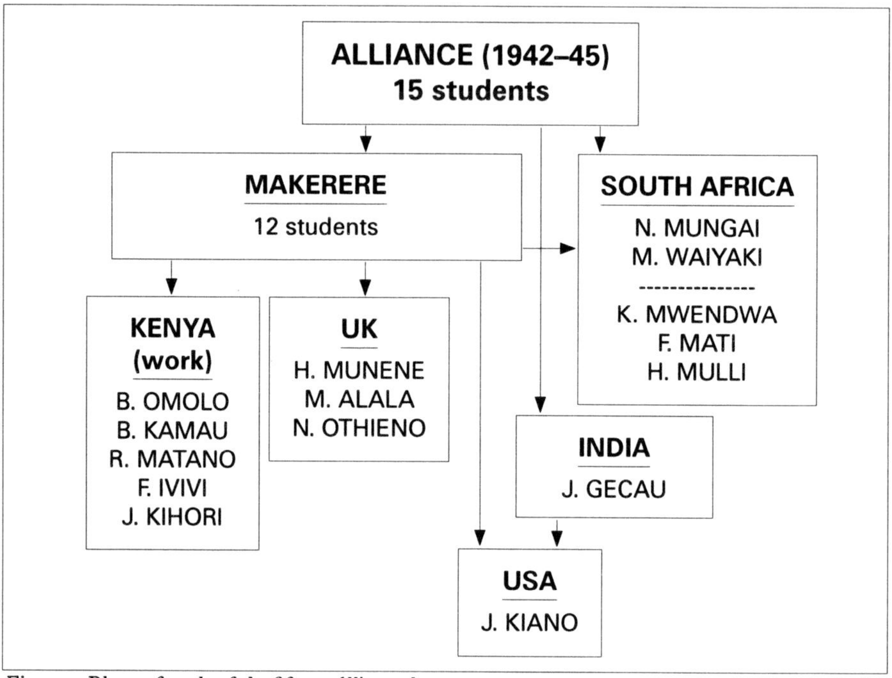

Figure 1. Places of study of the fifteen Alliance boys

one of the colonial schemes to study in the UK. However, only three actually followed the normal colonial procedure for higher education, whereas seven studied privately abroad. As we can see from the accompanying table (fig. 1), two groups of students can easily be identified according to their place and means of study.

Among the twelve students who entered Makerere, eight returned to Kenya after they graduated and worked for the colonial administration, mainly as teachers. Three were awarded bursaries to continue their studies abroad. After four years of teaching at Maseno School between 1949 and 1952, Moris Sika Alala was granted a Colonial Development and Welfare Act bursary to read for a BA and then an MA in math at St. Andrews University (Scotland). Nicholas Othieno, who was teaching at the Government African School in Kisii, also benefited from this scheme. Between 1950 and 1954, he read for a BA in science at Durham and then at Newcastle. Humphrey Kibuga Munene received a Government African Overseas Bursary to read at New Battle Abbey College in 1952. However, he failed his exams twice, and his bursary was withdrawn in 1953. Nevertheless, he decided to stay in the UK on a private basis. When he returned to the colony in 1954, Nicholas Othieno was posted to Alliance High School. Alala also returned to a teaching position when he returned to the colony in 1957. For those who stayed within the colonial boundaries of education, opportunities were few. Most of the Makerere graduates applied for colonial bursaries. For instance, Francis Ivivi applied three times for a Government African Overseas Bursary (in 1952, 1956, and 1957) but never qualified.[60] Jerome Kihori also applied for a Colonial

Development and Welfare Act Bursary in 1952.[61] In comparison, those who studied privately managed to get degrees very quickly.

Julius Gecau, who refused to take the Makerere examination, started to organize his studies abroad. He wanted to study in America, but it was difficult to get dollars and a passport. He started a small black-market business of *chang'aa* through which he earned enough to pay for his passage to India in 1949. He registered at the Erwings Christian College in Allahabad to prepare for the university matriculation examination. After two years he managed to get an Indian scholarship from a private foundation (MP Shah Scholarship) to read for an economics degree in 1951.[62] At the end of his studies in 1954, he was contacted by members of the Presbyterian Church of America who were looking for an African student for a tour in the United States. He subsequently managed to get a fellowship at the University of Chicago, where he read for an MA. In 1956 he joined the London School of Economics in London and returned to Kenya in 1957.[63]

Munyua Waiyaki passed the Makerere entrance examination but decided to study in South Africa. His father was rich enough to cover the expense. He prepared for university matriculation at Adams College and then enrolled at Fort Hare, where he read for a BA in hygiene (premedical studies). He continued his medical studies at St. Andrews in Scotland, at first as a private student, but in 1955 he was granted a Government African Overseas Bursary and the following year a Colonial Development and Welfare Act bursary. He returned to Kenya in 1958. Njoroge Mungai also studied medicine in South Africa. He could not study at Makerere for medical reasons. He had been infected with blackwater fever, so the climate was not suitable for him. He first went to Fort Hare and started a premedical course. He moved to Cape Town, but medical studies were too expensive, so he registered in commerce. He was still looking for admission to an American university. He finally received a positive response from Stanford University, where he studied medicine between 1951 and 1957. He subsequently spent two years at Columbia in New York and a further year at McGill in Montreal. He returned to Kenya at the end of 1959.[64]

As far as most students were concerned, the United States was the most attractive place to study. One of the Alliance students from this group actually managed to get there almost immediately after his studies at Alliance. Julius Kiano, like Gecau and Mungai, was busy writing to several American colleges to gain admission. When he received a positive answer from the Pioneer Business College in Philadelphia in 1948, he immediately left Makerere without even taking his exams. A long journey through the American universities commenced. As soon as he arrived in the United States he managed to find a better place. He registered at Storer College for a couple of months (the Nigerian politician, Nnamdi Azikiwe, started his American education in the same college). But these small black colleges did not satisfy his ambition, and Kiano finally managed to get a scholarship to Antioch College in Yellow Springs, Ohio, for an undergraduate degree in economics. After that he joined Stanford University, where he found Njoroge Mungai, and later proceeded to Berkeley to do a PhD. He was the first

Kenyan African to reach this level of education. He returned to Kenya in 1956 and was appointed lecturer at the Royal Technical College of Nairobi.[65]

Three other former Alliance students who decided to continue their studies immediately after leaving Makerere instead of joining the colonial service went to South Africa. Kyale Mwendwa enrolled at Fort Hare in 1949.[66] After three years of study in South Africa, he returned to Kenya with an undergraduate degree in math in 1951; he was appointed to Machakos, where he taught until 1960. Henry Mulli and Frederic Mati also read for a BSc and a BA respectively at Fort Hare from 1948. They received some support from the Akamba Union. Henry Mulli, for example, decided to proceed to South Africa in 1948, after he had finished his higher sciences degree (equivalent of high school graduation) at Makerere.

For this group of individual students, the path leading to university degrees was neither smooth nor direct. However, it seems that their struggles and determination in their academic peregrinations were rewarding. All of them succeeded in their studies. And it seems they exceeded their Alliance fellows who followed the colonial path: one PhD, two fully trained doctors. Indeed, the careers that members of this group of students undertook when they returned to Kenya at the end of the 1950s seem to confirm their success. All played a critical role in postindependence Kenyan politics.

The Making of an African Educated Elite and the Move toward Independence

Narratives from the former students about their education abroad underline the importance of specific factors in their success or failure. Social networks and political context played important parts in these individual stories. The group of young men who studied independently abroad shared common features. All of them are either Kikuyu or Kamba. Henry Munene, a Kikuyu, who first received a bursary to study in the UK, continued his studies privately. People from Central Province, and to a lesser extent from Eastern Province, seem to have had more connections with the various sources of colonial power (political, religious, or professional); these particular networks might have helped them in their pursuit of further education.

Kitale Mwendwa and Munyua Waiyaki were sons of chiefs who were wealthy enough to send their sons abroad. As already mentioned, political networks also played a crucial role in the education of Henry Mulli and Fred Mati, who were supported by the Akamba Union. Religious networks such as the Presbyterian Church of Scotland seemed also to have encouraged young Kenyans to study in their own network of schools and colleges. From its beginning, Alliance High School had strong connections with the Presbyterian Church of Scotland. The school had privileged links with Fort Hare College in South Africa, which belonged to the same network, and to a lesser extend with Erwings Christian College in India. It seems that in the United Kingdom, Scottish colleges such as St. Andrews, Robert Gordon in Aberdeen, and New Battle Abbey College were preferred by former Alliance High School students. In fact out of the ten students who studied abroad, nine at some point attended a Scottish school or university.

The Kenyan political context also influenced the individual choices and educational paths of the students. Between 1952 and 1960, Kenya was under a state of emergency. At very different levels, most of the former Alliance students were affected by these events. Jerome Kihori, who was serving as an appointed assistant district officer in Nyeri, was killed by the Mau Mau in July 1953.[67] The same year Henry Mulli, then working in Tanzania, was arrested on the grounds of his connections with the Akamba Association and the politician Paul Ngei, who was arrested with Kenyatta on October 20, 1952. He was detained for six years first at the Athi River Camp and then at Manyani.[68] Others feared arrest if they returned to Kenya. Julius Gecau recalls the rumor that all Kikuyu were being arrested. When he graduated in India in 1954 he did not want to return to Kenya and instead went directly to the United States.[69] For the sons of the well-integrated Kikuyu elite, who might have been Mau Mau's targets, being abroad was in some cases a way of safeguarding them.

Most of the students from the group of fifteen returned to the colony after 1956, by which time the war against the forest fighters was over.[70] Among the ten students who studied abroad, nine returned to the colony between 1949 and 1961, three before 1954, three in 1957, and three others sometime in the years 1956–58. In 1957 the first franchised elections were organized in Kenya to elect the eight African members of the Legislative Council.[71] The franchise system was designed after the Coutts' Report of 1955, which enabled certain categories of Africans to vote according to their wealth and level of education.[72] One single voter could cast up to three votes if he fulfilled three out of the ten identified criteria. Candidates to the election had to produce a certificate of proficiency in English or hold a university degree or a Makerere diploma. An amendment was actually introduced to exempt people who received a bursary overseas and successfully completed the selected course. It was known as the Mboya amendment as it entitled Tom Mboya, the Luo unionist and politician, to stand in (and eventually win a seat in) the election. Voters from Central Province had to prove their loyalty to the government during the Emergency.[73] These first elections in the Emergency context valorized a small section of wealthy, educated, and loyal Africans. About one-third of the population was eligible, but less than 10 percent registered in the eight constituencies. This poll actually formalized an invisible link between education and political influence. Out of the thirty-seven candidates authorized to run for the elections, twelve were teachers and thirteen had studied at Makerere; six held a degree from a United Kingdom university.[74]

Considering the general framework of African politics in Kenya in the late fifties it is not surprising to find a fair number of former 1945 Alliance students involved in postcolonial politics. As Benjamin Kipkorir pointed out in his thesis, ten former students of Alliance High School were part of the first postindependence cabinet of seventeen members. In 1966, they constituted twelve out of twenty-two.[75] Some of these early politicians were among the fifteen discussed in this chapter: Julius Kiano, Njoroge Mungai, Munyua Waiyaki, and Fred Mati. In fact, half of the 1945 Alliance fifteen became preeminent politicians, all of whom studied abroad independently.[76]

Julius Kiano returned to the colony in 1956 with a PhD and was appointed lecturer at the Royal Technical College. He was elected to the Legislative Council in 1958[77] and was reelected MP (Member of Parliament) onward until 1979. He served as minister of Commerce and Industry, minister of Education, and minister of Local Government. After he left politics, he was appointed chairman of KBC (Kenya Broadcasting Corporation). He died in 2003.[78] His American-educated colleague, Njoroge Mungai, also had a long political career. He returned to Kenya at the end of 1959 and started a clinic in Thika. He was first elected MP in 1963, lost his seat in 1983, but was elected again in 1988. He was appointed minister for Internal Affairs and Defence in 1963 and minister for Foreign Affairs in 1969. Later, under Moi's presidency, he was appointed minister for Natural Resources but resigned in 1991.[79] Njoroge Mungai is related to the Kenyatta family and as his personal physician was very close to Jomo Kenyatta. Munyua Waiyaki, who returned to Kenya in 1958 also as a medical graduate, first served as assistant minister in 1964 and as minister for Foreign Affairs in 1974. He was an MP from 1963 to 1983.[80] All these Kikuyu politicians were also strong KANU supporters. Frederick Mati also started a political career at the time of independence. He was elected MP in 1961 and was appointed minister of Health and Lodging the following year. From 1970 up to 1988 he was the speaker of the National Assembly. Henri Mulli, who also came from Eastern Province and studied in South Africa, was also elected to the National Assembly in 1961. However, he did not remain in politics but instead joined the diplomatic service, which led to postings in Beijing and Paris.[81] Kyale Mwendwa received a grant to study at Michigan State University in 1960. When he returned to Kenya in 1961, he became the first African district education officer; he was posted to Kitui. A couple of months later, he became director of education. When his brother Kitili Mwendwa, the former chief justice, died in a road accident he decided to "replace" him and entered politics. He was elected MP in 1986 and 1988.[82] Julius Gecau's career reflects another elite success story, not in the direct political spotlight but in the shadows of parastatal companies. After his studies in India and in the United States, he was hired by the British American Tobacco Company (BAT) when he was still a student in London. He returned to Kenya at the end of 1957, and after a couple of years with BAT, he was appointed executive director of Kenya Power and Lighting Company.[83]

All the seven students from Alliance who decided not to follow the slow colonial path to higher education and made their own way to university degrees started a political career. As far as politicians are concerned, Robert Matano appears as an exception. He did not go any further after his teaching diploma at Makerere. But in 1961 he was elected to the Legislative Council and continually elected until 1988. He served five times in the same constituency. In 1979 he was appointed cabinet minister for Social Services and Housing. Out of this group of fifteen, Robert Matano is the only one who entered politics without any higher education degree. Interestingly, the type of careers of the students who followed the colonial pattern of education is quite different. Morris Alala, who studied in Scotland, went for an academic career in math at the University of Nairobi; Nicholas Othieno remained a secondary teacher.

For this generation of students, it is clear that education and more specifically university degrees opened up new opportunities. The close relationship that was established under the colonial rule between education and power seems to have been strengthened by the first African students who benefited from the new opportunities. Many former students were actually involved in promoting education in Kenya or abroad. Mbiyu Koinange's experience with the African Teachers College Githunguri (1938–1952) and Eliud Mathu's independent school give clear examples of the educational commitment of the early educated African elite. As soon as he returned from the United States, Julius Kiano offered support to Tom Mboya's project of sending hundreds of students to America through airlifts. He was one of the founding members of the African American Students Foundation that arranged these trips. Other former students also started local education projects. Kyale Mwendwa is the founder of St. Austin's Academy in Nairobi; Henri Mulli started his own private school in Kitui. These different initiatives underline the specific contributions and commitment of this early cohort of educated youth to the development of education in Kenya as a privileged instrument of liberation and empowerment.

THE INDIVIDUAL STORIES of this group of fifteen students of Alliance High School, known as "the class of notables," emphasize the role of education among colonial youth. Within the colonial system, achieving education at a university level was a real struggle as there were no opportunities in East Africa apart from at Makerere, which prior to 1953 did not offer university degrees. Obtaining further education was for most of this ambitious cohort part of a recognition process leading to adulthood. It is because the colonial system treated Africans as children that education was desperately needed in order to challenge the colonial order.

Paradoxically, it is at Alliance High School, Kenya's foremost colonial school, that students measured the limits of the system and decided to fight back with their own weapons. It is in fact their experience at Alliance that fostered the identity of this cohort of youth, enabling them to play a critical social and political role in the independence process. Colonial secondary schools such as Alliance High School were one of the spaces of modernity—like urban centers—that were created by the colonial situation and that critically contributed to youth's empowerment.

Education was therefore highly political in the pre-independence years. It is not surprising to find most of these educated youth going on to achieve key positions in independent Kenya. From the individual stories of this group of fifteen, it seems that the more they challenged the colonial framework when studying in South Africa, India, or America, the more brilliant was their public career. But considering the social background of the young people who managed to get abroad without any colonial support, it could also be said that they managed to get there because they already had the social and financial support required. Education, then, was a means to greatly expand preexisting social capital. Connections made abroad were also important in the constitution of this group of students as an African elite after their return to Kenya in the late 1950s. Their stories show

how linked the struggle for education became to the struggle for independence. It was not only the story of escaping a paternalist and oppressive school system but also of acquiring national empowerment.

Notes

1. J. Comaroff and J. Comaroff, "Reflexions sur la jeunesse, du passé à la postcolonie," *Politique Africaine,* no. 80 (1990): 90–110.

2. The other was the Catholic Mangu High School run by the Holy Ghost Fathers and located in Central Province. There were also two junior secondary schools (two years of teaching): Maseno School (Anglican) and the Catholic St. Mary's School in Yala, both located in western Kenya. Education Department Annual Report, 1945, Public Record Office, London (PRO), Colony and Protectorate, CO 544/61; Education Department Annual Report, 1946, PRO, Colony and Protectorate, CO 544/62.

3. J. S. Smith, *A History of Alliance High School* (Nairobi: Heinemann Education Book, 1973), 148.

4. T. Kanogo, *African Womanhood in Colonial Kenya, 1900–50* (London: James Currey, 2005).

5. A couple of years later Archdeacon W. E. Owen was still opposed to this elitist view. He took a strong position on this matter in a text entitled "Corban in Kenya: A Criticism of State Financing of African Education" (1940), unpublished manuscript. Document quoted by J. M. Lonsdale "Some Origins of Nationalism in East Africa," *Journal of African History* 9, no. 1 (1968): 139.

6. B. E. Kipkorir, "The Alliance High School and the Origins of the Kenyan African Elite: 1926–1962" (PhD thesis, St. John's College, Cambridge, 1969), 81.

7. Maseno School was opened in 1906, twenty-five kilometers from Kisumu, by the Church Missionary Society with four pupils. It played an important role in the development of education in western Kenya, becoming a junior secondary school in 1938. However, it was eleven years (1949) before students from Maseno were able to take the Cambridge School Certificate.

8. Smith, *History of Alliance High School,* 10.

9. Ibid., 165. It is only in 1946 that Mangu was able to prepare students to the Cambridge School Certificate.

10. In 1926, twenty-four students out of a total of twenty-six were Kikuyu.

11. Between 1998 and 2007, I conducted interviews with six former students: Henry Mulli, Njoroge Mungai, Julius Kiano, Julius Gecau, Kyale Mwendwa, and Munyua Waiyaki.

12. Interview with Kyale Mwendwa, Nairobi, 2 May 2007.

13. Smith, *History of Alliance High School,* 125.

14. Interview with Kyale Mwendwa, Nairobi, 2 May 2007.

15. Georges Grieve was born in 1888 in Edinburgh. He arrived in Kenya in 1920 and taught for five years at the Church of Scotland Mission School in Kikuyu. In 1926, he was appointed the first headmaster of Alliance High School.

16. L. B. Greaves, *Carey Francis of Kenya* (Nairobi: Rex Colling, 1969), 17.

17. Ibid., 58.

18. Ibid., 59.

19. Interview with Julius Gecau, Nairobi, 19 January 1999.

20. Interview with Henry Mulli, Nairobi, 21 January 1999.

21. Interview with Julius Kiano, Nairobi, 15 January 2001.

22. Smith, *History of Alliance High School,* 26.

23. A prior attempt to remove the fez had been made in 1936 but was resisted (ibid., 101).

24. Kipkorir, "Alliance High School," 197.

25. Ibid., 198.

26. Interview with Charles Njonjo, Nairobi, 4 February 1999.

27. B. de Bunsen, *Adventures in Education* (London: Titus Wilson Kendal, 1995), 93.

28. Mr. Turner's Report on African Secondary Education, 1946, 54; Kenya National Archives, Nairobi (KNA), ED/1/2326; J. E. Goldthorpe, *An African Elite: Makerere College Students 1922–1960* (Nairobi: Oxford University Press, 1965).

29. The first degrees were delivered in 1948. On the history of Makerere, see C. Sicherman, *Becoming an African University: Makerere 1922–2000* (Trenton, NJ: Africa World Press, 2005).

30. Interview with Julius Gecau, Nairobi, 19 January 1999.

31. Interview with Munyua Waiyaki, Nairobi, 19 January 2001.

32. Interview with Julius Kiano, Nairobi, 21 January 2001.

33. Ibid.

34. P. H. Muraya, "The Kenya Teachers' College, Githunguri, 1939–1952" (MA thesis, University of Nairobi, 1972).

35. The college was opened in 1939, and its aim was to train qualified teachers for the Kikuyu independent schools' network. The Kikuyu independent school movement, started in 1929, can be seen as one of the various responses by the African population of the colony to the shortage of education. In other parts of the country, the Local Native Councils played a critical role in the development of education. The aim of Githunguri College was to provide an alternative for any African student who could not continue within the colonial system. The political meaning of such initiatives was clearly understood by the colonial government. All the Kikuyu independent schools were closed immediately after the Declaration of Emergency in 1952 and Githunguri was burned down.

36. Interview with Kyale Mwendwa, Nairobi, 2 May 2007.

37. Note from Carey Francis, 30 December 1953, KNA ED/1/2743.

38. Note from Norman Larby, Director of Education, 30 November 1948, KNA ED/3/2721.

39. Interview with Kyale Mwendwa, Nairobi, 18 January 2001.

40. Minutes from the selection committee meeting, 27 January 1949, KNA ED/1/2743.

41. Note from the Secretary of State for the Colony, 9 November 1949, KNA ED/1/2532.

42. De Bunsen, *Adventures in Education,* 81.

43. These figures are drawn from the population censuses of 1948 and 1962.

44. The Kikuyu Central Association was a political organization started in 1924 in Muranga. It was more radical than the old Kikuyu Association (1919). Most of its early members were young and educated.

45. *Petitions and Memorial, Kikuyu People,* 1940, PRO, CO/533/543/2.

46. 30 June 1945, KNA PC/NZA/3/6/162.

47. The Inter-State Native College was opened in 1916 in Natal Province in South Africa by the Church of Scotland Mission. For nearly twenty years it was the only

college of Africa offering external degrees to African students from all over the continent. Many of the future African ruling elite studied at Fort Hare (including Nelson Mandela, Robert Mugabe, Kenneth Kaunda, Julius Nyerere, and Hebert Chitepo).

48. For more details about Eliud Mathu see J. R. Roelker, *Mathu of Kenya: A Political Study* (Stanford: Hoover Institution Press, 1976).

49. Joseph Daniel Otiende was a contemporary of James Gichuru. They studied together first at Alliance High School and then at Makerere. He joined the teaching staff of the school in 1938. He taught music and used to make the pupils sing the ANC hymn: *Nkosi Sikelele Africa.* Of course when Carey Francis found out what the song was about, he decided to replace it with *God Save the King* (Kipkorir, "Alliance High School," 250).

50. Ibid., 240.

51. Interview with Julius Gecau, Nairobi, 19 January 1999.

52. H. Charton, "La genèse ambiguë de l'élite kenyane: Origines, formation et intégration de 1945 à 1963" (PhD thesis, Paris VII, 2002), 176. Thirty-eight students studied abroad under the Government African Overseas Bursaries scheme and thirty-four under the Colonial Development and Welfare Act scheme.

53. KNA PC/NZA/3/6/2.

54. Government of India's Scheme for the Award of Scholarships for the Promotion of Cultural Relations between India and Foreign Countries, 29 August 1949, PRO, CO/822/143/6.

55. Charton, "La genèse ambiguë de l'élite kenyane."

56. 18 June 1947, KNA ED/3/340.

57. Letter from the High Commissioner in India to the Commonwealth Relations Office, 8 August 1949, PRO, CO/537/4662.

58. Charton, "La genèse ambiguë de l'élite kenyane."

59. Interviews with N. Mungai (Nairobi, 17 January 2001) and J. Kiano (Nairobi, 15 January 2001).

60. Applications for Government African Overseas bursaries 1952/53, KNA ED/1/2743; Kenya Government Bursaries, 1956/57 and 1957/58, KNA ED/3/3020.

61. KNA ED/1/2532.

62. Interview with Julius Gecau, Nairobi, 19 January 1999.

63. Interview with Munyua Waiyaki, Nairobi, 19 January 2001.

64. Interview with Njoroge Mungai, Nairobi, 17 January 2001.

65. Interview with Julius Kiano, Nairobi, 15 January 2001.

66. KNA ED/3/2721.

67. H. Swanzy, "Quarterly Notes," *African Affairs* 52 (October 1953): 283.

68. Interview with Henry Mulli, Nairobi, 21 January 1999.

69. Interview with Julius Gecau, Nairobi, 19 January 1999.

70. The state of emergency was not terminated until 1960.

71. On the issue of the 1957 election see G. F. Engholm, "African Elections in Kenya, March 1957," in *Five Elections in Africa*, ed. W. J. M. Mackenzie and K. Robinson (Oxford: Clarendon Press, 1960), 391–461.

72. W. F. Coutts, *Report of the Commissioner Appointed to Enquire into Methods for the Selection of African Representatives of the Legislative Council* (Nairobi: Government Printer, 1955).

73. D. Branch, "Loyalists, Mau-Mau and Elections in Kenya: The First Triumph of the System, 1957–58," *Africa Today* 53, no. 2 (2006): 26–50.

74. Mackenzie and Robinson, *Five Elections in Africa,* 423.

75. Kipkorir, "Alliance High School," 2.

76. About the political careers of these elites see W. Kihoro, *Politics and Parliamentarians in Kenya, 1944–2007* (Nairobi: Centre for Multiparty Democracy, 2007).

77. This new poll was organized after the eight elected members of the LegCo boycotted the Lyttelton Constitution. New arrangements were made turning down the elected members system, and six new African members were elected (two in the new constituencies of Central Province).

78. Interview with Julius Kiano, Nairobi, 15 January 2001.

79. Interview with Njoroge Mungai, Nairobi, 20 April 2006.

80. Interview with Munyua Waiyaki, Nairobi, 19 January 2001.

81. Interview with Henry Mulli, Nairobi, 21 January 1999.

82. Interview with Kyale Mwendwa, Nairobi, 18 January 2001.

83. Interview with Julius Gecau, Nairobi, 19 January 1999.

5

Raw Youth, School-Leavers, and the Emergence of Structural Unemployment in Late Colonial Urban Tanganyika

ANDREW BURTON

IN 1958 AN article in the Tanganyika *Sunday News* singled out "workless youth" as a "problem of our future."[1] Its author showed great prescience in identifying joblessness among young Africans as an imminent threat. This was a pivotal time for urban economies throughout the region, when a problem of structural unemployment first emerged, which intensified after independence and has persisted up to the present.[2] The phenomenon was rooted in socioeconomic and cultural change occurring in African societies over the preceding half century, culminating after World War II in a generation that was the first to leave rural areas in such numbers as to create a position of urban labor surplus. By the mid-twentieth century forces arising from colonial rule exerted an increasing influence, resulting in significant shifts in the outlook and expectations of African youth. Whereas the transforming impact of colonialism among earlier generations—such as the one maturing in John Iliffe's "age of improvement," as discussed by Jim Giblin in chapter 3—had been confined to the handful of Africans at that time in direct contact with colonial institutions, by the 1950s these institutions had proliferated, and, partly as a consequence, a youth cohort had emerged among whom manifold "expectations of modernity" were widespread.[3] As discussed by Hélène Charton in the preceding chapter, the sociopolitical ambitions of an educated elite at the apex of this generation were often met by departing East Africa in pursuit of technical knowledge. The more modest economic and cultural aspirations of the majority of East African youth, on the other hand, appeared most easily addressed by a move to town, to which increasing numbers went in the run-up to independence. This phenomenon provoked mounting concern on the part of both the colonial government and African politicians and elders, for whom urbanization, particularly that involving young Africans, had long been regarded with deep suspicion.[4] Even at times of full employment, the perceived degeneration of African youth through exposure to the malign influences of the urban environment was a social process viewed with dismay. The mounting wave of young rural migrants building up in the course of the 1950s, when urban employment was at best static, was truly the stuff of colonial nightmares. They entered the towns at a critical point in the towns' (mostly) short histories.

The 1950s has been identified as a key decade for African urban economies. As Gavin Kitching observes, pre-1950 East African economies were characterized by a large *potential* reserve army of workers residing in rural areas, which might be induced into wage labor. In the 1950s the situation changed, with an *actual* reserve army of unemployed observable in towns by the end of the decade.[5] Frederick Cooper stresses the manner in which political calculations impacted upon growing joblessness in the 1950s.[6] A desire to mold "more productive and orderly" colonies after the war, alongside an increasingly demanding African workforce, and urban centers growing beyond colonial control, induced a shift in labor policy that emphasized stabilization. In contrast to prevailing low-wage, labor-extensive forms of employment, from the 1950s increased skill levels were rewarded by higher salaries. Paradoxically, this increase in wages formed a prime cause of growing urban poverty. According to Iliffe, it "attracted people into towns, encouraged employers to replace workers by machinery, and bred the unemployment, overcrowding, and ancillary problems which the authorities had intended to prevent."[7] A background context profoundly shaping the phenomenon was demographic change. Rapid African population growth from the mid-twentieth century, alongside a diminishing resource/population ratio resulted in a shift from famine-related "epidemic starvation for all but the rich . . . to endemic undernutrition for the very poor."[8] One of the most prominent forms in which this "structural" poverty manifested itself was the growth of urban joblessness among young Africans in particular.

This chapter provides a detailed account of structural causes that led to the emergence of unemployment among Tanganyikan youth, and the official response to this phenomenon.[9] A combination of factors resulted in widespread joblessness emerging in mid-1950s Dar es Salaam that spread to other towns, growing more acute as independence approached. Here too, an economic solution—increased wages—to the political problems arising from the growing demands of African labor, and to rapid urbanization, had dramatic repercussions. To offset the new cost of labor, local employers responded by reducing workforces and attempting to increase productivity. Unemployment was also fundamentally influenced by intertwined aspects of social and demographic change. By the 1940s, shifts in cash requirements, consumption patterns, and in African expectations of "modern" lives blessed by greater affluence, stimulation, and convenience—all contributed to an increase in numbers seeking waged employment. Most significantly, the postwar decades witnessed accelerated population growth, of which young Africans constituted an expanding proportion. This increasingly youthful population benefited from a substantial rise in colonial expenditure on education. As with the shift in labor policy, the expansion of education exemplified contradictions arising from late colonial developmentalism. It produced a generation of Africans who were not only better equipped for formal employment but also had greater expectations of obtaining waged work at a time when employment actually contracted. By the late 1950s officials identified a "school-leaver problem," with the numbers of educated Africans substantially outnumbering vacancies. However, school-leavers represented only part of the problem—just 47 percent of the school-age population attended school in 1957, and many failed to complete even lower primary.[10] The uneducated and poorly educated—identified as "raw youth" by trade unionist B. S. Kajunjumele—formed a considerably larger proportion of the young Africans pouring into towns for work.[11]

The phenomenon of mounting unemployment caused increasing anxiety among colonial officials and, in particular, Tanganyika African National Union (TANU) politicians as they acceded to power. A growing class of jobless youth was interpreted as a sociopolitical threat, resulting in desperate initiatives to address the problem in the first months of TANU rule. As was often the case with improvised policies aimed at addressing the unsettling effects of socioeconomic change on African youth, these initiatives did more to address official anxiety than the problem of unemployment itself. However, in time it became clear that the "unemployed" did not represent the threat that many feared.[12] These concerns arose from an ignorance of urban society. "Jobless" was perhaps a more appropriate description for many town dwellers lacking employment. Much urban work was characterized by its impermanence, and towns contained large numbers of individuals between jobs, participants in an emerging informal economy, and migrants from urban hinterlands looking for work in the agricultural off-season.[13]

The focus of official concern also highlights the gendered nature in which the "unemployment problem" was interpreted. Throughout the colonial period, employment *and* unemployment were overwhelmingly associated with men.[14] Women had for long entered urban centers and, with waged employment deemed appropriate for them restricted, provided a significant contribution to informal sector activity.[15] However, in the official imagination it was male youth who constituted a potentially insurrectionary unemployed class, who were more visible "loitering" on urban streets. The absence of female unemployed in surviving commentary reflects the gendered occupation of urban space. By contrast to young men, whose street presence has remained a concern up to the present,[16] women were more restricted to the home and/or the workplace. Nevertheless, in light of postindependence trends, when female urbanization and participation in the workforce increased,[17] it seems likely that the 1950s was a pivotal period for both young men *and* women, and that female unemployment increased at this time.[18] However, lack of consideration of this subject in extant sources allows only these speculative remarks: in the period under discussion, unemployment was conceived as a problem of male youth.

Work and Worklessness in Urban Tanganyika before 1950

Urban labor in Tanganyika arose within a broader historical context of work in predominantly agrarian societies. Nineteenth-century travelers to the region remarked on the time adult male Africans were able to devote to leisure. Juhani Koponen refutes the crude "idle native" stereotype presented in such accounts, while agreeing with the broader assertion that in many precolonial societies prolonged work routines were simply unnecessary. Local conditions allowed relatively short, and productive, periods of labor thanks to the climate, abundance of land, limited requirements of local peoples, and absence of any significant market for surplus.[19] In particular, work was marked by its seasonality. Such characteristics of agrarian societies were maintained in the early colonial period. While European administrators sought to promote rural industriousness through cash-crop cultivation or minimum acreage laws, earlier cycles of life persisted. Other forms of colonial extraction, alongside new incentives and opportunities arising from a cash economy, actually encouraged labor migration.[20] Nevertheless, waged employment was frequently articulated around established seasonal cycles. So, for example, Zaramo and Rufiji came to Dar es Salaam in large numbers to seek waged work in the agricultural off-season.[21] With land in Tanganyika relatively abundant, urban immigrants mostly retained strong rural links, and if all else failed a subsistence could be obtained from the family shamba. Pressures to conform to Western patterns of time and work discipline were not great.[22]

There were few signs of proletarianization in the first half-century of colonial rule, and unemployment remained rare. Although cyclical job shortages occurred, and from the colonial point of view "underemployment" was common, the principal characteristic of labor tended to be scarcity. African labor was certainly more abundant in the urban areas, notably Dar es Salaam and Tanga. Officials here bemoaned the numerous Africans shifting in and out of employment. Nevertheless, employers often encountered difficulties obtaining workers, especially skilled workers. The situation was exacerbated by peculiarities of the local workforce, which was held to comprise mostly "target workers," who, retaining an agricultural base, entered into employment with the aim of earning a fixed sum. Migrant labor prevailed, which employers used to justify strikingly low wages (at least as important a factor in perpetuating migrancy). Urban workers were often inclined to engage in employment only sporadically. For example, the relatively high wages received by dockworkers enabled them to evade pressure to work. In late 1940s Dar es Salaam most worked between fifteen and twenty days per month despite work being available for a "full month" (six days per week).[23] Workers temporarily leaving employment either lived off remaining wages or subsisted through petty trade and/or a peri-urban shamba. Africans could not only be choosy about when they worked but also about the type of work they engaged in. Dock work was favored because of the flexible routine and high wages. By contrast, more onerous work on sisal plantations surrounding Tanga and Dar es Salaam was deeply unpopular among town dwellers, even at times of high unemployment.[24]

When unemployment surfaced prior to 1950 it was conjunctural in character. Three serious bouts occurred between 1919 and 1950. The first arose from the slight depression after World War I but soon abated thanks to economic recovery.[25] More serious and lasting unemployment appeared during the Great Depression. By late 1931, 40 percent of Africans normally in work in Dar es Salaam were jobless.[26] The

1932 annual report recorded "thousands of natives out of employment, many living in or near . . . Dar es Salaam, who are unable to pay their tax and do not get one square meal a day."[27] Tanga suffered similar problems, where in 1931 the district commissioner (DC) complained that "trade depression has been responsible for the flooding of Tanga with natives . . . and the difficulty of obtaining work has led in, many cases, to the commission of thefts and acts of violence."[28] Nevertheless, by the middle of the decade urban economies had rebounded and joblessness eased.[29] The most serious bout, prior to 1950, emerged in the late 1930s. Although conjunctural, it was a harbinger of later events. Severe unemployment was identified in 1939. In Tanga, excess labor was blamed for low wages, to which a serious outbreak of strike-related disorder was attributed.[30] Similar conditions prevailed in Dar es Salaam, where the unemployed population was estimated at 1,500 to 4,000.[31] The situation was particularly grave in the capital, which from 1938 experienced an upsurge in rural-to-urban migration. Economic growth was insufficient to cope with this accelerated influx, and unemployment rose and living conditions deteriorated sharply. Nevertheless, improving economic conditions from the mid-1940s eased the problem. By the end of the decade, officials reported that although unskilled labor was abundant, there was work for all who wanted it.[32]

Surviving data give little impression of the age profile of those affected in these pre-1950 periods of unemployment. However, African youth must have featured prominently among the jobless. Many migrants to Dar es Salaam and Tanga—notably those without skills engaged in the casual work most affected by periods of economic downturn—were young African men who entered the towns in order to earn money to meet recently acquired responsibilities for colonial tax (or to evade its payment). There was also a smaller number of under-eighteens who engaged in child labor when available, who were especially vulnerable in recessionary times. Indeed, the growing visibility of this latter group in the second bout of unemployment in the late 1930s and early 1940s prompted a lively correspondence between officials on how to deal with the issue.[33] Though, as with unemployment, the problem appears to have receded by the end of the decade.

Rural-Urban Migration and a Changing Workforce

Structural causes of mass unemployment in 1950s Tanganyika had their roots in the previous decade, when the impact of colonialism was increasingly evident. One fundamental background factor was demographic expansion. A declining death rate resulted in population growth that had significant repercussions for urban centers.[34] Colonial measures aimed at "famine control and the eradication . . . of major epidemics and diseases . . . reduced mortality," leading to population growth from the 1920s at the earliest.[35] Juhani Koponen adds to this "a rise in fertility (at first hesitant, but accelerating with the approach of independence)" caused by various sociocultural factors, including an increased "demand for surplus labor imposed by colonialism."[36] Population growth accelerated in following decades, though deriving accurate figures from records before 1948 is impossible.

Judging by late colonial censuses, the population underwent substantial growth, increasing by 17 percent from under 7.5 to over 8.5 million between 1948 and 1957. At the same time, Tanganyika's towns expanded at unprecedented rates. The African urban population increased by 83 percent between 1948 and 1957, from 152,435 to 279,606.[37] The trend was most evident in Dar es Salaam. The capital's African population grew from approximately 26,000 in 1938 to over 93,000 in 1957. The population bulge meant that young Africans were the most prominent group among urban migrants.[38]

Other symptoms of colonialism contributed to rural-urban migration. The deepening penetration of the cash nexus forced growing numbers into the workplace.[39] Emerging consumer needs intensified the demand for sources of cash, as mass-produced products, from enamel bowls to bicycles, reached Tanganyika's remotest corners. Moreover, between 1928 and 1948 tax collected from Africans increased from £743,820 to £1,646,000.[40] With wages rising only marginally, this indicated a significant intensification of collection.[41] Demand for rural employment was negligible, thanks in part to the timidity of a colonial regime that stymied "the development of a class of rural capitalists,"[42] and increasingly Africans left their home areas in search of work. The trend was encouraged by heightened African mobility arising from improvements in transportation.[43] Between 1941 and 1951, migrant labor using government transit centers increased from 125,578 to 225,949.[44] Although the proportion of those destined for towns is inaccessible, and many were headed for plantations, a comparable increase in Africans seeking urban work certainly occurred. Towns, where potential earnings were greatest, were a popular destination for those seeking employment, even though the living conditions of most urban Africans remained grim.[45]

Other factors encouraging migration arose from shifts in attitudes. Towns formed a haven for young Africans, evading agricultural labor, colonial taxes, or simply tired of rural monotony and keen to sample urban life.[46] Western education played a crucial part in the changing outlook of African youth. Before 1940, educational provision had been negligible—under 10 percent of African children had access to schooling.[47] Furthermore, interwar "education for adaptation"[48] had an agricultural bias, which was "seen as a means of preventing the production of educated unemployed—the overriding concern of the Government at the time, 'the source of most of the world's social ills.'"[49] Even mission schools, which predominated in Tanganyika, pursued a similarly conservative system.[50] "[E]xtreme proponents of *Volksmission,*" observes Iliffe, "opposed any education in English lest it should produce an alienated elite which might flock to the towns and leave the rural areas to stagnate."[51] Nevertheless, this failed to prevent the emergence of young educated Africans for whom towns were a prime outlet for their energy and ambition. "Our school boys," observed an anxious correspondent to *Kwetu,* in 1942, "are fleeing from our fathers' *bomas* and try to avoid any racial customs."[52] Officials were equally concerned. "As one who sees a great deal of the young African townsman who has passed out of the schools in Standards VII and VIII," observed Tanga District Officer G. W. Hatchell, "I cannot escape a feeling of disappointment ... in the vast majority of cases their training does not seem to have enabled them to fit into any niche in life."[53] Armed with a Western education, albeit often incomplete, the tendency of school-leavers to scorn agricultural labor and drift to towns in search of employment befitting their self-perceived status was bemoaned by countless observers.[54]

The trend was intensified by educational expansion after 1940. Thanks to Colonial Development and Welfare Act funds, educational expenditure more than doubled between 1939 and 1945. New thinking emanating from the Colonial Office affected local policy, with a revised emphasis on "education for citizenship."[55] The ultimate objective was now a community "well-equipped by the advancement of education . . . to assume full responsibility for guiding and shaping the destiny of the country."[56] The "aim to ensure that as large a proportion as possible of the child population . . . would become literate" was also guided by "[t]he underlying view . . . that literacy would make labour and production more effective, and, therefore, should be considered as a form of capital investment."[57] Substantially greater resources were devoted to African education, increasing from £70,568 to £848,000 between 1936 and 1949, and approaching £4 million at independence. Enrollment of African students increased from 118,500 in 1946 to 515,375 in 1961.[58]

Increased educational provision not only enhanced African political awareness but also resulted in rising expectations among African youth, which, as far as many concerned, were best met through the move to town. Agriculture actually remained an important part of the syllabus in the primary and new, much-resented, middle schools, which aimed at producing "a rural middle class."[59] This met with considerable resistance from Africans who felt it "symbolized what they believed to be a deliberate . . . effort to retard the social and economic advance of their race." A propaganda campaign supporting agricultural bias was initiated. However, according to Morrison this had limited impact on people who regarded "education as a means of escaping rural life."[60] Restricted opportunities for primary school-leavers to go on to middle and secondary schooling provoked further frustration. "Middle" schools were allocated greater resources from the 1950s. However, despite an increase in secondary school-leavers from 1,418 in 1946 to 6,091 in 1961, secondary education received a fraction of departmental expenditure up to independence.[61] Lack of secondary places for the increasing numbers of Standard VIII–leavers actually sowed the seeds of unemployment.

Education was not the only factor influencing rising expectations. Africans were increasingly conscious of their political and economic entitlements.[62] The experience of war had a significant impact on participants and nonparticipants alike.[63] Not least, a combination of colonial rhetoric shifting tone from civilizing to developmental (among other things raising a state's responsibilities for public welfare) and significantly worsening economic conditions (in urban areas especially) led to an unprecedented degree of assertiveness on the part of African workers.[64] Trade unions emerged in the 1940s,[65] notably that of the dockworkers, which arose from a 1947 strike originating in Dar es Salaam that affected large parts of Tanganyika. The strike constituted an eloquent articulation of workers' grievances, resulting in important concessions by government and employers. It was, observes Iliffe, "the first real exercise of African power in Tanzania since the end of Maji Maji—an exhilarating and enlightening experience."[66]

Labor in Late Colonial Tanganyika

By 1953, Dar es Salaam's postwar boom was coming to an end; "noticeable unemployment" was reported for the first time since World War II.[67] With the population growing by over 6,000 annually and a faltering urban economy, the outlook was bleak. In the event, the situation was exacerbated by a pivotal shift in wages policy, resulting from demands by government, employers, *and* workers, that led to a contraction in employment with dramatic consequences for urban centers throughout Tanganyika.

Pressure, emanating from both local conditions and the Colonial Office, for a revision of policy had been growing since the late 1930s. Fundamental shifts in thinking on urban African administration occurred from the 1940s on, though often policies were not implemented until the following decade.[68] Modified attitudes toward African labor formed an important part of these wider policy shifts, though once again no change occurred until the 1950s, when a major reorganization was increasingly viewed as the solution to African workers' low output and miserable living conditions.[69] The first inklings of change came from a committee set up to investigate the "manpower position" in 1951.[70] Although initially articulating older prejudices, committee findings went on to signal a more optimistic appraisal of African capacities.

> The average African laborer has sprung from generations of men content to sit under the shade of the nearest tree and do little or no work whatsoever. . . . But, the African, while inherently lazy, is by no means beyond redemption. . . . If he can adapt himself to regular employment under conditions where food, accommodation, medical and other amenities are available, he can and does become worthy of his hire.[71]

At a time when demand for skilled labor was proliferating, enhancing the permanence, and thereby the performance, of African employees was important. Increasing wages, observed the influential 1954 "Carpenter Report" in neighboring Kenya, would "encourage the stabilization of labour and its effectiveness."[72]

Shifting policy also arose from and influenced a heightened consciousness among African workers. This had manifested itself in a number of disputes after 1939, most significantly the 1947 general strike. A second strike by dockers in February 1950 resulted in a pitched battle between strikers and other hangers-on and the police, leading to the dissolution of their union. Government stepped up efforts at molding a more moderate unionism.[73] This met with some initial success: post-1950 unions emerged among more skilled workers, and were "localized and craft-based."[74]

Moreover, the formation of the Tanganyika Federation of Labour (TFL) in 1955, with its educated African leadership, promised a handy partner through whom a revised labor policy could be negotiated.[75] However, as it turned out, relations between the TFL and government soured soon after its establishment.

Worker militancy was particularly evident in the capital, where strikes were a recurring feature of urban life from the mid-1950s.[76] Twenty-six disputes took place in the course of 1956.[77] The most serious occurred toward the end of the year, originating in the dismissal of four waiters accused of being drunk on duty.[78] The year 1957 began with Dar es Salaam in "a state of acute labour unrest" and government-labor relations deteriorating.[79] In January, the TFL announced that a territorial general strike would take place on 11 February in support of the reinstatement of laid-off workers. The threat of stoppages led to "lengthy negotiations" between the government, representatives of the principal employers' associations, and the trade unions. The strike was called off, and agreement reached to introduce a legal minimum wage in Dar es Salaam.[80] This was instituted in April 1957.[81] Although the minimum wage was primarily a government initiative, union leaders' ability to claim credit for its introduction was significant.[82] Moreover, the lack of clarity surrounding its eventual adoption is indicative of the mutuality of interests shared by a government committed to "a better wage for better work" and unions anxious to improve members' working conditions.

The enhanced terms accompanying the drive for increased productivity were to have unforeseen consequences. That these were not foreseen by both government and union officials is surprising. A substantial wage hike at a time when economic activity was slowing and increasing numbers seeking waged work, inevitably resulted in growing unemployment. Officials failed to anticipate its seriousness, and when evidence trickled in of urban joblessness, they downplayed its significance. As we have seen, periodic waves of unemployment had come and gone, which might help explain official complacency. The lack of foresight and later equanimity in the face of a major emerging social problem may also be attributed to the very persuasiveness of the new labor model. No doubt relieved to have abandoned a prewar discourse that dehumanized the African worker, the new policy was enthusiastically embraced by officials. That unionists, eagerly pursuing the restored dignity of African labor after an overwhelmingly negative work experience under colonialism, encompassing coercion, racial discrimination, and impoverishment, might not recognize the side effects of their members' gains is less surprising.[83]

Unemployment in Late Colonial Dar es Salaam

The introduction of a minimum wage had immediate repercussions. Lower-paid workers saw a swift improvement in their terms of employment.[84] There was also a noticeable increase in joblessness arising from a burgeoning flow of immigrants attracted by improved conditions. The completion of "big Government contracts," "tighter trading," and the "better utilization" of labor exacerbated the situation.[85]

In 1958 recorded employment in Dar es Salaam shrank to under 32,000,[86] and although a thousand jobs were created over the following year, this was woefully inadequate in the face of an urban population now growing at a rate of around 8,000 per annum.[87] Despite the negative side effects of the new policy, however, officials remained sanguine about its long-term impact.[88]

Concerns over unemployment were raised with government from various quarters.[89] In June 1957 an editorial in the *Standard* demanded action and condemned the Labour Department for underestimating the seriousness of the situation.[90] Definitions of unemployment, of course, had a major bearing in assessing urban joblessness. However, the "official" estimate of 5,000 adopted from John Leslie in February 1957 was progressively at odds with reality.[91] Nevertheless, this remained the figure trotted out by officials over following years, even though the figure was barely credible when taking into account the rural-urban tide, repeatedly bemoaned by the same officials, and the lack of job creation.[92] In 1958 unionists communicated a more plausible estimate of 10,000 unemployed to the Labour Department, which continued to play down the situation.[93] "I can't help feeling it's a problem on which we ought to be better informed," said an official in response to a growing outcry the following year, "if only to show that we know what we're talking about if we say the problem is not serious."[94]

According to another official, the problem was "not really unemployment as such but the creation of conditions of employment." Ironically, this represented the achievement of longer-term aims of extracting the African from his rural subsistence: "People have become conditioned to a cash economy but the opportunities for complete participation are limited."[95] Having formed the circumstances for an expanding supply of labor, the problem was suddenly one of creating demand. "[O]pportunities for employment . . . in Dar es Salaam," observed the labor commissioner, "appear to be diminishing rather than expanding." Those companies bucking the recession and establishing factories[96] were run on lines that would "not alleviate unemployment . . . to any significant degree."[97] "It is extremely unlikely that Government services, commerce and industry in the territory will be able to absorb half the boys . . . who will be leaving school in two or three years' time," reported a newspaper feature on "workless youth." "[F]arms and industrial concerns" found "labour costs too high," its author observed, "and are having to cut down. Machines are quickly replacing men and now a machine may well do the job of three or four men in half the time."[98]

By this time joblessness was increasingly evident on the streets of the capital, rendering official rationalizations increasingly unsustainable. In April 1958, the *Sunday News* reported that "[e]veryday the Employment Exchange in Dar es Salaam is packed out with men looking for work. . . . No sooner does a firm advertise that it needs labour . . . which will last perhaps only a few months—than the offices are swamped with men. Large queues can often be seen in Dar es Salaam outside some firm or another in the hope of getting a job as a casual labourer."[99]

The labor officer's monthly report for December 1959 observed the high number of applicants for jobs advertised through the employment exchange.[100] "Evidence of the existing situation" was even more apparent the following April. For two days, as contractors commenced operations on a building site on Main Avenue, "unemployed workers congregated in such numbers as to seriously disrupt normal road traffic."[101] Later that year, when a new East African Tobacco factory was scheduled to open, approximately three thousand congregated outside the premises, and the police were eventually required to disperse the crowd. Although the "mood of the crowd was orderly and cooperative," this and other incidents appear to have triggered alarm in the newly appointed TANU government.[102] With good cause: the problem was assuming increasingly serious dimensions throughout Tanganyika.

Emerging Unemployment in Urban Tanganyika

As late as 1957, at a conference in Dodoma, labor officers reached the conclusion that unemployment was confined to the capital, though there were "indications of some unemployment" in Tanga.[103] However, although minimum wage rates were not applied elsewhere until 1963, from the late 1950s symptoms of unemployment became increasingly evident in other urban centers. Initial concern was expressed over school-leavers entering towns who displayed a reluctance to engage in anything other than scarce white-collar work. "It is not thought that the large number of Standard VIII boys who are now leaving school will be able to secure the work they desire," observed Tabora's labor officer in January 1957. "[T]he number of people in this class . . . not content to return to agricultural life and unable to find clerical work will increase year by year." "The problem of the Standard VIII schoolboy is always with us," concurred his counterpart in Tanga. "[O]f this year's crop 25 are unemployed whereas all these could easily be placed in gainful employment . . . but [they] refuse to start at the bottom because they have 'education.'"[104] The situation was exacerbated by the inflation in qualifications demanded by employers as the education system produced more and better-educated school-leavers. While officials in Tabora and Tanga lamented Standard VIII "boys," their counterpart in Moshi reported difficulties placing those below Standard X.[105] The "voluntary unemployment" of the school-leaver—if this was a fair characterization—was to give way to a more serious problem of enforced joblessness. The educated unemployed, however, represented the tip of the iceberg. B. S. Kajunjumele, general secretary of the Tanganyika African Government Workers' Union (TAGWU), in 1959 distinguished between two "classes" of unemployed: "young men, literate or illiterate—who are without qualifications for any kind of work other than manual work; and young men with qualifications for some kind of work." The latter, he observed, constituted only around a tenth of "unemployed youth."[106] Whereas the frustrated ambitions of "school-leavers" were the cause of complaint and concern, it was the increase of "raw youth" in towns that constituted the heart of the problem.

The shift from labor scarcity to surplus was all the more dramatic and unanticipated outside Dar es Salaam. The labor officer in Mwanza, for example, in 1956 reported that although there was "always an element of unemployables" there was "no problem of unemployment in the true sense."[107] Indeed, employers throughout Lake Province bemoaned a labor shortage. The situation remained the same until 1959. In 1960, "a complete reversal of the trend" was reported: "Strikes have led to increased wages and better conditions of service; these in turn have attracted more labour . . . and at the same time forced employers to reduce their labour forces; the result has been a larger measure of unemployment than ever before."[108]

Its timing was all the more surprising given that in 1960 the cotton crop (which had absorbed the bulk of local labor, as well as that of neighboring provinces) was "one of the heaviest on record." Increased mechanization had a dramatic impact on labor demand. New, mechanized ginneries had been established by cooperatives employing around eighty men, compared to established ginneries that required around three hundred. Even older ginneries were said to be adopting new technology "as fast as possible." Moreover, improved utilization of labor and incentive schemes were another by-product of increasing wages.[109] As in Dar es Salaam, the changing nature of the African workforce was observed, now "becoming more dependent on its wages and less dependent on other sources of subsistence."[110]

Similar trends were observable elsewhere. A new agreement over conditions of service in the sisal industry in early 1960 led Tanga estates "to allow their labour force to run down and the demand for labour" thereby "dropped away."[111] SILABU, the recruiting organization set up to ease the process of obtaining workers from distant parts of the territory,[112] was "fast becoming an organization designed to convey workers home on leave and to return them to duty." Within twelve months, improved conditions of employment, alongside the lack of work in urban Tanga, resulted in noticeable shifts in the nature of the workforce, now increasingly composed of local labor.[113] As in Mwanza, with the increase in wages, employers sought value for the money.[114] In January 1961, the labor officer noted "indications that the numbers employed in the sisal and tea industries are falling and . . . there is a much greater degree of control being exercised by the management of the estates."[115]

Stabilization of workforces and introduction of labor-saving technology in rural *and* urban industries, alongside an ever-expanding and more educated population, fed the problem of unemployment. "The number of unskilled people and ex-school leavers . . . seeking employment is growing day by day," complained Tanga's labor officer in February 1961. The scale of the problem emerged in June when "[w]ord spread . . . that sixty temporary workers were to be engaged at the docks, and a crowd estimated between 500 and 600 formed near the dock area." Similar events were reported in Moshi, where "[f]ollowing a rumour that Tanganyika Breweries who ha[d] recently commenced construction of a new brewery . . . were seeking clerical and unskilled labour, the Labour Office was "besieged" by upwards of 300 persons seeking employment." Additional labor would in fact not be required for six months, observed the labor officer. It was, however, "symptomatic of the extent of the unemployment problem that such large numbers are able to appear 'out of the blue' and a conservative estimate of the number of unemployed in Moshi is in the order of 1,000." Mwanza's labor officer also reported a "deteriorating" unemployment situation, as evidenced by an incident at the Tangold Mining Company when police "had to be called in to remove a crowd of about 150 men seeking employment." Shortly afterward, between 25 January and 1 February 1961, a survey of urban unemployment was conducted by the DC and the town clerk. Almost 1,300 men and women registered as unemployed in the course of the week (when Mwanza's urban African population numbered 15,000).[116]

The Political Response to Emerging Unemployment

The relative equanimity with which the administration approached emerging unemployment formed a distinct contrast with the early years of the incoming African regime. Colonial complacence, though, was limited more to the social and political ramifications of unemployment rather than its administrative repercussions. Although officials were not unaware of the political strength TANU gained in the late 1950s by the mass attendance of unemployed and underemployed youth at rallies in Dar es Salaam,[117] this was never explicitly expounded as a reason for campaigns aimed at removing the "surplus" population.[118] The manner in which the *social* repercussions of unemployment were downplayed[119] can be explained by a number of factors: the temporary nature of previous outbreaks of urban joblessness, an officially conceived African penchant for irregular employment, alongside an awareness of the kinship support networks that were nevertheless bemoaned by officials keen to mold a discrete urban working class. A conviction that, although the new labor policy might have harsh side effects, in the longer term it would have a beneficial economic impact also played a part.

By contrast, as an *administrative* problem unemployment was viewed as one of crucial importance and various initiatives were taken in response. Colonial officials had long been concerned about the administrative consequences of large numbers of underemployed Africans.[120] If one of the main objectives of late colonial policy was the stabilization and enhanced productivity of an African working class, the other principal aim was to reduce the number of "undesirables" "infesting" urban centers.[121] The legislation employed to purge this urban "surplus" had a long history, but 1950s "*wahuni* raids" represented a significant intensification in its use.[122] The growing problem of joblessness in the late 1950s also inspired more novel initiatives. Leslie's social survey of Dar es Salaam was partly motivated by the need for "a more constructive approach" to the "problem created by the influx into the main centres of Africans in greater numbers than is economically necessary."[123] In late 1957, the so-called Vagrancy Committee was set up to investigate the growing presence of homeless and/or income-less Africans.[124] Twelve months on, a "Dar es Salaam Youth Employment Committee" was established. At only the second meeting of this committee, in July 1959, its dissolution was recommended on the grounds that "since youth employment was only one facet of the overall unemployment problem, the existing situation should be reviewed at higher levels."[125] Shortly afterward, in September 1959, when five TANU officials joined the highest government decision-making body, the Council of Ministers, emphasis was finally placed on the social and political repercussions of the phenomenon.

The consequences of growing unemployment had in fact been evident for some time. Africans, in particular, were acutely aware of its potential ramifications. In a letter to the *Standard* in July 1957, Josephine Mwasanyagi observed that it was "an uncontestable fact that unemployment in countries always brings catastrophic consequences, and we will sooner or later scent a state of unrestlessness [*sic*] if this phenomenon is not gone into." H. Mnkangaa concurred: Appealing to the administration "from a human point of view . . . to consider the present problem of mass unemployment," he considered it "the duty of a good Government to take care of the welfare of its citizens."[126] African unionists were also quick to recognize the problem, identifying six "Ways of Checking Unemployment" at their general council meeting in July 1957.[127]

Such expressions of African disquiet were to find official voice with the onset of TANU "self-rule" in September 1960, and were reinforced by politicians' concern over the inflated expectations of the African populace. At a Council of Ministers meeting on 3 November urban unemployment was discussed with particular reference to Dar es Salaam, where "political unease was being caused by a considerable workless population."[128] To address the situation the Ministry of Health and Labour quickly organized a Working Party on Unemployment, identifying a series of problems associated with joblessness.[129] Most urgent was disappointment of "expectation[s] that urban unemployment would cease immediately with responsible Government." This was designated "a psychological problem to be attacked by publicity methods." A less urgent, though enduring, problem of greater long-term importance was the existence of two categories of unemployed: "surplus uneducated labour" seeking urban employment and Standard VIII (and above) school-leavers with a strong preference for nonexistent skilled jobs. The former were to be addressed through "propaganda urging urban unemployed that it is their duty to accept rural jobs"; the latter by propaganda "showing it to be their duty to serve a period of voluntary 'national service' in settlement schemes." "A sense of constructive patriotism (building a new nation by sweat and toil)," the committee observed, "was not yet active enough, though the negative form of nationalism (repudiation of foreign rule) may be transformed into it."[130]

TANU ministers recommended the exploration of two practical solutions in particular—the initiation of labor-intensive government projects and the replacement of expatriates (of European, Asian, *and* African origin) in the local workforce[131]—thereby reflecting growing pressure exerted on them by both African unionists and the wider body of public opinion that unionists articulated. TFL leaders had outlined their answers to the problem of unemployment as early as 1957—which British officials happily ignored. First, the introduction of a territorial minimum wage to counter the principal source of rural-urban migration (low incomes in rural areas, plantations, mines, and small townships); second, Africanization of posts performed by "overseas" personnel; third, controlling immigration of manual plantation labor from neighboring countries;[132] fourth, the eradication of racial discrimination in industry; fifth, government was to undertake "economic schemes" that private industry was "unable to risk"; and finally, they urged a reduction in work hours for those in employment.[133] Unionist concerns were echoed in the popular press. The introduction of a minimum wage was vigorously supported by *Mwafrika*'s columnist Msemakweli ("The Truth Speaker"). "The African has had his blood sucked for long enough," he declared in September 1960, demanding a substantial increase in wages. "[T]hings must change so that people can see the effect of Uhuru [independence]."[134] Africanization formed another popular demand. In a scathing attack on "the new Government's policy," Stephano Mhina of Dar es Salaam complained that "the plums are for the foreigners." "If things get too hot," he observed in reference to an unemployment alleviation scheme in the Kilombero valley (see below), "our Government" can "send us to the Kilombero so that we can till the land to make room for Smith and Somji at the office desks."[135] More broadly, the papers also reflected rising concern over the growth of unemployment. Msemakweli spoke for many in his demand that it was a duty of government to address this "major problem." It was "no good shouting Uhuru na Kazi if there is no kazi," observed Habibu Dibibi, another Dar es Salaam resident, in reference to the widely broadcast TANU slogan emphasizing patriotic industriousness.[136]

TANU made vigorous attempts to address public concern. Under pressure from its political bosses, the Working Party recommended consideration of labor-intensive projects alongside the replacement of expatriate plantation labor. European committee members contradicted the reasoning behind new demands. Sanders observed that emphasis on labor-intensive work represented an inefficient deployment of existing resources, entailing the neglect of current plant and equipment and a spur to rising wages and rural-urban migration. Moreover, both he and Leslie, now permanent secretary in the Ministry of Health and Labour, pointed out the irrationality of mounting hostility toward "alien" plantation labor when many of those with "foreign names" were in fact long-established Tanganyikan residents and that with the rise in wages an increasing proportion of the workforce was in fact made up of local labor.[137] Political pressures on TANU, however, demanded action, and by the second meeting of the Working Party plans were in place for schemes that would create 1,300 jobs. In Dar es Salaam, the reclamation of the Msimbazi swamp, now prioritized ahead of a sewage scheme planned by the Public Works Department in Moshi, was to provide employment for 800. Various other sources of job creation were also under investigation.[138]

The most prominent initiative aimed at unemployment alleviation involved a rural project at Sonjo in the Kilombero valley,[139] which provided evidence that the government was taking both short- and long-term measures to address joblessness. The enlistment of 500 workers to engage in initial land clearing received considerable publicity. Recruits leaving Dar es Salaam were given a "heroic farewell" by the minister for agriculture and co-operative development, Paul Bomani.[140] However, whereas land clearance provided short-term work, the resources available were insufficient to offer everyone a place in the envisaged settlement schemes aimed at providing "a full community life and experience of cooperative farming" based on Israeli moshav cooperatives.[141] The alternative was to abandon plans for community development, public services, and amenities in Kilombero, and simply turn over cleared land to all workers. However, it was considered doubtful that the result—"subsistence farming with a low standard of living"—"would attract and retain on the land the type of men who have come to Dar es Salaam in search of employment, specifically to escape rural life of the traditional pattern." A further problem arose from the fact that Kilombero workers received wages that were comparable to those in Dar es Salaam, instead of prevailing Eastern Province rates. When subsequent attempts were made by the Ministry of Labour to employ 125 workers from Dar es Salaam for work in Morogoro at the local rate, it was rejected by recruits who demanded the same terms as those at Sonjo.[142] The propaganda value of the Kilombero scheme made it the principal initiative aimed at meeting both public concern over growing joblessness and the expectations of the unemployed. However, these expectations remained largely disappointed, with the urban unemployed demanding unsustainable wage levels for rural work and restive Kilombero recruits actually unhappy about conditions at Sonjo.[143]

Outgoing European civil servants, with long experience of the administrative problems arising from rapid urbanization, had counseled that such schemes were merely ameliorative and would do little to dampen expectations. With these early attempts at addressing the political ramifications of unemployment having minimal impact and now conscious of the limited resources available to tackle a deep-rooted and escalating problem, TANU officials were increasingly inclined to agree. Moreover, marginalized as they were, it turned out that the unemployed did not represent quite the sociopolitical threat originally anticipated. Urban joblessness did not translate into any significant outbreaks of disorder.[144] Although it contributed to the problem of over-urbanization by reducing the risks entailed by a move to the city, an expanding informal sector provided the jobless with opportunities to earn a subsistence (or better).[145] Street trading, in particular, although poorly remunerated, formed an important source of income with low entry barriers for rural migrants. It had existed throughout the colonial period, and from available qualitative evidence, petty trade appears to have expanded alongside accelerating urbanization.[146] The growth of the informal sector had a mitigating influence on the potentially restive unemployed. Instead, the principal political challenge to TANU lay with organized labor, which exercised an unsought influence on economic policy.

At the peak of their powers in the late 1950s and early 1960s, unions were highly successful in pressuring employers *and* government into meeting their demands. Between 1956 and 1961 the percentage of the labor force covered by collective agreements rose from 4 to 60 percent; over the same period the territorial average wage increased from Shs.51 to Shs.78, and by 1963 had reached Shs.138.[147] In the run-up to independence, the "responsible" TANU government conceded all unionist demands, notably appointing a territorial Minimum Wages Board in 1961.[148] At the same time, however, it viewed the employers' response to rising wages of economizing on labor, and the concomitant problem of growing unemployment, with mounting concern. The demands of those in employment were now viewed as selfish. Tanga's labor officer, in February 1960, observed that "the Unions are all now seeking to raise the standard of living and that the old cry of rising costs of living has been dropped," a sentiment with which TANU politicians increasingly sympathized.[149] In November 1960, Nyerere criticized those in employment scrabbling to improve their position when "there were more than 10,000 who would be satisfied with even Shs.2/- per day."[150]

With independence successfully negotiated, and TANU now fully responsible for the peace and prosperity of the new nation, politicians turned on their former unionist allies who oversaw an unabated strike wave continuing into the 1960s.[151] Nyerere decreed strikes were "evil things . . . the law of the jungle."[152] Various laws were passed aimed at curbing unions' power and by 1964 they were effectively nationalized. TANU was hampered not only by expectations of all sections of the African population, including both the employed and the unemployed, but also by the need to retain or attract (international and local) capital that was required to sustain economic growth under the liberal development policy adopted after independence.[153] In the event, unions were—in the "national interest"—reined in.[154] An African government was no better equipped to meet escalating demands of organized labor than the British. Meanwhile, the administrative response to urban unemployment soon displayed the familiar patina of colonial coercion, with roundups and repatriations re-commenced by 1964, if not earlier.[155]

IN THE EARLY 1950s, toward the end of the period of territorial labor scarcity, J. F. R. Hill and J. P. Moffett predicted that "[t]he future may well . . . render the African far more dependent upon the . . . economic development of his country [and hence waged employment] . . . and may in the process involve him in radical changes for his own ultimate advantage."[156] The extent and pace of change over the following decade was entirely unanticipated. Less than ten years on, anxiety over the limited number of Africans entering the job market was transformed into concern arising from the oversupply of labor. In 1960, although only one in five of the male, working-age population (430,000 out of 2 million) engaged in paid employment, this was sufficient to cause a serious and growing problem of urban joblessness. The problem arose from a revolution in rising expectations[157] that encompassed colonial officials, nationalists, unionists, and ordinary Tanganyikans—above all, young Tanganyikans. The British had anticipated that their new stabilization policy would have an invigorating effect on the territorial economy, which, as it turned out, never came to pass. Nationalists and unionists were allies in the grand project of restoring African dignity, notably that of African labor, which had suffered under colonialism. Those fortunate to obtain waged employment in the late colonial and early independence years did indeed experience dramatic improvements. However, as TANU politicians became aware on assuming government, with no dramatic economic expansion on the horizon the flipside of a more enlightened labor policy was increasing unemployment.[158] As for Tanganyikan youth, in the late colonial period their hopes had been raised not only by the expansion of education[159] but also by the developmental discourse of the colonial state and aspirational rhetoric of the nationalist movement. *Uhuru* was anticipated as a pivotal moment after which the miseries endured under colonialism would swiftly disappear. In the case of mass unemployment, however, the misery was only just beginning.

Notes

I am indebted to Jim Brennan, Tom Cadogan, Richard Waller, and two *JAH* readers for their comments on drafts of this chapter. An earlier version appeared as an article in the *Journal of African History* (*JAH*) 47, no. 3 (2006): 363–87.

1. *Sunday News* (*SN*), 15 April 1958.

2. Mass unemployment has been an important and enduring feature of postcolonial urban Africa. African towns attained independence with growing populations of "surplus" labor; reported unemployment rates in the 1960s ranged from 12 to 22 percent. They appear to have since expanded numerically and proportionately (J. Iliffe, *The African Poor: A History* [Cambridge: Cambridge University Press, 1987], 241). It should be noted that, partly due to shifting definitions of the term, unemployment statistics are often unreliable. In Dar es Salaam unemployment has grown from around 11 percent at independence to an estimated 46 percent in 2000–2001 (Note on unemployment in Tanganyika, Labour Department, 24 February 1960, Tanzania National Archive, Dar es Salaam [TNA], 460/1049; Economic Survey 2002, http://www.tanzania.go.tz). The accuracy of these figures is, of course, open to question. The 1960 figure was probably a considerable underestimate (see pp. 116–18), whereas the latter figure probably fails to account for (at least some) informal sector activity. For a recent regional discussion of unemployment, see Afrobarometer, "Africa's Unemployment Crisis," www.afrobarometer.org.

3. The phrase is borrowed from J. Ferguson, *Expectations of Modernity: Myths and Meanings of Urban Life on the Zambian Copperbelt* (Berkeley: University of California Press, 1999).

4. A. Burton, *African Underclass: Urbanisation, Crime and Colonial Order in Dar es Salaam* (Oxford: James Currey, 2005).

5. G. Kitching, *Class and Economic Change in Kenya: The Making of an African Petite-Bourgeoisie* (New Haven: Yale University Press, 1980), 379.

6. F. Cooper, *On the African Waterfront: Urban Disorder and the Transformation of Work in Colonial Mombasa* (New Haven: Yale University Press, 1987); *Decolonization and African Society: The Labor Question in French and British Africa* (Cambridge: Cambridge University Press, 1996).

7. Iliffe, *African Poor,* 171.

8. Ibid., 6. Iliffe (utilizing Gutton) outlines two forms of poverty that have emerged in the history of sub-Saharan Africa: structural, long-term poverty arising from individuals' "personal or social circumstances" and conjunctural, "temporary poverty into which ordinarily self-sufficient people may be thrown by crisis." Thanks to "increases in wealth, diversified sources of income, more effective government, better transport, wider markets, and improved hygiene and medicine," the latter has declined substantially over the past century. Structural poverty, in contrast, has persisted if not deepened.

9. For associated phenomena in Kenya and Uganda, see A. G. Dalgleish, *Survey of Unemployment* (Nairobi: Ministry for Labour, Social Security and Adult Education, 1960); C. Hutton, *Reluctant Farmers?* (Nairobi: East African Publishing House, 1973).

10. Around 30 percent of those entering Form I each year between 1951 and 1953 did not complete Form IV. Education Annual Reports (ARs); A. Coulson, *Tanzania: A Political Economy* (Oxford: Clarendon Press, 1982), 91.

11. Comments on Youth Employment Committee, 31 July 1959, TNA 460/SS2/75/01.

12. For Kenya, see Kitching, *Class and Economic Change in Kenya*, 375–77.

13. See Burton, *African Underclass*, 53–54, 65–69, 153–63, 197–98. The role of the informal sector in the provision of livelihoods was largely unacknowledged up to its christening by Keith Hart in a paper originally presented in 1971, and its subsequent adoption by an International Labour Organization (ILO) team to Kenya. See Keith Hart, "Informal Income Opportunities and Urban Unemployment in Ghana," *Journal of Modern African Studies* 11, no. 1 (1973): 61–89; ILO, *Employment, Incomes and Equality* (Geneva, 1972).

14. For fragmentary, though tantalizing, comments on shifting gender patterns of employment in Mwanza, see Mwanza labor reports 1956–60 (TNA 460/12/10/II), which record the "sphere of employment open to [women] . . . widening steadily" (at the same time as employment of children is decreasing).

15. See, e.g., Burton, *African Underclass*, 56.

16. For colonial *wahuni* (undesirables), see ibid.; for "jobless corners" in the 1970s, A. G. M. Ishumi, *The Urban Jobless in Eastern Africa* (Uppsala: Scandinavian Institute of African Studies, 1984); and for *wamachinga* (street traders) in contemporary Dar es Salaam, E. Moyer, "In the Shadow of the Sheraton: Imagining Localities in Global Spaces in Dar es Salaam, Tanzania" (PhD thesis, University of Amsterdam, 2003).

17. A. M. Ivaska, "In the Age of Minis: Women, Work and Masculinity Downtown," in *Dar es Salaam: Histories from an Emerging Metropolis*, ed. J. R. Brennan, A. Burton, and Y. Lawi (Dar es Salaam: Mkuki na Nyota/British Institute in Eastern Africa, 2007), 213–31.

18. In the 1967 census, in the six main towns of mainland Tanzania, thirty-five hundred women over age fifteen (2.8 percent) identified themselves as unemployed. United Republic of Tanzania, *1967 Population Census*, vol. 2: *Statistics for Urban Areas* (Dar es Salaam: Government Printer, 1970).

19. J. Koponen, *People and Production in Late Precolonial Tanzania: History and Structures* (Helsinki: Finnish Society for Development Studies, 1988), 60, 292–95, 301–4. In the case of the Nyamwezi, through whose country the slave and ivory routes passed, trading activity actually resulted in early engagement in waged labor. Nyamwezi porters' "marching songs ridiculed those who preferred to stay at home 'to be idle with the women'" (J. Glassman, *Feasts and Riot: Revelry, Rebellion and Popular Consciousness on the Swahili Coast, 1856–1888* [Portsmouth NH: Heinemann, 1994], 59, quoting Mtoro bin Mwinyi Bakari). Nevertheless, on arrival at coastal destinations such as Bagamoyo or Pangani, they usually spent several months unoccupied waiting for an opportunity to join a caravan bound upcountry. On Nyamwezi labor see Stephen J. Rockel, "A Nation of Porters: The Nyamwezi and the Labour Market in Nineteenth-Century Tanzania," *JAH* 41, no. 2 (2000): 173–95. For porterage and wage labor in nineteenth-century sub-Saharan Africa, see J. Iliffe, *The Emergence of African Capitalism* (London: Macmillan, 1983), 14–17.

20. J. Iliffe notes a significant extension of migratory labor from around 1908, which continued under British rule (*A Modern History of Tanganyika* [Cambridge: Cambridge University Press, 1979], 151–63, 305–11). Thaddeus Sunseri likewise observes several hundred thousand laborers engaged on plantations, as porters, or in other capacities by 1910, though, significantly, he emphasizes a prevailing context of labor scarcity (*Vilimani: Labor Migration and Rural Change in Early Colonial Tanzania* (Portsmouth, NH: Heinemann, 2002), xxi et passim).

21. Burton, *African Underclass*, 197–98.

22. Moreover, sporadic demand for labor in rural communities may well have influenced migrants' responses to urban economies dominated by various forms of casual work.

23. R. Sofer and C. Sofer, "Report on a Possible Sociological Survey of Dar es Salaam," 2 April 1951, TNA 18950/Vol. III, 48. The same was true of colonial Mombasa. See Justin Willis, *Mombasa, the Swahili, and the Making of the Mijikenda* (Oxford: James Currey, 1993), 163; and especially Cooper, *On the African Waterfront*.

24. For example, Dar es Salaam District Annual Report (Dsm DAR) 1922, 8; 1928, 17; TNA 54; Frederick Kaijage, "Alternative History and Discourses from Below: Social History in Urban Tanga," University of Dar es Salaam, Department of History, seminar paper, 30 November 2000.

25. E.g., Dsm DAR 1921. It was paralleled in other African territories, see Iliffe, *African Poor*, 170.

26. Dsm DAR 1931, 2.

27. 1932 Eastern Province AR (EPAR), 9.

28. Tanga DAR 1931, 4. For depression-related unemployment elsewhere in Africa, see Iliffe, *African Poor*, 155–56.

29. Burton, *African Underclass*, 68.

30. Tanga PAR 1939, 94; "Report of the Commission appointed to enquire into the disturbances which occurred in the port of Tanga, August 1939," para. 13, Public Records Office, London (PRO), CO/691/179/42191/13.

31. Pike, "Report on Native Affairs in Dsm," 5 June 1939, TNA 18950/Vol. II; notes on McLeery Report, ca. 1940, TNA 26177.

32. Burton, *African Underclass*, 214–18.

33. This paragraph is based on Burton, *African Underclass*, 70–73, 95–97.

34. J. Iliffe, *Africans: The History of a Continent* (Cambridge: Cambridge University Press, 1995), 238–42. Although declining death rates were probably the dominant factor behind population growth, Iliffe observes that the phenomenon had diverse causes. For accelerating urbanization in Eastern Africa from 1940, see A. Burton, "Urbanization in Eastern Africa: An Historical Overview, c. 1750–2000," introduction to *The Urban Experience in Eastern Africa, c. 1750–2000*, ed. A. Burton (Nairobi: British Institute in Eastern Africa, 2002).

35. C. J. Martin, "Estimates of Population Growth in East Africa, with Special Reference to Tanganyika and Zanzibar," in *Essays on African Population*, ed. K. M. Barbour and R. M Prothero (London: Routledge and Kegan Paul, 1961), 49–61.

36. In the late precolonial and early colonial periods the population is thought to have declined. Juhani Koponen, "Population: A Dependent Variable," in *Custodians of the Land: Ecology and Culture in the History of Tanzania*, ed. G. Maddox, J. Giblin, and I. N. Kimambo (Athens: Ohio University Press, 1996), 19–37.

37. Martin, "Population Growth," 56.

38. Burton, *African Underclass,* 84, 194.

39. Even before World War II, Iliffe observes, "the need for cash—for tax, bridewealth, school fees, imported goods—was the essential stimulus to migration" (John Iliffe, "Wage Labour and Urbanization," in *Tanzania under Colonial Rule,* ed. M. H. Y. Kaniki [London: Longman, 1979], 284).

40. D. A. Low and A. Smith, eds., *History of East Africa,* vol. 3 (London: Oxford University Press, 1976), appendix 3, table 14.

41. Expansion of cash crops may have provided additional rural sources of income, but prices were volatile and large parts of Tanganyika were unsuitable for cash-crop production. Moreover, land shortages arose in some areas where commercial agriculture flourished (Iliffe, *Modern History of Tanganyika,* 347–48).

42. A 1950s shift in policy that aimed to nurture a class of prosperous "yeoman" farmers came too late to have any fundamental influence on the rural economy (S. Mueller, "The Historical Origins of Tanzania's Ruling Class," *Canadian Journal of African Studies* 15, no. 3 [1981]: 475, 481).

43. See ibid., 84–86, 194–96.

44. J. F. R. Hill and J. P. Moffett, *Tanganyika* (Dar es Salaam: Government Printer, 1955), 283.

45. Burton, *African Underclass,* 67–68, 91–95, 219–20.

46. A. Burton, "Urchins, Loafers and the Cult of the Cowboy: Urbanization and Delinquency in Dar es Salaam, 1919–61," *JAH* 42, no. 1 (2001): 199–216.

47. Coulson, *Tanzania,* 88.

48. As outlined in United Kingdom, *Education Policy in British Tropical Africa* (London: H.M.S.O, 1925).

49. L. Buchert, *Education in the Development of Tanzania, 1919–1990* (London: James Currey, 1994), 20. The quote is from a 1925 Colonial Office education report.

50. Coulson, *Tanzania,* 86.

51. Iliffe, *Modern History of Tanganyika,* 339.

52. *Kwetu,* 18 September 1942, 3.

53. Note on the Education and Training of Africans, 8 September 1945, TNA 450/404.

54. For example, N. Langford-Smith complained in 1946 that the "present educational system . . . is producing a class of 'black-coated workers'" upon which "[n]o sound national economy has ever been based. . . . Black-coated workers don't produce wealth, they exhaust it" ("The Education of African Rural Communities," *Tanganyika Notes and Records* 22 (1946): 3–4, quoting the governor of Uganda. See also Burton, "Urchins, Loafers and the Cult of the Cowboy," 204–5).

55. See Buchert, *Education in the Development of Tanzania,* chap. 4.

56. *1947 Tanganyika Report to the United Nations,* quoted ibid., 58.

57. Ibid. Frederick Cooper notes more broadly of British imperial policy, that through its adoption of "human capital theory" it "turned attention to the productionist side of the development-welfare nexus" ("Modernizing Bureaucrats, Backward Africans, and the Development Concept," in *International Development and the Social Sciences,* ed. Frederick Cooper and R. Packard [Berkeley: University of California Press, 1997], 68).

58. Ibid., 22, 24–25, 62, 64–65.

59. Iliffe, *Modern History of Tanganyika,* 444–45.

60. One demand of a 1952 TANU delegation to the UN was the abolition of a new agricultural syllabus introduced in 1952 (D. Morrison, *Education and Politics in Africa: The Tanzanian Case* [London: Hurst, 1976], 84–85). According to Tom Cadogan, the

association of schooling with urban centers was actually exacerbated by the introduction of compulsory primary education in towns from 1947 ("Students and Schools in the Southern Highlands: Education in Tanzania, 1890s to the Present" [PhD thesis, University of London, 2004], 164–66).

61. In 1961 secondary schools received just 7.18 percent of the departmental budget (Tanganyika, *Annual Report of Ministry of Education 1961* (Dar es Salaam, 1962), Statistics, vii). Thanks to Tom Cadogan for providing this figure.

62. See Cooper, *Decolonization and African Society.*

63. See N. Westcott, "The Impact of WWII on Tanganyika" (PhD thesis, Cambridge University, 1982).

64. See J. Iliffe, "A History of Dockworkers of Dar es Salaam," *Tanzania Notes and Records* 71 (1970): 119–48; J. R. Brennan, "Nation, Race and Urbanization in Dar es Salaam, Tanzania, 1916–1976" (PhD thesis, Northwestern University, 2002), chap. 3; Burton, *African Underclass,* chap. 4.

65. By 1948, there were five unions registered in Dar es Salaam (Brennan, "Nation, Race and Urbanization in Dar es Salaam," 202).

66. Iliffe, "History of Dockworkers of Dar es Salaam," 134.

67. Labour Office AR, Dsm, 1953, 2, TNA 61/503/III.

68. Burton, *African Underclass,* chaps. 4 and 11.

69. See ibid., 226–35; and for British/French Africa, Cooper, *Decolonization and African Society.*

70. A copy of the Report of the Manpower Committee is in PRO, CO/859/403.

71. *Tanganyika Standard* (*TS*), 6 September 1952, 4.

72. Reported in *TS,* 12 June 1954, 12.

73. I. G. Shivji, *Law, State and the Working Class in Tanzania* (London: James Currey, 1986), 182.

74. W. H. Friedland, *Vuta Kamba: The Development of Trade Unions in Tanganyika* (Stanford, CA: Hoover Institution Press, 1969), 21.

75. Coulson, *Tanzania,* 107.

76. Moreover, strikers more often than not made gains as a result of their action. For the outcome of strikes by wharf laborers, quarry workers, and municipality employees see *SN,* 16 October 1955, 1; Secret despatch by Labour Commissioner, 24th January 1957 (LC Despatch), PRO, CO/822/1625.

77. 1957 EPAR, 42.

78. Supportive action organized by the Domestic and Hotel Workers' Union resulted in approximately 40 percent of urban domestics (approximately 2,400 individuals) and 450 hotel employees striking in December 1956. Sympathy strikes, resulting from what the TFL regarded as unfair Labour Department intervention, called by the Commercial and Industrial Workers' Union and the Eastern Province Building and Construction Workers Union were "well supported," resulting in a peak of around 10,000 workers out of an approximate urban workforce of 37,000 joining the strike. Further action was threatened by the Transport and Allied Workers' Union and the Dockworkers and Stevedores Union.

79. 1957 EPAR.

80. LC Despatch; Friedland, *Vuta Kamba,* 22; Governor Twining to Colonial Office, 11 December 1956, PRO, CO/822/1129; Coulson, *Tanzania,* 116.

81. An earlier minimum wage had been set, for government workers only, from 1940. Its value was rapidly eroded by inflation. See Burton, *African Underclass,* 92–93.

82. Labor activism stretching back to 1939 undoubtedly played a part in the introduction of the minimum wage. However, a Minimum Wages Board had been appointed by government the previous May to set a suitable rate, and it seems TFL intervention may, at most, have expedited its introduction and/or led to the adoption of a higher rate (Tanganyika Intelligence Summary, January 1957, PRO, CO/822/1625).

83. They did recognize a growing problem of joblessness but, unsurprisingly perhaps, apparently failed to connect it to rising wages.

84. Nevertheless, many employers ignored the order.

85. In some cases staff were now shared—employers of night watchmen, for example, banded together to employ a single guard instead of appointing one for each premises (1957 AR of Senior Labour Officer [SLO], Dsm, TNA 460/1051; Mins., Labour Department Conference, Dodoma, 5–7 June 1957, 4, PRO, CO/822/1625).

86. Down from 36,000 in 1952 (Burton, *African Underclass,* 216).

87. 1958 AR of SLO, TNA 460/1049; 1959 EPAR, 49.

88. "[O]ne of the most valuable results of the minimum wage," observed Leslie shortly after its introduction, "was that it drove a number of unnecessary men out of employment—a harsh human fact but economically speaking a tonic to both worker and employer, forcing the latter to prune staffs, consider schedules, tighten up supervision and begin to make a real effort to get value for money; where this happened the moral effect on remaining workers of having enough to do was equally advantageous" (J. A. K. Leslie, *Survey of Dar es Salaam* [Oxford: Oxford University Press, 1963], 134).

89. For unionists' complaints, see extract from LO's report, January 1957, TNA 460/1049.

90. *TS,* 9 July 1957.

91. When asked to assess the unemployment rate, Leslie, who had recently completed fieldwork for his social survey, estimated it at 16 percent, which worked out to around 5,000 (SLO to Labour Commissioner [LC], 30 May 1957, TNA 460/1049).

92. E.g., 1958 Labour AR, para. 32; LC, K. L. Sanders to Permanent Secretary, Minister of Education and Labour (PS, MEL), 18 November 1959; "Note on Unemployment in Tanganyika," Labour Department HQs, 24 February 1960, TNA 460/1049. Labour Department underestimates were no doubt influenced by the conviction that a large proportion of urban workers were voluntarily underemployed, preferring to work only intermittently (e.g., Sanders to Humanities, Dsm, 21 August 1958, TNA 460/1049). In a 1961 minute, one official estimated the unemployed at about 4,500 and the underemployed at 8–12,000.

93. 1958 AR, SLO, Dsm, 31 December 1958, TNA 460/1049.

94. Minutes to EL(1), 24 November 1959, TNA 460/SS2/75/01. Officials viewed the situation as not so much an urban problem as a rural one—those without work were increasingly deemed as having no legal place in the town. In both 1957 and 1958 over 2,000 "undesirables" were removed to "their villages." Unemployment was a key trait of those repatriated. See Burton, *African Underclass,* esp. chap. 12.

95. Min. by EL(1) to PS (Labour), 23 November 1959, TNA 460/SS2/75/01.

96. In 1959 this included a Bata shoe factory, three knitwear factories, and razor blade, cigarette, and cement bagging factories.

97. Mins. of Second Meeting of the Dsm Youth Employment Committee (YEC), 31 July 1959, TNA 460/1049; Sanders to MEL, 14 July 1959; TNA 460/SS2/75/01; SLO Report, December 1959, TNA 460/1051.

98. *SN,* 15 April 1958.

99. Ibid.

100. One advertisement for 16 drivers holding "C class licenses" (a rare qualification) for three days' employment "produced 70 suitable applicants in a matter of hours."

101. Work was, in fact, unavailable, as all labor requirements were met prior to commencement through the employment exchange.

102. SLO Report, Dsm, December 1959; April 1960; October 1960, TNA 460/1051.

103. Departmental Conference Mins., 5–7 June 1957, TNA 460/1049.

104. LO Monthly Report, Tabora, January 1957; 1957 AR, LO Tanga. See also reports from LOs in Lindi, Iringa, Mbeya, and Korogwe, TNA 460/1051.

105. Extract from Monthly Report, January 1957, TNA 460/1051.

106. Comments on second YEC, 31 July 1959, TNA 460/SS2/75/01. Twenty years on, a survey of unemployed youth numbered those with a secondary education also at 10 percent (Ishumi, *Urban Jobless in Eastern Africa,* 48).

107. The following account is based on SLO's Annual Reports for 1956–60, TNA 460/12/10/II.

108. Excluding the territorial postal and railway strikes, 31,130 man-days were lost in the course of twenty-five notified strikes (though there were considerably more strikes for which figures were not obtained), compared with 18,008 man-days in 1959, AR 1960, Lake Province.

109. A reported "drive to increase output per man and to make increased wages above a certain level dependent upon skill or output rather than upon length of service as has been the case in the past" was "not welcomed either by the Unions or the workers."

110. Labor turnover at Williamsons Ltd., a diamond mining company operating in Lake Province, dropped from around 200 per month in 1958 to 30 per month in 1960, at which point they had "a waiting list of over 200 men seeking to bring their families to the mine rather than leave them at home to till the land."

111. The following is based on monthly reports by the SLO, Tanga, TNA 460/9/2.

112. Workers—from western and southern Tanganyika in particular—had been recruited in place of local labor, which was notoriously reluctant to work on the plantations, preferring to market garden or work in Tanga town.

113. Lack of work in the town may have deterred individuals from the sisal-growing areas entering Tanga. Even urban labor showed signs of a change of heart toward plantation work: the May 1961 report on the urban employment exchange recorded "72 unskilled placed to a sisal estate, which is quite unusual." Though the estate had requested more than this, many seeking work continued to prefer to take their chances in town.

114. The sisal agreement stipulated cutters' "tasks" be raised to ninety bundles of thirty leaves. Unhappy workers evaded the new requirements by producing ninety bundles containing fewer than thirty leaves. In response, the growers' association commissioned a survey to explore further mechanization in the industry.

115. In Eastern Province, where the other main plantations were located, similar patterns were observed in the wake of the sisal agreement: "[N]ormal labour wastage without corresponding recruitment," with turnover reducing and signs that "the new terms have laid the foundation of a more stable labour force in the industry" (1960 EPAR, VIII, 3. Copy in TNA research room).

116. The day after the survey ended, another large crowd arrived and was turned away, leading the DC to conclude that it was "possible that several thousand more may be unemployed" (Tanga SLO's monthly reports for February, April, and June

1961, TNA 460/9/2; extracts from LO's reports, Moshi, February 1961; and Mwanza, December and January 1960, TNA 460/1051; *TS*, 13 February 1961).

117. E.g., CS to W. A. C. Mathieson, CO, 11 November 1957, PRO, CO/822/1795.

118. Overstretched urban services, (Africans') economic irrationality, and/or rising crime rates were instead raised to justify the raids.

119. Officials did occasionally express concern over the social welfare of urban populations; nevertheless, it was the social *order* of urban Africans that was uppermost.

120. See, e.g., Provincers' responses to the proposal to extend the application of "Removal of Undesirables" legislation to towns throughout Tanganyika (10 September 1952) in TNA 21616/Vol. III.

121. See Burton, *African Underclass.*

122. *Wahuni*, literally translated as "hooligans," was the Swahili label applied to unemployed and informally employed Africans officially regarded as surplus to urban populations.

123. Draft memo for ExecCo by CS, 25 April 1955, TNA 460/SS2/7/011.

124. CS to W. A. C. Mathieson, 11 November 1957, PRO, CO/822/1795.

125. Minutes, Second Youth Employment Committee.

126. Letters to *TS*, 16 July 1957 and 19 August 1958. Mnkangaa's letter, in which mass unemployment was described as "not an epidemic of one town only . . . [but] for the whole of the territory," produced a flurry of activity in the Labour Department in order to assess the existence or nonexistence of "mass" unemployment.

127. Resolutions of General Council, Tanga, 4–6 July 1957, TNA 460/1049; see also TAGWU General Secretary, Kajunjumele's "Comments on Second YEC," 31 July 1959, TNA 460/SS2/75/01.

128. Extract from CoM mins., 3 November 1960, TNA 460/HL2/29/031.

129. The Working Party was a peculiar product of the interstitial twilight of colonial Tanganyika, composed solely of British officials (including Leslie and Sanders), now reacting to a political agenda largely set by their new African masters.

130. Notes for Working Party on Unemployment, 25 November 1960, TNA 460/1051/II. Groups throughout the country, mobilized by the TANU Youth League, often responded positively to this propaganda. From late 1960 more than five hundred "spontaneous farming schemes" were initiated by young men moving from urban centers. Few survived beyond a year, however. One of those that did survive developed into the Ruvuma Development Association (L. Schneider, "Developmentalism and Its Failings: Why Rural Development Went Wrong in 1960s and 1970s Tanzania" [PhD diss., Columbia University, 2003], 141).

131. Referred to in Sanders to PS, MHL, 23 November 1960, TNA 460/1049.

132. Immigrant laborers purportedly accepted lower wages and poorer conditions and were described as "a menace to the economic development of this country." Official hostility to the presence of non-Tanzanians at a time of high unemployment has persisted to the present, as evidenced by periodic purges of foreign workers (notably Malawians) from Dar es Salaam.

133. Resolutions of General Council, Tanga, 4–6 July 1957, TNA 460/1049. With the onset of "responsible" government TFL demands remained largely unchanged (see, e.g., "Proposals for Reducing Unemployment," J. D. Namfua, Secretary, TFL, to Chief Minister, 30 November 1960, TNA 460/1051/II.

134. *Mwafrika,* 3 and 17 September 1960. References to newspapers here and below are extracted from translations in Summary of the Vernacular Press, TNA

460/931/4. For a discussion of metaphors of vampirism and economic exploitation in Tanganyika/Tanzania see J. Brennan, "Sucking with Straws: Exploitation and Urban Citizenship in Tanzanian Nationalist Thought and Rhetoric, 1958–76," *JAH* 47, no. 3 (2006): 389–413.

135. Smith and Somji refer to the European and Indian communities (*Ngurumo*, 30 September; 1 November 1960).

136. *Mwafrika*, 29 October 1960; *Ngurumo*, 27 October 1960. *Uhuru na kazi* (independence and work) had been adopted in 1959 partly at the urging of the British, to check what colonial officials—and increasingly their TANU successors—viewed as a widespread perception of independence as representing a free-for-all in which colonial taxes and laws would be abandoned and colonial wealth would be redistributed among the long-suffering African population.

137. Sanders to Leslie, 23 November 1960; Leslie to Secretary, Federation of Tanganyika Employers, 5 December 1960, TNA 460/1051/II.

138. These included the utilization of more manual labor on existing road-building schemes and on soil tests for the site of the proposed university (Unemployment Working Party Mins., Second meeting, 25 November 1960, TNA 460/1051/II).

139. It was sited in the vicinity of a cooperative settlement established by TANU in 1959. The Kilombero valley lies southwest of Morogoro, several hundred miles from Dar es Salaam. Unless otherwise indicated, information in this paragraph is from "Alleviation of Urban Unemployment: Contribution by the Ministry of Agriculture and Cooperative Development," November 1959, TNA 460/HL2/29/031.

140. Leslie recalled this as an attempt "to harness political enthusiasm by shipping lorry-loads [*sic*] off to open up the *pori* [bush], singing party songs" (personal communication, 4 October 2000; LO Makukita, Kilosa to LC, 3 February 1961, TNA 460/HL2/29/031).

141. It was estimated that initial work by the five hundred recruits from Dar es Salaam would clear land for only fifty pioneer settlers, and only considerable further expenditure might provide space for a further thirty to sixty over the following year.

142. Working Party on Unemployment, minutes of second meeting, 25 November 1960, TNA 460/1051/II.

143. When S. R. M. Makukita, labor officer for Kilosa, visited Sonjo in late January 1961, workers bemoaned the poor rations received, lack of amenities and recreational facilities, alongside the fact they hadn't acquired cleared land for their personal use as anticipated. Others complained they were treated like convicts (Makukita to LC, 3 February 1961, TNA 460/HL2/29/031).

144. Despite spiraling joblessness, such outbreaks have remained rare in postcolonial Dar es Salaam; the rioting and looting that occurred in the wake of the army mutiny in 1964 represents a rare example.

145. A survey of urban "self-employed" in 1971 found 55 percent had never had waged employment, and a slender majority were earning more than the minimum wage. Of those surveyed, 43 percent had arrived in town before 1961, and a further 19 percent before 1968 (M. Bienefeld, "The Self-Employed of Urban Tanzania," Economic Research Bureau Paper, University of Dar es Salaam).

146. See Burton, *African Underclass*, 65–67, 158–63.147. Shivji, *Law, State and the Working Class in Tanzania*, 204.

148. Its recommendations were not implemented until 1963. See the *Report of the Territorial Minimum Wage Board* (Dar es Salaam, 1962).

149. Monthly Report by SLO, Tanga, February 1960, TNA 460/9/2.

150. *Mwafrika,* 7 November 1960.

151. A total of 417,000 man-days were lost in 1963 alone. Time lost was also high by international standards: in 1960 total man-hours lost stood at 1.29 percent compared to a British figure of 0.2 percent (Mueller, "Historical Origins of Tanzania's Ruling Class," 487; Colin Leys, "Tanganyika: The Realities of Independence," in *Socialism in Tanzania,* ed. L. Cliffe and J. S. Saul [Dar es Salaam: Dar es Salaam Publishing House, 1972], 1:195n).

152. *TS,* 25 June 1962. Quoted in Shivji, *Law, State and the Working Class in Tanzania,* 227.

153. Bienefeld observes that "it was the increasing incompatibility of calculations based on private interest [including that of capital and workers], and the Government's notion of what was needed to serve the public interest, which led to the policy shift embodied in the Arusha Declaration" ("Trade Unions and Peripheral Capitalism: The Case of Tanzania" [copy in University of Dar es Salaam library], 25).

154. For the unions and their relations with the state, see also Friedland, *Vuta Kamba;* Coulson, *Tanzania;* D. Jackson, "The Disappearance of Strikes in Tanzania: Incomes, Policy and Industrial Democracy," *Journal of Modern African Studies* 17, no. 2 (1979): 219–52; and Bienefeld, "Trade Unions." There are interesting parallels with other parts of Africa. In Francophone West Africa, for example, Cooper notes that unions had before independence articulated "an ideology that subordinated 'class struggle' to 'national liberation,'" thereby denying "the labour movement an autonomous space from which to question labor leaders/labor ministers." "Out of power," observes Cooper, "this was a call for anti-colonial solidarity; in power, it was a rationale for repression" (Cooper, *Decolonization and African Society,* 416).

155. See A. Burton, "The Haven of Peace Purged: Tackling the 'Undesirable' and 'Unproductive' Poor in Late Colonial and Postcolonial Dar es Salaam," *International Journal of African Historical Studies* 40, no. 1 (2007): 119–51. The organization of the TANU Youth League formed another official response to the problem of unemployment, both through its provision of gainful activities to unemployed youth and through its urban policing role in the roundups and repatriations. See Jim Brennan's contribution to this volume.

156. Hill and Moffett, *Tanganyika,* 270.

157. This phrase is taken from a criminological literature that identifies the heightened expectations of ordinary citizens (for televisions or video recorders as everyday items, for example) as one cause of crime.

158. Colonial employment trends persisted into the postindependence period. Between 1960 and 1965, while wages increased by 80 percent (65 percent in real terms) employment decreased on average by 3 percent annually (ILO, "Wages, Incomes and Prices Policy," Govt. Paper no. 3, 1967, 4; A. Van de Laar, "Growth and Income Distribution in Tanzania since Independence," in *Socialism in Tanzania,* ed. Cliffe and Saul [Dar es Salaam, 1972], 1:107). For similar phenomena elsewhere in Africa, see Cooper, *Decolonization and African Society,* 458–59.

159. Strikingly, the *Labour Force Survey of Tanzania, 1965* (Dar es Salaam, 1966), found that Tanzania's urban unemployed population had on average more education than those who were employed.

6 Bad Boys in the Bush?

Disciplining Murran in Colonial Maasailand

RICHARD WALLER

IN MID-1918, the military authorities in Nairobi finally decided to conscript Maasai *murran* (warriors), as the Officer in Charge of the Masai Reserve (OiC) had long been urging.[1] Plans were made to take 250 for the Kings African Rifles (KAR) and 50 for the police. However, when recruiting began in Narok at the end of August, it was met with a "defiant attitude" on the part of the Purko murran of Il Meiruturut, the senior circumcision group of the age-set Il Tareto.[2] The murran refused to discuss the matter; they announced that they had repudiated their elders and spokesmen and vowed to die rather than submit. KAR reinforcements were hurriedly dispatched to enforce compliance while the murran gathered and withdrew into the forest.[3]

At dawn on 9 September, a military patrol surrounded the *manyatta* (camp) of ILaimer *sirit* (warrior company) near Melelo, northwest of Narok. The intention was to arrest murran who were said to be there. However, as their officers went forward to reconnoiter, the *askaris* opened fire without orders. There were no murran in the manyatta, but two women and ten head of cattle were shot dead and two other women and an elder wounded before order was restored. Two days later, some three hundred murran, drawn from all six Purko sirits, attacked the patrol in camp near Ololulunga. They were driven off with the loss of perhaps thirty killed and up to a hundred wounded.[4] They then dispersed over a wide area, but, apart from some looting and isolated murders, no further incidents were reported. The Keekonyukie murran, whose attitude had been "uncertain," did not join their Purko allies, and negotiations began as government officials, Maasai elders and spokesmen, and Lord Delamere, who had organized Maasai scouts during the war and knew the area, attempted to contact the rebels and persuade them to come in for talks. Finally, toward the end of October, a representative meeting of murran accepted a government ultimatum to pay compensation and to provide sixty recruits for the KAR. In return, the government agreed to allow them to select their own recruits, to exempt the stock of those in service from requisitioning, and to take no further action over Olololunga. However, it took a further six months of patrolling, pressure, and persuasion before all the murran were rounded up. Few recruits materialized, and that demand was eventually allowed to lapse.[5] The 1918 Rising had followed what would become a familiar pattern: initial defiance and confrontation followed by withdrawal and then negotiation and reluctant acquiescence. But Il Meiruturut had made their point. They had sustained their resistance to compulsion—something that they had apparently determined on at their *Eunoto* (promotion to senior murranhood) ceremony in 1917—and they had forced both government and elders to take them seriously.

Olololunga was neither the beginning nor the end of conflict with murran. Thomson's portrait of "Moran," the "perfect military masher [dandy], ready for love or war," with its overtones of violence and sexuality, reminds us that there were "bad boys" in Maasailand long before colonial rule, and trouble continued into the 1950s.[6] The Purko, the largest and most recalcitrant of the Kenya Maasai sections, were always at the forefront, but there were conflicts in most other sections as well.[7] This chapter charts the troubled course of relations from the different perspectives of murran, elders, and administrators; and examines the vacillations of government policy as it sought, at various times, to co-opt, eradicate, contain, and remodel murranhood. Age relations were relations of power, and during the colonial period murranhood was a highly contested field. Different interests struggled for control, not merely over the lives of murran but, since murranhood was an almost iconic sign of Maasai-ness, over what it meant to be Maasai. At stake was the local authority of the colonial state and that of the elders it supported, the future of the Maasai, and the survival of an institution that appeared to embody much of their past.

Beyond this local study, lie two larger issues. One is the nature of youth violence; the other the impact of external intervention and change on age organization itself. Maasai murran were not the only young men disturbing the colonial peace. Unrest in Nandi, Kipsikis, and Samburu, for example, caused as much, and sometimes more, concern. While recent literature has focused on towns, colonial rule first encountered idle and belligerent youths in the countryside, and many of the elements in official stereotypes of urban delinquency were first applied to warriors in the bush. Colonial rule did not create youthful rebellion, but it did change the terms of debate by altering the structure of opportunity that made young men patient and their elders more tolerant and by proposing new models of responsible behavior and its opposite. Negative images of "modern" youth and calls for its control often emerged as an expression of unease about the meaning and direction of colonial progress, its impact on "traditional society" and the apparent erosion of "tribal discipline."[8] Maasai murran were not "detribalized," but they were certainly undisciplined and increasingly out of step with colonial trajectories of development. Officials saw discipline as "progress"; elders recast it as "tradition." Both in effect collaborated to create the idea of delinquent youth and then to actualize it by defining certain youth behaviors as transgressive or criminal, but they differed in how they viewed them. Elders were more concerned with disobedience and lack of respect, whereas the colonial administration focused on raiding as a particularly outmoded feature of murranhood that merited stern punishment.

Despite the glamour of youth, it was age that brought the things that really mattered: control over household and herd and a voice in the community. Commissioner Eliot's "republic of young men" was, in reality, an oligarchy of old men.[9] But murranhood was an integral part of the larger social organization of age and an important stage in the process of "becoming Maasai."[10] It thus became a focus of argument over both the orderly management of maturation and the extent to which "tradition," of which murranhood seemed the most visible part, could and should be retained. Here, as elsewhere, the colonial administration found itself drawn into the business of making and remaking tradition in the pursuit of social order and legitimacy.[11] In Maasai, and later in Samburu, however, government was first forced to intervene more directly and drastically to impose law and order. Early experience of what was revealingly described as the "moran system" led to the belief that it was a self-contained military organization that was now both obsolete and dangerously out of control. Realization that it produced responsible adults, not merely warriors or juvenile delinquents, came much later. When it did, administrators strove to rebuild a system that they now believed had been seriously damaged by their earlier intervention.

Alliance and Confrontation

The course of relations between murran, elders, and administrators can be divided roughly into four stages, each corresponding to one of four successive age-sets: Il Twati (c. 1894–1917), Il Tareto (1910–23), Il Terito (1926–37), and Il Nyankusi (1939–54). The first was a period of alliance.[12] It began in 1895 with a stand-off in the Kedong Valley between murran, who had just massacred a caravan transporting government loads along the newly established and highly vulnerable artery of what would become Kenya, and nervous officials, who realized that they could not command, let alone punish, these angry young men. All they could do was to rely on the negotiating skills and self-interest of their spokesmen and elders. In fact, interests ran parallel, for the expansion of the conquest state required local military manpower and opened up opportunities for those who supplied it. Murran, directed by the British but fighting under their own leaders and for themselves, were able to restock their families' herds and so "bring the Maasai back to life" after the disasters of the early 1890s, while at the same time enhancing their own prestige and power.[13] While some officials doubted the wisdom of using allies who were independent and uncontrollable, they did not yet see murranhood itself as threatening or dysfunctional. Indeed, they owed their initial position in much of central and western Kenya to the very system that they later sought to destroy.

As the pace of conquest slackened and the British became more confident of their own power and less reliant on that of their allies, they and the Maasai began to disengage. After the suppression of Nandi resistance in 1905, they no longer needed Maasai spearmen, and the murran had achieved their immediate object of acquiring stock. Although Maasai were seemingly one of the "martial races" from which the Empire was accustomed to draw its military recruits, attempts to incorporate them into regular army formations were a failure: murran wanted to take enemies' livestock, not the "King's Shilling."[14] Attitudes were beginning to change. Early officials had often been impressed by the murran they dealt with, but Eliot thought "Masaidom" "a beastly, bloody system, founded on raiding and immorality," best left to anthropology.[15] In 1904, the Maasai were concentrated in two reserves, one south of Nairobi, the other on Laikipia, leaving the Rift Valley floor to white settlement.[16] Significantly, agreement had been reached with elders, not warriors. Power was shifting across a generational divide, and a new understanding between government and Maasai was emerging, based on the subcontracting of authority, not force.

The second stage was one of confrontation. It began with the second Maasai Move (1912–13), when Maasai on Laikipia were returned to join their fellows in a single reserve. There were resentments over the loss of grazing and at government attempts to control raiding, both indications of a new colonial order in which murran would now be subordinated. Purko, especially, were bitter over their removal from Laikipia, and their dissatisfaction with the land they had been allotted in Narok District persisted. Drought and the spread of disease among both herds and people after the Move emphasized what the Maasai had lost and what murran had failed to prevent.[17] Il Meiruturut had been perhaps too recently initiated to offer concerted resistance to the Move, especially in the absence of support from elders and the senior murran of Il Twati, but the nominal plaintiffs in the celebrated court case that sought to overturn the treaty that legitimated the Move were junior murran, and some made at least one abortive attempt to return to Laikipia.[18]

Hemsted, OiC of the Reserve from its establishment in 1913 to 1923, was not sympathetic toward murran and took a consistently tough line in his dealings with them. In particular, raiding was heavily penalized. Between 1913 and 1917, Maasai lost at least three thousand eight hundred head of cattle and over £10,000 in fines, a total equivalent to some nine thousand head, for a series of raids, murders, and stock thefts. Purko were especially hard hit, losing nearly four thousand head.[19] These were not the only losses Maasai suffered through government agency or its lack. During the war, more than thirty thousand bullocks and three hundred thousand sheep were requisitioned for military supply. Maasai living on the border lost stock to German raiding parties that the military could not intercept.[20] To some extent, therefore, murran were attempting to recoup stock losses, but raiding by Il Meiruturut and their fellows in other sections had a greater symbolic significance. They were building their own cohesion as an age-set, advancing their prospects for adulthood, and seeking to emulate their predecessors, Il Twati. They had much to live up to, for Il Twati, and especially the dominant right-hand circumcision, had a considerable reputation. Several of their leading spokesmen, such as ole Gilishu of Purko, had made a name for themselves as leaders of levies in punitive expeditions and were now influential junior elders.

The outbreak of war in 1914 had seemed an ideal opportunity. The British clearly needed Maasai armed assistance against the Germans, and, although the government had no intention of returning to the days of punitive expeditions, some of its actions in a time of confusion were open to misinterpretation by eager murran. Some were given rifles and instructed to guard the Magadi Railway from German raids; others were enlisted in troops of irregular scouts led by settlers whom they knew.[21] The distinction between scouting and raiding was perhaps unclear, and it seems that older networks of patronage, alliance, and enmity were reactivated in the temporary absence of formal oversight.[22] However, as the war progressed, government regained its grip. Intelligence work was brought under central control (with a concomitant reduction in pay, rations, and scope for the Maasai scouts), irregulars were disbanded, rifles recovered, and raiders intercepted and arrested.[23] It seemed that murran would not after all be able to accumulate stock for their families and renown for themselves but were instead being offered the choice between discipline and punishment.[24]

However, the war offered other, longer-term, prospects. By May 1916, northern Tanganyika had been cleared of Germans, leaving an administrative void filled only by isolated Political Officers with meager resources.[25] Maasai began to cross the border to settle as well as to raid, seeing this as an opportunity to escape drought and to reestablish patterns of grazing and occupation that had been destroyed by the creation of colonial boundaries and reserves. By early 1919, Purko and Loitai camps could be found as far south as Ngorongoro.[26] At the same time, Purko were attempting to drive Loitai off the plains into the Loita Hills, thus resuming the advance halted by the conclusion of the War of Morijo in 1902 and expanding their own grazing areas after the loss of Laikipia.[27] After Ololulunga, some sirits moved southward, partly to escape arrest but also to continue raiding, and they were joined by murran of other sections. At the beginning of March 1919, mounted infantry arrived in Narok to enforce a further government ultimatum, which now included a demand that all Purko sirits should move their manyattas close to Narok *boma*, give up ringleaders, and disarm. Patrols operated both in Loita against dissident murran and south of the border, rounding up camps and driving them back into Kenya. By the end of May, 1,150 Purko and 250 Loitai had surrendered and nearly 3,000 head of cattle, 2,500 sheep and goats, and 200 donkeys had been seized in fines or compensation. It was a bitter end for Il Meiruturut, who were finally forced to disband a year later, but an incomplete victory for the government.[28]

In his annual report, the chief native commissioner (CNC) noted confidently that the Maasai had been taught a much-needed lesson.[29] Yet, almost as he was writing, Il Kitoip, the junior circumcision, were gathering and beginning to try their mettle in fights with their seniors. Evidently, they intended to follow the path of Il Meiruturut. By the middle of 1922, the district commissioner (DC) Narok was reporting "an appalling state of lawlessness" in his district and forwarded an impressive list of offenses committed by the murran in the first five months of the year. The administration responded as before with police, arrests, and punishments, but this time it went further.[30] Hemsted was already determined to "break the [moran] system of the Masai," and he now requested legislation that would, in effect, criminalize murranhood by prohibiting the carrying of arms, the formation of manyattas, and even the eating of meat in the bush.[31]

Il Kitoip held their Eunoto in March–April 1922. A month later they were ordered to disarm and disband, and police patrols broke up manyattas. The reaction of the murran was much as it had been in 1918. Immediately after the police had withdrawn in July, fifty murran of Ilaiteti sirit, who expected arrest for building an illegal manyatta, announced their intention of raiding once more or dying in the attempt, "as the district was unfit for heroes to live in." They were turned back by elders, but the rest of their sirit then joined them. They were dispersed, and the ringleaders arrested.[32] The immediate trigger for an uprising came early in December when three Ilaiteti murran, recently escaped from Narok jail and joined by three others, ambushed a police party sent out to rearrest them or confiscate their stock. The sergeant in charge was killed, and one of the assailants shot, but the others made off with the confiscated stock. The rest of Ilaiteti, some three hundred murran, then gathered in the forest near Narok and sent out parties to attack trading centers in the area. Meanwhile, another sirit, Il Kanyara, had also gathered to defy government and to loot. Two traders, a Maasai elder, and a Kikuyu were killed. An emergency was declared in Narok, and a KAR detachment hurriedly sent in. On 17 December, Dorobo scouts located the Laitteti camp at Oloipange, and at dusk the next day it was stormed by the KAR with six murran killed and two thousand head of cattle captured. The day after, the returning patrol encountered a group of murran who had been away raiding when their camp was attacked. The patrol opened fire and inflicted further casualties. The murran then scattered as they had in 1918, and a roundup commenced. By the end of 1923, 198 murran had been arrested. Hemsted noted: "The moran system, with its attendant evils . . . may be said to have been abolished."[33]

Shaken by events and no longer constrained by wartime conditions, the government took severe reprisals. The earlier collective fine, reduced by half, was reimposed, and the Purko were also made to pay the costs of the operation plus compensation for the looted stores. Some £4,300 worth of captured and confiscated stock was eventually sold and the rest, two thousand five hundred head of cattle and fifteen hundred sheep, returned.[34] One hundred sixty-eight murran were convicted of unlawful assembly, and each sentenced to two years' imprisonment; seven were charged with murder.[35] Confiscated shields, spears, and headdresses were publicly burned, a symbolically definitive act that made a deep impression on murran who witnessed it; and Il Kitoip were registered for tax and given *kipandes* (registration certificates)—perhaps as a pointed substitute.

Different groups drew their own conclusions from the troubled career of Il Tareto. For the administration, their defiant and seemingly irrational behavior—especially, the apparently motiveless violence of 1922—seemed to justify the decision to abolish murranhood. It was a "social evil impossible to underrate," a "constant menace to . . . peace and good order," and an obstacle to orderly progress.[36] Unsurprisingly, murran had no place in Hemsted's vision of the future. He expected the Maasai to contribute to the economic development of the colony through their herds, and saw disciplined young men contributing their labor to the enterprise. Discipline was best served by bringing young men firmly under the control of their fathers in the family homestead and to this end, Hemsted intended both to abolish manyattas and to bolster the authority of elders through sectional councils and a central consultative Masai Council.[37] If the mode of Maasai government was to be gerontocratic, elders must be protected from the "methods of terrorism" employed by murran on the rampage and encouraged to assert their authority over the young.[38]

Colonial Office officials took a similar view, if more cautiously. They were aware that Maasai had some legitimate grounds for grievance over land and that repeated cattle fines might come to be seen as "tyranny rather than punishment." The balance between justice and strict administration was a delicate one to hold.[39] They therefore welcomed a shift from punishment to progress, a theme emphasized in the report of the committee set up to investigate Maasai affairs in the aftermath of 1922, and echoed in local editorials.[40]

Elders were less cautious. As Chief Masikonte of Purko told the Enquiry Committee: "[I]f there were no more Moran, there would be no further trouble." They were concerned about the maintenance of their authority, collectively as elders and individually as fathers and household heads. Defiance threatened both. Il Meiruturut and Il Kitoip had disobeyed their elders, rejecting their attempts to mediate and physically threatening them.[41] Moreover, it was elders who ultimately paid the price of disobedience, since fines levied on murran, some £900 a year from 1925 to 1939, came from their family herds.[42] Elders may also have been anxious to secure closer control over their sons' labor in a period of more frequent droughts, since, with access to grazing and water restricted by reserve boundaries, herding in Maasailand was becoming more arduous than before. Finally, "bad behavior" attracted the unwelcome attention of government, and its intervention, even if ostensibly in their support, infringed on the elders' right to rule their own affairs. Bringing murran out of the bush and back into the homestead thus served a double purpose. With their sons firmly under the "paternal yoke," as Spencer terms it, elders would exercise their authority in the household and over the community unchallenged by either youthful disobedience or government interference, and the unruliness of juniors would be tamed by the discipline of herding for their fathers.[43]

Murran did not see their behavior as irresponsible or irrational. Rather, they felt that they had been betrayed by equivocating elders and an alien government, their honor trampled, and their rights infringed. As protectors of the land, its people and herds they had been unable to prevent loss and disruption; they had failed to win new grazing areas; and they had not been able to build a foundation for themselves as prospective herd owners and household heads. Instead, they had been punished for trying to do what was their duty. Even their time as murran, the experience that gave life meaning, had been abruptly ended. Their responses had thus been angry and defensive, rather than delinquent, but murran, and their seniors and rulers, had yet to find an alternative to a pattern of coercion and resistance.

Interwar Uncertainties

With the forced retirement of Il Tareto, murranhood ceased—officially—to exist, but the problem of what to do with young men remained: they could not similarly be abolished. Responses to the uprisings had been extreme; attitudes now moderated.[44] If young men were to become obedient and productive members of the community, some framework would have to be left in place to manage the difficult but vital transition from unruly adolescence to responsible adulthood. The alternative was a permanent and dangerous alienation. Abolition was tacitly abandoned, and, in 1926/27, with the initiation of a new age, Il Terito, a third stage began.

To make sense of the past and to guide policy in the future, administrators situated murran at the intersection of two discourses about the Maasai and their present state. The first was a narrative of decline. Although the Maasai might once have been the "lords of East Africa," they were now in decline, their vitality and distinctiveness sapped by intermarriage with neighboring peoples, their birth rate low, and their physique deteriorating. They had not progressed under colonial rule and were now backward and vulnerable. The continuation of murranhood was at the root of the problem. Murran no longer had a military function, thanks to the imposition of the colonial *pax,* but they refused to find another. The qualities of bravery, discipline, and intelligence that earlier travelers and officials had admired had been corrupted by idleness. "[They] perform no work of any kind, boys and Natives of other tribes even being employed to herd their cattle for them while they themselves lead idle, vicious lives in sexual intercourse with young immature girls." Clearly, they now lacked discipline, moral and physical, as well as purpose, and it was the responsibility of their rulers to instill both.[45]

The second thread of discourse also addressed indiscipline but situated it in the context of overprivilege. In the past, Maasai had been treated too leniently. They had been spared punitive action, and their young men had not been forced out to work. Protected by government, they were rich in stock but did not use their wealth productively. They were the "spoilt child[ren] of the Protectorate": "beautiful to look at . . . [but] never . . . of any use to any living soul."[46] Murranhood would continue in spirit while fathers could afford to keep their sons in idleness.[47] For many critics of an indulgent Maasai policy, especially settlers who feared insurrection and envied Maasai wealth, the cure for indiscipline lay in compulsory labor and an "economic squeeze" to break the connection between wealth and idleness: "[I]f they will not work, then make them pay."[48] In less overtly punitive ways, work and discipline were to be the keys to progress and the new vehicles of socialization.

Both of these interconnected, though neither entirely consistent nor uncontested, discourses were couched in strongly moral terms. They contrasted present idleness, "insolence," and degradation with a future of industry and civic virtue under colonial tutelage. Once the "Moran system" had been dismantled, young men might be taught husbandry and civic responsibility, and their competitive energies channeled through athletics and public works. Yet, memories of a warrior past, suitably redacted, still had a place. Speaking at the official opening of the Masai Council Hall in 1926, an occasion that was intended to bring official closure to the recent and coercive past, Governor Grigg drew attention to the shields hanging on the walls, now symbols of valor and tradition rather than implements of war, and noted that it was Tribal Police, agents of order, who now carried the murran spear.[49]

Accordingly, for the next two decades, administrators looked for ways to incorporate, rather than alienate, young men, in the hope that murranhood would eventually fade out of its own accord. It was "too much to expect" that there would be "no recrudescence of tradition demanding the resurrection of these obsolete customs," but it was hoped that the "acknowledged authorities of the tribe" now had no wish for "their disinterment from the grave in which they have been buried by the forces of progress and enlightenment."[50] Murranhood, suitably modified and overseen by elders and administrators, would continue.

What emerged, however, was an uneasy and shifting compromise as murranhood became negotiable, dependent on good behavior.[51] At times, administrators even found themselves defending the young against the old in the pursuit of stability. In 1929, for example, Purko murran, faced with compulsory retirement, appealed secretly to the DC for support against their sponsoring elders: they wished to repudiate them and come directly under government control. The DC's decision to allow them manyattas against the wishes of leading elders apparently led to a split between "the *murran* of Ole Gilishu" who obeyed their elders and those "of Major Dawson [the DC]" who did not.[52] The dangerous ambiguity of such a policy, which left enforcement to the discretion of individual administrators and headmen and depended on "bluff," was captured by the DC Kajiado in 1932. Failure to enforce the rules governing murranhood weakened authority and appeared to countenance lawlessness; yet "capricious" enforcement might itself provoke confrontation. Government, he argued, should decide whether or not it wished to suppress murranhood completely and then act decisively, accepting the possibility of resistance.[53]

Yet, there seemed good reason for compromise and negotiation. Lack of resources made the kind of surveillance and policing necessary to prevent "recrudescence" impossible. Disarmament, mandated since 1921, was not completed until 1925–26 and was enforced only sporadically thereafter.[54] Raiding continued. Although Jennings's equation of murranhood with organized crime may have been extreme, he had an impressive crime sheet to point to, including murder, assaults, and a raid on Musoma from which only eight out of the eighty-nine head stolen were recovered.[55] Moreover, a series of incidents suggested that control over the young was still far from secure. In 1928–29, there were confrontations between elders and murran in Purko and Keekonyukie.[56] Early in 1930, Loitokitok murran launched five separate raids on Taveta and Teita, taking some three hundred and fifty head of cattle.[57] In June 1935, a major riot, involving Purko murran of both circumcisions, erupted on a road-building project at Rotian. It was ignited by taunts directed by the senior circumcision against their juniors, but it revealed a deeper anger over both directed labor and early retirement.[58] Finally, in 1936, about fifty Purko left-hand murran, including fugitives from the riot and others who refused to retire, established an outlaw manyatta at Kirtalu, in Loliondo just across the Tanganyika border, from which they raided Musoma and Maswa. Following a tense visit from the DC Narok, the murran were lured out of the manyatta, arrested by Tanganyika police, and repatriated.[59]

Curtailing murranhood was creating more problems than it solved: indeed, it was helping to produce the delinquent behavior that intervention was intended to suppress. In its attempts to impose order, the administration had concentrated its attention on "the moran system" in isolation, but because the experience of murranhood was integral to the life-long process of becoming a Maasai, intervention was beginning to have further-reaching effects. From the early 1920s, the orderly and continuous progression of initiations and retirements had been disrupted, and the loose synchronicity of age organization across Maasailand was suffering as each section followed its own course. Significantly, disruption was greater in Narok, where the Purko had been the main target of official intervention, than in Kajiado, where age relations were smoother.[60]

By the 1940s, three important and interrelated changes had occurred.[61] "Custom" had been modified and, in particular, the closed period (*Endungore*), during which no initiations could be held, had been abandoned;[62] the age of initiation had dropped; and the period of formal murranhood itself had been cut by at least half.[63] An age organization that depended on creating and managing distinction and succession was losing its meaning. Categories of maturation no longer reflected the reality of age: boys were now murran and young men elders. Men had once been initiated in their late teens and had not become junior elders until their early thirties, but teenagers could now become twenty-one-year-old elders, thanks to early initiation and retirement and to the fact that, in some sections, boys might join a circumcision almost up to its Eunoto.[64] Murranhood was threatening to become "a complete farce."[65] The abandonment of Endungore, together with the hastening of promotion and retirement, also erased the distinction between senior and junior murran and the overlap between them that had once been a prominent feature of murranhood and had structured opposition between adjacent age-groups.[66] In some sections, senior (i.e., post-Eunoto) murranhood had almost ceased to exist, and in all sections a new age-set did not now begin to form until its predecessor had retired. This telescoping, with resentment on one hand and impatience on the other, made tensions between senior and junior circumcision groups and between adjacent age-sets more overt than before.[67]

Hemsted, like Thomson, had believed that once murran retired "their entire outlook on life changes and they settle down to become law-abiding and reasonable members of the community."[68] This optimistic view, however, depended on a lengthy apprenticeship in manyatta. With the period of murranhood now drastically shortened, the community had to deal with angry young men who were neither socially nor psychologically ready to return to their fathers' households. In 1933, some of the murran who had ostensibly retired the year before were sequestered in the forest stealing stock and assaulting any who opposed them.[69] Nor were they necessarily able to marry, even if their fathers agreed, since the outlawing of raids made it more difficult for ex-murran to acquire the assets necessary to establish themselves as marriageable men and future household heads, especially at a time when herds were being thinned by drought and disease.[70]

Inevitably, murran who resented their forced retirement continued to behave as the young men they really were. Misbehavior had not ceased; it had merely changed its locus. Il Terito, retired in the late 1930s, continued to raid as elders. The administration saw this as a sign of weakening respect for "tradition," for elders did not normally go on raids, but what was changing was elderhood itself. For similar reasons, the shift in attitude following retirement that Hemsted had hoped for did not take place. Young men in their twenties could not be expected to behave with the restraint of elders; nor, it seemed, would they have the authority, the experience, and the cohesion to manage murran in their turn.[71]

There were problems at the point of recruitment as well as retirement. With initiations delayed, uncircumcised boys (*ilayiok*) became more truculent. In 1924, the OiC had noted that, although abolition had strengthened the elders' authority, it had led to "indiscipline" among the layiok, now that murran were not there to keep them in order. In 1928, they had become so unmanageable that Purko elders agreed, with serious consequences, that the next Eunoto would have to be brought forward and the current murran retired to enable a new initiation to take place. Avoiding the "Charybdis of moran hubris," as the DC Narok later warned, risked shipwreck in the "Scylla" of uncontrolled boys. Yet, simply initiating boys younger would not solve the problem and would make the transition to mature elderhood even more difficult.[72]

Administrators were not the only ones attempting to control murran. With the inauguration of a new age in 1926, a new set of sponsoring elders (*ol piron*), Il Twati, took over. It was their task to guide and discipline their charges as they negotiated murranhood. As ol piron, Il Twati were more disciplinarian than their predecessors. Their intransigence exposed the weakness of government policy and pushed the administration, caught in the middle, into conflict with both elders and murran.

Crisis erupted over the Purko right-hand Eunoto. In June 1928, following a decision by the ol piron that the ceremony should be held as soon as possible, ole Gilishu, their chief spokesman, with the reluctant agreement of his age-mates, directed that the *laibon*'s (prophet) blessing should be dispensed with and the date fixed for September. Expecting opposition, he did not inform the murran, and attendance was sparse. The chief murran spokesman, Ngarabali, a man of considerable influence with his age-group, denounced the ceremony and the ol piron and stated that the murran intended to consult their laibon, Kimoruai, in the proper way and then hold their own Eunoto.[73] Ole Gilishu then threatened to force the murran to drink milk (and retire) immediately and to "treat them as criminals" if they refused, and turned to the administration for support since the murran were openly defying their elders.[74] The situation was defused by ole Gilishu's age-mates, who forced a compromise. However, in April 1929, he returned to the charge and ordered the murran to retire within two months. The murran took to the bush and refused to have any further dealings with their sponsors, appealing in turn and in secret to the DC to support them and uphold "custom." A meeting of all Purko spokesmen persuaded ole Gilishu to revoke his order.[75] However, in June, seventy murran of Il Merisho sirit again defied orders and established a manyatta at Mosiro, with the blessing of Kimoruai, who had been brought in earlier by the DC to support the elders. Il Merisho sent a deputation to the DC offering to disband but refusing to accept the authority of the elders. However, when so ordered, they refused either to disband or to come in to Narok for a meeting. They did so only when persuaded by Ngarabali and their own spokesman, and Kimoruai, who had now been pressured into withdrawing his protection. Eventually, the matter was settled, and the DC, thoroughly outmaneuvered, presided over a feast of reconciliation at Mosiro.[76]

The events of 1928–29 reveal some of the complexities involved in disciplining the young. The Eunoto crisis had been defused because the ol piron had been willing to restrain ole Gilishu and reach compromise. While they agreed on the need to reduce the murran to obedience, behind the collective rhetoric of denunciation, few shared ole Gilishu's determination that murranhood must be abolished completely—and the age organization thereby fundamentally changed. Like the administration, they were uncertain and divided over the issue, but their understanding of the problem was deeper and more immediate, and their attitudes correspondingly more ambivalent.

There were several reasons for ambivalence. The experience of murranhood itself was one. Although in their view murran were irresponsible and lacked respect (*enkeanyit*), elders were not immune to the glamour of murranhood—they had once basked in it themselves.[77] Moreover, as fathers and household heads, they recognized that arrogance in the bush was the price paid for order at home. Although collectively they spoke the language of paternal discipline, individually they were often reluctant to deal with truculent young men in their own households.

Yet, for elders, murranhood was merely an episode, if a vivid one, in a much longer career focused on managing the family herds. The timing of sons' initiations, like their marriages, was therefore a matter of long-term calculation. The social progression of fathers was linked to that of their sons, and, as he got older, a father would need the support of sons mature enough to play an increasingly important part in herd management. Circumcising a son early into an age-set which was beginning to close accelerated the process of maturation in some ways, but it meant that the son would be unlikely to make his mark among older age-mates; delaying circumcision so that a son would be among the first and oldest of the next age had corresponding advantages and disadvantages. With murranhood in disarray, calculation became more complex. Initiating sons younger avoided tension at home; delay gave fathers more control over their labor and kept them out of the government's way but also risked confrontation.[78] The power of ruling elders depended in part on the fact that their corporate authority within the hierarchy of age was reinforced by their individual authority as fathers and household heads. Yet, individual elders might find their private interest opposed to that of the public consensus. Private interest has always chafed against the need for public solidarity, but here colonial demands increased the friction and sharpened conflict. The issue of murranhood was both a focus for dispute and a matter that demanded a collective response. In mid-1936, for example, the Matapato chief reported that some elders were pressing for a new age to be inaugurated despite a Local Native Council (LNC) resolution that this be delayed. The DC supported the chief, but the elders eventually agreed to a compromise: Il Twati might circumcise their sons, but the younger elders of Il Tareto must wait.[79]

Defense was also a concern. Although the British believed that a warrior organization was outdated, the Maasai knew better. Maasailand remained insecure, its western border areas especially subject to almost continuous trespass and raiding. In 1929, for example, Purko murran were involved in major clashes with Kipsikis raiders; and when Kipsikis war parties struck again in 1936, penetrating as far south as Loliondo and showing "a contemptuous spirit both of the Masai and the Government," the DC pointed out that, if government could not guarantee peace, Maasai elders would conclude that dismantling their own means of defense had been a mistake.[80]

The Maasai were not of course guiltless, for their murran also raided, and this too raised questions for the elders. Although they knew that raids were costly, not only through the retaliation they invited but also through the loss of cattle in fines and sons to prison or the spear, herd owners were not averse to adding stolen animals to their holdings, nor were they likely to turn in raiders unless it was unavoidable: they had been raiders themselves. Despite their public disapproval of raiding, they were often complaisant, if not privately complicit: "Present elders and chiefs were once thieves of cattle; their present moran are also thieves. Who is worse, the present thief or the former?"[81] Local herd owners were also interested parties in clashes between murran of different sections over access to grazing and water. Publicly, elders deplored the fighting and dismissed it as "nothing but the foolishness of the moran who are children," but privately they wanted to keep murran on call to defend their section's resources.[82]

Underlying the elders' cautious handling of the murran was the question of how their authority should be exercised. Although the young should show at least outward deference to their seniors, the latter in turn should exercise restraint and judgment in their dealings with their juniors. In fact, elders, collectively and individually, possessed a battery of formidable sanctions to bring recalcitrant young men to heel, ranging from verbal intimidation at public meetings, to disinheritance and the denial of marriage, to the ultimate weapon of the sponsors' curse. Power generally lay in the threat rather than the action, but government pressure had raised the temperature of intergenerational relations. The defiance of young men strained elders' authority and patience to the utmost, and a dangerous form of brinkmanship developed. In November 1921, an elder had allegedly cursed a large raiding party of some two hundred Purko that had crossed into Tanganyika against the express orders of the ol piron. The "Shameful Raid's" disastrous failure—less than half returned, and the survivors were arrested and imprisoned—raised the question of how far the elders were willing to go in disciplining murran.[83] Later, in the time of Il Terito and in the context of confrontations over manyattas, the Loitai ol piron allegedly threatened publicly to "break the firestick" if their charges did not submit, an extreme act of repudiation with incalculable consequences for the age-set concerned and even for the community as a whole. At the same time, however, Il Terito murran had rejected their sponsors and had threatened, assaulted, and even killed individual elders. These were all actions of great symbolic significance, and it is impossible to be sure that all of them actually occurred. Yet, their central place in the collective memory of the time is a powerful indication of perceived dislocation and crisis.[84]

Given the complexity of the issues, it is not surprising that the elders appeared unwilling to take action. In fact, by negotiation and delay, supporting government measures in public but doing little to implement them, they were attempting to protect the core relations of power and authority in Maasai society from both murran and government, using the threat of state power to cow their juniors and to bolster their own authority, and shifting the burden of implementing unpopular and possibly dangerous measures onto official shoulders. Officials were equally determined that it would be elders who enforced administrative edicts.

Laibons were also competing for the allegiance of the young. Like the "moran system" itself, they were part of a past that had not passed. Their interest lay in the fact that they provided both legitimate blessings for the ceremonies of murranhood and (now illegal) charms for raids. Although their services may have been essential to the well-being of the community, elders regarded them with great suspicion, and the administration followed suit, for theirs was a power that could be neither ignored nor safely co-opted.[85] Despite their suspicions of Kimoruai's "evil influence," officials attempted to use him in 1929 and again in 1935, in both cases unsuccessfully.[86] But laibons too were divided, and intensely jealous of rivals. Some, like Senteu, had secure positions as the recognized prophets of sections and thus some interest in cooperation; others, though recognized, felt insecure and might thus side with murran to improve their positions, as Kimoruai did in 1929 and perhaps 1935; and still others were opportunists, men who had neither position nor prospects and whose ambition led them to encourage raids for the payments and prestige that accrued. It was to them that dissident murran went in search of charms and direction.[87] The Loitokitok raids in 1930, for example, were incited by the laibon Ntitika. Apart from gifts of raided cattle, he may have been hoping that the Loitokitok murran would transfer their allegiance from the Kisongo laibon, Mbeiya, who lived across the border. If so, his plans went disastrously wrong. Although the raids were successful, the administration reacted vigorously. Ntitika himself was fined eighty head of cattle and was exiled for a time, and his son, with three other raiders, was hanged for murder. Similarly, the

Kirtalu manyatta was under the protection of another opportunist, Oruma ole Nailyang.[88] The influence of laibons added yet another element of tension.

Like administrators, both elders and murran had versions of the past to which they could appeal. All agreed that there had been a glorious and distinctive warrior past, but differed in how, if at all, that past might inform the present. Youths had been men then, not boys. Danger and exertion had kept them disciplined, respectful, and obedient, so elders claimed, and both community and household had benefited from the combination of old men's wisdom and young men's valor. Now the young were idle and heedless of their duties. Maasai were ruled by others partly because they could not rule themselves. Young men saw it differently. It was they whose predecessors had "ruled the land" and made that glorious past, sometimes in defiance of timorous and selfish elders, and it was they who both exemplified and maintained the "tradition" that made Maasai. If they were disrespectful, it was because elders did not deserve respect. If elders would behave like elders, then murran could again be murran. Both sides, of course, had got their history partly wrong. Youth had not always been obedient nor age commanding; force had not always been tempered by authority; young men had been reckless and old men foolish; and there had been tension and confrontations. In other words, the Maasai past had been as messy and conflicted as any other. But this is not how generations under pressure remember and argue over their pasts. Yet, the argument was not an equal one, for elders now had the upper hand and murran were marginalized. The elders' version would therefore be authoritative, while murran could only draw on theirs to legitimate their anger and alienation. This clash of memory partly explains why the administration, which had once sought to erase the past but now wished to co-opt it, was ultimately unsuccessful in reviving and modernizing murranhood.

Postwar Revival

The next age, Il Nyankusi, was inaugurated in the early 1940s. It began inauspiciously, at least in Purko, where spokesmen of Il Tareto, the new ol piron, demanded that murranhood be hurried through or, better, abolished. Their language echoed Masikonte's twenty years before. The administration disagreed: murranhood would continue, and it would be directed either by the elders or, if necessary, by the government itself.[89] This did not signal another change of policy, but it did indicate a new determination to make the "system" "work." The generational chaos of the interwar period had convinced the administration that young men could not be socialized or controlled except within the frame of murranhood. A change in tone becomes apparent in discussions of the "problem" of murran. Although Hemsted was still being quoted, officials no longer saw murranhood as a direct threat to colonial authority. Instead, they looked for positive aspects to build on: "the spirit of comradeship and interdependence," self-confidence, and leadership. Even "lessons learnt on raids contribute[d] to virility," though other "manly pursuits" like lion hunting were to be preferred. Like generations of elders before them, officials were learning to live with the young, though the sometimes complacent tone of reports suggests an unwillingness to recognize how deeply violence was engrained in murran culture.[90]

The demands of law and order as well as the search for a new model of murranhood led to a reevaluation of the role of the manyatta. Murran pushed to the margins, literally as well as metaphorically, were difficult to police. In 1932, the OiC had drawn a contrast between what he saw as a period of disciplined communal life before Eunoto and what amounted to anarchy afterwards; his successor linked an outburst of stock raiding to the breakup of manyattas in Kajiado which had led to the dispersal of "small undisciplined parties," "free of all restraint," and bent on stock theft. Congregated in one place, murran could be more easily watched.[91] Policy was supported by an enhanced policing capability. From 1943, Kenya Police were available to back up Tribal Police in the Reserve, and reinforcements could be called in by telephone or wireless. By 1950, the Masai Police Division had an establishment of ninety-four.[92] Manyattas were searched for stolen stock, lists of wanted men circulated, and, if necessary, ceremonies held up until they were produced; and murran with records were served with supervision orders.[93] Purged and supervised by resident elders, manyattas were now commended as sites of virtue, not vice, instilling discipline and cohesion in the young, and offering a better model of appropriate socialization than a marginal life in the homestead or the bush. "When the *manyatta* system becomes a cross between a School of Animal Husbandry and a youth camp the problem is solved."[94]

The administration's enthusiasm for a revival of murranhood was not shared by the elders. At a joint meeting in January 1947, just before the inauguration of the junior circumcision of Il Nyankusi, Il Kamaniki, Purko elders again proposed that murranhood be abolished. Despite warnings about the likely consequences, the proposal was agreed upon. This threatened to halt progress and unleash yet more alienated and angry young men, and the administration took steps to ensure that the abolitionists did not get their way.[95]

Officials linked the proposal to a recent incident where the Purko ol piron had attempted to force newly circumcised youths who were gathering to form the new junior circumcision to drink milk and return home. Many refused, and the elders then called on Il Kalikal, the senior circumcision, to enforce their orders. The youths won the ensuing fight and later toured homesteads, calling on those who had obeyed the elders to return and join them in defiance.[96] Relations between sponsors and wards had been troubled from the outset. By 1944, they had broken down completely, with ol piron refusing to deal directly with murran and using junior elders as intermediaries. The DC had to intervene to effect a reconciliation.[97] Il Tareto had been the first age-set whose career had been disrupted by government intervention, and their cohesion may have been impaired as a result. In Purko, they were now split into two factions, led by ole Sankale, who followed ole Gilishu's hard line, and ole Lemeen, who adopted a more conciliatory attitude.[98] Although the two were rivals for the position of senior chief and were probably using the issue of murranhood to gather support and advance their own claims, the differences in attitude that they represented were real enough and not confined to Purko.

Reform was bringing underlying conflicts to the surface. If Maasai youth was to be transformed and take its place in a developing colonial order, as administrators intended that it should, the cooperation of elders was essential, but this was not always forthcoming. Officials had often thought elders weak: now they came to see them as passive resisters, unwilling rather than unable to exert their authority, at least in support of the government, and evading their "hereditary responsibilities." The Moran Officer was convinced that elders had the power to control murran more effectively than government if they chose to use it—which they did not.[99] The blame for unrest was shifting from the young to the old as the administration took an increasingly active role in determining and managing murranhood, in effect becoming ol piron themselves.[100]

Elders responded to what they saw as the usurpation of their own role and the erosion of their authority over the young partly by withdrawing from active involvement, leaving the business of managing murranhood to the officials who insisted on maintaining it. From their point of view, murranhood was a burden that they were now carrying on behalf of the government, which ignored their concerns and advice and whose changing enthusiasms they found difficult to follow. Defiant and disrespectful youths assaulted their dignity and sometimes their persons, and, as raiders, placed their fathers' herds in jeopardy. Government support for murranhood merely encouraged the bad behavior that elders were expected to curb but forbidden to eradicate.[101] Moreover, they differed sharply with government over the ends as well as the means of socialization. Whereas government hoped to mold young citizens able to play an important part in the modernization of their community, elders wanted obedient sons who would help manage the family herds under their fathers' direction. Citizens and sons were not the same, however: elders wanted young men tamed, not transformed.

Inevitably, conflict centered on manyattas, where murranhood as an ethos was produced. Most elders did not want to see murranhood as an age-grade abolished completely, but they did want it curtailed and the period in manyatta reduced to the minimum necessary to enable the vital ceremonies of maturation to be performed. Perhaps based on their own past experience, they saw manyattas as places where their sons learned disobedience, where raids were planned, and seductions celebrated. Unlike the administration, they believed that manyattas encouraged rather than reduced lawlessness and that young men could be better controlled at home. Since the government did not agree, they took their own action, by dispersing manyattas as soon as they could, by forbidding their sons to join them or by undermining them indirectly. Particularly in Purko, not all murran (and even fewer elders) now actually lived in the manyattas: they were either at home or in the bush, thus defeating the new purpose of manyatta life. Partly this was because murran were well aware that living in a manyatta made them more accessible to the police, but it also appeared that the herds attached to manyattas were often too small to support a large resident population, especially in dry conditions.

Some fathers were refusing to send either cattle or wives (the mothers of the murran) to the manyatta. Their boycott was effective, for without cattle and women manyattas could not exist.[102]

This revealed another aspect of the complex interplay between collective action and individual self-interest that had influenced elders' responses to murranhood in the past. Especially for men with small households, sending cattle and wives to the manyatta involved a significant sacrifice. Such domestic tensions had always been present, but in the past elders had accepted that manyattas were a central feature of the process of maturation and that their own convenience should ideally be subordinated to the general good. The present conflicts over murranhood, however, gave them the opportunity to consult their own interest as household heads while at the same time expressing their collective opposition to the continuation of manyattas as elders. Ultimately, the struggle over manyattas was a struggle over authority. Fathers wished to discipline and mold their sons at home; they did not want government to do it for them elsewhere. For the administration, on the contrary, the interests of law and order and development were best served by communal discipline outside the household, since fathers would not control their sons. Manyatta and homestead were now opposed as sites of control and socialization.[103]

The crisis over abolition led the administration to bring Tanganyika, where murranhood had been left more or less undisturbed, into the discussion, partly in the hope that Purko "extremists" would be overborne by more moderate opinion and partly because administrators wanted a uniform murran policy, backed by law, throughout Maasailand.[104] At a meeting of Maasai representatives at Monduli in August 1947, the first of several, it was agreed that, while murranhood would not be abolished, its term would be reduced to three years for each circumcision. Neither administration thought this sufficiently long, but they were constrained by the elders' unanimous decision. Subsequently, it was decided that the least disruptive way of making the change was to get murran to drink milk and disperse immediately after Eunoto. Although the hardliners had not won, they had now gained official endorsement for measures that their predecessors had tried to impose against government wishes.[105]

A year later, the administration took another step. It was already under pressure from the central government to get murran finally under control, and a resurgence of violence, in which Il Kalikal were heavily involved, led to the appointment of a Moran Officer. His duties were intended to be primarily supervisory—getting in touch with murran, overseeing their activities and compiling systematic data on manyattas—but Holford-Walker was an enthusiastic and talented ethnographer, and he quickly became a main source of detailed information about the workings, past and present, of the age organization.[106] He was soon ready with an overview and recommendations; for the first time the administration had access to information that it needed. Holford-Walker's findings, based on visits to every manyatta and the close questioning of elders in all sections, confirmed what administrators already suspected: that attempts to abolish murranhood in the 1920s had been a huge mistake and that elders' control and solidarity had been undermined and "custom" "corrupted" as a result. His recommendations for how it might be "purified" and adapted were in line with the policy of reform and were accepted as the basis for a new abbreviated, but still valid, murranhood.[107] Early in 1949, the Masai Council approved a set of proposals, initially drafted by Holford-Walker, for "unifying and strengthening the customs associated with the Moran system." Essentially, these embodied his recommendations that Endungore should be reintroduced, that two circumcisions (right and left) of equal length should be the norm for each age and that synchronization between sections should be restored. A committee of ol piron and murran spokesmen would oversee murranhood. Additionally, murran would be made to work on development projects—with sports thrown in for the "glamour aspect."[108]

This, however, was as far as the new policy would go. The administration, still concerned about the "dangerous period" between drinking milk and settling down, pressed for a longer manyatta period, but the Masai Council refused to lengthen murranhood. In 1952, over the objections of Il Terito, who would be the ol piron of the next age, the Council again decided to end manyattas and to compress all ceremonies into two years. Murranhood thus remained suspended between reform and abolition.[109] The debate dragged on throughout the 1950s, against the background of a breakdown of "tribal discipline" in Kikuyuland far more threatening to the colonial state than anything that the Maasai administration could have imagined. New voices joined in the argument. The Secretariat counseled extreme caution in making any further changes; so too did the Tanganyika administration, which hoped that murranhood would simply fade away and did not intend to interfere. Young, educated Maasai attacked it on the grounds that it was retrograde and an obstacle to both social and economic progress.[110] Faced with this clamor, and the continued opposition of the elders, the administration retreated. By the end of 1952, the OiC was signaling that if the elders pressed for abolition, he would not oppose it. He thought that murranhood might be beyond saving after all.[111]

The postwar struggle over the future of murranhood was full of contradictions and ironies. An administration that had once been determined to destroy murranhood and had outlawed manyattas was now defending both against elders, who had been manyatta murran themselves but did not intend their sons to be so. It might be tempting to conclude that elders and administrators had merely changed sides, but it was more complicated than that. Elders were no modernizers, but they were willing to adapt in the present in order to avoid worse in the future. Officials recognized that those who were most intransigently opposed to their development plans were also the most effective at controlling murran. Nor were administrators committed to tradition per se: modernization would inevitably change it. To pursue their aims, both sides adopted convenient rhetoric. Elders used the arenas opened up by colonial rule to argue that murranhood had outlived its usefulness and that murran were lawless as well as disobedient. In doing so, ol piron were adapting an old style to new ends, threatening and overawing their wards and appealing to consensus while thwarting or diluting government policy.[112] This new form of brinkmanship, however, might go too far, alienating sons, dividing fathers, and stirring rivalries between sets of elders. Administrators proclaimed the virtue of traditional discipline, but public support for traditional authority might imply that elders held the decision-making power and could thus bend government policy to suit their own ends. Neither side forgot that the real conflict was over authority. A common concern with the control of the young concealed this deeper and more divisive issue. Deference to elders' opinion on "customary matters" notwithstanding, tradition would be determined and enforced by the government.

To a colonial state anxious to show that it was mindful of the need to preserve social cohesion in the midst of rapid change, murranhood had a larger appeal. It offered a demonstration of how "tradition" might be revitalized and made to "work." In Maasailand, young men were being put to work not just as laborers for the public good but also as actors in a colonial drama of "tribal" regeneration. With the emergence of the "bad boys" into the limelight, another layer of irony falls into place. The Kaputiei Eunoto of 1949—with or without riot police—was filmed by the Government Information Office.[113] Murran also featured in a documentary film made by the American Museum of Natural History in 1953. Among other things, the film included re-creations of acts that would in reality have landed all participants in jail: a raid and a consultation between murran and laibons beforehand.[114] With images of young men in arms shifting from the threatening to the picturesque, we should perhaps leave the murran, still undisciplined, to fade into the ethnographic sunset.[115]

Searching for Alternatives

In the late 1950s, a former Moran Supervisor reviewed the failures of murran policy: "One may say, 'Do away with Moran system' [but] the question [then arises] 'Replace it with what?'"[116] Neither hard work at home, the elders' remedy, nor education, sports, and communal labor, government's ideal, could compete with manyatta life in attracting the enthusiasms of the young. At first, it was enough to break up murran formations to prevent raiding, but from the 1930s onward, administrators realized that an opportunity was being lost. One OiC thought it "lamentable that we can do nothing with [murranhood] but break it up." "The fundamental idea," he argued, "is not to oppose Masai institutions but to use and mould and develop them into an educational system."[117] An alternative frame of socialization and a different model of male maturity were the elements needed. Their absence in Maasailand reminds us how important their presence was elsewhere, where government could look to missions and schools for help in molding young colonial citizens.

The Africa Inland Mission, the only mission in Maasailand until the 1950s, was always marginal, ignored by Maasai and their rulers alike. Its first success had, in fact, been with an influential murran spokesman, Malonket ole Sempele, but conversion separated him from his age-mates and the opportunity of working with murran was lost and never recovered.[118]

Nor were schools any more successful. Education in Maasailand began as part of a larger modernization effort.[119] A school was opened at Narok in 1921 and another at Kajiado in 1926. The latter moved to Loitokitok in 1929 and merged with Narok in 1940. In the late 1930s, the first LNC primary schools appeared, but, by 1940, education was still confined to "a few tiny . . . islands existing in a wide sea of apathy." The principal at Narok thought the history of education in Maasailand "a series of disappointments" and its pupils' achievements "equally uninspiring."[120]

There were several reasons why schools failed to strike root. The first was the compulsion involved. Chiefs were given quotas to fill. Small boys were then rounded up and sent to serve what must have seemed like a three-year detention sentence far from their families. Absenteeism was common, and truants were tracked down by the Tribal Police. Fathers needed their younger sons to herd at home, since older sons were away in manyatta, and therefore resisted conscription and shielded truants.[121] In 1931, the DC admitted that, without compulsion, attendance at Narok Government Masai School would not reach double figures.[122]

Another difficulty was that school preceded rather than replaced murranhood. Most of the boys were between eight and fourteen and would still be laiyok when they left school. They were thought to be more tractable and easier to influence, but in a competition to reach boys before they became young men the school was bound to lose. As initiation approached, boys became "restless" and lost interest in school work. With circumcision, a "marked change" took place, and when ex-pupils joined the murran, they lost "any good which [their] education may have done [them]." They had, in effect, been re-socialized.[123]

Education had a larger purpose as a moral alternative to murranhood and a means of regenerating Maasai society. The fear that the continuation of murranhood might mean the end of the Maasai gave the project a special urgency.[124] The opposition between school and manyatta, the future and the past, explicit by 1926, had been implicit from the beginning. Some claim that Il Meruturut rose in 1918 primarily because they feared that government intended to steal children away [to attend school]. As protectors of the community, it was their duty to prevent this. While it is unlikely that it refers specifically to events in 1918, the claim makes sense in terms both of memories of murran resistance and forced schooling and of perceptions of the real purpose of education. Administrators believed that the new disciplines and skills of education would remake Maasai: Maasai believed that they would unmake them, turning them into *il meek* (non-Maasai).[125]

Finally, it was not clear what practical value education might have, even for those who persevered. The intention was for school-leavers to take up employment in the Reserve, but this expectation was dashed, partly because many ex-pupils preferred to return home, become murran, and then take their place in the family enterprise, but also because there were few jobs to be had.[126] While young educated men elsewhere were able to make a life for themselves, their counterparts in Maasailand had few opportunities, either to better themselves or to influence others.[127] Pastoralism remained not only the most satisfying but almost the only life.

The failure of alternatives must be placed against the background of the involution of the Maasai economy between the wars. Because there was little development in Maasailand, there was no point in making youth more productive. Getting murran to work for the community had been a key part of Buxton's development scheme for Narok in the mid-1930s, and he had wanted enrollment in school, training schemes, or labor gangs made compulsory. The Rotian Riot did not dent his enthusiasm, but the economic progress that might have sustained it did not materialize.[128] Postwar development plans, however, offered a chance to combine discipline with improvement. Murran could be employed building roads, cattle crushes, and dams, and clearing bush. Young men and elders were less keen. Despite the trappings of tradition—murran were mobilized as sirits under their own spokesmen and fed with cattle donated by their fathers—they were still being forced to do manual work that they despised. Their fathers saw it as another aspect of the struggle to control the young, in this case their labor. They claimed that their sons were already fully employed with the family herds and then demanded that murran should not be rewarded as a group but paid individually for their labor, an indication that they saw the work not as community service but as wage labor from which they were entitled to a share.[129]

Ultimately, the question of what to do with young men remained unresolved. One DC hoped that murranhood might evolve into a form of "National Service" with citizenship and sports thrown in, but most murran continued to lead "the aimless lives which must perforce be their lot in modern times until a more useful function can be found for them."[130]

Honor and Violence: Murran as Gangs

Murran were young men in a world that seemed weighted in favor of the old. Together with the "girls of the *manyatta*," they formed a youth culture: cohesive, defiant, and impenetrable. To look at murran as youth gangs is to read somewhat across the grain of earlier ethnography. Yet, the detailed catalog of thefts, assaults, affrays, and confrontations available in late-colonial reports especially can be read as an external record of gang behavior. Sirits, like gangs elsewhere, had their own territories and jealously guarded boundaries, their own particular dress fashions, songs and dances, their own codes of honor, their own histories, and their own intergroup feuds.[131] Relations between them, even within the same section, could be tense, especially at the time of Eunoto when they gathered together for the first time, but murran might ally against rivals of another section or age-group.[132] Gaining access to this world is difficult. Much of what we know about murran comes from those who tried to punish or change their behavior. Murran themselves remain shadowy figures, seen in the mass rather than as individuals, silent and acted on rather than acting, except in ways that fit the negative image of deviance that their elders and rulers had created.

Elders and murran lived in separate and contrasting worlds, both spatially and morally. Elders lived at home in the cattle camp (*enkang*), immersed in the business of managing herds, households, and community: murran roamed outside, based on manyattas hidden in the bush (*entim*). Their world might seem rebellious and anarchic, but it was governed by strict rules and norms of behavior, as some early observers noted.[133] It was, ideally, a world of altruism, equality, and solidarity that extended even to the consumption of food—a closed moral universe of self-denial and brotherhood, defined by honor. Honor lay in personal bravery and in upholding the ideals of murranhood. Its rewards came in recognition by peers, in the admiration of women, in cattle raided, and in grazing and water resources seized and defended. As murran saw it, the values of the manyatta opposed and in some ways surpassed those of the enkang, even though their path toward maturity inevitably took them from the one to the other. Becoming an elder meant exchanging the companionship of youth for the private concerns of the household, and the beginning of a descent into the selfishness of old age—or, as elders saw it, leaving behind the impulsive irresponsibility of youth and behaving with respect, prudence, and restraint, exchanging the warrior's honor for that of the householder. There was, however, some truth in the contrast between the altruism of youth and the selfishness of age. Although the rhetoric of authority stressed the seamlessness of household and community power, it could not disguise the fact that wealth and accumulation—and the differentiation they brought—operated in the private sphere, whereas forms of equality were reserved for the public sphere. It was murran who best upheld the ideals of equality, not the elders who preached and benefited from it.[134]

Murran and elders thus had their own domains, semiautonomous but not equal. Murranhood was subordinated to elderhood by the passage of time; and whereas the young might have the physical force to confront their elders and the wit to ridicule them, the old had the power to command and to punish. It was they who controlled the passage to maturity and access to the family herds. However, the frustration and alienation of murran arose from the fact that their domain was now not merely subordinate but steadily marginalized. The priorities of colonial rule supported the power of elders and the peaceful accumulation of wealth. As Spencer has pointed out, tensions between war and peace as alternative modes of accumulation have always been present. One belonged to the world of the murran and the other to that of the elders. The two were never equally balanced, for, except in very unusual circumstances, careful husbandry built a herd faster than raiding ever could. Nonetheless, raiding had its place, especially in regard to inheritance, since murran could hope to establish some right to the offspring of animals that they had contributed to the family herd. By outlawing war and promoting husbandry, colonial rule, in effect, further consolidated paternal authority by ensuring that control of the stock economy, and thus of the avenues of accumulation, would be entirely in the hands of elders.[135]

Heavy-handed attempts to control murran invaded their world in a number of ways. Forbidding manyattas disrupted the moral geography of murranhood. They had once been located with an eye to expansion and defense, and they were the focus of a territory that successive sirits regarded as especially "theirs."[136] With the postwar revival of manyattas, locations had to be approved and accessible by a track, cut if necessary by the murran themselves, and they might be moved to avoid confrontations between rival sirits.[137] Confiscating shields, forbidding the carrying of the white spear, and shaving off the characteristic murran pigtail, "pinprick[s]" as the DC Kajiado put it, destroyed potent symbols of warriorhood and threatened to erase important aspects of group identity and differentiation. Shield markings conveyed important information about the bearer and his sirit and sectional allegiances; the white spear was a jealously guarded privilege, and pigtails were closely associated with the ceremonial shavings that marked important points in the progression of murranhood. To be forcibly disarmed or untimely shaved was a personal violation.[138] The prohibition on raiding struck at a vital aspect of the warrior's honor, for both individual prowess and group solidarity could be displayed, and celebrated afterward in powerfully evocative songs with coded meanings that became part of the group's identity.[139] Raids continued, nonetheless, and the need for concealment and the possibility of arrest may have offered new avenues of honor. The administration attempted to enlist the warrior's honor on the side of law and order, but it was by now an outlaw honor and, unlike their Samburu counterparts, Maasai did not come to accept military service as a worthy substitute for raiding. In the 1940s, there were probably as many murran in jail as in uniform.[140]

Between 1920 and 1950, colonial intervention changed the world of the murran, but it is difficult to get a clear sense of how murran themselves were changing. We might look to three areas. The first is the structure of leadership. Despite its egalitarianism, the manyatta was not flat terrain: some murran were influential, with reputations for courage or generosity to their age-mates; others were not. Each sirit had a spokesman, chosen by his age-mates for his influence and negotiating skills. Spokesmen were supported by assistants and by a group of advisors, but they had no power to compel their age-mates except by reasoned argument. A chief spokesman for the entire age group was chosen earlier by the ol piron.[141] As relations between murran, elders, and administrators became more conflicted, their position as mediators became more difficult, as Ngarrabali discovered. Two of his predecessors, ole Pere, spokesman of Il Meruturut and ole Sankale, spokesman of Il Kitoip, had been threatened and driven out by their age-mates intent on confrontation in 1918 and 1922.[142] Administrators expected spokesmen to be "loyal" and able to control "their" murran, and this too undermined their authority. As spokesmen lost ground, leadership may have passed to more intransigent murran like the "diehards" discussed by Spencer, much as elders were increasingly being influenced by hardliners.[143] But, like their sponsors, not all murran were unreasonable or confrontationally minded, and splits developed over what stance to adopt, with a consequent loss of group cohesion. The "republic of young men" was eroding from within. Thus, at a time when young men were thought to be out of control, changes within their domain made it more difficult for them to refute the accusation and to move beyond violence and rebelliousness to find a new and agreed-on path to maturity.

Signs of the erosion of solidarity can be found in changing patterns of raiding. During the interwar period, raiding changed from being a communal and public activity in which the majority of murran participated, though probably never all, to a private and clandestine one in which relatively few took a regular part. Il Tareto was the last age to mount large-scale coordinated raids (*injorin*).[144] Their successors shifted to "snatches" by small groups that were more stock theft (*empurrore*) than war (*enara*). In part, this shift was a natural response to the spread of colonial policing and was paralleled by changes in the patterns of stock theft elsewhere, but it also suggests both that raiding was becoming an act of defiance and assertion, rather than a sanctioned part of the process of group cohesion and identity formation, and that there were now wide variations in the experiences and expectations of individual murran. Although stock theft never became fully commercialized, there is some evidence from the late 1930s onward that individual murran were beginning careers as professional stock thieves. These were the "bad hats" that the administration was trying to remove from manyattas in the 1940s.[145] Some were probably sons from poor households who had limited prospects of inheritance, but others may have been either "diehards" or "bulls," murran for whom battle was the supreme test of virtue.

It is also worth considering whether violence was increasing during the colonial period. Were murran in fact behaving more like gangsters than warriors? Violence had always been a part of the world of murran. Indeed, it was their prerogative to take action if the community was threatened. Arusha murran had shed blood to cleanse their land in 1896, and Maasai murran may have had similar intentions when they attacked the government caravan in 1895 and "those who wear clothes" (i.e., Europeans and Indians) in 1922 and 1935.[146] This was legitimate, but other types of violence, against Maasai of allied sections, for example, were less so.[147] Several factors might have made outbreaks of violence more likely. The contraction of the boundaries of Maasailand brought adjacent sections and sirits closer together; and the disruption of the cycles of murranhood had a similar effect on relations between adjacent circumcisions and age-sets. Additionally, as they sensed that their honor was diminished, murran reacted violently to perceived challenges and felt justified in taking extreme action to defend what remained. This might explain the apparently spontaneous attacks on Buxton at Rotian in 1935 and a Moran Supervisor in 1952.[148] Changes in patterns of raiding may have altered norms of behavior. In the past, custom had protected noncombatants, and murran had kidnapped rather than killed women and children. Although it is difficult to know how far this reflects heroic narrative rather than reality—the brutality of murran on punitive expeditions shocked British officers—it is likely that small groups of clandestine raiders had less time for the niceties. Certainly, Kikuyu elders thought that Il Nyankusi murran in the 1940s had violated accepted norms, "murdering for amusement," as Chief Josiah Njonjo put it.[149]

Murran were not merely young, they were also male. Ethnography now rightly insists that we see pastoral societies as gendered, though colonial administrators seemingly did not. This raises questions about the construction of masculinity and how struggles over its definition should be included in studies of youth, especially in the context of gang machismo. It requires us to consider the role played by women and girls in the world of the murran and the shaping of its culture, for, as Spencer notes, each step in the maturation of men involves a transformation of their relations with women.[150]

There were two contrasting constructs of masculinity in Maasai, linked by the process of transition from murranhood to elderhood. One was the overt and brash masculinity of the murran; the other the more muted—but much more authoritarian—masculinity of the patriarch. Over their time as murran, young men were expected to learn respect, an important element of which involved proper relations with women, and to begin the shift from one register of masculinity to the other. Colonial intervention disrupted this transition. By curtailing and controlling murranhood, it struck at key aspects of young men's masculinity. Could murran who had never raided "properly" or lived in a manyatta still become men? Colonial ideas of proper manliness could encompass some aspects of murran masculinity—the disciplined courage of the past, the physicality admired by early travelers, or the comradeship that late colonial administrators hoped to co-opt—but not others. "Real men" were not idle, nor were their relations with women "vicious." Manyattas were first seen as places where disciplined masculinity degenerated into sexual license, and promiscuity was allegedly leading to the spread of venereal disease, infertility, and, ultimately, "race suicide." Disapproval was sharpened by the belief that the girls concerned were underage.[151] In fact, this lurid picture was somewhat wide of the mark and perhaps owed more to the affront that youthful sexuality offered than to any real knowledge of what went on. Even in 1948, when the age of female circumcision had been lowered, many of the unmarried women in the manyattas were sexually mature. Moreover, although casual sex was allowed, girls had recognized murran lovers whose honor was invested in their protection.[152] But they would not marry their lovers: they were destined to become the wives of older men, a sometimes traumatic demonstration of the power and prerogatives of age and of the superior claims of procreative masculinity.

Clandestine liaisons between murran and the wives of elders, however, challenged the subordination of youthful sexuality that marriage demonstrated. Adultery was doubtless partly bravado, but it could also be a weapon. It breached the rules of respect and the separation between entim and enkang that supported elders' authority in a way that exposed husbands to ridicule if they took public action, for the adultery of his wives undermined a man's claim to rule his household. In 1929, at the height of tension in Purko, a rumor apparently circulated that Ole Gilishu's intransigent attitude was due to the fact that, some years earlier, laiyok had slept with his wives in protest at his attempts to delay their circumcision. He had never forgiven the insult. Whether true or not, the story pointed a moral. The boys' action was both rash and unpropitious, but it was also a protest against what they saw as the selfish use of power and the denial of their rights.[153] Conflicts over sexual access to women sharpened intergenerational tensions between men but also emphasized the solidarity of age. Private knowledge of each other's adulteries strengthened bonds between murran; elders allowed visiting age-mates to stay with their wives. In discussions during the course of the 1930–31 medical survey, elders blamed the spread of venereal disease on the lack of sexual restraint by adulterous murran. Murran did not deny their adulteries, but argued that elders too were to blame because they gave their wives to age-mates.[154] Behind the moral outrage were larger issues. Elders claimed that adultery was on the increase due to the disbanding of the manyattas that kept young men in the bush and away from married women in the camps. Colonial intervention presented elders with a dilemma: forcing murran to retire prematurely might strengthen their control, but it also left them more open to sexual retaliation. For elders, then, the "dangerous period" after murran formally disbanded had a different meaning. In 1936, at a formal intergenerational meeting in Narok, Il Twati had to defend their wards against the anger of Il Tareto junior elders who accused the recently retired murran of seducing their wives.[155] Some of the wives would, however, have been "girls of the manyatta" until their marriages. For murran, hospitality might look more like communal appropriation, as elders took women from them and shared them with each other.

If murran remain in the shadows, the "girls of the manyatta" are virtually invisible. Despite its concern with murranhood, the administration paid little attention to the women who were part of it. The record shows men arguing with—and fighting—each other over women, but gives the latter neither agency nor individuation. Yet, women, as lovers and mothers, played an important role in the life of the manyatta and the culture of murranhood. Girls were both a focus of honor and an encouraging audience for its public assertion as murran sang of their exploits.[156] Married women managed the affairs of the manyatta and, as the wives of elders at home, were complicit in the rebelliousness of adultery. Neither women nor girls can have been merely passive spectators or victims in a male-dominated world, however coercive and unequal gender relations may have been. Spencer argues that it is women's "rituals of rebellion" as much as those of younger men that counter the corruption of patriarchal power, and he suggests that girls and their mothers in the manyatta acted as custodians of its ideals.[157] The colonial record gives us little tangible to work with, but it is worth asking whether young women themselves had a conception of honor, other than that derived from their lovers, and whether they shared the alienation felt by young men, for, if young men felt themselves subordinated in the colonial world, girls had even less control over their fate. The selfishness of age had a more direct impact on their lives as daughters and future wives, and they had good reason to celebrate and even encourage the defiance of the murran.[158]

Social and sexual disorder arose, as elders saw it, from lack of respect among the young. Indeed, murranhood was failing the expectations of all parties, albeit in different ways. This was not merely a crisis of maturation, but of age itself. Age organizations are highly resilient and adaptive to both internal and external pressures, but they cannot easily withstand the sheering apart of biological and social age and the selective excision or compression of one stage of "becoming."[159] By 1940, murran were younger, spent less time in manyatta, and retired sooner. Since their proper path to maturity had been blocked, they had less reason to learn respect and demonstrate restraint and less time to do so. By now, some young men may really have been delinquent, and murranhood had become what its critics had always supposed it to be, a dangerous anachronism.

Notes

Earlier versions of this paper were presented at the African Studies Association Conference in 2003 and in a workshop in Oxford in 2007. I am grateful to participants and to Tom Spear, John Lonsdale, and Andrew Burton for their helpful comments.

Maasai is the current orthography, but was written as Masai during the colonial period. I have kept the colonial orthography where necessary.

Note on Citations

Kenya National Archives:

Masai Province:

Annual Reports (MPAR): 1913–39 (vols. I–II): PC/SP 1/2/1–2, and (vol. III): DC/NRK 1/2/1; 1942–52: PC/SP 1/2/3.
Monthly Intelligence Reports (MPIR): 1933–37: PC/SP 3/1/1.
Handing Over Reports (MPHOR): 1936–52: PC/SP 2/1/1.

Kajiado District:

Annual Reports (KDAR): 1927–33: DC/KAJ 2/1/1; 1941–1952: PC/SP 1/5/3.

Narok District:

Annual Reports (NDAR): 1914–23: DC/NRK 1/1/1; 1925–34: DC/NRK 1/1/2; 1938: PC/NKU 2/1/14; 1939–52: DC/NRK 1/1/3.
Monthly Intelligence Reports (NDIR): 1939–45: PC Ngong 1/1/1.
Handing Over Reports (NDHOR): 1945–54: PC/SP 2/2/1.
Interviews are cited as M(aasai) T(ext)/M(aasai) with a sectional code.

	Damat (DT)	
5	Mure ole Kasino	Il Terito (R)
8	Katato ole Lekwarri	Il Terito (L)
	Loitai (LT)	
4	Kanjori ole Kisunyei	Il Terito (R)
7	Rankau ole Mashati	Il Terito (R)
13	Oloimoja ole Kikonya	Il Terito (R)
	Purko (P)	
1	Letuluo ole Dikirr	Il Tareto (R)
7 and 35	Ntiako ole Koonyo	Il Tareto (L)
8	Sakaina ole Koru &	Il Terito (L)
	Olorkisoi ole Nchoe	Il Terito (L)

20	Atteti ole Nkarara	Il Terito (R)
	Sironkei ole Nkoie &	Il Terito (R)
	Seiro ole Rakwa	Il Terito (L)
21	Nampararany ole Nabaala	Il Tareto (L)
25 and 39	Senjura ole Nchoe	Il Terito (R)
31	Rumpeni ole Yiankere	Il Tareto (L)
36	Ole Korongoro	Il Tareto (L)
40	Kerotare ole Nkuruma	Il Tareto (L)
41	Ole Paratet	Il Terito (L)

1. G. Sandford, *An Administrative and Political History of the Masai Reserve* (London: Waterlow and Sons, 1919), 129–30; Officer in Charge (OiC) to Chief Secretary (CS), 6 February 1916 and CS to District Commissioner (DC) Ngong, 30 March 1916, DC/KAJ 9/1/1/1, Kenya National Archives (KNA).

2. Most Maasai sections had both senior (right-hand) and junior (left-hand) circumcisions (initiation groups). The two merged into one age-set at a final ceremony after the end of murranhood.

3. Official accounts of events in MPAR (1918/19); NDAR (1918/19); Kings African Rifles (KAR) Intelligence Reports (KIR), September–December 1918, KAR 3/3/1, Malawi National Archives; Barth to Long, 15 October 1918, with encls., London, National Archives (PRO), CO 533/198; Sandford, *Administrative and Political History*, 73–81. Maasai accounts in MT/M/P21, 31, 35.

4. Exact casualty figures are unknown. Fourteen dead were left behind, but the retreating murran carried away all but one of their wounded.

5. There had been resistance to recruiting in Ngong District also, and both the new governor and Colonial Office officials thought that conscription had been a mistake, poorly conceived and motivated more by a desire to force the Maasai to contribute labor to the war effort than by any military necessity ("Recruitment into KAR," in Ngong Political Record Book [NPRB], Part A, DC/KAJ 1/2/1; minutes on Barth to Long, 15 October 1918; Northey to Milner, 30 April 1919 and minutes, CO 533/209). See also Berkeley Cole to Editor, *Leader of British East Africa*, 21 September 1918.

6. J. Thomson, *Through Masai Land* (London: Frank Cass, 1968), 243–61.

7. Purko had by far the largest number of murran, some seven hundred in 1952 in three sirits in the left-hand circumcision group and probably more in the five recently retired sirits of the right. Together, Purko and Keekonyukie accounted for nearly a third of approximately three thousand murran in Maasailand. No other section had more than five hundred, and the general average per section was half that. Figures for 1918 are slightly higher (Moran Officer's Handing Over Report [MOHOR], June 1952, Appendix C, KNA PC/SP 4/2/1; Sandford, *Administrative and Political History*, 6–7).

8. See, e.g., A. Burton, "Urchins, Loafers and the Cult of the Cowboy: Urbanisation and Delinquency in Dar-es-Salaam, 1919–61," *Journal of African History* (*JAH*) 42, no. 2 (2001): 199–216, and R. Waller, "Rebellious Youth in Colonial Africa," *JAH* 47, no. 1 (2006): 77–92. Negative images persist. For a trenchant critique of modern constructs of "lumpen" youth in pastoral societies, see D. Eaton, "Youth, Cattle Raiding, and Generational Conflict along the Kenya-Uganda Border," chapter 2 in this volume.

9. Introduction to A. Hollis, *The Masai* (Oxford: Clarendon Press, 1905), xvii; "Memo. on the Masai," and "Further Notes on the Masai," n.d., KNA, Native Affairs Dept. Mss, 19/iii/48.

10. P. Spencer, "Becoming Maasai, Being in Time," in *Being Maasai,* ed. T. Spear and R. Waller (London: James Currey, 1993), chap. 7. P. Spencer, *Time, Space and the Unknown* (London: Routledge and Kegan Paul, 2003), provides a vital ethnographic perspective.

11. For an illuminating discussion of colonial tradition making, see T. Spear, "Neo-Traditionalism and the Limits of Invention in British Colonial Africa," *JAH* 44, no. 1 (2003): 3–27, and also C. Ambler, "The Renovation of Custom in Colonial Kenya: The 1932 Generation Succession Ceremonies in Embu," *JAH* 30, no. 1 (1989): 139–56.

12. R. Waller, "The Maasai and the British, 1895–1905: The Origins of an Alliance," *JAH* 17, no. 4 (1976): 529–53. The best overview of the conquest period is still J. Lonsdale, "The Conquest State, 1895–1904," in *A Modern History of Kenya 1895–1980,* ed. W. Ochieng (Nairobi: Evans Brothers, 1989), 6–34.

13. R. Waller, "Emutai: Crisis and Response in Maasailand 1883–1902," in *The Ecology of Survival,* ed. D. Johnson and D. Anderson (Boulder, CO: Westview, 1988), 110–11.

14. A Masai Company of the KAR, established in 1902, was disbanded five years later, and the army remained skeptical of their suitability thereafter, having concluded that murran were too resistant to discipline and too lacking in "ambition" to make good soldiers (Eliot to Lansdowne, 20 March 1901, with encls. and minutes, PRO, FO 2/446; KAR Inspection Reports (1906 and 1907), PRO, WO 106/24; Sandford, *Administrative and Political History,* 73; NDAR (1946). For "martial races," see T. Parsons, *The African Rank and File* (Portsmouth, NH: Heinemann, 1999), 53–59.

15. F. Jackson, *Early Days in East Africa* (London: Edward Arnold, 1920), 201, 293–94, 329; Jackson to Lansdowne, 12 July 1902, FO 2/573. Eliot to Lansdowne, 9 April 1904, FO 2/835; *Report by HM's Commissioner on the East Africa Protectorate,* Cd 1626 (1903), 8. Eliot was not impressed by Maasai strength and thought his officials too partisan.

16. For the Maasai Moves and Treaties, see M. Sorrenson, *Origins of European Settlement in Kenya* (Oxford: Oxford University Press, 1968), and L. Hughes, *Moving the Maasai* (Basingstoke: Palgrave Macmillan, 2006). Ostensibly, the move was to prevent possible clashes between murran and settlers.

17. MPARs (1914/15–1918/19), vol. II; Sandford, *Administrative and Political History,* 60–65, 120; Hughes, *Moving the Maasai,* chap. 5, 174–75. Other sections also suffered, but it became an official commonplace that it was their memory of the Moves that made Purko particularly suspicious and difficult to administer (see, e.g., NDAR [1928] and NDHOR, February 1951). For a parallel, see D. Ellis, "The Nandi Protest of 1923 in the Context of African Resistance to Colonial Rule in Kenya," *JAH* 17, no. 4 (1976): 555–75.

18. Sandford, *Administrative and Political History,* 121. Three plaintiffs were Purko and five Keekonyukie, including their leading spokesman, Kairrak ole Saitaka (Civil Case 91/1912, ibid, 186 ff.).

19. Summarized in Sandford, *Administrative and Political History,* chap. 7. These were communal fines imposed under the Collective Punishment Ordinance (1909); the total does not include individual fines.

20. "Masai and the War," in NPRB, Part A. Between May 1917 and March 1918, Maasai also lost more than one hundred thousand head of cattle and a million sheep and goats to disease (Sandford, *Administrative and Political History,* 59).

21. Sandford, *Administrative and Political History,* 126–27.

22. For example, DC Ngong to OiC, 24 April 1916, DC/KAJ 9/1/1/1. For the organization of raids, see reports in same file. Browne, ex-DC Ngong, organized his own

armed Maasai followers when he was appointed Political Officer Arusha, and these were rumored to be raiding on their own account as well as operating under his direction (DC Ngong to OiC, 22 March 1916 and statement by Ndogo, encl. in DC Ngong to Military Intelligence, 15 April 1916, DC/KAJ 9/1/1/1; "Masai and the War").

23. MPAR (1915/16). Rifles had been haphazardly distributed in the first months of the war and then used on raids. In some cases it took the threat of police action and fines to recover them (DC Ngong to OiC, 22 March 1916 and reply, OiC to CS, 11 April 1916, DC/KAJ 9/1/1/1; Sandford, *Administrative and Political History*, 127).

24. Raiders also suffered losses in collisions with alert and armed defenders south of the border. It was rumored that only one of the first Matapato raiding party to cross the border had returned alive, and in July 1915 Sukuma handed in sixty-five Maasai heads, probably Purko and Keekonyukie, to the Germans (DC Ngong to OiC, 22 March 1916; P. von Lettow-Vorbeck, *East African Campaigns* [New York: Robert Speller and Sons, 1957], 65).

25. C. Hordern, *Military Operations: East Africa* (London: HMSO, 1941); Chief Political Officer, "The Administration of Occupied Territory in German East Africa," 1 December 1916, encl. in Byatt to Long, 2 January 1917, CO 691/4.

26. KIR, March 1919; memo by McCall, 24 September 1919, encl. in Hollis to Milner, 2 October 1919, CO 691/24. German policy had confined Maasai east and south of the Arusha-Dodoma road, leaving a large area south of the border vacant.

27. For the "War of Morijo" between the Purko and Loitai alliances and their rival prophets, Olonana and Senteu, see Waller, "Maasai and the British," 540–41. At least two threatened Purko attacks, fueled by the continuing power struggle between Senteu and the sons of Olonana, were averted, in 1917 and 1920 (NDAR [1920/21]; OiC to DCs, 22 March 1922 in NPRB, Part A).

28. MPAR (1918/19); KIR, September 1918, January, March, and May 1919; Northey to Milner, 30 April 1919; "Political Events of the 1920s," in NPRB, Part A. Murran in other sections were also retired by the end of 1920.

29. Native Affairs Dept., *Annual Report* (NADAR) (1918/19), CO 544/10.

30. DC Narok to OiC, 7 May 1922 and OiC to Chief Native Commissioner (CNC), (?) 6 May 1922, both encl. in Coryndon to Churchill, 19 October 1922, CO 533/283. A collective fine of ten thousand head was approved, but queried in London, and its collection was deferred (Devonshire to Coryndon 6 December 1922 and reply, 15 February 1923, CO 533/283 and 293).

31. CNC to Attorney General (AG), 17 October 1921 and OiC to CNC, 5 October 1921, KNA AG 25/17. Legal opinion was doubtful, especially about the proscription of meat feasts—"exceedingly draconic." The proposed legislation was watered down, and some subsequent prosecutions were quashed (Crown Counsel to CNC, 19 December 1921 and draft rules, ibid.; MPAR [1922]).

32. NDAR (1922). Some Maasai accounts attribute the defiant mood to harassment by "Koroja" ("Hump-back"—possibly Mood, ADC Mara Bridge), who chased and beat murran and broke up a meat feast by dragging women in and upsetting the soup (MT/M/P21, 31).

33. Summary of events in OiC to CS, 7 and 13 December 1922, DC/KAJ 9/1/1/1 and KIR, December 1922; Maasai accounts in MT/M/P21, 31, 35; NDAR (1923); MPAR (1922).

34. Bowring to Devonshire, 1 August 1923, CO 533/296; Coryndon to Thomas, 13 March 1924, and minutes, CO 533/309. Hemsted had wanted the murran treated as

outlaws and called for the use of Kipsikis levies to track them down. Even the Colonial Office lost patience—"hunt these people down ruthlessly" was one opinion—but later concluded that the Purko had been "hammered and fined out of all proportion" (OiC to CS, 7 December 1922 and CS to AG, 13 December 1922, AG 1/575; Bottomley minute on Coryndon to Devonshire 19 January 1923, CO 533/292; minute on Parliamentary Question, 10 March 1924, CO 533/322). For a critical view of government action, see "The Masai Scandal," n.d. in file G137, Anti-Slavery and Aborigines Protection Society (APS) Papers, Rhodes House, Oxford.

35. Most of those convicted of unlawful assembly were released after a year. Four accused of murdering a Kikuyu were convicted but had their sentences commuted to terms of imprisonment, and two who murdered a Goan trader received eight years each. The murderer of the police sergeant did not give himself up until 1926 and then received three years for manslaughter (*East African Standard,* 15 December 1923; Denham to Thomas, 14 August 1924 and encl., CO 533/312; papers in AG 1/575; Returns of Death Sentences, encl. in Coryndon to Amery, 4 January 1925, CO 533/328; NDAR [1926]).

36. MPAR (1921); CNC to AG, 17 October 1921, AG 25/17.

37. CNC to AG, 23 December 1921, AG 25/17; Sandford, *Administrative and Political History,* 57–58. Details of councils in NPRB, Part B, Native General, xi, DC/KAJ 1/2/2. They reproduced the hierarchy of age, but included murran spokesmen.

38. OiC to CS, 13 December 1922, DC/KAJ 9/1/1/1. Hemsted, however, had a low opinion of elders in general, describing them as "comatose, conservative, reactionary old men," a view that their juniors might well have shared (MPAR [1920/21]).

39. For example, see extract of letter from Parkinson, 14 September 1918, in CO 533/198; Bottomley minute, 7 December 1923, on Bowring to Devonshire, 1 August 1923; minute on Parliamentary Question file, CO533/322.

40. Minutes on Coryndon to Devonshire, 19 January 1923 and Parliamentary Question file, CO 533/292 and 322; *Masai Enquiry Committee Report* (Nairobi, 1926); "The Masai," *East African Standard,* 27 August 1926. The published report said little about the causes of murran unrest, ostensibly precluded from doing so by its terms of reference, and concluded that the uprising was due to "an excess of animal spirits" and had no wider significance. Unofficial members of the committee, however, claimed that witnesses had been pressured and evidence suppressed to exonerate government, and refused to endorse the report (*Report,* 2, 6, NADAR [1923], 5; Cooke to Goldfinch, 23 September 1924, APS Papers, G137; correspondence in file AG 1/576; *Legislative Council* [*LegCo*] *Debates* [1925], vol. I, 242 ff. and [1926], vol. I, 8 ff., 22).

41. *Enquiry Committee Report,* 4. In 1922, murran had killed an elder who "remonstrated with them" and seized his stock, and apparently threatened to kill chiefs and other elders (OiC to CS, 7 December 1922, DC/KAJ 9/1/1/1).

42. Calculated from returns in MPARs passim, vol. II. Technically, murran themselves had no property to attach (ADC Ngong to DC Ngong, 11 April 1916 and DC Ngong to OiC, 29 April 1916, DC/KAJ 9/1/1/1).

43. P. Spencer, *The Maasai of Matapato* (Bloomington: Indiana University Press, 1988), chap. 13.

44. In the mid-1930s, however, Samburu suffered equally savage reprisals for continuing murran violence, including a massive communal fine, a KAR patrol and the imposition of a Police Levy; see Samburu and Laikipia-Samburu Districts, *Annual Reports,* KNA DC/SAM 1/2; and P. Spencer, *Nomads in Alliance* (Oxford: Oxford University Press, 1973), 160–65.

45. H. Johnston, *The Uganda Protectorate* (London: Eyre & Spottiswoode, 1902), 2:798; Bowring to Devonshire, 1 May 1923; Sandford, *Administrative and Political History*, 2, 4; MPARs (1918/19, 1921, 1922).

46. Sandford, *Administrative and Political History*, 7; MPAR (1922); Lord Cranworth, *Profit and Sport in British East Africa* (London: Macmillan, 1919), 55, 58.

47. MPAR (1931). The OiC drew a comparison with Somali and Kalenjin, where arid conditions or land shortage made youth work hard.

48. See, e.g., "Important Meeting at Nakuru," *Leader*, 5 October 1918. Settler discourse had embedded in it a sharp critique of "Masai-maniacs," whose own wealth and privilege was reflected in their patronage and defense of the Maasai (see editorial, 27 September, and exchange between Cole and Clutterbuck, all printed in the *Leader*, 28 September 1918).

49. "Precis of Masai baraza," encl. in Grigg to Amery, 20 July 1926, CO 533/348. See also "Masai Pride: Masai Misfortunes: Masai Future," MPIR, October 1936.

50. NADAR (1927), 13.

51. In 1935, for example, the OiC gave two proscribed Keekonyukie manyattas the opportunity to "justify themselves by good works," and in 1937 the DC Narok reported that the Purko murran were being advised by their seniors that, if they wanted manyattas, they must "buy" them from government [by undertaking road work] (MPHOR, January 1936; MPIR, April 1937).

52. NDAR (1929); MPIR, April 1937. It was allegedly the latter who caused trouble.

53. DC Kajiado to OiC, 22 June 1932, DC/KAJ 2/1/5; Storrs-Fox to Lambert, 1 November 1932, DC/KAJ 2/1/7; NDAR (1934). There were sharp differences between administrators: Dawson had been sympathetic, but Jennings believed that allowing murranhood was "tantamount to recognising organised crime" (NDARs [1931, 1934]).

54. MPARs (1925, 1926).

55. NDAR (1934).

56. NDAR (1929) and pp. 145–46, above.

57. Details in file KNA, PC Coast 1/1/257; KDAR (1930).

58. Wade to Macdonald, 25 July 1935, with encls., CO 533/459/12; MT/M/P8, 20, 39. Two murran were killed and two wounded when police opened fire on the rioters.

59. Details in file KNA, DC Ngong 1/1/21. The situation was complicated by the facts that manyattas were permitted in Tanganyika and that the DC Narok did not have jurisdiction south of the border.

60. This also reflects significant differences in organization between "northern" and "southern" Maasai sections—discussed in Spencer, *Time, Space and the Unknown*, chaps. 7–8, esp. 197–201.

61. Much of what follows is summarized from the Moran Officer's reports in files PC/SP 6/2/1B & 2 and 4/2/1 (see p. 152, above).

62. Endungore had separated successive groups of coevals. In many sections, Il Terito was the last age to which it applied.

63. Storrs-Fox had thought that most were spending only four or five years as murran, but, increasingly, many were spending even less time in manyatta (D. Storrs-Fox, "Further Notes on the Masai of Kenya Colony," *Journal of the Royal Anthropological Institute* 60 [1930]: 451). For a different view, see Spencer, *Time, Space and the Unknown*, 213–16.

64. Premature elderhood, in which boys were, in effect, initiated directly as elders, had always existed as a response to exceptional household circumstances. It was anomalous and required specific approval, but "exceptions" were now multiplying as

sanctions against the practice weakened. Some murran were even marrying before retirement, their wives in some sections allowed to live in manyatta on sufferance and in others remaining at home under the control of their fathers-in–law (Spencer, *Maasai of Matapato,* 80–81, 172–74).

65. Moran Officer's Safari Diary, November 1948, PC/SP 6/2/1B.

66. See P. Spencer, "Opposing Streams and the Gerontocratic Ladder: Models of Age Organisation in East Africa," *Man* 11 (1976): 153–75.

67. Moran Officer's *Annual Report* (MOAR) (1950), PC/SP 6/2/2. In some respects, circumcisions were replacing age-sets in the structuring of murranhood.

68. MPAR (1921); Thomson, *Through Masai Land,* 258–59.

69. MPARs (1933–34), vol. III. Although the timing of initiation, promotion, and retirement had always been flexible, murran who joined the senior circumcision could once have expected up to six years before Eunoto and slightly more after. By the end of this period, the majority would be glad to move on into adulthood. Arguing in 1952 for a lengthening of the period of murranhood, Holford-Walker drew attention to the contrast between the Kaputiei murran, who, after ten years in manyatta, were demanding to be allowed to retire, and the situation in Purko where the elders' determination to hold Eunoto as early as possible and to force murran to retire immediately afterward had created turmoil throughout the 1940s (Spencer, "Becoming Maasai," 149–52; MOHOR, June 1952, chap. 3).

70. For example, see NDAR (1920/21) and KDAR (1933). Concern that the cessation of raiding might permanently blight the prospects of young men, especially those from poorer households, was long-standing (R. Waller, "Pastoral Poverty in Historical Perspective," in *The Poor Are Not Us,* ed. D. Anderson and V. Broche-Due [Oxford: James Currey, 1999], 35–37).

71. NDAR (1942); Moran Officer's Safari Diary, January 1949, PC/SP 6/2/1B.

72. MPAR (1924); NDAR (1928); MPIR, April 1937; MPARs (1936–37). Displays of bravado by layiok were a normal part of the impetus that moved age-sets up the ladder of seniority, but the premature retirement of murran created a void. A similar dynamic operated as a new group of murran proved itself against their seniors (Spencer, *Maasai of Matapato,* 68–70, 82–86).

73. Ngarabali was angry at being ignored but even more concerned at the mystical danger to his age if their Eunoto was held without the laibon's blessing. He died young, and it was believed that he had been cursed (MT/M/P21, 41; Spencer, *Time, Space and the Unknown,* 154).

74. MT/M/P1, 36, 39. Drinking milk alone instead of in the company of other murran marked the first step toward retirement. For its psychological impact, see Spencer, *Maasai of Matapato,* 174–75.

75. Ole Gilishu then withdrew in disgust. A man of great authority, his intransigence and bullying approach to guiding the murran lost him ground with both his age-mates and administrators, who disapproved of his "wild-cat schemes" to terminate murranhood permanently. He continued to advocate abolition and the disciplining of young men by their fathers at home, forbidding his own sons to join the murran. He may simply have believed that murranhood no longer reflected either the ideals of his own age or the needs of the present (MPAR [1929]; NDAR [1929]; NDAR [1938]; MPAR [1939]; MT/M/P7, 25, 41).

76. NDARs (1928, 1929). For a different resolution of a related dispute in Matapato, see Spencer, *Maasai of Matapato,* 101. For tensions in other sections, see, e.g.. MT/M/DT5, 8; MT/M/LT4, 7.

77. Such divided sentiments are evident in memories of the period. The governor appealed shrewdly to them in a speech to the elders at Ngong, announcing a new policy of tolerance: "Your young men ask for the same privileges as you yourselves enjoyed at their age. I ask you to consider what you would yourselves have done had these privileges been denied to you" ("Notes for HE's speech," 23 July 1941, DC/KAJ 4/1/1).

78. The size and strength of sirits would be reduced if boys were held back until the next age-set. Newly formed murran are remembered as taking direct action to prevent this by seizing laiyok and having them forcibly circumcised over the protests of their fathers (MT/M/P36; see also NDHORs, September and December 1947).

79. MPIR, June 1936; DC Kajiado to OiC, 1 June, with circular to chiefs, and 6 August 1936, DC/KAJ 2/1/7. Some elders were apparently prepared to have their sons circumcised in Kikuyu to avoid the ban. A decade later, however, it was sons themselves who went to Kikuyu to escape their fathers (DC Kajiado to OiC, 15 June 1936, DC/KAJ 2/1/7; Moran Officer's Safari Diary, January 1949).

80. NDAR (1929); MPIR, August 1936. See also Narok District, Monthly Intelligence Report (NDIR), November 1942; reports in files KNA PC/NZA 3/18/4/1 & 3/1318 (current reference unknown), and Stock Theft Enquiry Report, March 1943, KNA MAA 7/751.

81. KDARs (1932, 1933); DC Ngong to OiC, 12 April 1916, DC/KAJ 9/1/1/1; MPAR (1934); OiC to CS, 17 July 1936, DC Ngong 1/1/21; Moran Supervisor's Safari Report, March 1957, PC/SP 6/2/3.

82. See, e.g., minutes of Kajiado LNC, 30 June–2 July 1932 and 12 August 1932, DC/KAJ 5/1/2&3; KDARs (1939, 1946), PC/SP 1/5/2 and 3. These disputes arose from the emergence of defined sectional boundaries.

83. NDAR (1921); MT/M/P21, 35. The curse was not formally lifted until 1944 (NDIR, August 1944).

84. MT/M/LT4, 13. See also MT/M/P36, 40.

85. See R. Waller, "Kidongoi's Kin," in *Revealing Prophets,* ed. D. Anderson and D. Johnson (London: James Currey, 1995), 44–48, and Spencer, *Time, Space and the Unknown,* 102–4.

86. DC Narok to OiC, 2 and 3 April 1929, and "Kimuruai ole Lenana," 18 March 1936, KNA PC/NKU 2/15/24; DC Narok to OiC, 16 July 1935, and OiC to CS, 20 July 1935, PC/SP 6/2/1A. Kimoruai was suspected of involvement in the 1918 and 1922 Purko uprisings, as well as in the Rotian Riot of 1935. He was banned from Narok but never prosecuted (MPAR [1922]; NDAR [1929]).

87. Waller, "Kidongoi's Kin," 38–44.

88. KDAR (1930); DO Monduli to DC Kajiado, 10 February 1933, DC/KAJ 2/1/7; "Oruma ole Nelian," Appendix B in ADO Loliondo to DO Monduli, 23 June 1936, DC Ngong 1/1/21.

89. NDAR (1940). The OiC had his decision, and the elders' agreement, read into the LNC records (Minutes of Narok LNC, 28–29 November 1941, DC/KAJ 2/1/11).

90. MPAR (1946); NDARs (1944, 1946–47); Narok District, HOR, October 1946, PC/SP 2/2/1.

91. OiC to DCs, 30 December 1932, DC/KAJ 2/1/7; MPAR (1934); minutes of DCs Meeting, 1 February 1932, DC/KAJ 4/1/1; KDAR (1933); Kajiado District, HOR, December 1938, MAA 2/3/5.

92. Handing Over Notes, Masai Division, n.d. KNA, PC Ngong 1/18/7. In July 1949, a fight at the Kaputiei Eunoto was broken up by the Nairobi riot squad with armored cars summoned by telephone from Athi River (KDAR [1949]).

93. KDAR (1947); Moran Officer to DC Kajiado, 30 May 1952, PC/NKU 2/1/25; MOAR (1950); NDHOR, October 1946. Convicted stock thieves could be served with an order requiring them to report regularly to the DC or local chief.

94. NDHORs, March and October 1946; minutes of Narok LNC, 30 April 1942, DC/KAJ 2/1/11. A draft training scheme captured the new approach. Newly circumcised youths would be brought together under the eye of an ex-KAR sergeant-major for a month's camp where they would be put through a program of drill, bush-clearing, sports, lectures, and films. Ol piron would be on hand to instruct on tribal custom (Minutes of Narok LNC, 13 July 1945, KNA DC/KJD 3/4/1).

95. OiC to CS, 21 January 1947, MAA 7/705; minutes of Narok LNC, 23 January 1947, DC/KJD 3/4/1; KDAR (1947). The Purko elders' aggressive stance was not fully supported elsewhere, however. Kajiado representatives later told the DC that they had accepted the proposal—"Narok business"—only because they did not wish to oppose the Purko elders ("The Kenya Masai Moran," n.d., encl. in OiC to DC Monduli, 7 August 1947, MAA 7/705).

96. OiC to CS, 21 January 1947; NDARs (1946–47); minutes of Narok LNC, 17–18 June 1947.

97. NDIRs October–November 1940, February–March 1941; NDARs (1944–45). In 1943, the OiC, seriously concerned about the breakdown of law and order, had reluctantly requested extra police and advised that the elders' suggestion, that the murran be conscripted en masse, be considered if unrest persisted (OiC to CS, 15 April, with minutes, 12 May and 12 June 1943, MAA 7/735).

98. NDAR (1945); NDHOR, February 1945. Ole Sankale, now chief spokesman for Il Tareto, had been brought out of semiretirement to deal with the murran in 1944. He had allegedly been circumcised by force and later rejected by his fellow murran, and he may have held a grudge (MT/M/P21, 35, 36).

99. MOARs (1950–51) and MOHOR, June 1952, chap. IV; NDARs (1947, 1950); NDHOR, March 1946.

100. Such was the view of one Maasai assistant: "The influence of the elders is complete inertia. It looks from the face of it that Government is now the father and the ruler" ("Moran System: An Alternative Approach," n.d., KNA DC/NRK 3/1).

101. MOAR (1950); KDAR (1951); Kajiado District, Monthly Intelligence Reports, August 1951 and January 1952, extracts in PC/NKU 2/1/25; NDHOR, February 1945; Moran Officer to OiC, 6 May 1951, PC/NKU 2/1/25.

102. In 1950, less than a quarter of Narok murran lived in a manyatta, while in Kajiado the majority still did so. The position improved after murran were offered tax exemption if they resided in a manyatta, and elders were assured that manyatta herds would not be attached, as they feared (MOARs [1950–51]). Mothers looked after their murran sons and brought with them their unmarried daughters, who became the "girls of the manyatta" (see NDHOR, December 1947, MOHOR, June 1952, chap. II, and Spencer, *Maasai of Matapato,* 82–94).

103. For the conflict between parental and governmental control, see MOHOR, chap. III.

104. "Note on Policy to Be Adopted for the Oncoming Age of Masai Moran," 19 March 1941, encl. in OiC to DO Kajiado, 7 July 1941, DC/KAJ 2/1/7; minutes of Secretariat meeting, 1 March 1947, PC/NKU 2/1/12; MPARs (1947–48).

105. OiC to CS, 2 September 1947, and "Future of the Moran," encl. in OiC to CS, 29 September 1947, MAA 7/705; Clarke to Sweatman, 3 September 1947, PC/NKU 2/1/12.

106. "Note on Moran Policy," NDAR (1949), Appendix A; OiC to DCs, 4 October 1948, PC Ngong 1/8/1; OiC to CNC, 25 May 1951, MAA 7/705. Holford-Walker's view was, however, colored by the concerns of elders who gave him information.

107. A. Holford-Walker, "Masai Social Customs: Past and Present: The Moran System and Proposals for Its Control," 23 June 1949, Native Affairs Dept. Mss, 19/iii/206 and expanded in MOHOR, June 1952, chap. III; MPAR (1948); minutes of DCs' meeting, 29 December 1948, DC/KAJ 4/1/1; NDHOR, February 1951; OiC to CNC, 15 July 1952, enclosing MOHOR, MAA 7/705.

108. Minutes of Masai Council meeting, 22–23 February 1949, MAA 7/705; "Draft Resolution for Control of Moran," n.d., Native Affairs Dept. Mss, 19/iii/206; MPARs (1949–50).

109. Minutes of DCs' meetings, 6 December 1950 and 28 February 1951, DC/KAJ 4/1/1; extract from minutes of Masai Council, (?Jan.) 1951, Moran Officer to OiC, 6 May 1951, OiC to DCs, 5 September 1952, minutes of African District Council, Ngong, 18 December 1952, all in PC/NKU 2/1/25; MPAR (1952). The administration at first intended to override the refusal to lengthen murranhood but reluctantly accepted the elders' views (Minutes of Masai Council, 1951; Narok District, Monthly Intelligence Report, May 1951, extract in PC/NKU 2/1/25; OiC to DCs, 7 November 1952, PC/NKU 2/1/25; OiC to CNC, 8 April 1953, MAA 7/705).

110. The opinions of "young progressives" carried weight, perhaps because they made the case against murranhood in developmental terms, and it was their views that were later quoted by the OiC ("Note of a Meeting (26 September 1952) to Consider the Future of the Moran System," and OiC to CNC, 26 January 1953, PC/NKU 2/1/25).

111. OiC to CNC, 26 January 1953, PC/NKU 2/1/25. Not all shared his pessimism, however. See, e.g., Moran Officer to OiC, 12 and 14 October 1952, and DC Kajiado to PC Southern Province (the OiC), 10 August 1953, PC/NKU 2/1/25.

112. Elders' public decisions over murranhood might also be seen as rhetorical devices as much as statements of actual intent. See Moran Supervisor's Bi-Monthly Report, Narok, December 1953, PC/SP 6/2/1B.

113. MPHOR, March 1950. Its predecessor had been broadcast (KDAR [1943]).

114. Moran Officer's Monthly Reports, December 1952 and January–February 1953, PC/SP 6/2/1B. The laibons Kone and Musonik ole Senteu acted "brilliantly": both had previous convictions for providing murran with charms. In the same year, a thousand Samburu warriors, provided by the district administration, provided an exotic backdrop for Clark Gable and Ava Gardner in *Mogambo* (T. Gavaghan, *Of Lions and Dung Beetles* [Ilfracombe: Stockwell, 1999], 202–3).

115. The re-creation of murran as ethnographic objects recalls Fabian's comments on the kinship between anthropology and museums (J. Fabian, "Culture, Time and the Object of Anthropology," in idem, *Time and the Work of Anthropology* [Philadelphia: John Benjamins, 1991], 194–96).

116. "Moran System: An Alternative Approach," DC/NRK 3/1.

117. OiC to DCs, 30 December 1932, DC/KAJ 2/1/7.

118. R. Waller, "They Do the Dictating and We Must Submit," in *East African Expressions of Christianity*, ed. T. Spear and I. Kimambo (Oxford: James Currey, 1999), 83–126.

119. The best summary is in R. Tignor, *The Colonial Transformation of Kenya* (Princeton: Princeton University Press, 1976), 281–87.

120. Ibid., 284; Government Masai School (GMS) Narok, *Annual Report* (AR) (1941), Reports file, Narok School, seen by kind permission of the headmaster.

121. *LegCo Debates* (1925), vol. I, 244; Inspection Report: GMS Narok, March 1945, Miscellaneous file, Narok School; MPAR (1930); GMS Narok, *AR* (1941). Fathers were made legally responsible for their sons' school attendance and could be fined.

122. NDAR (1931). In 1933, only three of the sixty-three pupils at Narok were volunteers (MPAR [1933]).

123. Education Dept., Annual Report (AR) (1927), 53, 57; MPAR (1933). By 1930, three-quarters of the boys were under twelve (Report on GMS Loitokitok, 1929–30 in Education Dept., *AR* [1930], 56–57; DC Kajiado to OiC, 22 June 1932, DC/KAJ 2/1/5).

124. See, e.g., MPARs (1931, 1936).

125. DC Ngong, "Estimates for Kajiado School," KNA, Education Dept. Deposit 1 (current reference unknown), file 419/26; "Bringing Practical Education to the People," *East African Standard,* 27 August 1926; Tignor, *Colonial Transformation of Kenya,* 79, 282; MT/M/P1, 7, 8, 20, 25; D. Hodgson, *Once Intrepid Warriors* (Bloomington: Indiana University Press, 2001), 251–53. Narok GMS was not established until after the uprising (Bowring to Churchill, 3 July 1922, CO 533/279).

126. GMS Narok, *AR* (1923); MPAR (1933). Of about fifty ex-Kajiado GMS pupils in the district in 1931, only five had jobs. The principal was disappointed by their "lack of ambition and interest" (Kajiado GMS, Half Year Report, June 1931, Education Dept. Deposit 1, file 419/29). Some pupils became teachers, and, as the size and scope of administration expanded, there were posts for clerks and assistants.

127. See R. Waller, "Acceptees and Aliens," in *Being Maasai,* ed. Spear and Waller, 243–46.

128. NDAR (1936), copy in Buxton Papers, Rhodes House; MPAR (1936); DC Narok to OiC, 26 July 1935 and OiC to CS, 20 July 1935, PC/SP 6/2/1A. Buxton thought the first day of road work in May 1935 an event of "outstanding importance in the annals of the Masai" (DC Narok to OiC, 27 February 1936, PC/NKU 2/1/14).

129. Moran Officer's Safari Reports, November 1948 and February 1949, PC/SP 6/2/1B.

130. NDAR (1950); KDAR (1951). Elsewhere too, there were experiments with "traditional" forms of communal labor to similar ends, but a national youth service had to await the arrival of the nation.

131. For a useful discussion of gang culture, see C. Glaser, *Bo-Tsotsi* (Portsmouth, NH: Heinemann, 2000).

132. See, e.g., Spencer, *Maasai of Matapato,* 157; NDIRs, February–March 1945; Moran Officer's Report, October–November 1952, PC/SP 6/2/1B; KDARs (1947–48).

133. See, e.g., M. Merker, *Die Masai* (Berlin: Dietrich Reimer, 1910), chaps. 10–11.

134. Spencer, *Time, Space and the Unknown,* chap. 2. For honor, see J. Iliffe, *Honour in African History* (Cambridge: Cambridge University Press, 2005), and P. Spencer, *The Samburu* (London: Routledge, 1965), chap. 5.

135. P. Spencer, *The Pastoral Continuum* (Oxford: Oxford University Press, 1997), chap. 1; Tignor, *Colonial Transformation of Kenya,* 85–86.

136. The 1936 Kirtalu manyatta, as well as being beyond Kenya jurisdiction, was established in a strategic border area that Il Meruturut had occupied in 1918–19 and to which Purko still laid claim. The dissidents were thus asserting their spatial autonomy, their links with the past, and their determination to fulfill their duty as guardians of the grazing frontier.

137. In 1948, following clashes between Matapato and Kaputiei murran, the Kajiado LNC ordered that all manyattas were to be sited in the middle of sections, not on the borders (KDAR [1948]). See also Moran Officer to OiC, 23 May 1952, PC/SP 6/2/1B for conflicts over the siting of Loitokitok manyattas.

138. DC Kajiado to OiC, 22 June 1932, DC/KAJ 2/1/5. As the DC noted, however, the most humiliating measures had been relaxed by then.

139. Some songs have survived; see, e.g., Hollis, *Masai,* 352–56; MPIR, August 1937, Appendix.

140. NADAR (1929), 16; NDAR (1929); MPAR (1935). For KAR recruitment see Parsons, *African Rank and File,* 57–59, 96; Spencer, *Nomads in Alliance,* 163–64. Fewer than 250 Maasai served during the Second World War, compared with some 400 Samburu.

141. Spencer, *Time, Space and the Unknown,* 153. For an early description of murran debate, see J. Macdonald, *Soldiering and Surveying in British East Africa* (New York: Edward Arnold, 1897), 59, 68–69.

142. MT/M/P1, 7, 40. Others, however, like ole Saitaka, ole Pere's counterpart in Keekonyukie, encouraged their age-mates' defiance (NPRB, Part B, Native General, xiii).

143. "Diehards" were murran who took the Spartan aspects of the ethos of murranhood to extremes and formed a small enclave in the manyatta, apart from its conviviality. They found it particularly hard to make the transition to elderhood and perhaps had most to lose from curtailment and reform (Spencer, *Maasai of Matapato,* 125–27).

144. For injorin, see J. Berntsen, "Pastoralism, Raiding and Prophets: Maasailand in the Nineteenth Century" (PhD diss., University of Wisconsin, 1979), 240–52.

145. NDHOR, February 1945. Professional stock theft requires a fuller discussion elsewhere.

146. T. Spear, *Mountain Farmers* (Oxford: James Currey, 1997) chap. 3; Northcote to Amery, 26 May 1925 and encls., CO 533/331; DC Narok to OiC, 16 July 1935 and [chiefs] to DC Narok, 1 July 1935, PC/SP 6/2/1A.

147. Waller, "Emutai," 78, 80.

148. DC Narok to OiC, 16 July 1935, PC/SP 6/2/1A. In June 1952, the Supervisor and two policemen were attacked by two hundred Narok Keekonyukie murran. The incident occurred just before the Keekonyukie Eunoto when the sirits from Narok and Kajiado had established manyattas close to each other. The night before, the Narok murran had allegedly planned an assault on the Kajiado manyatta ("Assault on Moran Supervisor" and NDIR, July 1952, PC/NKU 2/1/25).

149. R. Meinertzhagen, *Kenya Diary* (Edinburgh: Oliver and Boyd, 1957), 66–69; extract from Kiambu LNC Minutes, 21–23 August 1944, in Champion Report, February 1946, MAA 7/736. See also ibid., Report, Findings, MAA 7/736, and Mathu to CNC, 16 January 1950, PC Ngong 1/8/2. For views of what constituted permissible violence on raids, see Kikuyu-Masai Border Committee Minutes, 7 October 1947, PC Ngong 1/8/2, and papers in *R. v. Sironga ole Kindi and 3 Others,* esp. Assessor's comments, and DC Narok to Executive Council, 28 December 1952, KNA MLA 1/454.

150. D. Hodgson, "Gender, Culture and the Myth of the Patriarchal Pastoralist," in *Rethinking Pastoralism in Africa,* ed. D. Hodgson (Oxford: James Currey, 2000), 1–28; Spencer, *Maasai of Matapato,* 7.

151. MPARs (1921, 1931). A 1931 medical survey thought gonorrhea "probably universal" among Maasai ("Dr. Philip's Medical Survey of Masai Reserve," draft copy in

CO 533/416/3). For the connection between sexuality and disease in colonial moral discourse, see M. Vaughan, *Curing Their Ills* (Stanford: Stanford University Press, 1991), chap. 6.

152. Moran Officer's Monthly Reports, passim; Spencer, *Time, Space and the Unknown,* 152–53. For a later and more sympathetic view of murran as adolescents rather than deviants, a view that critiqued the narrative of promiscuity and infertility, see memo by Fosbrooke, Tanganyika Government Sociologist, "Abolition of Moran System as Suggested by Kenya," 2 March 1953, MAA 7/705.

153. NDAR (1929). The liaisons crossed the line drawn by circumcision and were dangerously anomalous, like the pregnancy of uncircumcised girls. Some informants denied the story.

154. "Philip's Medical Survey," CO 533/416/3 The OiC came to the conclusion that disease was spreading because murran were giving up the custom of cohabiting with young girls and were being infected by married women instead. Fosbrooke thought that the problem lay partly with the age disparity between elderly men and their much younger wives (MPAR [1931]; "Abolition of Moran System," MAA 7/705).

155. MIR, September 1936.

156. For example, see Spencer, *Samburu,* 125–27.

157. Spencer, *Maasai of Matapato,* 7, 113. See also idem, *Time, Space and the Unknown,* 35–37, 43–50. This is not to deny the high levels of sexual predation and violence associated with gangs, but to look beyond victimhood in order to recover agency. See L. Thomas, *Politics of the Womb* (Berkeley: University of California Press, 2003), and B. Shadle, *Girl Cases: Marriage and Colonialism in Gusiiland, Kenya, 1890–1970* (Portsmouth, NH: Heinemann, 2006).

158. There is little in the literature, but see M. Llewelyn-Davies, "Two Contexts of Solidarity Among Pastoral Maasai Women," in *Women United, Women Divided,* ed. P. Caplan and J. Bujra (Bloomington: Indiana University Press, 1979), 206–37; B. Straight, "Cutting Time: Beads, Sex and Songs in the Making of Samburu Memory," in *The Qualities of Time,* ed. W. James and D. Mills (Oxford: Berg, 2005), 269–77, and T. Chieni and P. Spencer, "The World of Telelia: Reflections of a Maasai Women in Matapato," in *Being Maasai,* ed. Spear and Waller, 157–73. Telelia was born c. 1913.

159. See R. Waller, "Age and Ethnography," *Azania* 35 (1999): 135–44.

7

Youth, Elders, and Metaphors of Political Change in Late Colonial Buganda

CAROL SUMMERS

"THE YOUNG AFRICAN," argued Robert Kakembo in a 1946 pamphlet calling for sweeping changes in Uganda, "will no longer tolerate the old out-of-date chiefs. They must give room to the young generation."[1] In his progressive vision of Uganda's politics, modern "youth," qualified in new ways, were agitating against senior leadership and for new opportunities. Late colonialism, for Kakembo as for colonial officials, experts, and church leaders, was an era of youth, which Kakembo described with blunt and modern metaphors: "We are born in a queer age—an age of speed; it is a flying age. We are very impatient, because we want to grow overnight. We want to get the steering of our country from the old shaky faltering hands, and drive away at a break-neck speed. It is all right—it is a quality of all things young. We shall only learn by making mistakes. . . . That is the opinion of the African young men of today."[2]

Reading Kakembo and a variety of other Ugandan, missionary or official observers of the simultaneously hopeful and perilous "break-neck speed" of the 1940s, youth seems a natural analytic category, a metaphor used by historical actors to interpret conflict as the growing pains of adolescence. Here, though, I seek to complicate simple ideas of youth. I briefly explore the idea of Buganda as a young or "adolescent" nation, an idea that was proffered in late colonial Buganda by missionary and official actors as well as by specific Ganda activists. I then reread Kakembo's metaphors in a specifically Ugandan context by looking at patterns of Ganda politics and historical tales to show how Ganda social thinkers had at least two additional, alternative ways of thinking about the metaphor of youth—ways they continued to use during the turmoil of the 1940s and 1950s. The first of these provided an internal logic for the "Bataka Union," as activists saw youth as politically significant through their integration into a community of clan members as inheritors and stewards, responsible for communal resources. Youth inherited not just individual fates, but the community itself from "old shaky faltering hands" that had once been strong but could no longer steer. Second, in uniting to demand the return of Mutesa II as kabaka during the crisis of the

1950s, Ganda loyalists drew on a model of youth, particularly the youth of the king and the elite, as a volatile, dangerous time of struggle that—far from being simple delinquency—allowed for both the emergence of brilliant individuals and a cyclical strengthening and remaking of the kingdom. Kakembo's invocation of "break-neck speed" and his statement that "We shall only learn by making mistakes" simultaneously acknowledged the dangers of this disruptive struggle and its creative necessity.

Together, the existence of these three models—the developmentalist one of adolescence and the alternative Ganda ideas of youth as heirs or challengers—complicates any vision of youth as a straightforward category. Instead, the category's heterogeneity suggests questions about how a variety of historical actors used the idea of youth for their own social ends. This study of assumptions encoded in the metaphor of youth thus encourages us to think about the history of youth as an intellectual and cultural history, rather than a description of what youth did. And this sort of history may offer new insights into changes and continuities in values and power in a specific historical context.

Liberal Colonialism and Buganda as an Adolescent Nation

During the 1930s and throughout the 1940s, British officials, missionaries, and even some Ganda activists, referred to Buganda as an "adolescent."[3] In doing so, they responded to the challenges of a difficult time: the men who had made the alliance between Britain and Buganda in 1900, as young men, were aging and sometimes dying, but not retiring gracefully.[4] The country's wealth and its leaders' investments in schools and governance meant that a rising generation of young men were ambitious and saw resources available for their visions of individual and group progress. Thus, as the Anglican bishop of Uganda complained, "[T]he Baganda are in a very difficult adolescent period . . . [e]merging from childhood where they were willing to be controlled but not yet having reached sensible thinking manhood."[5] The bishop's vision of history was perhaps too rosy in its evocation of a past paternal guidance, but he sought to explain a turbulent present. In a time of national adolescence, the slightest of causes could trigger disorder—the queen mother's marriage, for example, or upheaval at Budo school. The label "adolescent," applied to both "the Baganda" as people and "Buganda" as a nation, offered a relatively blame-free explanation for why a model colony where the Baganda once administered themselves prosperously, effectively, and at minimal if any cost to the British exchequer, had become unexpectedly turbulent: turmoil was a sort of growing pain.[6] And the metaphor of adolescence suggested hope that such turbulence was finite and would end with the adolescent achieving maturity and the ability to stand alone, independent and self-supporting. For the bishop and the British officials who deployed the term, these were important connotations. For the Ganda activists such as Robert Kakembo who also adopted it, ideas of an adolescent Buganda offered a way to legitimize rebellion and opposition to British guidance. An adolescent, after all, is more than a child. He or she knows more, understands more, and is on the verge of adulthood and maturity. Adolescents achieve maturity, moreover, not through the dutiful obedience and acceptance of subordination of a client, but by rebelling, pointing out injustice, seizing resources, and developing the experience to hold their new positions, sometimes by "making mistakes." Adolescence was a stage on the path to self-determination, self-sufficiency, and independence.

The power of adolescence as a progressive trope—a way of reconceptualizing the relation of colonizer and colonized from parent/child to master/apprentice or journeyman with an emphasis not on control and nurture, but on preparation for adult responsibilities and autonomy—comes through clearly in the time of colonial stress when, between the Great Depression and the aftermath of the Second World War, Britain's position in Uganda was vulnerable rather than powerful. The power of adolescence as a metaphor—its ability to provoke rethinking of racial and colonial institutions, relationships, rights, duties, and futures—alerts us to the significance of some of the metaphors that Baganda thought with as they debated the kingdom's power structure, moral values, and networks of patronage, clientage, and obligation.

Unlike the language of child and parent, phrases intuitively obvious and classically a part of politics and philosophy in discussions by such theorists as John Locke, the term adolescence came from the social science-based pastoral and caring professions of the early twentieth century, and it carried a gloss of modernity and precision. Early users included activists in religious education and the Sunday school movement in Britain and the United States, who faced the problems of instilling moral values and independent selves in modern urban youth.[7] Secular experts on educational sociology were also prominent, delineating "the adolescent" as a problem addressed in a substantial literature of research, textbooks, books, book reviews, and policy implications.[8] The idea of adolescence was a response to the increasing inadequacy of more conventional, romantic, and conservative ideals of patriarchal family life, maternal guidance, and child rearing. It acknowledged a need for policies to cope with physically mature, but unmarried, youth as individuals, rather than as sons and daughters, husbands and wives, or fathers and mothers. And it implied that though state and church policy was an important factor, the youth must also be involved in the learning and developing of new, modern, self-based maturity. Furthermore, from its origins in the Child Study movement of the 1890s onward, advocates such as G. Stanley Hall explicitly saw the maturation of an individual and the maturation of a society or nation as parallel processes that followed the same distinctive format.[9]

A specific, distinctive metaphor—"adolescence"—thus offers us an array of questions and possibilities to explore in seeking to understand not just specific policies of late colonialism, or the interests that actors pursued, but what was thinkable. Metaphors, especially metaphors that involve basic social categories, are very much worth taking seriously. Contextualized, they offer potential insight into past mentalities, ways that contemporaries understood basic social values, goals, and processes.

This chapter is part of a larger project on radicalism in Buganda from 1939 to 1956, and I was originally entranced by colonial leaders' metaphor of adolescence. The significance of adolescence in Buganda as a way of explaining and neutralizing the political, social, and economic clashes of late colonialism suggests the power of metaphors in a context where they have not been much studied. The image of adolescence that the bishop and others invoked is a telling one, offering hints of a specific challenge to conventional images of a parental colonial authority and a childlike African population. Historians of colonialism have explored the paternal images of the antislavery movement and liberal imperialism and noted the pervasive conceptualization of Europeans as adults and Africans as children in multiple genres, all of which make clear the huge gulf and great deal of work and guidance between childhood and adulthood.[10] The image of adolescence reshapes conflict from childish ingratitude to a stage of maturation. Like the Maasai *murran* described by Richard Waller, youth was disruptive to specific colonial policies. But liberal colonial actors did not see this as a challenge to colonial hierarchies.[11]

Even as images of adolescent Ugandans and an adolescent Ganda nation both legitimated and defused tensions between Ugandan subjects and their colonial parents, they de-legitimated conflicts that broke this model, such as those among senior men who demanded rights and protections rooted in precedent. If social parenthood was to be progressive, it must be assigned to colonial authorities, educated men, and experts. The senior men who bemoaned lost land, honor, rights, and values became political fossils, irrelevant to the new Uganda, no matter how modern their methods or critiques of specific policies. Major historical figures such as Apolo Kaggwa and Semei Kakungulu struggled with British constraints in the 1920s. And a more ordinary elder who condemned life in the 1950s compared to the days of his youth was reinterpreted by a *ggombolola* chief as "when the old man was young people had few needs. When they did want anything extra, they just went to Bunyoro and robbed someone. Now they cannot do that."[12] The elder's complaints about the effect of markets, of immigrant labor, Indian middlemen, and problems with inequitable land ownership disappeared in the new analysis, and the elder appeared only as a reflexive reactionary disgruntled by law, order, and progress. Even Sir Apolo Kaggwa, radically innovative and political in his heyday, was dismissed by a protectorate government that characterized him as obsolete, sick, and backward.[13]

"Adolescence" as a concept had little to do with real young people on the verge of adulthood. It was part of a vision of how social change paralleled individual maturation. It legitimated one set of progressive hopes and struggles for a modern Uganda, and de-legitimated politics rooted in indigenous histories. It was not, however, the only metaphor for social change or values in circulation in Buganda, or even the only metaphor that invoked ideas of youth. As my project has moved from straightforward examination of official documents and mission materials to explorations of security files, anthropological fieldwork, and writings by Ugandan intellectuals and activists, I have remained convinced of the power of ideas of adolescence but come to acknowledge that the idea—though occasionally adopted by elite Ganda in communications with the church or the protectorate—was only one of several ways in which Ganda used very distinctive ideas of youth and generation to rethink politics, political values, and possibilities for change. The colonial metaphor of adolescence, and indeed the entire colonial framework of progress, blocked recognition of other ways Ugandans in this period understood power, politics, and change. As we explore the metaphors and *mentalité* of a historical context, it is important to look not merely at a dominant, colonial-sponsored vision but also at some of the dissident ways other actors thought with and used alternative visions and metaphors of youth—ideas that involved fundamentally different understandings of time, maturity, rights, and inheritance.

During the late colonial era, a time when youth was repeatedly invoked by a wide range of social and political actors, it had more than one potential meaning. Despite the resonance of the image of adolescence in the colonial literature, Ganda, trying to explain the challenges and changes of politics and society, deployed at least two alternative and fundamentally different ideas of youth that deviated from the liberal model of progress and maturation of the individual self. These two alternatives offered very different ways of thinking about politics and morality. Reconstructed from the translated and mediated phrases of Ganda activists, notes of anthropological fieldworkers, and other highly suggestive but far from definitive sources, these alternative metaphors offer glimpses of just how culturally specific and radical seemingly natural categories such as "youth" and "change" can be. For at least some Baganda, their ideas of youth fit not in developmental models of the maturing youth or progressive nation but in Ganda visions of time—a time of continuities marked by the stewardship and inheritance of grandfathers and grandsons within patrilineal clans (Bataka), and a time of disruption and individual ambition associated with the life cycle of kings.

The Bataka movement of the 1940s, explicitly invoking ideas of grandfathers and grandsons, used the distinctive idea of intergenerational alliance between elderly stewards and youthful heirs to oppose the greed of fathers. It offered a powerful critique aimed less at British overrule than at the "progressive" leaders of colonial Buganda. And, alternatively, Ganda understood what it meant to be a kingdom under a kabaka who would inherit while young, greedy, potentially violent, experimental, and almost certainly dangerous: with each king-centered cycle, they could expect the king's youth to open the kingdom to new influences and changes as it had in the time of long-ago kings, and more recently the reigns of Muteesa I, Mwanga, Daudi Chwa, and Muteesa II. Upheaval, conflict, innovation, and violent change constituted no linear development toward progressive kingship, or disintegration of local authenticity, but part of a classic pattern of cyclical kingship that drew on the life cycle of the king to reconstitute and renegotiate the kingdom's social contracts and associations on a regular basis. Muteesa II, like Daudi Chwa, Mwanga, and Muteesa I before him, inherited not smoothly and benignly, but with turmoil and civil unrest that eventually provoked a remaking of the kingdom. In looking beyond the real youth of colonial Uganda, or conventional ideas of youth as progressive or disruptive forces in the twilight of an era, we can see the creativity of alternative politics in the kingdom, alternative visions of time, generation, and change that survived the colonial encounter, and allowed people to continue to think creatively about what should be, rather than drawing entirely on Northern models of progress and ideas of linear change.

Grandfathers, Grandsons, and the Bataka

During the 1940s, radical Ganda activists in the Bataka movement developed a modern mass politics, drawing on ideas of the corporate rights and responsibilities of Buganda's clans, but developing them into a new politics and a new model of Ganda citizenship.[14] They published newspapers, had mass meetings of thousands, developed a "Buganda National Anthem," reconstructed personal associations with a greeting and chant of "BU" (Bataka Union), and communicated their new consciousness within the group in youth organizations, choirs, covert networks, and fundraising appeals, and to the world at large through sponsoring Ssemakula Mulumba as a lobbyist in London, writing regular petitions and briefings for Protectorate and Colonial Office officials, and attempting to reach beyond the British Empire with overtures not simply to the kings of Ankole and Toro but to the Khedive of Egypt, the foreign minister of the Soviet Union, and the trusteeship council of the United Nations. Both the scale and tactical modernity of the movement was impressive, and, somewhat shaken, British intelligence officers and officials became the Bataka Union's most enthusiastic duplicators and translators, collecting and analyzing telegrams, petitions, speeches, spy reports on meetings, and Luganda language newspaper reports. The movement reached a public high point in the 1949 unrest, which provoked its banning, mass arrests and trials for its leaders and associates, more intelligence efforts to sort out what the people sought, and changes in the Bataka Union's rhetoric that led British analysts in the 1950s to see the group not as a form of early, progressive, Ugandan nationalism, but as a reactionary and incoherent collection of the disgruntled and wronged.[15]

The enthusiasm of the Protectorate's intelligence efforts, though, combined with the systematic anthropological work of colonial anthropologists, provides an opportunity to look more carefully at the actual message the Bataka of the 1940s generated—who they were and what they sought. In their own speeches, telegrams, petitions, and publicity materials, Bataka activists identified themselves repeatedly as grandfathers and grandsons. This was no accident: it was a set of claims about youth and generation that had a particular moral force within Ganda politics. Grandfathers, both real and imaginary, laid claims not simply to age and respect, but to economic wisdom and stewardship. Within the context of Buganda in the 1940s, the men who called themselves grandfathers and chided the young about politics, land sales, and betrayal, stood for a vision of Uganda's economic and social life as something that must be nurtured and sustained, not invested in, developed, or consumed. In the famous (banned) 1944 pamphlet *Buganda Nyaffe,* one self-identified grandfather chided the country's fathers and asserted, "[I]t is your responsibility to preserve this land which should not be fragmented until you depart from it and bequeath it to your grandchildren. . . . Money is easily expended and exhausted whereas our native land remains permanently."[16] *Buganda Nyaffe* went on to caution Baganda about the dangers of betrayal. The real risks, the pamphlet asserted, were not from the British, but from Baganda who cooperated with them, working as their "dogs" and pets in controlling the people and seizing their resources. The Bataka party managed to assert legitimacy and citizenship in both "traditional" and democratic ways by emphasizing that as a member of a clan, each Muganda had both rights and obligations, rights as inheritors of their grandfathers' land and resources and obligations to pass those resources on to the future. These rights and obligations came from the Bataka—the clans and people—rather than being given (and potentially curbed) by the king and bureaucracy. They were not a vision of "human rights" in the Northern sense, but certainly a version of human dignity in a culturally specific metaphor.

Bataka leaders called for a politics of grandfathers and grandsons that resonated with older Ganda visions of family, moral responsibility, and good behavior and went beyond any simple colonial dichotomy of "tradition" and "modernity." Living grandparents, such as Jemusi Miti, whose house was an important gathering point, provided legitimacy to activists, as they remembered a time before clan resources had been seized by those in the Buganda government who did deals with the Protectorate. Ancestors and figurative grandparents were ways of emphasizing how the resources of the country belonged to all, as everyone had grandparents, was a member of a clan, and should expect to receive something as an inheritance that they would, in their own turn, pass onward.[17] Grandparents were thus the people's guarantors.

Like the metaphor of grandfathers, the trope of grandsons, also at the core of the Bataka movement, carried substantive emotional weight. Grandsons were the inheritors of the clan and the hope for the future. But they could be good heirs for the family, as opposed to advocates for themselves, only if they were properly raised, fostered in the homes of their grandparents, shown affection but also discipline and the need for service, and taught manners that marked them as members of patrilineal clans (Bataka), rather than simply as ambitious individuals. Grandsons were important because they were vulnerable and malleable and thus able to function as resources and representatives of their clans.

A politics of grandfathers and grandsons was thus very different from one of fathers and sons. Fathers were distant and could be harsh disciplinarians. And they were often seen as struggling for their own positions—marrying, acquiring offices, developing estates. Sons, in surveys during the 1950s, regularly expressed nervousness and fear of their fathers. Traditionally, fathers had good reason to fear their sons as well, as sons pressured fathers for tuition, resources, and help that took away from a mature man's efforts to establish himself and enjoy his status and success. A politics of fathers and sons was thus a politics of competition, consumption, and demands, as both father and son sought resources, used those resources to build their own status, and made demands on the other for help, labor, and respect. It was also a politics of individuals. Grandfathers and grandsons, as political figures if not always in reality, represented benign cross-generational inheritance, cooperation, and nurture. They emphasized the power of the clan and society—Bataka—rather than the achievements of specific individuals. And they stood for a sort of power and politics that preserved human and material resources rather than consuming them in a struggle for individual prosperity, achievement, or change.

In the context of the British protectorate of Uganda, the politics of grandfathers and grandsons was indeed radical, as it condemned the greed of elite Baganda who cooperated with the British and governed Uganda, called for protection of the people's inheritance, and evoked a vision of the future rooted in Buganda's history (reinterpreted as democratic) and not British paternalistic ideas of progress. They repudiated two concepts essential to Protectorate rule: first, that Baganda were simply subjects of the kabaka and chiefs rather than citizens and members of a Ganda community; and second, that Baganda should be guided toward modernity and progress along British models. If we take the metaphor of grandfathers and grandsons seriously, we as historians thus gain a glimpse of a Ganda historical consciousness and politics that challenges standard assumptions about nationalism, socialism, citizenship, politics, and legitimacy. It offers a vision of democratic participation rooted not in opposition to colonialism and Northern power, but in an indigenous oppositional tradition of community, stewardship, inheritance, and respect.

Young Kings

Thinking about the British metaphor of adolescence illuminates colonial visions of Ugandan independence and exploring the Bataka's metaphor of a politics of grandfathers and grandsons offers insights into a local vision of rights, obligations, and citizenship. If we wish to understand Ganda ideas of innovation, restructuring ,and national power, though, it is appropriate to look at another major metaphor of generation in Buganda, that of the kabaka/king, in the context of the normative life cycle of a monarch. By looking at how sometimes-violent intense competition, struggle, and ruthless ambition were part of the socialization of individuals into both achievement and service to the king and state, we see how Ganda rejected the Northern model of vulnerable or delinquent youth in favor of a less developmental model of competitive achievement where children and youth's actions and responsibilities paralleled those of adults. Results, rather than chronological age, were all-important as observers assessed specific patterns of violence, aggression, and self-promotion. The violent struggle of the young, and especially of young kings, was a routine stage of the succession, worked out temporarily in the process of a king's maturation with the expectation that upheaval and renegotiation can be expected to recur as his kingship passes to a successor. This violence, though, was understood not simply as stage to endure but also as a time of opportunity and creativity for ambitious men.[18]

"Traditional" normative ideas of child rearing among elite Ganda families beyond the Balangira (princes) differed radically from the psychology- and social science–influenced ideas dominant in the North and used by British officials when they invoked ideas of paternalistic colonialism or late colonial adolescence. Instead, Ganda norms taught even very young children about the absolutely central importance of relationships, manners, and hierarchies, and did so not by emphasizing nurture and affection, but by making negative sanctions—both from adults and other children—crystal clear. Successful Baganda men reminisced in their life histories about the elaborate hierarchies children built and enforced. Joswa Kivu, an important 1940s radical, described how in his youth he had lived in the household of his aunt, where about thirty boys of ages of six to seventeen organized intricate structures while herding. "We elected our 'chief' by show of hands or shouting," he remembered, "and other chiefs were appointed under him. . . . 'Commoners' built grass huts for our chiefs, but every boy had the right to build himself one also. I was seven years of age at the time, but I was chosen as the Sabawali of the fourth chief in order of rank. All complaints had to pass through me before they were heard by our leader. Although I used to hear cases, I had no power to give judgment. After I had listened to the case I had to refer the matter to the chiefs above me who were allowed to pass sentence."[19] Nor was this simple playing. Children as officials judged cases, took responsibility for the loss of goats, allocated work, and even organized "fighting games," not casually, but with kings, generals, and officers. Kivu's memoir emphasized, above all else, that children made their own social worlds, worlds with real consequences. Kivu's elaborate memories fit well with descriptions of growing up in ambitious chiefly households from other members of Buganda's elite. W. P. Tamukedde, for example, was proud of being named for his grandfather, an important military leader, benefited from his father's status as a *ggombolola* and eventually *ssaza* chief, and early on expressed an interest in following in such illustrious footsteps, so that his father bought two hundred acres of land for Tamukedde when the boy was only eight years old, automatically making him a *mutongole* chief—a real one—at a markedly young age. Tamukedde emphasized that, though his father appointed a steward, "as I grew up I took keen interest in the affairs of the village and in the chiefship as a whole." The young Tamukedde was further trained for office and status by being sent to live in the household of Prince Suna, where he was disciplined in proper behavior.[20] Both Kivu and Tamukedde also attended school, but their real training was as children fostered to an important household and holding practice (and real) offices.[21]

Audrey Richards's team of anthropologists at Makerere pushed these sorts of anecdotal notes further with a survey of children and those who worked with them at some of Buganda's most elite schools. Their results delineated an approach to raising responsible children that was markedly rigorous and unromantic but widely understood as essential within Buganda's elite society. A sampling of 177 boys indicated that 54 percent of Baganda boys had been sent away from home (for fostering) before their twelfth birthdays, leaving at varying ages grouped around seven or eight, and spending an average of more than three years away from home. Richards interpreted this to mean that they had been sent away as part of early training and character formation before their years of schooling (which often took place in boarding schools). And of those who offered an opinion, 88 percent of the boys sent said that their fostering was a good thing. They had learned and experienced more of the world, becoming members of their families (probably patrilineage/*mutaka*), and not simply possessions of a mother and father, or beloved babies.[22] Richards's respondents in the 1950s saw fostering and moral training as something of an old tradition that was fading. And they regretted its loss. One survey respondent from the elite Catholic school St. Mary's Kisubi complained that "[today's youth] are being spoilt by being let so loose—being treated in a European way. They even freely use their father's chairs."[23] Harsh discipline was particularly important in the raising of elite boys. One rebellious girl at Gayaza school complained bitterly about her family's treatment of her, but voiced the conventional sentiment about boys: "Boys were accepted [*sic*] to learn hard works. To stand at attention when talking with a person old than himself and better still to kneel."[24]

Growing up, elite Baganda children experienced more than simply herding goats or serving their aunts, though. They also went to school. Schools, though, continued very culturally specific patterns of youth organizing and responsibility that occasionally resembled British models (e.g., prefects, debate teams, scouting, sports) but above all reinforced basic Ganda lessons about hierarchy, group membership, and competitions. Hierarchies within a given school might differ from those outside its bounds—Tamukedde, for example, gleefully remembered how Prince Muteesa, soon to be crowned as Muteesa II, had swept his cubicle for him at King's College, Budo[25]—but they were carefully delineated by youth who understood ranking and hierarchy as real and worthwhile, whatever their attitude toward the British colonizers. A 1941 Budo school club that called itself "Nazi" (it was recognized as legitimate by school sponsors as it asserted that "Nazi" meant coconut in Kiswahili, and that its members were interested in boxing and social activities, not politics) nevertheless apparently felt the need to organize around officers (unfortunately titled "Hitler," "Himmler" and "Goering") and seek official school recognition.[26] And school clubs of a more respectable variety offered clear and smooth connections with the adult world of work and officialdom, connections emphasized by both the Old Budonians and the Old Boys of Saint Mary's Kisubi, clubs of elite school alumni with powerful social and financial connections.[27]

Autobiographies of the elite, and materials from surveys intended to ferret out information about Ganda ideas of leadership training, provide a vision of what it meant for a child to mature in Buganda which differed starkly from the vision implied in the literature on adolescence, of a youth seeking to find himself at a time between childhood and adulthood, with uncertain status and fragile economic resources. Elite Ganda youth, at least in "traditional" terms, had no business being adolescents or even children. Instead, they were on a clear route to the connections, roles, and responsibilities that enmeshed them in clan, social group, patrons, and competitors, within which they would define themselves for their entire adult lives. They were junior adults, not different in kind from their seniors, simply not as far along the path.[28]

Without the Northern view of children as helpless, needing protection, nurture, and guidance to mature as moral and social individuals, Ganda norms for elite youth seem to have expected levels of violence, sexuality, volatility, and ambition that sometimes shocked and dismayed Christian missionaries. Ganda seniors, despite the occasional grumbling about what youth were up to, seem to have understood violence, sexual activity, and ambition as ordinary and expected among elite youth. Such practices and attitudes did not block a future of achievement and power and might indeed foreshadow success. The structure of kingship, with a regular pattern of succession by a young king who rocked the kingdom and only with maturity settled down, seems to have adapted to and perhaps taken advantage of this vision of elite youth volatility as normative rather than a violation. Pulling together comments on this from surveys, one of the East African Institute of Social Research (EISR) researchers noted that they had effectively been told repeatedly that "[w]e sink all differences and support the king because, though he may be a nasty young man, he represents Buganda. . . . [we] condoned, and even admired, the Kabaka's cruelty, not just because anything he did was legitimate, but rather because the absolute, common end was the expansion of Buganda and a fierce Kabaka served and embodied that end."[29]

Drawing their examples from precolonial history, stories of Buganda's past have observed repeatedly that not only was the succession period after the death of one king and before the installation of the new one dangerous as a time of no law,[30] but the period of the young king was also potentially rocky, likely to be full of military action, sexual alliances, and innovations in the kingdom's structures and relationships. In the process, a successful young king, like Muteesa I in the nineteenth century, could expand his kingdom geographically and demographically in conquering new lands, capturing clients, cattle, and women.[31] He could kill his brothers as potential rivals, and demand women from the clans of Buganda and from among the captives of his wars. And he could renegotiate basic structural elements of the kingdom—not simply things such as who held what office, but the balance of power between clan heads and appointed chiefs, structures of taxation, land allocation, education systems, and trading initiatives. Muteesa I, who reigned from the mid-1850s until his death in 1884, was perhaps the best exemplar of the idea of kings as dangerously innovative and able to use the innovation and volatility of youth in their early years but shifting to other means as they aged. Muteesa's youth was popularly remembered as so violent and disruptive that he had to apologize to his people, change his name, and begin to marry his sisters off to his clients as an unprecedented form of compensation.[32] Those years, though, allowed him to deal successfully with Swahili traders and European missionaries, importing new weaponry to simultaneously modernize the kingdom's armaments and make them pay by allocating guns to elephant-hunting adventurers such as Semei Kakungulu.[33]

While Northern anthropologists and historians have emphasized the bureaucratic structure of the Ganda kingdom, Ganda historians both academic and popular have emphasized the ways in which succession and inheritance of young kings remade the kingdom with each generation, avoiding any calcification. In Kiwanuka's history, wars of expansion (mostly against Bunyoro) and succession (between brothers) shaped a pattern of kabakaship that demanded any kabaka be a warrior, not simply a statesman. Successful warfare, further, allowed a new king to reward his followers with the new lands and loot of conquest, putting together a corps of chiefs and officials to counterbalance the grandfathers and Bataka elders who held older areas of the country and subscribed to older norms.[34] Expanding kingdoms, too, offered new opportunities that leaders took advantage of. Kiwanuka noted the implications of early conquests by Ssakabaka Mawanda and Junju, which seized control over rich iron deposits and skilled ironworkers. Buganda's fighters also conquered lands with cattle, which could be easily distributed among the winners. And beyond the tusks of elephants in conquered areas, the king acquired the power to grant permission to hunt them, for which applicants paid. Even new manufacturing skills arrived in Buganda as a result of these conquests—not just better ironware, but better barkcloth, new grains to supplement *matooke,* and so on.[35]

And all this warfare and its spin-off innovations both economic and social—even in the nineteenth century, as sources improve—was associated in the minds of Ganda observers with youth. An anonymous Ganda author wrote a particularly articulate discussion of this, citing his father, and concluding that Buganda needed war when:

1. "the country was in poverty or needed more cattle";

2. "the country had lots of young men who might cause trouble, the way to get rid of them was to declare war; some would be killed and others would return back rich in cattle and women which they have plundered from other tribes";

3. "if there was a rival chief with Katikiro [prime minister] whom he wished to get rid of he may cunningly suggest to Kabaka to declare war and give command to that rival young man; if he returned he would become a good man as he would be rich enough; if he died that would be the easiest way of getting rid of him";

4. "if there was a new chief who was not rich enough the Katikiro might suggest to the Kabaka or even the Kabaka might appoint him as a General to raid a tribe and if he was successful he came back rich with cattle and women.

   "I may add here that at present [1950s] Uganda is in time where many young men are badly in need of getting rich quickly this would have been appropriate time—in older days to make a war to any tribe in order to get rid of the most ambitious young men or to make them rich if they were successful in the war."[36]

Of the stated reasons for war, all but one (chiefs who were not rich enough) were explicitly or implicitly associated with youth and succession. And Ganda elders who remembered their years in the civil war under Mwanga's explicitly violent and disruptive rule were remarkably mild in their assessments of those years and of Mwanga's prospects as a king. Reverend Bartolomeyo Zimbe, for example, despite being a Christian who described with pride both how he had participated in the end of the slave trade and given up a chiefship in favor of the ministry, offered a description of the young Kabaka Mwanga that differed starkly from critical historians' observations: Mwanga, he argued, had been a very good friend to the kingdom's young men. In Zimbe's history, Mwanga was a violent but promising young ruler who struck out against the Christians because they threatened to remove the young men whom he saw as key to his establishment of control. Zimbe acknowledged that Mwanga was violent—beating Apolo Kaggwa, sending the youth that was "second in command of the palace" off to be castrated when he failed in his obedience, and ordering a killing of the young boys who "learned religion" as they were causing trouble and in effect rebelling against the kabaka.[37] But Zimbe also remembered that Mwanga sent out young raiders who despoiled even grandparents, and after successful raids established *bitongole* chiefships of young men, clients of Mwanga, rather than his father, mother, brothers, or sisters. "We the young men indeed had freedom during this reign," Zimbe recalled. Even when Mwanga needed a general, he was sensible enough to consult his soldiers rather than precedent. Despite all the destruction and warfare Mwanga's violence unleashed, Zimbe emphasized that "[t]he fact that Kabaka Mwanga was brought back to his throne three times is a very sure sign of the love for him."[38] And (somewhat to the anthropologist's dismay) Mwanga, and the love people had for him, came up repeatedly in interviews about the deportation of Muteesa II in the 1950s. Muteesa II was widely viewed as "just like Mwanga" in a variety of ways—unable to love, violent, hanging around with the young, and unable to get on with elders, but also a man with "shining eyes" so that one could not look away.[39]

Violence, sexual adventurism and abuses, and genuine failures of judgment were part of what one expected in a young king, and like it or not, they were not understood by most Ganda observers as a reason to depose the king or change the system. Ganda observers, both in the time of Mwanga and of Muteesa II, rejected the sorts of prudery and disciplined standards put forward by Northern missionaries and government agents. Instead, they saw young kings, in all their violence and misrule, as the remaking of the kingdom. And a kingdom without this time of violence, exuberance, and experimentation was a fearsome prospect—it would be controlled by old men and dwindle in old men's schemes and conservatism. The chaotic violence of the transition meant both generational turnover, and individual opportunity. Mwanga's civil wars provided the context for Semei Kakungulu, Apolo Kaggwa, and others, to emerge as powerful, innovative leaders. In the turmoil around young Muteesa II's exile, activists from across the political spectrum, from Amos Sempa to E. M. K. Mulira, Apolo Kirondo, and others struggled to emerge as the new spokespeople and leaders of Buganda. The turmoil of a young king's reign—which encouraged selfishness and ambition, separated individuals and families, and foregrounded martyrs and diplomats—was important to the kingdom in ways that were distinct from the visions of stewardship and continuity put forward by Bataka and activists who emphasized grandsons as the inheritors of their grandfathers' resources and the hopes of their families.

In turmoil and danger, actual or political warfare, young men in a time of new kings vied for offices and scrambled for economic resources. In pursuing individual goals, they often trampled on the larger collectives of elders, clans, and families. In Mwanga's time, Semei Kakungulu, Apolo Kaggwa, and others remade Buganda. In Mutesa II's time, Kivu, E. M. K. Mulira, Ssemakula Mulumba, Apolo Kironde, Ernesiti Kalibala, and many others sought to do likewise not as delinquent adolescents (a category that made no sense in the context of Ganda tolerance for hierarchy, violence, sexuality, and ambition among the young) but as individuals whose visions were not simply ones of collective national benefits, clan solidarities, and tradition, but of achievement, respect, position, and leadership—making names for themselves in ways that would position them as the great men of their generation.

Thinking with Youth

Youth and generational change are categories that historians and anthropologists often consider obvious and natural. We think we know youth when we see it. And we assume that the problem of generational change is fairly universal in a species that is born, socialized to maturity, and socializes the next generation to inherit. This set of assumptions about the "naturalness" of a category is very similar to the assumptions historians once made about sex and gender: it exists and is basic. Even within Northern models of the life cycle, though, ideas of youth, parental power, and change may be reshaped by the rise of new social science ideas of institutions and of the value placed on self-formation and individuality as opposed to family roles. Liberal imperialists thus found in modern visions of adolescence an ideal progressive metaphor for the tumult of Ugandans' politics as Baganda rejected ideas of colonial paternal guidance. The metaphor of adolescence allowed them to fight—if they even perceived—the creativity and diversity of Ganda activists' initiatives as the Bataka invoked indigenous models of community and inheritance, rights and responsibilities in a vision of popular ownership of a democratic nation with long historical roots. And it privileged order—a progressive order at that—over the intense ferment, uncertainty, danger, and opportunity that Baganda had historically associated with young kings and dynastic transition.

When I first started looking at Ugandan history, back in the 1980s, I was struck by the way colonial officials, missionaries, and Baganda discussed gender and sexuality. Missionaries in particular were intent on seeing women and sex as either being good—promoting effective motherhood and nurturance within basically monogamous relations—or bad and shameful. Baganda, though, and the colonial officials they influenced, proved remarkably resistant to the Northern-style moralizing of basic gender and sex categories. My early work on syphilis suggested some of the reasons why such an obvious, natural set of categories about women and sex failed to translate directly into Ugandan policy.[40] And my more recent look at Eastern Ugandan women suggested that colonial and mission categories of women could be rewritten in a context where local realities challenged Northern images of women's essential characteristics.[41] Here, I suggest that another equally simple, obvious, and natural category—youth and generation—suffers from similar problems. An analysis in which youth or adolescents are understood as inherently timeless even while times change risks missing the creative contestation over the category itself.[42] Instead therefore of marking out good youth (progressive, nation-building, education-oriented, innocent/uncorrupt, and productive) versus delinquent youth (violent, selfish, destructive, far too numerous, and poor), it is more interesting to ask how else we can think about youth and generation, drawing on local, indigenous models, and paying close attention to the politics and values delineated with our models of what youth is, should be, and can achieve.

Above all, though, in looking at youth through the eyes of liberal imperialists, Ganda activists, and historians of Ganda kingship, I see metaphors and ideas of youth that differ so radically that they fundamentally undermine any effort to see youth as a natural category with logical and straightforward consequences. Even efforts to produce a slightly more complicated model—looking at youth as alternatively progressive and hopeful to those seeking a just and democratic future, or as disruptive, violent, and demanding, undermining order and producing chaos—fail to fit the historical perspectives described above. Instead, perspectives on youth from Buganda included the colonialists' progressive ideas of adolescence that emphasized the individuality of Ganda actors in a time when Ganda politics was emphasizing integration and cooperation against the British. One of the most democratic and reformist threads of Ganda politics emerged through an explicit linking of grandsons and youth to elders and the community of Bataka, rather than to progressive and individualistic colonial politics. And the historical narratives offered by Baganda from a variety of generations rejected childhood and youth as a protected category of vulnerability in favor of seeing it as potentially, in a context of kingship, a sort of violence that shaped individuals' competition and ambition into forces that ultimately strengthened the king and Buganda's resources as a state, in opposition to the moral and communal connectedness of the clans and family.

Few actual youth show up in this essay. Here, I have written about metaphors, ideas, ideals, and concepts of social order. Partly, this is for a practical reason: when I have written specifically about individuals portrayed as youth, I have often been unable to determine how old they actually were. But even in autobiographical narratives of individuals such as W. P. Tamukedde or Joswa Kivu, where individuals born to Christian families did know their ages, and offered memoirs of maturation that make it possible to work out the individual's age at a given time, chronological age often failed to fit social age in terms of employment, responsibilities, status in family and inheritance, and so on. Thus Joswa Kivu was born in 1895, inherited his father's lands and became a chief at age ten, organized a successful strike as a schoolboy, worked as a county chief's clerk when he was fifteen, and subsequently enrolled at King's College Budo, where he was considered rather young. After a varied career, he "decided to become more active in politics" in his thirties, while working as a driver in Kampala, and was a major force in the 1945 general strike (especially in his telling of events). Though arithmetic suggests he was fifty by the time of the strike, he was nevertheless a leader of young men and something of a youth himself compared to senior men such as his uncle, Jemusi Miti.[43] There seems to have been no dramatic transition between childhood and adulthood, as adult responsibilities and resources arrived early, his involvement in politics and labor began before his teens, and his status as a client of senior men persisted into his fifties. W. P. Tamukedde, born a generation later in 1919, described a similar trajectory of important responsibilities begun early and a status as a client that persisted even into his years as a chief and authority.

Real youths, as individuals, were important to history. But they were important as Muteesa I, Mwanga, Apolo Kaggwa, Muteesa II, Joswa Kivu, W. P. Tamukedde, E. M. K. Mulira, and so on. The category of youth connected to these men's lives and historical significance only occasionally and tactically, and often for those who were not especially young, be they colonial missionaries, educators, officials, or Ganda activists.

The concept of late colonial Buganda as an adolescent nation is a vivid one for historians today, just as it was for progressive Ganda activists and colonial planners in the 1940s and 1950s. But it is not a simple, natural, or hegemonic metaphor able to illuminate all aspects of the political turmoil of late colonial Buganda. Baganda—and Ugandans—have deployed multiple ideas of youth and generation as they have both proclaimed and challenged their country's policies and political leadership. Youth, adolescence, and generation, like gender, must be understood by historians as political labels with varied associations used by constituencies who may contend violently as they use these concepts to mark out "natural" qualities and moral expectations.

Notes

1. R. Kakembo, *An African Soldier Speaks* (London: Edinburgh House Press, 1946), 44.

2. Ibid.

3. For examples, Bishop of Uganda to the Archbishop, 30 October 1943, and Cyril Uganda, "The Budo Disturbance" [undated], CMS Archives, Birmingham University (hereafter CMS), G3 A7 d1, G3 A7/e 1; Denis Herbert [headmaster, Budo school] to Hooper (CMS), 15 May 1943, CMS G3 A7/e 1; Ssemakula Mulumba to Bishop Stuart, 26 July 1948, Fisher Papers, 49:380–88, Archbishop of Canterbury's archives, Lambeth Palace.

4. Efforts by specific British officials, such as acting Provincial Commissioner J. R. P. Postlethwaite, to encourage retirements could provoke articulate rejections at the

highest levels. See, for example, Kabaka Daudi Chwa to Mr E. B. Jarvis, 9 January 1926, A/G Box 259, London, School of Oriental and African Studies, Council of British Missionary Societies Archives (hereafter CBMS), which complained that Postlethwaite was "too anxious to get rid of my old and trusted Chiefs and Advisors . . . and he even exhibits open dislike towards them. His present policy appears to be the wholesale dismissal of my old chiefs and the appointment in their place of his young native favourites, he advocates this principle so openly that naturally all the young educated natives flock round him, while my old and important chiefs naturally avoid him. In order to further his policy he has shewn marked favour towards all and sundry young educated as well as uneducated natives; and in certain instances he has even gone as far as to invite them to tea and to discuss with them all the confidential and important matters affecting the Native Government of Buganda and then promise to secure them appointments or promotions to some of the most important posts in the Native Government. . . . I have every reason to believe that there is no question or subject of a confidential nature affecting the Native Government, which he discusses with me or my Ministers, which he does not disclose to his young native friends, with the natural result that all the important questions affecting the policy of the Native Government are talked about in the streets even before we have had time to discuss or deal with them in the Lukiiko. From the foregoing, it is quite easy to understand that this policy is the direct cause of the endless trouble and difficulties which confront me and my Ministers in the matter of appointment or promotion of my chiefs."

5. Bishop of Uganda to the Archbishop, 30 October 1943, CMS G3 A7 d1.

6. In Buganda, after all, the British protectorate was established in the Uganda Agreement of 1900, a treaty effectively negotiated by a faction of the Ganda elite to end the civil war. And in the early years of British Uganda, Ganda administrators, generals, clergy, teachers, and even traders had been prominent in administering not simply Buganda, but the protectorate as a whole, especially in the north, in Bunyoro, and the east. The most successful examples of this were Jemusi Miti in Bunyoro, and Semei Kakungulu in the east. See J. Miti, "History of Buganda," English version, Files 1–3, Makerere University Library AR MI 8/3; M. Twaddle, *Kakungulu and the Creation of Uganda* (London: James Currey, 1993).

7. For U.S. examples, see N. Richardson, ed., *The Religious Education of Adolescents* (New York: Abingdon Press, 1918); J. L. Alexander, *The Sunday School and the Teens: The Report of the Commission on Adolescence (authorized by the San-Francisco Convention of the International Sunday School Association)* (New York: Association Press, 1913), and J. L. Alexander, *The Teens and the Rural Sunday School, Being the Second Volume of the Report of the Commission on Adolescence* (New York: Association Press, 1914). British sources include Edward Arthur Burroughs (Bishop of Ripon), "Education and Religion," a course of lectures given in the Bristol Cathedral, 1924; E. F. Braley, *Sir Hobbard de Hoy: The Religious Education of the Adolescent* (London: Macmillan, 1920).

8. A cursory search on WorldCat or JSTOR identifies enough of this literature to make it clear that any professional educational policymaker in the English-speaking world of the 1930s or after would be exposed to the central concept of adolescent, and the notion of managing it as a dangerous period of human development. See, for example, "Report of the Consultative Committee on the Education of the Adolescent" (London, 1926) and the articles and book reviews of publications such as *The American Journal of Sociology, Child Development, Social Forces,* and the *Journal of Educational*

Sociology. Sociologists' materials went to a wider interested audience in textbooks and journals such as *Scientific Monthly* and *School Review*.

9. David Leary, personal communication, June 2006.

10. An obvious example is Rudyard Kipling's "White Man's Burden"; and I discuss mission paternalism in colonial Zimbabwe in C. Summers, *From Civilization to Segregation: Social Ideals and Social Control in Southern Rhodesia* (Athens: Ohio University Press, 1994), esp. 262–63.

11. See preceding chapter, Richard Waller, "Bad Boys in the Bush? Disciplining Murran in Colonial Maasailand."

12. A. I. Richards, interviewing the "old man" in the presence of the chief, 3 February 1951, Mutuba III, AIR Fieldnotes from Busiro land survey, London School of Economics, Audrey Richards Papers (hereafter LSE, Richards Papers), 6/18.

13. See the correspondence in Public Record Office, London (PRO), CO 531/141.

14. On the moral significance of grandfathers and grandsons in the politics of the 1940s, see C. Summers, "Grandfathers, Grandsons, Morality, and Radical Politics in Late Colonial Buganda," *International Journal of African Historical Studies* 38, no. 3 (2005): 427–47. This discussion draws on my analysis in that piece.

15. D. Apter, *The Political Kingdom in Uganda* (1961; London: Oxford University Press, 1997), 124. The published literature on the Bataka movement is thin and rests principally on D. A. Low's work and his anonymous journalism for *The Times* (of London). Low had the advantage of proximity to events. See D. A. Low, *Buganda in Modern History* (Berkeley: University of California Press, 1971), and D. A. Low and C. Pratt, *Buganda and British Overrule, 1900–1953* (London: Oxford University Press, 1960). Scholars such as T. V. Sathyamurthy, *The Political Development of Uganda: 1900–1986* (Aldershot, UK: Gower, 1986), 300–346, and S. R. Karugire, *A Political History of Uganda* (Nairobi: Heinemann Educational Books, 1980), 123–70, offer little hint of additional sources. Working with other sources now declassified, my articles on the Bataka include "Grandfathers, Grandsons," cited above; "Radical Rudeness: Ugandan Social Critiques in the 1940s," *Journal of Social History* 39, no. 3 (2006): 741–70; and "Young Africa and Radical Visions: Revisiting the Bataka in Buganda, 1944–54" (2004 draft paper, presented in various seminars). G. Thompson's *Governing Uganda: British Colonial Rule and Its Legacy* (Kampala: Fountain Publishers, 2003) covers the same time period, but with a very different focus.

16. D. S. K. Musoke, "Buganda Nyaffe, 1944," in *Mind of Buganda*, ed. D. A. Low (Berkeley: University of California Press, 1971), 119.

17. For an indication of just how powerful this expectation was, see the negotiations over the Uganda Agreement of 1900. Even in the act of making the Agreement (which was subsequently seen as a betrayal by many Baganda) the kingdom's leaders explicitly noted the need to preserve land and resources for the youth who married and, by implication, their children (The Regents of Buganda to F. J. Jackson, 16 January 1900, in Low, *Mind of Buganda*, 35).

18. See Richard Reid, "Arms and Adolescence: Youth, Warfare, and Statehood in Nineteenth-Century Eastern Africa," in this volume for a discussion of the vigor and violence associated with Kabaka Mutesa I's youth and more broadly with other successions to youthful kingship.

19. J. Kivu, "Autobiography," LSE, Richards Papers, 6/16.

20. W. P. Tamukedde, "My Life as a Chief and a District Commissioner," in *Uganda's First Republic*, ed. A. F. Robertson (Cambridge: Cambridge University Press, 1982), 53–75.

21. Ibid.

22. These statistics are not rigorous. Variability from school to school was huge (at Aggrey Memorial, for example, boys were generally sent away at three to five years of age, for around three years). Their value is that they hint at assumptions and understandings about childhood and training that differ markedly from bourgeois Northern norms, more closely resembling British aristocratic or elite ideas ("Discipline and Attitudes to Authority in Buganda Schools" 4 February 1956, LSE, Richards Papers, 6/26).

23. Survey response, St. Mary's School Kisubi. Respondents ranged from nineteen to twenty-three years in age. Of the thirteen respondents, twelve agreed with the notion of disciplining children sharply because punishments "made better characters" (LSE, Richards Papers, 6/27).

24. Florence Namulier, Gayaza, survey response [1956], LSE, Richards Papers, 6/28. Other girls also discoursed on the importance and enforcement of kneeling.

25. Tamukedde, "My Life as a Chief and a District Commissioner," 55.

26. See, for discussion, C. Summers, "'Subterranean Evil' and 'Tumultuous Riot,' in Buganda: Authority and Alienation at King's College, Budo, 1942," *Journal of African History* 47, no. 1 (2006): 93–113, esp. 107.

27. I discuss this more in C. Summers, "Catholic Action and Ugandan Radicalism: Political Activism in Uganda 1930–1950," *Journal of Religion in Africa* 39, no. 1 (2009): 1–31.

28. They fit better, in other words, with the image of young children as simply small adults that P. Aries, controversially, applied to the "pre-modern" world in *Centuries of Childhood: A Social History of Family Life* (New York: Vintage, 1962). This characterization potentially applies to girls as well as boys, though evidence for girls is scantier, and sexuality and potential fertility were probably more central to girls' efforts to establish status in new marriages and elite polygynous households. See, for hints of this, Nakanyike Musisi, "Women, 'Elite Polygamy' and Buganda State Formation," *Signs* 16, no. 4 (1991): 757–86.

29. Comments (L. A. Fallers?) on "The Political Values of the Ganda," LSE, Richards Papers, 5/15 (undated, c. 1953). The commentator emphasized that fighting against a kabaka—such as Mwanga during the civil war—did not seem to have been considered illegitimate. People did not see a kabaka as inherently special. They demanded results. And if they did not receive them, in loot, for example, they sought a new king.

30. Such statements were probably reflections of fears and ideology, not reality, but they were voiced and recorded by anthropologists even before the kabaka crisis gave them a new relevance. See, for example, L. Mair, *An African People in the Twentieth Century* (New York: Holt, Rinehart and Winston, 1934, 1965), 178. See also Richard Reid, "Arms and Adolescence: Male Youth, Warfare, and Statehood in Nineteenth-Century Eastern Africa," chapter 1 in this volume.

31. H. Hanson, *Landed Obligation: The Practice of Power in Buganda* (Portsmouth, NH: Heinemann, 2003), esp. 78–104, describes the expanding kingdom, and the ways conquest and loot transformed relations within the elite hierarchy of king and chiefs, and the wider web of the elite's connection with ordinary people. The centrality of young kings to this expansion can be seen in M. S. M. Kiwanuka, *A History of Buganda: From the Foundation of the Kingdom to 1900* (New York: African Publishing House, 1972), which emphasized the succession conflicts as important in restructuring the kingdom in the nineteenth century.

32. See, for example, A. Kalule Sempa, "A Short History of Buganda at the Advent of Whitemen," 23 July 1954, Sir (William) Keith Hancock Papers, 29/1/6, Institute of Commonwealth Studies (hereafter Hancock Papers, ICS), London, Sempa argued that when Mutesa I became king he was cruel and self-important, but "for a new King cruelty might have been the only recourse by which he could break in reactionary tendencies on the part of some of his subjects, for later on, after he had gained control . . . , he changed his name to "Mutesa" meaning Peace-maker." See also Rev. Bartolomayo Musoke Zimbe, "Buganda ne Kabaka: Ebyafayo Eby'obwa Kabak bwe Buganda" (Mengo: Gambuze Printing and Publishing, 1939), translated by Simon Musoke, 40: Zimbe gives a list of the relevant marriages and summarized: "That was the way in which Kabaka came to terms with his people by giving away princesses to them."

33. See Twaddle, *Kakungulu and the Creation of Uganda.*

34. See, e.g., Kiwanuka, *History of Buganda,* 98–100, 108, et passim. A. I. Robertson emphasized, "It has been said so many times in the vernacular literature that a king made war to stop his chiefs fighting," but Robertson contested this interpretation, emphasizing instead the role of the king's wars in building state power—both military and economic (A. I. Robertson, Notes on Wrigley, "Changing Economic Structure" [195?], LSE, Richards Papers).

35. Kiwanuka, *History of Buganda,* 149–50.

36. [Author confidential: possibly W. P. Tamukedde], "Leadership Study: The Powers of the Katikiro in Buganda in the Past," Hancock Papers, ICS 29/1/6/4. The author was explaining what he had been told by his father.

37. According to Zimbe, Kaggwa survived because he was too useful to kill. And Mwanga ordered the death of the person who botched the castration of his former servants, two of whom died. Bishop Hannington, in this version, was killed for violating the king's orders. And Mwanga's actions were all in a context in which he had been warned by the Arabs that Europeans "begin by saying they are teaching, and end by ruling." Mwanga's violence, for Zimbe, was a desperate effort to preserve his people. Converts were dangerous. Hearing of yet another elite young man's absence from court for prayer, Mwanga reportedly complained: "With whom shall I rule if the Katikiro's son Muwafu whom I expected to put in his father's place has taken the religion?" (Zimbe, "Buganda ne Kabaka," 141–43).

38. Many historians would provide a different explanation, probably emphasizing a combination of realpolitik, a shortage of heirs, and factions within the oligarchy. What's striking here is not the accuracy of Zimbe's judgment, but the fact that despite his careful description of Mwanga's violence, abuse of friend and enemy, and provocation of violent civil war, the young kabaka was nevertheless beloved and should not be condemned.

39. For examples, Joshua Kamulegeya (The Mugema), 28 June 1954, LSE, Richards Papers, 7/5; and talk with Kyingi 10 November 1954, LSE, Richards Papers, 7/6.

40. C. Summers, "Intimate Colonialism: The Imperial Production of Reproduction in Uganda 1907–1925," *Signs* 16, no. 4 (1991): 787–807.

41. C. Summers, "Whips and Women: Forcing Change in Eastern Uganda during the 1920s," paper presented at the Global Partners Symposium, University of Nairobi, July 2000, available at http://www.global-partners.org/africa/2000/papers/csummers/. The paper explores how local colonial officials and Mill Hill missionaries articulately and persistently advocated violence against women as a progressive

development strategy, rejecting imperial ideals of a "civilized" restraint on the corporal punishment of women.

42. Consider, for example, Dave Eaton's thoughtful discussion in "Youth, Cattle Raiding, and Generational Conflict along the Kenya-Uganda Border" (chapter 2, this volume) of youthful cattle raiding, which reclaims the history of youthful contention with elders over bridewealth accumulation and opportunities. But Eaton concludes that "[t]he relationship between the elders and the young warriors in the North Rift has not been transformed recently" without exploring how people understood these categories and who they included.

43. Kivu, "Autobiography"; Tamukedde, "My Life as a Chief and a District Commissioner."

8 Youth, the TANU Youth League, and Managed Vigilantism in Dar es Salaam, 1925–73

JAMES R. BRENNAN

THIS CHAPTER EXAMINES the underappreciated role played by male youth in the political history of Dar es Salaam in particular and Tanzania in general. It demonstrates how colonial and postcolonial political authorities constructed and manipulated male youth, and how young men formed an increasingly powerful political force in their own right. The chapter also looks into the larger questions raised by the political history of youth, such as creating meaningful citizenship in a colonial and one-party state, the manipulation of patron-client networks to mobilize underemployed urban youth for political ends, and finally wider questions about the legitimacy of violence, other forms of coercion, and their political intelligence in a system where youth and party distrust yet also rely on a state bureaucracy. It also raises questions relevant to our understanding of the contemporary dilemmas of political violence among male youth in urban Africa today. Networks of patronage underwrote the work of the nationalist party's Youth League in Tanzania, but sharp limits to the patrimonial capacity of both state and party in postcolonial urban Tanzania had already revealed themselves by the 1970s, opening a new and still unfinished chapter of youth politics, characterized by the gradual fragmentation of centralized party-state controls over the violence, vigilantism, and intelligence gathering of young men.

"Youth" here is understood as both an abstract social category and an empirically definable group whose members are eligible to participate in specific institutions. Borrowing Insa Nolte's description, youth is "not so much circumscribed by biological age as by status and behaviour: the group includes all those who do not (yet) have the material means and the recognition to establish themselves as providers for others."[1] As both category and group, "youth" was changing rapidly during the twentieth century, defined "less by a set of inherited discursive constructs as by unique historical circumstances and narratives that set their generation apart from others before or after."[2] Also in flux during this period were the instruments and organization of legitimate violence. Channeling the violent energies of male youth through sharply defined generational duties of defensive or destructive labor is a signature dynamic of several African age systems.[3] In the colonial context, harnessing the dissatisfactions of potentially violent male youth had become a common strategy of emerging nationalist parties during the late 1940s and 1950s. This was realized institutionally within most African nationalist parties through the creation of "Youth Wings" responsible for the more coercive activities of mass political mobilization.[4] This chapter focuses primarily on a period in African history (1945–73) characterized by a strong faith in state-led development projects and single party domination over national political structures.[5] The theoretical ambitions and institutional capacities of parties and states to manage the coercive powers of youth toward normative unitary ends seem to have passed with this era.

This chapter proceeds chronologically in three sections. The first section (1925–54) examines how a group of young African bureaucrats in Dar es Salaam, seeking to set themselves apart from local "elders" claiming traditional authority, shifted the very meaning of generation and youth by pioneering a form of racial politics that enabled outsiders to become urban citizens. The second section (1954–64) investigates how the political victory of African nationalism was realized in Dar es Salaam and elsewhere in part through the strategic deployment of coercive youth in the form of the TANU (Tanganyika African National Union) Youth League. The third section (1964–73) considers the dilemmas of managing Youth League vigilantism in a one-party state in the decade following independence. As with most African cities, the public space of Dar es Salaam today is overwhelmingly male, young, and occasionally punctured by bursts of vigilante justice.[6] Explanations of vigilantism and other forms of violence in contemporary Africa where youth take a leading role need to be situated within the specific historical contexts in which they emerge. Tanzania has largely avoided the horrors of child soldiers and nihilistic urban gang culture, but male youth today play a central role in the increasingly fractious political competition on the mainland and particularly Zanzibar, as new ideological motivations and patron-client chains take shape. To a large extent the dangers of violence among political youth are intrinsic to the nature of youth itself—what have changed are the strategies and structures created by relationally "elder" elites to channel the violence and other coercive powers of youth.

Politics and Generational Mobility in Colonial Dar es Salaam, 1925–54

Generational conflict between old and young men has long been recognized as a foundational feature of many African societies. In polygynous societies where access to bridewealth held the keys to political power and social fulfillment, youths chafed under the gerontocratic authority of elders while, dangerously, being entrusted with access to means of violence.[7] In East Africa, this social dynamic was formalized, particularly among pastoralists, through functioning age-class systems.[8] While formal generational structures were less apparent in the coastal towns of East Africa, elder men still exercised enormous power over male youths through their monopoly of bridewealth and offices. The notion of who constituted youths (in Swahili, *vijana*) in this context reflected not only biological age but also the subordinate status of outsiders to the exclusionary patrician hierarchies of the *mrima* coast of modern-day northern Tanzania.[9] Thus, the category of vijana on the coast of nineteenth-century East Africa implied patrician domination through the overlapping structural exclusions of generation, class, and citizenship.

The basis of generational authority in Dar es Salaam underwent enormous change in the decades following its founding by Sultan Majid of Zanzibar in the early 1860s.[10] The town developed as part of the social fabric of adjacent Swahili "Shomvi" and Zaramo villages of the *mrima* coast. Youth born both on the coast and in interior fought for adulthood and inclusion in Dar es Salaam and its nearby villages through traditional means of production such as farming or fishing, as well as through opportunities offered by artisan trades or caravan work in regional commercial networks. After a period of decline in the 1870s and 1880s, Dar es Salaam had revived by 1891 when it became capital of German East Africa. German authorities spatially reconfigured the city through a tripartite system of racial segregation for its European, Indian/Arab, and African residents, and introduced a new system of political authority for the urban and peri-urban African residents based on direct rule through nonlocal Arab and African *akida* (political agent) administrators. During this period, the spheres of political influence in Dar es Salaam were bifurcated between an official realm of state authority, personified in African neighborhoods and outlying areas by alien akidas, and a marginalized realm of traditional authority among displaced Shomvi and Zaramo elders (Swahili, *wazee*).

The reconstitution of political authority in Dar es Salaam under the British after the First World War revealed the continued racial character of colonial rule, as well as desultory attempts to revive African gerontocratic authority in colonial towns. The town's racially heterogeneous population obviated any strategies of indirect rule. Dar es Salaam's European and Indian communities insisted that a representative Township Authority administer their respective neighborhoods, while African neighborhoods and peri-urban settlements went neglected. After initially relying on the inherited German system of akida administration,[11] the township authority in 1925 appointed two officers to oversee courts and tax collection in town, one operated by an Arab *liwali* (appointed governor) presiding over the township, and the other by an African *mwenyemzi* (political agent) presiding over peri-urban Dar es Salaam. The town's first and only mwenyemzi, a young, competent clerk with no local hereditary status, was rejected by several Zaramo and Shomvi town elders. The district office responded by abolishing the office of mwenyemzi in 1930, absorbing its court into that of the liwali, now head of urban "native" administration.[12] The rejection of the young African outsider by self-styled *wenye mji* (literally, "owners of the city") composed of long-resident Zaramo and Shomvi, demonstrated that age and heredity counted in the colonial calculus of political authority.

The language of identity in Dar es Salaam was itself a debate over generational authority. The term *wenye mji* (indigenes) and its antonym, *watu wa kuja* (immigrants), suffused local discourse in colonial Dar es Salaam and overlapped along ethnic, generational, and educational lines. Wenye mji were generally but not exclusively Shomvi and Zaramo elders lacking Western education but claiming first-comer status; watu wa kuja were generally, but not exclusively, younger and often Western-educated Africans lacking claims to local lineage-based authority.[13] The term frequently used by wenye mji to assert their traditional rights over Dar es Salaam was *wazee wa mji,* meaning "town elders,"[14] the term *wazee* (elders) connoting gerontocratic authority. In its use, *wazee wa mji* stood as a discursive antonym not only to *watu wa kuja*, but also to the more generation-specific epithet *wahuni,* the young unmarried men who lacked authority, wealth, and responsibility. The striking ubiquity of the term *wazee wa mji* in interwar Dar es Salaam had also to do with conclusions administrators drew about the decentralized social structure of the surrounding Zaramo society and the salient role of village elders in matters of political authority.[15] The government turned these conclusions to its fleeting experiments with Dar es Salaam's local administration by constituting an official elders' council (*baraza ya wazee*). In practice, the term *wazee wa mji* was used by mostly Zaramo or Shomvi political figures to indicate first-comer claims of authority over Dar es Salaam.

Racial politics offered young, educated African outsiders a potential bridge over the divide of age and first-comer status. In 1930 the colonial government proposed to replace Dar es Salaam's retiring Arab liwali with another Arab. The recently formed African Association objected, explaining that "[a]n Arab always looks down upon an African within or without, as a slave or putting it frankly an 'inferior' in all respects and therefore what justice and good treatment can the latter expect from the former unless a European Officer spends his whole time checking him."[16] This position reflected popular sentiment among the African Association's Western-educated, bureaucratically employed constituency, but traditional authority based on seniority and lineage proved amenable to the government's nomination. The elders' council ratified the appointment of a new Arab liwali, a man with deep family roots in Dar es Salaam.[17] Whereas the liwali's Arab identity was racially unacceptable among the immigrant watu wa kuja of the African Association this was in the eyes of wenye mji an acceptable reaffirmation of local political and religious authority. The Township Authority formalized the elders' council in 1934 by appointing its members to the town's native advisory board, although this structure was dismantled three years later to restrict the potentially dangerous principle of representation.[18] Lacking any formal political representation, younger men responded by forming a number of urban "tribal" organizations, such as the Wazaramo Union, to provide some modicum of welfare such as burial services. Although these organizations relied on the support of older figures, leadership rested decisively in the hands of Western-educated male youths, many of whom were government clerks.[19]

Major shifts in urban demography and colonial policy in the 1940s created conditions that enabled young African bureaucrats to gain new measures of political authority. The radical increase in African migration to urban areas after 1940 raised colonial fears of a "moral chaos" unfolding in Dar es Salaam. The anxious watchword was "detribalisation," which meant the loosening of rural elders' control over urbanizing youth.[20] In Dar es Salaam, colonial engagement with this process revolved around Sisyphean efforts at rural repatriation and desultory experiments with African political authorities.[21] Heavy-handed expatriations of under- and unemployed youth became a regular feature of life in Dar es Salaam, sharpening African youths' hostility to colonial rule and highlighting the struggle of Africans to secure urban citizenship.[22] Keenly aware of growing discontent among African civil servants and the generational challenge of youth, the postwar colonial government offered political initiatives to increase African involvement in local administration. In Dar es Salaam, the administration instituted a township ward council in 1945 to afford Africans a constitutional mode of political expression.[23] The provincial commissioner explained:

> The political consciousness of the African, particularly of the younger intelligencia (many of whom are Government employees in various departments), who are in the majority in these associations, is rapidly awakening, and is becoming very vocal and active. . . . In my opinion, the time is now ripe to obtain their goodwill and to harness their energy and enthusiasm to the Government chariot. If left to their own devices there is little doubt that their activities will tend towards the undermining of the local native authorities and opposition to, and a feeling of resentment towards, Government.[24]

The African Association and a number of "tribal" organizations were invited to join.[25] A group of wenye mji elders, feeling marginalized by the youthful leadership of the ward councils, demanded the reconstitution of the elders' council, without success.[26] Despite its revival in the 1930s, the elders' influence was waning, as was the significance of the division between watu wa kuja immigrants and wenye mji indigenes. Swelling African migration to Dar es Salaam made the town increasingly representative of the whole territory, while generational tensions became increasingly territorialized. Well-traveled youth, enjoying greater access to Western education and cash wages, were more willing to challenge the authority of state-appointed chiefs and elders of regionally bound "tribes" in Tanganyika.

It was young men in their twenties who most effectively seized the intellectual and political opportunities offered in the 1940s. Julius Nyerere, then a twenty-one-year-old student at Makerere University, argued in 1943 that "[o]ur population is mainly African and the African being naturally socialistic, economics in East Africa should be based on socialistic principles." He exhorted better-educated Africans to save less fortunate Africans from wartime deprivation through selfless leadership in welfare bodies, cooperatives, and unions.[27] One youth group asked older African political veterans "to hand over the work to our youth, who bear all the bluntness of ill-treatment from the foreigners. . . . This is our country, our inheritance, why are we deprived of our own bread?"[28] Realizing their African "inheritance" meant taking control of the meager institutions of "tribal" and racial politics, particularly the African Association. The core of the African Association leadership consisted of entry- and mid-level African civil servants, who, as an urban group, were hardest hit by the wartime economy. Salaries were capped without adjustment to inflation, eroding mid-level civil servants' economic status in towns during the 1940s.[29] This boded poorly for the swelling number of Western-educated African youth seeking bureaucratic posts. This group lost faith in the African Association's senior leadership and responded by taking leadership initiatives in branches throughout Tanganyika. By 1948, a British intelligence report stated that this younger leadership had started a campaign "for the removal of all old and illiterate chiefs and sub-chiefs throughout the territory and their replacement by young and educated men—i.e., themselves."[30] In 1950, the rechristened Tanganyika African Association (TAA) expanded its ambitions by proposing that the party offer Africans what the state was failing to provide. A branch secretary wrote, "The Union should teach Africans to do things for themselves and not expect Government to do everything for them. In order to build the new Africa, all African patriots should hope for a better understanding and friendly relationship between the various tribes in Tanganyika."[31] In April 1953, Julius Nyerere was elected president of TAA by a younger group of activists calling themselves the "Action Group," who rejected the remnants of the association's aging and conservative leadership.[32]

The Creation of TANU and Its Youth League, 1954–64

On 7 July 1954, the Tanganyika African National Union (TANU) formed in Dar es Salaam as a reorganization of the TAA, again led by the young Action Group. Molded by Western education and comfortable with urban life, this new generation promised pan-ethnic, African racial empowerment by challenging existing state structures while also promising extrastatist welfare through the party. Beginning their campaign in Dar es Salaam and its peri-urban areas in late 1954, TANU closely followed pathways already blazed by the Wazaramo Union by appealing to Africans' racial resentment against Indian traders and promising to short-circuit these middlemen through party-created African cooperatives and shops. Earlier hopes of pioneering a racial politics of African empowerment were rapidly fulfilled in the mid-1950s. Nationalists interpreted African development as African self-sufficiency and freedom from non-African economic forces.[33]

The lightning political success of TANU from 1955 raised two enduring problems: To what extent would the party provide extrastatist welfare and maintain political legitimacy as TANU took up power within the colonial state? And what role would young men play in a party seeking both the vitality of youthful challenge and the stability of elders' authority? *Maendeleo* (development) emerged as the new pole of public discourse in the 1950s, as did its discursive antonym *fujo* or "disorder." Preventing fujo became the shared concern of TANU nationalists and the colonial administration.[34] TANU public meetings in Dar es Salaam were remarkable for their public order, though occasionally petty racial violence accompanied them. Fearing this hooligan or "spiv" element would be emboldened by TANU rhetoric, the colonial government enjoined party leaders to make obedience to law and order a central topic of public meetings.[35] Despite conflict between TANU and the state, which stands at the center of nationalist accounts, TANU largely adopted the colonial government's commitment to bring maendeleo and prevent fujo as it took up state power in the late 1950s. Within this ideological transformation, the social category of young bureaucrats, who during the interwar years lacked the authority of "traditional" elders, now emerged as a relationally "elder" nationalist elite to the swelling numbers of African youth throughout Tanganyika, the vast majority of whom lacked the opportunities to obtain similar bureaucratic qualifications.

From the viewpoint of nationalist leaders, order was to rest on party discipline, not state controls. Party authority flowed from the party's central committee in Dar es Salaam down geographically to its branches and socially to its familial auxiliaries defined by generation and gender. The motion to create a youth and women's section within the TAA was put forward in early 1954 by younger activists, and in 1956 the youth section was formally constituted as the TANU Youth League. According to John Iliffe, the Youth League provided the party "vigorous support and numerous disciplinary problems" by young men who had disproportionately "failed to enter middle or secondary school."[36] In rural areas, the TANU Youth League frequently filled traditional generation roles. TANU Youth League branches in Sukumaland took on the tasks of *basumba* (young men) responsible at the village level for discharging communal labor tasks, while also performing the party work of membership recruitment, self-help projects, and tax collection.[37] In Dar es Salaam, the Youth League attracted the town's numerous under- and unemployed youth constantly disparaged by the state and anxious African middle classes. For the growing numbers of male youths lacking the bureaucratic bona fides of educational qualifications, membership in the Youth League offered immediate if minuscule wages, enhanced social status, and potential for promotions to higher offices within the party, as well as the possibility (albeit remote) of salaried state employment. There was also a women's section within the TANU Youth League who did party work as singers, guards, messengers, intelligence gatherers, and food preparers, and dressed in similar green uniforms.[38] But TYL membership and ethos would prove to be overwhelmingly male and masculine, particularly in how the organization tasked itself with the regulation of women's public sexuality.[39]

Youth gained an enlarged role as both a social category and a group of political actors within TANU in January 1958, when Nyerere was negotiating with the colonial government over elections during the party's annual conference in Tabora. Most TANU members initially rejected the tri-racial electorate offered by the government and in anticipation organized a national civil disobedience campaign to be enforced by the Youth League (or "Volunteer Corps"), led by Julius Nyerere's brother, Joseph Nyerere.[40] The anticipated disobedience campaign was obviated by an agreement between Nyerere and the government to participate in elections—dissenters formed the opposition Tanganyika African National Congress (ANC) party—but the TANU Youth League (TYL) never lost sight of its initial mission, to enforce party discipline in public areas and attack formal opposition to TANU. The ANC publicity secretary complained in 1961 that the TYL had "taken the law into their own hands and have arrested, tried and convicted people; they have drilled like soldiers with imitation rifles, have entered houses and ejected the occupiers and have stopped and searched motor-cars etc."[41] Sharply race-conscious, Youth League members searched Asian shops suspected of purchasing produce illegally, and detained non-Africans consorting with African women.[42]

According to Thomas Burgess, the advent of TANU in urban areas such as Dar es Salaam offered youths the opportunity to "win the acceptance of more established African residents" by performing security work, maintaining discipline at nationalist rallies, and assuming other physical tasks desired by party leaders. "All this," Burgess argues, "was active distancing on the part of youth from the taint and stigma of criminality."[43] Throughout the colonial period, the African areas of Dar es Salaam had received scant police attention, except for raids to seize tax evaders and repatriate under- or unemployed wahuni youth living illegally in town.[44] Before the arrival of the Youth League in the late 1950s, there is little evidence in Dar es Salaam of any analogy to communal policing initiatives or gang control that had emerged on the violent urban terrain of the South African Rand.[45] From its base in Dar es Salaam, Youth League policing quickly became territorial. The colonial state anxiously identified TYL supporters as "vigilantes," and according to Burgess, "Vigilantism was an unambiguous assertion and very public statement of young men's respect for law and order."[46]

In the twilight of colonial rule, party coercion extended itself deeply into the normative domains of the bureaucratic state. British officials worried that Youth League vigilantism undermined the authority of the legally appointed native authorities.[47] In late 1960, Governor Richard Turnbull considered the group "an embarrassment rather than a danger," and elaborated the spectrum of motives driving Tanganyika's young vigilantes:

> At one end of the scale we have groups of enthusiastic young men who feel that it is their duty to take active steps to bring about that climate of enhanced social responsibility which they consider the new regime demands, and who honestly think that they are behaving in a most commendable and self-sacrificing way if they patrol the streets and try to enforce what they regard as a proper code of behaviour. At the other we have unscrupulous corner boys and street corner keelies who take advantage of the general atmosphere to intimidate the ordinary public and extort danegelt and protection money from the Asian trader and the non-Party man. In between are those who have claimed to be invested with Police powers, those who have attempted to hold unlawful courts and so on.[48]

By this time, Dar es Salaam's police force and the TYL held a joint meeting and passed a series of resolutions following the release of three detained Youth League members. One of the detained had earlier arrested an African woman for accompanying a European. After bringing the woman to the police, he told them that his job as a Youth League member was to patrol the city and arrest anyone who might break the law. While it was agreed that only police could arrest lawbreakers and citizens were limited to the prevention of law-breaking, it was also agreed that police now required new training, as a number of officers had been trained poorly by the colonial government.[49]

TANU was confronted with two interrelated questions of statecraft as it accrued constitutional powers between 1958 and independence in late 1961, one Weberian and one epistemological. Where does the monopoly of legitimate violence lie if TANU proclaims the colonial state as illegitimate yet simultaneously bans any fujo that might embarrass the state? And how can one define and assess threats of illegitimate violence? The party took tremendous pride in controlling the violence associated with rallies through Youth League policing—sources brim with approving remarks of how well the Youth League controlled party events.[50] But Youth League policing initiatives could also degenerate into cynical freelancing. In the Southern Highland town of Njombe, a TYL district secretary was imprisoned for two years following his attempt to extort five hundred shillings from an Indian shopkeeper by otherwise threatening a boycott.[51] Chiefs and elders with interests vested in the British regime were particularly alarmed by what they viewed as the metastasizing role of the TYL in TANU activities between 1958 and 1961. Although the policy decision to eliminate the position of chiefs had long been a core principle of TANU, by early 1961 Nyerere—in a timely volte-face—began instead to solicit their support. In a reorganization of the party that year, TANU announced that although European countries recognized rank more than age, TANU would combine both rank and age. From now on, elders would receive more respect.[52]

Youth League violence was most consistently directed at identifiable political competitors and almost never at the colonial state. In Morogoro District, Youth League members threw stones at the car chauffeuring Chief Patrick Kunambe, who then stood as the African candidate on the conservative United Tanganyika Party ticket.[53] When another oppositionist political party, the All Muslim National Union of Tanganyika (AMNUT), formed in May 1959 by anxious Muslims fearing a Christian-dominated TANU government after independence, TANU's provincial chair in Dar es Salaam threatened that "the TANU Youth League would carry out investigations" of the new party.[54] Most dramatically during this period, TANU Youth League members regularly disrupted African National Congress meetings throughout Tanganyika.[55] Indeed, ANC sources provide some of the most vivid pictures of TYL militancy in Dar es Salaam. The registrar of societies, in the hands of TANU by early 1961, refused to register an ANC Youth League, arguing that it would "likely to be used for purposes prejudicial to or incompatible with the maintenance of peace, order and good government."[56]

This was a crippling blow to the ANC, as the Youth League had demonstrably played a critical role in TANU's success. ANC's Dar es Salaam district chairman complained that TANU youth leaguers entered houses forcing people to produce their voting registration certificates so that they may be kept in safe custody in TANU offices.[57] ANC president Zuberi Mtemvu pinned the blame of his poor electoral performance on TANU Youth League intimidation; he described the Youth League as a vigilante organization that was "arresting people, caning them and imprisoning them without authority from the government."[58]

With independence won on 9 December 1961, Youth League members sought to extend the exercise of their ambiguous police powers by continuing to hound Tanganyika's meager political opposition. Unsurprisingly, opposition parties became champions of an independent bureaucracy. Mtemvu told an ANC rally that only police can arrest suspected criminals, while TANU and ANC youth could only arrest when crimes were being committed.[59] But formal political opposition was weak, and more police work had to be found. By mid-1962, Youth League members began to challenge the will of senior TANU officials. Edward Barongo was removed from his position as regional commissioner of Tanganyika's Northern Region because of "a disagreement with the TANU Youth League for taking police power into their own hands."[60] Dar es Salaam youth leaguers carried out a thorough check on all shops to find those still selling boycotted South African goods and report them to party headquarters.[61] They also threatened a number of shops and took to arresting people for petty offenses, such as riding bicycles without lights. The *Tanganyika Standard* complained that the ranks of the TYL "include many who can be described only as *wahuni* using the T.Y.L. for nefarious intentions."[62] Dar es Salaam police intervened again to explain the limits of citizen arrest power to the Youth League, only this time the new African commissioner of police ordained a formal alliance between the two bodies in policing Dar es Salaam, requesting only that the TYL bring the arrested immediately to police stations.[63]

Imposing party control over urban "policing" by young men became increasingly necessary in the first years of independence. Vigilante activities, the acknowledged province of the TANU Youth League, briefly became the province of other freelancing male youth in Dar es Salaam. This "volunteer policing zeal" among Dar es Salaam's male youth found an independent existence in the Tata Kabwera Foola Union of the city's Ilala neighborhood. This was a short-lived organization that took up the task of expelling the urban unemployed to "remove this shame" from town. The union sought party permission for its activities but wanted to exist outside the TYL.[64] Although the organization was quickly disbanded, the dangers of overdemocratizing coercive powers to youth became clear to the postcolonial government and party. The caricature of wahuni hooligans terrified the postcolonial urban imagination as well as the colonial; the potential for political instability unleashed by urban youth violence would also continue to shape the urban policies, and more critically the security policies, of the postcolonial TANU government and party.

Dilemmas of Umoja (Unity): Party Discipline, Intelligence, and Generational Conflict, 1964–73

After TANU dispensed with opposition parties in 1963, the Youth League's ambition to appropriate the instruments and organization of legitimate violence parallel to that of the state grew considerably. Patron-client chains between deployable youth and powerful party figures similarly grew in significance, offering paths to political citizenship otherwise denied to uneducated and often urban-bound young men. The Youth League scored an important success with its partial inclusion in new state programs, particularly with the gargantuan growth of the Ministry for National Culture and Youth. Led by Lawi Sijaona, this ministry established the National Youth Corps (or National Service) in July 1963 for nation-building exercises such as road-building and agricultural projects. The TYL had successfully lobbied for the establishment of this national service program as the TANU government was drawing up its national defense policy in 1963, allowing the TYL to rechannel energies of unemployed party youth who found themselves mostly redundant after the termination of opposition parties.[65] The ministry hoped that the National Youth Corps would form three hundred battalions with military powers to complement and, in some cases, to supplement the Tanganyika Rifles.[66]

Looming questions of how best to manage legitimate violence and to gather intelligence about security threats came to a climax on 20 January 1964, when the Tanganyika Rifles mutinied in demand for accelerating Africanization of officer ranks and raising soldier pay. The previous week had witnessed the Zanzibari Revolution and Nyerere's unequivocal pronouncement that merit rather than race would guide government hiring and promotions. When the mutiny broke out, Nyerere and Vice President Rashidi Kawawa went into hiding for two days, and the soldiers' demands were negotiated primarily with Oscar Kambona, minister of External Affairs and Defence since early 1963. It was the greatest rupture of public order in Dar es Salaam's history. When Nyerere reemerged and began negotiations with the mutineers, rumors swirled that the Police Field Force Unit were set to mutiny as well. Facing a complete security breakdown, Kambona and Nyerere agreed to call in British military assistance to restore law and order.[67] Several shops were looted the following day, and in total some fifty people, many of them Arab shopkeepers, were killed in the violence.

While historians of the mutiny generally agree that the soldiers' motivation was "higher pay, better living conditions, and more rapid promotions,"[68] lingering questions about postcolonial approaches to violence and intelligence remain. Nyerere had largely shrugged off the need for an effective security service or Special Branch. In early 1962, the Special Branch identified potential mutineers in the army who were quietly and effectively removed from their positions. But in 1963, Oscar Kambona at Defence and Home Minister Job Lusinde had broken up the Special Branch as an unseemly reminder of the preceding colonial government. This decision may have been influenced by Nyerere's realization in September

1962 of a liaison between Tanganyika's Special Branch and MI5 in a regional network that also included Southern Rhodesian intelligence interests.[69] In its place, according to a British colonel's report on the mutiny, Kambona and Lusinde had substituted "a sort of party-political police manned by inexperienced members of the TANU Youth League, whose main function seems to be eavesdropping in bars for rude remarks about Ministers."[70] Such informal intelligence networks overlapped with chains of patronage within the Youth League, leading upward to important party and state figures. TYL political spies, however, had made no effort to obtain security intelligence from the army—Kambona later explained that he had thought it was the responsibility of military intelligence to uncover subversion in the army. The British colonel investigating the mutiny concluded that "whereas Tanganyika Ministers have learned much since independence about politics, it is doubtful even after the mutiny whether they yet understand the first principles of security or of military precepts and discipline."[71] Although such an assessment may be dismissed as mere postimperial scoffing, it does point to the continuing crisis of how nationalists conceived of violence, its knowledge, and its monopolization.

Indeed, the political history of Tanzania in the subsequent decade after the mutiny turned on Nyerere's reconceptualization of the role of violence and its control by party and state. His first move after the mutiny was to disband the Tanganyika Rifles entirely and to create a new Tanzania People's Defence Force (TPDF)—a shift away from a professional, "pure army to a developmental militia."[72] Nyerere called on TANU Youth League members—who had been the first to rally in his support after the mutiny—to register for army service. The president built the new TPDF on TANU Youth League recruits, six hundred graduates of Tanzania's National Service program, and three hundred Zanzibari recruits taken quite literally off the streets of Zanzibar in the days immediately following the April 1964 union between the islands and mainland that created "Tanzania."[73] The former commander of the Tanganyika Rifles, Brigadier Patrick Sholto Douglas, worried that such a mass recruitment drive would "upset the careful tribal balance the British had tried to maintain in TR and would necessarily center on unemployed Dar-es-Salaam youth which he considered a most unreliable lot."[74]

Although issues of "tribe" certainly remained in Tanzania's new army,[75] the greater tension in the military and other institutions of legitimate violence lay between youth and professionals, reflecting larger tensions between party and state. Binding the TYL to the new national army was the first of several moves Nyerere would make to simultaneously draw on the TYL for security while attempting to limit its independence. The new TPDF required that all recruits first join TANU and be scrutinized by the TYL, while undergoing a uniform political education designed to reduce elitism and arrogance.[76] TANU also wanted to ensure that the military no longer enjoyed a monopoly over training and weapons, and that the party was on an equal security footing with the state. In 1965 the Tanzanian parliament passed legislation that formalized the role of the TYL in the nation's paramilitary training and instituted the Jeshi la Mgambo, or People's Militia, a volunteer force controlled exclusively by the party.[77] This act accorded well with the new 1965 constitution, which enshrined the one-party state and eliminated vestiges of civil service autonomy by giving the president freedom to "appoint, demote, transfer, or fire any one in government service, including members of the Cabinet."[78] While the government shut down formal spheres of political dissent, the party worked to eliminate political opposition on the ground. In the middle of 1964, TANU began to coerce civil servants and police to join the party, and Tanganyikans in several regions were denied medical care or crop-selling privileges unless they could produce a TANU card. At the end of the year, TANU launched a system of ten-house cells for urban areas organized through ward development committees, increasing the party's ability to survey and ferret out political opposition.[79] This new regime of political regulation and intelligence gathering effectively guaranteed a one-party state in Tanzania but raised the troubling question of how to manage—and who should manage—Youth League policing in the postmutiny security system.

By 1964, the Youth League had developed an unfavorable reputation throughout Tanzania for interfering in people's ordinary lives by assuming police functions without legal permission or political accountability. They often took aim at unpopular minorities. In the southern coastal town of Lindi, youth leaguers in the mid-1960s forcibly awoke Shi'a Ithnasheri Indians—including old women and children—at between four and five a.m. to make them work on communal projects. One notable Ithnasheri remembered that there was simply "too much enthusiasm on [the] part of youth without direction," and that they "took [the] law into [their] own hands," actions which drove Ithnasheri and other Indian groups to relocate to larger cities.[80] African farmers simply tired of Youth League interference. By 1964, TANU officials in Sukumaland had turned away from the "militant and often tactless Youth League contingents," and toward groups of elders in order to resuscitate local participation in party activities, which had lagged considerably since independence.[81] TYL members in Arusha District threatened to strip naked any ethnic Arusha or Maasai caught wearing traditional dress and ornaments.[82] In Kilosa, youth leaguers were criticized for inserting themselves as unwanted judges in local disputes, randomly arresting people without cause to extract five shillings, and generally carrying out activities only for the sake of filling their own bellies (*kupenda tu kujaza matumbo yao*).[83] Much of this "enthusiasm" was officially sanctioned from the top. Encouraging greater youth participation in Tanzania's agricultural schemes, Julius Nyerere told a meeting at South Mara that, "as an indirect way of forcing idlers to comply with cotton regulations, Tanu youth could cut and burn the cotton stumps of people who had failed to do so in time and then collect goats or cows from them in payment."[84]

It is difficult to recapture the simultaneous optimism and paranoia that surrounded the decade following Tanzania's independence. Despite the unambiguous political victory of a bureaucratic elite, many cabinet and party leaders were only in their thirties or even late twenties, and the larger question of generational authority remained open. Andrew Ivaska has argued that "a persistent ambiguity characterized this renegotiation" between youth and political authority. On the one hand, the state "explicitly raised the visibility of 'youth' as a political category, establishing a cabinet portfolio for youth, mobilizing institutions like the National Service and the party's Youth League," while on the other, party and government officials also sought to "marginalize youth who potentially posed challenges to that vision" by positioning themselves in a "vertical rivalry" with this elite.[85] National Service stood as the centerpiece of youth development since its inception in 1963. It was to be a transformative experience that would not only inculcate national values but also eliminate elitism. Nyerere told a TYL annual conference meeting in Dar es Salaam that Tanzania needed a "gentlemanly discipline" which could be best provided by a mandatory two-year National Service stint.[86] Students at University College were "lukewarm" toward TANU generally, and TYL failed to establish a branch there in 1965—only ten of the five hundred–odd students at the college were committed to TANU.[87] Moreover, few secondary school-leavers had joined the National Service since its establishment in 1963, finding its hard manual labor unappealing and a needless digression from career advancement. Distraught at this nationwide attitude, Nyerere told an audience in Moshi that school-leavers should not expect their education to entitle them to white-collar jobs but should "be prepared to work on the land."[88] After the National Assembly passed legislation instituting mandatory two-year National Service that included university graduates and secondary school-leavers, it was met with serious resistance by University College students. G. D. T. Lusinde, a teacher at Kivukoni College, TANU's ideological school in Dar es Salaam, boldly stated a gerontocratic case in favor of National Service. In the distant past of African ancestors, he explained, "The youths of those days accepted and carried out the laws passed to them by the elders. . . . The youth must really thank our elders for taking us from the unknown darkness (colonialism) to freedom. It is the duty of every youth now to protect this freedom. And this freedom will not be protected by pen, ink and paper only but by working hard."[89]

That October, a large group of students marched from the university to the city center to protest the new mandatory requirement, and 393 students attending the protest were expelled immediately and rusticated for two years (later reduced to one).[90] Over the next few days, a number of marches led by the TYL condemned the students and supported Nyerere and National Service. Green Guards—named after their Chinese counterparts and for their green shirts, the color of TANU—made their force felt throughout Dar es Salaam, taking control of traffic checkpoints surrounding the city.[91]

At stake was the creation of an urban space that was neither public nor private, but *national.* Youth League vigilantes entered into the living rooms of African voters and behind the counters of Indian shopkeepers, as well as into the public spaces of markets, bars, parks, and bus stations. TYL policing created and maintained a national space in Dar es Salaam by projecting their coercive powers on areas of the city otherwise filled with loitering, profiteering, drunkenness, thieving, prostitution, lascivious dress, racial segregation, and other enduring antinational recidivisms. The scope for such national space-making through volunteer policing only increased in February 1967 with the Arusha Declaration of Tanzanian socialism and self-reliance, which called for greater development and vigilance.[92] Youth leaguers immediately asked Nyerere for rifles and hoes to carry out the Arusha Declaration—hoes were more forthcoming.[93] The months and years that followed the Arusha Declaration witnessed what Andy Ivaska terms the "intensification of the Janus-faced nature of official constructions of youth as both key to the nation's health and development, and the potential core of its rot." Ivaska continues, "[I]f official rhetoric alternately portrayed 'youth' as heroes and saboteurs, the TYL was meant to deal with both: provide a model of austere, rurally oriented, hard-working nation builders, and serve as the main agents for policing perceived decadent, lazy and corrupt manifestations of youth in the capital."[94]

Maintaining public order and discipline became a widely shared goal of both African youth and elders, and opened further opportunities for the policing thirst of young urban males first unleashed in the late 1950s. But such policing often ran ahead of Nyerere's own policies. Following the nationalization of the Dutch bank in Dar es Salaam shortly after the Arusha Declaration, youth leaguers barged into the bank and pulled down a portrait of Dutch Queen Juliana to march with it in protest. Embarrassed by this insult to a personal friend, Nyerere asked two newspaper editors, "What was he to do with 'those young men.'"[95] The most revealing example of TYL "vigilance" in Dar es Salaam was "Operation Vijana," a campaign against indecent dress and adornment announced in October 1968. The campaign consisted of a ban on "mini-skirts, wigs, women's bleaches, and tight male [*sic*] trousers," and sought to defend "Tanzania's culture and further . . . the aims of the Arusha Declaration."[96] The plan, designed and implemented by the TYL at the urging of its chairman Lawi Sijaona, instructed male youths to patrol urban areas and "arrest all women wearing [indecent] clothing and artificial hair."[97] Drawing heavily on the rhetoric of China's Cultural Revolution, Sijaona promised that Operation Vijana would "wipe out all lumpen and renegade practices, foster national culture and carry forward the Tanzanian revolution," and further warned those who claimed TYL was exceeding its authority that "[t]heir time is yet to come."[98] The campaign extended to the dormitories of the University of Dar es Salaam, where all-male TYL vigilantes held placards that apparently threatened specific women, one reading, "Two devils in Hall 3, your days are numbered."[99] By this point, the university's TYL branch had some 150 members, whose influence was "due to its connections with the ruling TANU party and its consequent potential threat to the highly privileged existence of University College."[100] In Zanzibar, a similar campaign against modern dress of Zanzibari women was carried out by the Afro-Shirazi Youth League during 1968–76, only there the Youth League guidelines were more explicitly Islamic. Burgess argues that new fashions were deemed decadent in part "because they suggested generational autonomy from the new development ideology rather than devotion to nation building."[101]

Much of the Youth League's vigilantism was managed along the lines of its internal hierarchy. Lawi Nangwanda Sijaona, a mission-educated Christian from

Tanganyika's Southern Province and a former civil servant, was the dominant figure in the TYL. He initially rose to prominence in TANU as the first Youth League secretary in 1956. After having relinquished the post in 1960, Sijaona garnered significant strength as minister of National Culture and Youth in 1962 just as TANU leadership ascribed to youth a fundamental role in the country's development, security, and intelligence activities. He took effective power when he became TYL chairman in September 1967, though Julius Nyerere's brother Joseph remained its official leader as TYL secretary. By 1967, Sijaona was attempting to distance himself from close links to Oscar Kambona as well as FRELIMO (Frente de Libertação de Moçambique, or Liberation Front of Mozambique) defectors by pushing forward increasingly radical youth initiatives.[102] He had been one of the earliest TANU visitors to China, and throughout 1968 championed TYL links with communist countries—in one instance presenting the North Vietnamese chargé d'affaires with 634 cartons of corned beef in sympathy with their struggle against imperialists.[103] The militant language of socialist vanguardism adopted by Sijaona not only suited the Youth League's esprit de corps, it also articulated an alternative leadership vision within TANU, backed by the cultivated loyalty of deployable Youth League activists.[104]

Despite the resounding popular political success of the Arusha Declaration in 1967, by 1970 the TANU leadership was sharply feeling security worries. Political intelligence remained in the hands of two groups—the apparently ineffectual Tanzanian Police and Security Service (TPSS) and more informally within the ranks of the TANU Youth League. Six major TANU figures were arrested and charged with treason in late 1969 after the TPSS director of intelligence, Emilio Charles Mzena,[105] connected them with helping to finance a planned coup to be led by Oscar Kambona, exiled from Tanzania since 1967, and supported by a variety of factions within Southern African exile liberation movements. The treason trial again steeled government's resolve to eliminate dissent—it responded by passing a National Security Bill providing for a sentence of life imprisonment for espionage and sabotage.[106]

As with the 1964 mutiny, Nyerere responded to this security crisis by augmenting the role of the party and especially its youth to mobilize and renew "vigilance" against potential enemies within the country. At this point, an all-out battle for the TYL broke out. In April 1970, Joseph Nyerere resigned as TYL secretary, declaring that its main problem now was "to control the inflow of youths into urban areas by making living conditions in rural areas viable to their youthful aspirations."[107] He quit because he had been outmaneuvered in competition for control over the organization. As chairman, Lawi Sijaona had exercised effective control over TYL since the mid-1960s, in no small part because of his skills as an effective patron.[108] Sijaona was strongly supported by Chedial Mgonja, then minister of National Culture and Youth, who publicly argued that "youth must be armed" and that "the meaning of education is to make pupils competent in the use of revolutionary tools," even to the extent of encouraging student drills and exercises emphasizing hatred of foreign "imperialists."[109]

Competition for TYL leadership intensified considerably after Joseph Nyerere's departure. A letter from the youth group Tanzanian Friends of China was circulated in August 1970 denouncing Nyerere's type of socialism and identifying China as Tanzania's "only friend and comrade in the battle against modern revisionism and US imperialism." The TYL denounced the letter as a forgery and political trick, which it undoubtedly was—but its existence shows how youth groups were widely viewed as the softest entry point for radical challenge to TANU leadership.[110] In the paranoid aftermath of Idi Amin's coup in Uganda in January 1971, the TYL asserted itself with greater and greater force into national security issues. It opposed a proposed new Hilton hotel because it would "overlook State House and Defence Headquarters and the port with its new naval berths."[111] As the tenth anniversary of independence approached and fears of a coup mounted, TANU called on the Youth League to be extra vigilant and discount swirling rumors of a possible government overthrow.[112]

Fearing that Sijaona and Mgonja were exercising too much power and transforming the Youth League into a militantly socialist "vanguard," Nyerere ordered the government to reduce TYL funding. A confrontation of sorts took place at the Youth League biennial conference in Dar es Salaam, August 21–24, 1971. Acting on Nyerere's behalf, Vice President Rashidi Kawawa offered the TYL the carrot of "building and defending the nation" by taking over all the country's night watchman contracts on "security grounds," as a part of getting youth out of the cities and into the country to work on *ujamaa* villages (socialist villages). The corresponding "stick," however, was for the TYL to accept a new rule to require an age limit of thirty-five for all active TYL leaders—which would remove the forty-three-year-old Lawi Sijaona and several of his supporters on its general council. Sijaona responded by giving a dramatic plea for greater assistance to southern African liberation groups, which brought an "emotional outpouring of contributions from the delegates." And the next day, a number of Sijaona supporters stood up to denounce the age limit proposal.[113] The issue was passed to the TANU central committee, which on 11 September ruled (undoubtedly on Nyerere's behest) that no one over thirty-five may be elected to any office in the TYL—which effectively removed thirty-one of the sixty-one TYL district committee heads in Tanzania who were over thirty-five.[114] In theory this restored advancement channels for youth within the TYL membership, then numbering 156,550; in practice this succeeded in removing Sijaona, who had succeeded too well in creating political support independent of TANU leadership. Party leaders redefined "youth" in terms of biological age not only to separate potential rivals from a dangerous patrimony, but to clarify and reaffirm the higher status of the Youth League's bureaucratic elders.

WITH THE REMOVAL of the highly popular Sijaona, the TANU Youth League, which had long reflected party leadership hopes for a volunteer-led program of nation-building, found itself stripped of its independence. Its quasi-policing and quasi-military activities were now to be put aside in favor of a nationwide militia aimed at rooting out internal subversion.[115] In order to "pump new life" into the neutralized Youth League, the party devised elections that placed a new set of Youth League leaders in power in hopes of restarting grassroots activism.[116] But by 1973, the TANU Youth League had become a more passive body. TANU leaders would continue to call on the Youth League to wipe out enemies such as bandits and economic saboteurs, and the rhetoric of TYL leaders remained militant as ever, yet independent action became less frequent.[117] Youth League power was ebbing away. In 1974, National Service was taken away from the Ministry for Youth and Culture and brought under control of the Tanzania People's Defence Forces.[118] Both party and state turned their attention and resources to villagization. Immigration to Dar es Salaam kept apace throughout the 1970s and thereafter, but neither party nor state would ever have again the proportional resources to manage and act as patrons for young, employment-hungry men who continued to constitute the bulk of urban migrants.

The role of youth in the history of Dar es Salaam has been one characterized by alternately idealistic and opportunistic political leaders who valued the transformative power of politicized youth but who also sought to avoid reaping the whirlwind of rising, unmatchable expectations. While the Youth League had been critical to TANU's success, after independence it became an experimental tool for a one-party state unable to effectively meld party and state on account of their conflicting goals of mass social transformation and bureaucratic stability. The repeated yet desultory experimentation with politicized youth to create urban order and eliminate political dissent raised fundamental questions of what constituted legitimate violence in the postcolonial state. The result has been the creation of an unstable national space in Dar es Salaam where vigilante justice is more common and popularly legitimate than the violence of state authorities, whose capacity to serve as patrons to young urban clients began its long erosion in the 1970s.

Notes

This chapter is based on doctoral research conducted in Tanzania, Great Britain, and the United States between 1998 and 2002, and subsequent research thereafter. I am indebted to Gary Thomas Burgess, Andrew Burton, and Andy Ivaska for their valuable work on youth in Tanzania. I also thank them, as well as Karin Barber, Richard Sherrington, and the anonymous referees of the journal *Africa* for their comments on earlier drafts. This chapter first appeared as an article in *Africa* 76, no. 2 (2006): 221–46.

1. I. Nolte, "Identity and Violence: The Politics of Youth in Ijebu-Remo, Nigeria," *Journal of Modern African Studies* 42, no. 1 (2004): 62.

2. T. Burgess, "Introduction to Youth and Citizenship in East Africa," *Africa Today* 51, no. 3 (2005): x. See also the introduction of this volume.

3. B. Bernardi, *Age Class Systems: Social Institutions and Polities Based on Age* (Cambridge: Cambridge University Press, 1985), 29; J. Lamphear, "Brothers in Arms: Military Aspects of East African Age-Class Systems in Historical Perspective," in *Conflict, Age and Power in North East Africa: Age Systems in Transition*, ed. E. Kurimoto

and S. Simonse (Oxford: James Currey, 1998), 79–97; S. Heald, *Controlling Anger: The Anthropology of Gisu Violence* (Oxford: James Currey, 1998), 150.

4. T. Burgess, "Youth and the Revolution: Mobility and Discipline in Zanzibar, 1950–80" (PhD diss., Indiana University, 2001); J. Allman, *The Quills of the Porcupine: Asante Nationalism in an Emergent Ghana* (Madison: University of Wisconsin Press, 1993), 28 ff.; C. Glaser, *Bo-Tsotsi: The Youth Gangs of Soweto, 1935–1976* (Portsmouth, NH: Heinemann, 2000); K. Phiri, "A Case of Revolutionary Change in Contemporary Malawi: The Malawi Army and the Disarming of the Malawi Young Pioneers," *Journal of Peace, Conflict and Military Studies* 1, no. 1 (2000), www.uz.ac.zw/units/cds/journals/volume1/number1/article3.html.

5. F. Cooper, *Africa since 1940: The Past of the Present* (Cambridge: Cambridge University Press, 2002), 91 ff.

6. See R. Sherrington, "Developing Disparities: Consumption and Social Differentiation in Post-Adjustment Dar es Salaam" (PhD diss., University of Manchester, 2005), 203–36.

7. For reflections on this, see Burgess, "Introduction to Youth and Citizenship in East Africa," ix ff. See also this volume's introduction; Richard Reid, "Arms and Adolescence: Male Youth, Warfare, and Statehood in Nineteenth-Century Eastern Africa," chapter 1 in this volume; Dave Eaton, "Youth, Cattle Raiding, and Generational Conflict along the Kenya-Uganda Border," chapter 2 in this volume; and J. Lindstrom, "Age and Generation: A Study of Some African Age- and Generation-Class Systems" (Working Paper no. 16, Department of Social Anthropology, University of Gothenburg, 1978).

8. M. Aguilar, "Gerontocratic, Aesthetic and Political Models of Age," in *The Politics of Age and Gerontocracy in Africa,* ed. M. Aguilar (Trenton, NJ: Africa World Press, 1998), 3–29.

9. J. Glassman, *Feasts and Riot: Revelry, Rebellion and Popular Consciousness on the Swahili Coast, 1859–1888* (Portsmouth, NH: Heinemann 1995), 158 ff.

10. For an overview of Dar es Salaam's history, see J. R. Brennan and A. Burton, "The Emerging Metropolis: A History of Dar es Salaam, circa 1862–2000," in *Dar es Salaam: Histories from an Emerging Metropolis,* ed. J. R. Brennan, A. Burton, and Y. Lawi (Dar es Salaam: Mkuki na Nyota/British Institute in Eastern Africa, 2007), 13–75.

11. Between 1919 and 1925, Dar es Salaam's native administration consisted of a *liwali,* who oversaw legal matters, marriages and divorces, and questions of Islamic law; an *akida,* who collected taxes and oversaw "the task of controlling the very mixed population of the town"; and five *majumbe,* who worked under the akida's orders (Orde-Brown, Dar es Salaam District Annual Report [DAR] 1923, Tanzania National Archives, Dar es Salaam [TNA], 1733/26, Secretariat Minute Papers [SMP]). The akida was "subordinate to the district administrative officer without any hereditary right to his position" (Brett, Dar es Salaam DAR 1921, TNA 1733/7).

12. Fryer to Provincial Commissioner (PC) Eastern, 25 November 1930, TNA SMP 26150/13; E. C. Baker, "Memorandum on the Social Conditions of Dar es Salaam, 4 June 1931," 71–72. Copy of report at SOAS library special collections; Ronayne to PC Eastern, 6 January 1934, TNA 61/207/I/48.

13. Other terms refer to this division between local indigenes and outsiders, particularly *watu wa pwani* (coastal people) and *watu wa bara* (upcountry people). See J. R. Brennan, "Nation, Race and Urbanization in Dar es Salaam, Tanzania,

1916–1976" (PhD diss., Northwestern University, 2002), 93–118. For a cultural history of Dar es Salaam that considers this dynamic, see T. Tsuruta, "Popular Music, Sports and Politics: A Development of Urban Cultural Movements in Dar es Salaam, 1930s–1960s," *African Study Monographs* 24, no. 3 (2003): 195–222.

14. D. Anthony, "Culture and Society in a Town in Transition: A People's History of Dar es Salaam, 1865–1939" (PhD diss., University of Wisconsin, 1983), 119.

15. See the Kisarawe District Book, which reports that the origin of Zaramo village structure was "the settlement there of a group of members of the same family or clan who acknowledged the authority of their elders" ("Wazaramo," n. a., n. d. [ca. March 1930], Kisarawe District Book, TNA).

16. Cecil Matola to Chief Secretary (CS), 22 April 1930, TNA 61/207/I/12.

17. Fryer to PC Eastern, 28 April 1930, TNA 61/207/I/15.

18. Ronayne to PC Eastern, 6 January 1934, TNA 61/207/I/48; Helps to PC Eastern, 6 January 1936, TNA 61/207/I/67; Hartnoll to Municipal Secretary, 12 January 1937, TNA 61/207/I/74.

19. Mohamed Omari et al. to PC Eastern, 31 March 1937, TNA 61/207/I/124; *Tanganyika Standard,* 6 August 1938; *Mambo Leo,* November 1938.

20. For an extended analysis of this in Tanzania, see T. Burgess, "Mobility and Discipline: Colonial Age Discourse in Tanzania," in *Rethinking Age in Africa: Colonial, Post-colonial and Contemporary Interpretations of Cultural Representations,* ed. M. Aguilar (Trenton, NJ: Africa World Press, 2007), 45–82; and A. Burton, "Urchins, Loafers and the Cult of the Cowboy: Urbanization and Delinquency in Dar es Salaam, 1919–1961," *Journal of African History* 42, no. 2 (2001): 199–216.

21. See Burgess, "Mobility and Discipline," 55–60; and Andrew Burton, "Adjutants, Agents, Intermediaries: The Native Administration in Dar es Salaam township, 1919–61," in *The Urban Experience in Eastern Africa, c. 1750–2000,* ed. A. Burton (Nairobi: British Institute in Eastern Africa, 2002), 98–118.

22. Brennan, "Nation, Race and Urbanization in Dar es Salaam," 155 ff; A. Burton, *African Underclass: Urbanisation, Crime and Colonial Order in Dar es Salaam* (Oxford: James Currey, 2005), 250 ff.

23. PC Eastern to CS, 27 September 1945, TNA SMP 28946/8; PC Eastern to CS, 9 January 1946, TNA SMP 33136/12. See also A. Burton, "Townsmen in the Making: Social Engineering and Citizenship in Dar es Salaam, c. 1945–1960," *International Journal of African Historical Studies* 36, no. 2 (2003): 331–65.

24. Cheyne to CS, 10 August 1946, TNA SMP 28946/27.

25. PC Eastern to District Commissioner (DC) Dar es Salaam, 20 December 1946, TNA 540/3/75/A/1; Liwali of Dar es Salaam to DC Uzaramo, 30 December 1946, TNA 540/3/75/A/2; Secretary, African Association, to PC Eastern, 20 July 1946, TNA 28650/5; Secretary, African Association, to PC Eastern, 10 February 1947, TNA 540/3/75/A/11.

26. Wazee wa mji wa Dar es Salaam to CS, December 1948, TNA SMP 37417/27A.

27. "African Socialism," by JUKANYE, Kampala, *Tanganyika Standard,* 23 July 1943.

28. Letter of "African Youth," *Tanganyika Standard,* 19 July 1946.

29. N. Westcott, "The Impact of the Second World War on Tanganyika, 1939–1949" (PhD diss., Cambridge University, 1982), 299.

30. East African Political Intelligence Report, July to September, 1948, London, Public Record Office (PRO), Colonial Office (CO) 537/3646/36/17. For a discussion of the African Association's development, see J. Iliffe, *A Modern History of Tanganyika* (Cambridge: Cambridge University Press, 1979), 405–35.

31. East African Command Fortnightly Intelligence News (EACFIN), no. 56, 1 August 1950, PRO, CO 537/5920/16.

32. "Tanganyika African National Union," enclosed in Stapledon to Gorell Barnes, 26 November 1955, PRO, CO 822/859/37.

33. Brennan, "Nation, Race and Urbanization in Dar es Salaam," 292 ff.

34. From his observations of 1956–57, J. A. K. Leslie concluded that the top leaders of TANU in Dar es Salaam "are desperately anxious to prove themselves on the side of the angels, able to control the mob, and to show themselves responsible and disciplined" (J. Leslie, *A Survey of Dar es Salaam* [London: Oxford University Press, 1963], 270).

35. Kisarawe DAR 1956, TNA Library.

36. Iliffe, *Modern History of Tanganyika,* 532.

37. G. Macguire, *Towards "Uhuru" in Tanzania: The Politics of Participation* (Cambridge: Cambridge University Press, 1969), 317–19.

38. S. Geiger, *TANU Women: Gender and Culture in the Making of Tanganyikan Nationalism, 1955–65* (Portsmouth, NH: Heinemann, 1997), 118–19, 148.

39. On this, see especially Andrew Ivaska, "'Anti-Mini Militants Meet Modern Misses': Urban Style, Gender, and the Politics of 'National Culture' in 1960s Dar es Salaam, Tanzania," *Gender and History* 14, no. 3 (2002): 584–607.

40. Grattan-Bellew to Mathieson, 12 March 1958, PRO, CO 822/1362/197.

41. Omido to Kahama, 21 July 1961, TNA 540/20/69. See also press release of Omido, 12 August 1960, TNA 561/17/21.

42. Extract from Tanganyika Intelligence Report—October 1960, CO 822/2126/10; letter of Sydney (no surname given) entitled "Church and Political Situation: The Church's Attitude to Politics and Nationalism," dated 10 May 1961, Oxford, Rhodes House (RH), MSS Afr. s. 1604/14.

43. Burgess, "Mobility and Discipline," 62.

44. A. Burton, "'Brothers by Day': Colonial Policing in Dar es Salaam under British Rule, 1919–61," *Urban History* 30, no. 1 (2003): 65, 91.

45. D. Goodhew, "The People's Police Force: Communal Policing Initiatives in the Western Areas of Johannesburg, c. 1930–62," *Journal of Southern African Studies* 19, no. 3 (1993): 447–70; G. Kynoch, "Politics and Violence in the 'Russian Zone': Conflict in Newclare South, 1950–7," *Journal of African History* 41, no. 2 (2000): 267–90.

46. Burgess, "Mobility and Discipline," 63.

47. Ibid., 61.

48. Turnbull to Monson, 21 November 1960, CO 822/2061/12.

49. *Mwafrika,* 19 November 1960.

50. See, inter alia, letter of Sydney, "Church and Political Situation: The Church's Attitude to Politics and Nationalism," 10 May 1961; Macguire, *Towards "Uhuru" in Tanzania,"* 256–57; but see also R. Sadleir, *Tanzania: Journey to Republic* (London: Radcliffe Press, 1999), 231. On the question of legitimate or illegitimate youth violence, see Reid, "Arms and Adolescence," chapter 1 in this volume.

51. *Tanganyika Standard,* 2 November 1960.

52. Letter of Sydney, "Church and Political Situation: The Church's Attitude to Politics and Nationalism," 10 May 1961.

53. M. Longford, *The Flags Changed at Midnight: Tanganyika's Progress to Independence* (Leominster: Gracewing, 2001), 288.

54. "Extracts from Tanganyika Intelligence Summary Report—May 1959," PRO, CO 822/1363/267.

55. See correspondence from ANC Dodoma office to Mtemvu from 25 February 1961 onward, TNA 540/27/28 ff.

56. General Notice no. 657, *Tanganyika Gazette,* 17 March 1961; Sanga to Turnbull, 8 March 1961, RH MSS Brit. Em 365 Box 121/4/160. For a full account of the ANC, see J. R. Brennan, "The Short History of Political Opposition and Multi-Party Democracy in Tanganyika, 1958–64," in *In Search of a Nation: Histories of Authority and Dissidence in Tanzania,* ed. G. H. Maddox and J. L. Giblin (Oxford: James Currey, 2005), 250–76.

57. "Big Bid by A.N.C. in Poll," *Tanganyika Standard,* 23 December 1961.

58. Statement by Zuberi Mtemvu to the Fourth Committee at its 1098th meeting, n.d. (c. March 1961), TNA 540/33/no folio.

59. Presidential speech by Zuberi Mtemvu, ANC, n.d. (c. October 1962), TNA 540/PP/3/no folio.

60. John Miller to Department of State (DOS), Washington, D.C., 26 October 1965, United States National Archives II, College Park, Maryland (USNA), RG 59, Box 2690.

61. *Tanganyika Standard,* 4 July 1962.

62. Ibid., 19 July 1962.

63. Ibid.; letter of Lugano Mwasomola, ibid., 24 July 1962; letter of Emmanuel K. Lwamgira, ibid., 1 August 1962.

64. Circular of Tata Kabwera Foola Union, by Bakari Kondo et al., dated 25 March 1962, Chama Cha Mapinduzi archive (Dodoma) Accession 5/57/27. Buguruni was home to much quasi- and extralegal policing—in 1969, twelve "land rangers" were selected from local TANU Youth League members to police against the growth of squatter settlements in this (largely squatter) community, with little success (R. Stren, *Urban Inequality and Housing Policy in Tanzania: The Problem of Squatting* [Berkeley: University of California Institute of International Studies, 1975], 67).

65. See G. Thomas Burgess, "To Differentiate Rice from Grass: Youth Labor Camps in Revolutionary Zanzibar," chapter 9 in this volume, for a simultaneously connected yet also comparative case.

66. Hennemeyer to DOS, 6 June 1963, USNA RG 59, Box 4057, Pol 13; C. Tungaraza, "The Transformation of Civil-Military Relations in Tanzania," in *The Military and Militarism in Africa,* ed. E. Hutchful and A. Bathily (Dakar: CODESRIA, 1998), 299. On the problems of structural unemployment in Dar es Salaam, see Andrew Burton, "Raw Youth, School-Leavers, and the Emergence of Structural Unemployment in Late Colonial Urban Tanganyika," chapter 5 in this volume.

The Tanganyika Rifles formed on Tanganyika's independence (9 December 1961) out of 6th and 26th Battalions of the King's African Rifles stationed in the territory (Tanzania People's Defence Forces [TPDF], *Tanganyika Rifles Mutiny January 1964* [Dar es Salaam: Dar es Salaam University Press, 1993], 25).

67. The Tanganyika Mutiny, C.R.O. Ref.: 2EA 55/22/4B Copy 149, 18 March 1964, PRO, Dominions Office (DO), 213/56/124A.

68. T. Parsons, *The 1964 Army Mutinies and the Making of Modern East Africa* (Westport, CT: Praeger, 2003), 140. See also TPDF, *Tanganyika Rifles Mutiny,* 106–9.

69. Ph. Murphy, "Intelligence and Decolonization: The Life and Death of the Federal Intelligence and Security Bureau, 1954–63," *Journal of Imperial and Commonwealth History* 29, no. 2 (2001): 121.

70. The Tanganyika Mutiny, C.R.O. Ref.: 2EA 55/22/4B Copy 149, 18 March 1964, PRO, DO 213/56/124A.

71. Ibid.

72. A. Mazrui, *Violence and Thought: Essays on social tensions in Africa* (London: Longman, 1969), 33.

73. Leonhart to Secretary of State, 27 January 1964, USNA RG 59, Box 2687, Pol 23–9; *Tanganyika Standard,* 27 January 1964; Report by Defence Adviser, United Republic of Tanzania for the period 11 March–30 September 1964, Colonel B. G. Pugh, PRO, DO 213/160/1.

74. Leonhart to Secretary of State, 4 February 1964, USNA RG 59, Box 2687, Pol 23–9.

75. For example, Colonel Amin Kashmiri, an Asian officer in the TPDF, informed a U.S. State Department official in 1972 that there was a widespread feeling in "influential circles" that there were too many Chagga and Arusha in the TPDF officer ranks and that orders had been made to recruit from all tribes, not just the allegedly "martial tribes" of Tanzania such as Kuria, Ngoni, and Hehe (Paul Kreisberg to DOS, 14 July 1972, USNA RG 59, Entry 1613, Box 2616).

76. Tungaraza, "Transformation of Civil-Military Relations in Tanzania," 293; Report by Defence Adviser, United Republic of Tanzania for the period 11 March–30 September 1964, Colonel B. G. Pugh, PRO, DO 213/160/1.

77. H. Bienen, *Tanzania: Party Transformation and Economic Development* (Princeton, NJ: Princeton University Press, 1970), 377; Tungaraza, "Transformation of Civil-Military Relations in Tanzania," 301–3.

78. J. Kees van Donge and A. Liviga, "Tanzanian Political Culture and the Cabinet," *Journal of Modern African Studies* 24, no. 4 (1986): 623.

79. *Kiongozi,* 1 August 1964; Gordon to DOS, 10 October 1964 and 29 December 1964, USNA RG 59, Box 2689.

80. Interview by Martha Honey with Seyyid Saeed Akhtar Rizvi, Dar es Salaam, 18 February 1974, notes of interview in author's possession.

81. Macguire, *Towards "Uhuru" in Tanzania,* 371.

82. *Mwafrika,* 9 June 1962. For a history of the Maasai dress campaign, see L. Schneider, "Developmentalism and Its Failings: Why Rural Development Went Wrong in 1960s and 1970s Tanzania" (PhD diss., Columbia University, 2003), 480–540.

83. Letter of L. C. C. Chinkunta, *Mwafrika,* 15 May 1963.

84. *Tanganyika Standard,* 8 October 1963.

85. A. Ivaska, "Negotiating 'Culture' in a Cosmopolitan Capital: Urban Style and the Tanzanian State in Colonial and Postcolonial Dar es Salaam" (PhD diss., University of Michigan, 2003), 157.

86. "Disciplined Youth Needed—Nyerere," *Nationalist,* 17 May 1965.

87. Richardson to Hobden, 27 August 1965, PRO, DO 213/103/50.

88. "No Unemployment in Tanzania," *Nationalist,* 17 August 1965.

89. Letter of G. D. T. Lusinde, *Nationalist,* 19 October 1966.

90. For an authoritative account, see Andrew Ivaska, "Of Students, 'Nizers,' and a Struggle over Youth: Tanzania's 1966 National Service Crisis," *Africa Today* 51, no. 3 (2005): 83–107.

91. "Youths Back Mwalimu," *Standard,* 24 October 1966; Ch. Swift, *Dar Days* (Lanham, MD: University Press of America, 2002), 16.

92. *Standard,* 2 October 1967.

93. *Ngurumo,* 6 February 1968; letter of Bakari Seleman Bakari, *Ngurumo,* 14 February 1968.

94. A. Ivaska, "Negotiating 'Culture' in a Cosmopolitan Capital" 206–7.

95. Brendon Grimshaw, *A Grain of Sand: The Story of One Man and an Island* (Nairobi: Camerapix Publishers International, 1996), 39. The two men were Grimshaw, editor of the *Standard,* and Benjamin Mkapa, editor of the *Nationalist.*

96. "TANU Youths Ban 'Minis': Sijaona announces 'Operation Vijana,'" *Standard,* 3 October 1968, cited in Ivaska, "Negotiating 'Culture' in a Cosmopolitan Capital," 130. For an authoritative account see Ivaska, "Anti-Mini Militants Meet Modern Misses," 584–607.

97. *Ngurumo,* 23 September 1968, cited in Ivaska, "Negotiating 'Culture' in a Cosmopolitan Capital," 211.

98. *Nationalist,* 30 December 1968.

99. Ivaska, "Anti-Mini Militants Meet Modern Misses," cited in Ivaska, "Negotiating 'Culture' in a Cosmopolitan Capital," 223.

100. Hart to Holmes, 30 January 1969, PRO, Foreign and Commonwealth Office (FCO), 31/435/9.

101. T. Burgess, "Cinema, Bell Bottoms, And Miniskirts: Struggles over Youth And Citizenship In Revolutionary Zanzibar," *International Journal of African Historical Studies* 35, no. 2/3 (2002): 301–2.

102. J. Liebenow, *Colonial Rule and Political Development in Tanzania: The Case of the Makonde* (Evanston, IL: Northwestern University Press, 1971), 245, 258–59, 315; biographical note of Lawi Nangwanda Sijaona, enclosed in Hart to Holmes, 6 June 1969, PRO, FCO 31/434/18.

103. *Standard,* 20 April 1968.

104. Ross to DOS, 30 January 1971, USNA RG 59, Entry 1613, Box 2616.

105. Emilio Charles Mzena, a former officer in the colonial police force, was appointed director of intelligence (or "Special Branch") in April 1962. Mzena was replaced as director of intelligence in 1973 by Lawrence Mtazama Gama, a former TANU Youth League member who never had an intelligence assignment, but was married to President Nyerere's sister (Carter to DOS, 6 February 1973, USNA RG 59, Entry 1613, Box 2617.

106. Matlock to DOS, 18 February 1970, USNA RG 59, Entry 1613, Box 2618. There is no adequate history of the treason trial and its background; until there is, see Geiger, *TANU Women,* 175–79, 182–83.

107. Ross to DOS, 2 May 1970, USNA RG 59, Entry 1613, Box 2617.

108. Ibid.

109. Ross, "Quarterly Analysis of Politico-Economic Trends in Tanzania: October–December, 1970," USNA RG59, Entry 1613, Box 2616.

110. Ross to DOS, 11 Aug. 1970, USNA RG 59, Entry 1613, Box 2617.

111. Phillips to Le Tocq, 7 April 1971, PRO, FCO 31/968/7.

112. "Vijana wawe macho," *Uhuru,* 6 December 1971. The fear was that Oscar Kambona would launch another coup attempt—a fear considerably increased when leaflets were dropped over Dar es Salaam on the tenth anniversary supporting Kambona and challenging Nyerere's fitness to rule.

113. Ross to DOS, 4 September 1971, USNA RG 59, Entry 1613, Box 2617.

114. Ross to DOS, 15 September 1971, USNA RG 59, Entry 1613, Box 2617; Ayres to Holmes, 5 October 1971, PRO, FCO 31/968/14. The apparent victor of this contest was Edward Sokoine, who was the only person to oppose Sijaona for the TYL chairmanship, and who would later go on to be prime minister and Nyerere's favored

successor until his death in a car accident (much speculated to have been no accident) in April 1984.

115. W. B. Carter, "Tanganyika African National Union: What Makes Tanzania Run," in American Embassy Dar es Salaam to DOS, 14 December 1973, USNA RG 59, Entry 1613, Box 2617.

116. "Report of Third Quarter 1972, Tanzania," in Carter to Department of State, 20 October 1972, USNA RG 59, Entry 1613, Box 2616.

117. "Militiamen Urged to Wipe Out Banditry," *Daily News,* 10 November 1973; "Operesheni kupe kuenezwa kote—TYL," *Uhuru,* 9 January 1973.

118. H. Lupogo, "Tanzania: Civil-Military Relations and Political Stability," *African Security Review* 10, no. 1 (2001), www.iss.co.za/pubs/ASR/10No1/Lupogo.html.

9

To Differentiate Rice from Grass

Youth Labor Camps in Revolutionary Zanzibar

G. THOMAS BURGESS

UNDERSTANDING HOW ZANZIBAR'S revolutionary regime sought in the 1960s and 1970s to discipline youth helps scholars theorize the postcolonial state in Africa in new ways. Jean-François Bayart's evocative, vegetal, "politics of the belly" serves as a reference to how political scientists in particular commonly describe African political life.[1] Achille Mbembe characterizes the postcolonial era as "an age of nervous exhaustion, greediness, and desire. . . . The spectacle of a world marked by unbridled license . . . an age that exults, so to speak, in suffering, festivity, and drunkenness mixed together." The postcolony, he writes, is "a world hostile to continence, frugality, sobriety."[2] This hardly describes Zanzibar after the revolution. Guided by African nationalist aspirations and socialist techniques, revolutionary elites evolved their own discourse of values in which discipline, applied to the worlds of labor, consumption, and leisure, became an intended prerequisite for public service. Corruption was not the single unifying truth of the regime; instead, through a series of policies and institutions such as youth labor camps, revolutionary officials sought to promote a citizenship ethic that exalted discipline as the means by which to build the nation.

This essay is about how nationalists in Zanzibar chose to exercise power after the revolution. They expended considerable resources in an attempt to create a new generation for whom hard physical labor would be a deeply felt need, an essential condition of an honorable life. The citizens of the new world would be characterized by modesty and selflessness. The camps were meant to serve as mirror opposites of the postcolony Mbembe describes; they were to be free of decadence, ostentation, and beyond the sphere of the economy of desire. They would produce a formative experience: a period of seclusion from ordinary life during which youth could develop a commitment to labor and the revolution that would protect them for the rest of their lives from all the perceived seductions and deceits of the capitalist and imperialist worlds. Although I foreground elite nationalist perspectives on the camps, I also seek to recover something of the nature of the camp experience for the individual. I hope that this essay will stimulate further research on the meaning, for youth, of the nationalist camp experience, one shared by millions of men and women in contemporary Tanzania.

In precolonial Africa it was common practice to seclude youth from the ordinary routines of life in order to produce an exceptional experience that would initiate young people into a new phase of life: that of the warrior, adult, or elder.[3] The guiding purpose of such seclusion was social reproduction, even if it meant the toleration or even promotion in such camps of a culture of youthful dissent from the social norms of the family and village. A generic understanding of such periods of seclusion would emphasize the pedagogical nature of the experience: the lessons imparted were meant to ensure the preservation of the social status quo and maintain the security of the clan, village, or ethnic group. And yet Richard Waller (in this volume) has shown that for the Maasai, *murran* encampments were sites where young males enacted an autonomous and alternative moral universe to that of their elders, characterized by outsiders as "rough" and anarchistic, but which was also one of "extreme solidarity" and "self-denial." Certainly in precolonial societies the production and reproduction of knowledge, sensibilities, and power through periods of seclusion led at times to disputes over questions of duty and the very essence of local notions of 'tribal" discipline.

For its own purposes, and according to its own techniques, the colonial state also secluded youth, at least in relatively small numbers. Boarding schools presented the colonial state an opportunity to uproot young people and immerse them in a competitive environment at a time in their lives when the desire for peer approval and acceptance is intense. Away from home and family, students were relatively open to new habits, routines, knowledge, and procedures. Through the boarding school the colonial state could enact constant surveillance over their young dependents within an enclosed, artificial space; they provided an opportunity to distribute students by ranks and assess them according to examinations. Memories of school in Zanzibar dwell on discipline, hard work, and regimentation, as well as youthful rebellion and pranks. Even with the occasional scandal or escape at night there was limited space for idleness, conspicuous consumption, or ostentation.[4] Schools produced an experience that compelled most students, at least temporarily, to practice a measure of discipline in their habits of labor, leisure, and consumption.

Youth discipline appeared only unevenly in colonial Zanzibar as an explicit objective of state policy. It sometimes emerged as British officials sought to maintain the health and vitality of the clove economy through a constant supply of labor during the harvest season.[5] They were usually concerned, however, with more mundane public works projects and the collection of taxes than they were with ambitious ideas of reshaping public and personal attitudes towards labor, leisure, and consumption. Nevertheless, beginning in the 1940s discipline emerged as a more common reference point in colonial discussions; the concept was often invoked when the topics of youth idleness and delinquency were considered. And yet, in contrast to territories on the East African mainland, British officials in Zanzibar never considered these serious problems; colonial era innovations such as Western schools, sports leagues, and scout programs took young men off the streets and, at least in colonial eyes, inculcated forms of self-discipline.[6] Only in the early 1960s, in the last few years of colonial rule, did officials in the islands elevate youth idleness and delinquency to the stature of, at least potentially, a national crisis for which existing associations and institutions had few answers. Even then the proposals such worries engendered—to extend the colonial state's rather rudimentary disciplinary apparatus through the establishment of a series of youth labor camps—never gained the endorsement of the highest authorities in the islands. Such proposals—initially forwarded by Zanzibari civil servants in 1962 and then discussed by their British expatriate colleagues—expressed the need to protect society from the perceived autonomy and shiftlessness of young loiterers in Zanzibar Town.[7]

The presence of underemployed youth in the capital wasn't anything new; rather, colonial officials in the islands were now making the conceptual link already made by officers on the East African mainland between youth underemployment, urbanization, and undesirable political agitation.[8] As reflected in the proposals and resolutions of an international conference on unemployed youth in Dar es Salaam in 1962 that drew representatives from over a dozen African territories and newly independent states, the idea of secluding youth in rural labor camps was gaining currency just as colonialism faded into history.[9] Labor camps would not only be a means by which to convince youth—school leavers in particular—to stay away from the cities and adopt farming as a profession, they would occupy a no-man's-land between town and country. Such intermediate spaces would be well suited to the liminal social positions of unemployed youth, neither children nor adults, no longer rural nor yet fully urban.

Such proposals, never acted upon in the period of colonial rule in Zanzibar, presaged the radical experiments undertaken only a few years later. African nationalists who led the revolution shared many of the same concerns as the colonialists and conducted experiments in nation building in Zanzibar and in other African states no less ambitious or coercive than the colonial "civilizing mission." Their youth camps represented a conscious attempt to remove "the scars of colonialism" from society, which they uniquely interpreted as, among other things, an acceptance of underdevelopment. An antidote to such acceptance was time spent in a labor camp; in such an interval the state could impart citizenship lessons and seek to instill a disciplinary code premised on the idea that labor and sacrifice were inevitable and necessary to build the nation.

Thus while the idea of youths gathering in rural camps might appear a natural echo of precolonial social institutions, their purpose had changed dramatically. Nationalists regarded change—enacted on the *national* level—as a moral imperative in a way their ancestors did not. And although the idea of youth camps had been discussed briefly in the last years of colonialism, the actual inspiration for Zanzibar's postcolonial interventions came less from the colonial past than from the socialist present. By the 1960s youth labor camps had become common currency in the socialist world, from Cuba to China. In a separate but related development, they were in the process of being established on the Tanzanian mainland. To mobilize and discipline youth, Julius Nyerere's regime established a system of National Service, or "economic conscription," in which young people went to labor camps and endured army-style discipline in a spirit of volunteerism.[10] Service in such camps was mandatory from the later 1960s through the 1970s and 1980s. Ali Mazrui remarked that "the demand for dedicated exertion, the suspicion of certain forms of consumption, the eulogization of the virtues of frugality and self-denial" characterized life in the camps.[11]

Reflecting on the power, wealth, and knowledge of socialist societies in the mid-twentieth century, many nationalists in Zanzibar as well as mainland Tanzania were convinced that their apparent success was partially a consequence of their advanced methods for inculcating youth discipline. Socialism appeared to offer a series of innovations by which to create a new type of citizen, devoted to production more than consumption. They also found in youth camps and associations a series of disciplinary rituals and procedures that gave modern institutional form to historical memories of patriarchal control. Through the medium of socialist technique nationalists sought to enact age-based forms of clientelism on the national level. In this respect nationalists had an edge over colonial officials: they could remind youth that they had delivered the nation from colonial rule, and that youth ought to show their appreciation for such a gift through national service. If they did so, nationalists promised youth eventual full inclusion within a society that claimed to be in the process of removing all privileges of race and class. Such inclusion was only possible, however, through service; the state sought to make patronage function according to a service ethic. Employment in the state bureaucracy would be contingent on a willingness to volunteer and to accept the deferment of rewards. The appearance of discipline, however unevenly enforced and rewarded, was considered the means by which neopatrimonial logic could be reconciled with the development imperative. Politics of the belly—and official elitism—could be abolished or avoided altogether as long as, for example, enough young people circulated through the labor camps and learned their correct duties as citizens. They would learn to look to the state for rewards, but to only seek rewards as a consequence of their perceived contribution to nation building. That was the idea, at least. Andrew Ivaska and, in the preceding chapter, James Brennan have reconstructed how the announcement in 1966 of imminent compulsory National Service—time spent in labor camps—was met with organized hostility among university students in Dar es Salaam.[12] To what extent National Service provoked such resentment and resistance in the camps themselves awaits further research.

Zanzibar's experiment with youth labor camps was not completely unique in postcolonial Africa, but it was exceptional. The islands' minuscule size afforded relatively easy communications, so that official directives could be passed on to the most remote village locales within a day or two. It was unusually difficult in Zanzibar for individuals to withdraw from the state; the East German–trained security apparatus constructed during the era of President Abeid Karume, under the direction of his trusted lieutenant Seif Bakari, chairman of the -Shirazi Party Youth League, was ever-vigilant. The Volunteers—also known on the Tanzanian mainland as the Green Guards—were encouraged to be suspicious and intrusive. Even with the sea a border less permeable and more finite than any land boundary, islanders understood their only recourse from such surveillance was actual exile, an option pursued by thousands after the revolution. Yet despite such openings it wasn't difficult for nationalists in Zanzibar to imagine their islands as a bounded experimental terrain for the sort of disciplinary innovations they sought to impose. The clove boom of the 1960s and 1970s also facilitated the disciplinary project, in that it provided the state unusual resources with which to invest in such institutions as youth labor camps. The Zanzibari Revolution in 1964 added another exceptional impetus; the uprising appeared to legitimize a decisive departure from the ruling norms of the past and to permit a radical restructuring of society. This would involve, among other things, an intended cultural revolution, in which the state encouraged or coerced citizens to reconsider and reform their daily habits in light of perceived national interests.

How the state defined these interests in the islands was an extension of nationalist thought, informed by socialist precepts. Zanzibar's embrace of socialism was not merely lip service but a key element of the revolutionary project and a long-term engagement with the ideas, historical precedents, aid, and advice of the socialist world. The unusual degree, at least in postcolonial Africa, to which Zanzibar experimented with socialist disciplinary techniques was partially a function of socialism's distinguished provenance and reputation in the mid-twentieth century as the best means by which to achieve rapid development. It was also a function of the islands' cosmopolitanism; Zanzibar had for centuries attracted an almost uninterrupted flow of people, commodities, and new ideas from throughout the Indian Ocean world. Even though socialism was a rather more exotic plant, it had already established roots in island society by the time of the revolution. A cohort of young Zanzibaris had, through their travels and studies in the 1950s and 1960s introduced the islands to socialism to a degree not seen in other East African territories, provoking American and British fears that Zanzibar would emerge as the "Cuba" of East Africa.[13] The comparison contained some meaning; the revolutionary regime in Zanzibar came to share with Cuba and other members of the socialist family of nations a common emphasis on social discipline as an essential characteristic of any society seeking accelerated development.

Labor camps had both a bureaucratic and a romantic appeal. In the nationalist imagination, they were meant to serve as patronage devices, as means to relieve the towns of urban loiterers, and as a way to impart practical skills. In an early publicity statement, President Karume's regime explained its primary motivations for opening the camps: "[T]he emerging young generation should be integrated with the productive occupations of the country," which were primarily agricultural. Second, "the people of Zanzibar should exploit fully their arable land by cultivating food crops" in order to make the country self-sufficient. Third, "[a]part from their economical value, the schemes also have character-training value.

The young people learn self-reliance and become hardened by camp life. They also learn to work selflessly and to be of service to their country."[14]

The camps were also supposed to level the differences between youth from town and from the countryside. Ali Sultan Issa, as minister of Youth, Education, and Culture from 1965 to 1968, took a leading role in establishing the labor camps. His ministry shared responsibility with the Youth League of the ruling Afro-Shirazi Party (ASPYL) for the camps. He remembered:

> There was a problem also with idle youth, whom we wanted to make more productive. We had to contain the multitude of our youngsters swarming from the rural areas into town after the revolution. We couldn't have them roaming the streets, doing nothing, so we decided they should go back to the country and cultivate. We should put them in labour camps, like in the socialist countries. . . . These camps already existed in China, Ghana, Cuba, Israel and other places. . . . We eventually brought over a Ghanaian expert named E. A. Hawkson to come run the youth camps along lines already developed in Ghana.
>
> The camps would take the youth off the streets, organize and discipline them, train them with practical skills, and, finally, give them ideological and military training. From the Chinese we also had the idea of sending people from town to the countryside, so we could break down the differences between the urban and the rural. How can we have a more homogeneous society, and more unity? How could the urban people know the hardships of the rural areas if they did not go there? The intelligentsia here would look down on the peasantry as inferior, but they relied on them for their food.[15]

The camps were thus, among other things, intended to function as spaces of social integration, where young Zanzibaris shared common living conditions and worked and sang together. Issa remembered that although youth from town "hated the camps, we made them go; they had to differentiate between rice and grass. . . . We had to minimize the differences between rural and urban youth, so the contradictions would be eliminated, so the urban youth didn't look down on rural youth."[16] The differences between rural and urban youth were historically marked both in terms of living conditions and exposure to hard physical labor. The slave economy as it developed in Zanzibar in the nineteenth century allowed most members of urban patrician families to regard agricultural work in particular as lacking social prestige. Since state officials sought to exalt physical labor as the primary engine of national development, they felt they needed to reeducate citizens whose ancestry, wealth, and urban residences had in the past largely relieved them of strenuous labor requirements.

Such attitudes would not do in a revolutionary society; in nationalist eyes Zanzibar Town, with its numerous ethnic enclaves and commercial networks, its public and private displays of cosmopolitan consumerism, its dependence on poorer outlying neighborhoods and the countryside for its productive labor, was what young people needed to escape in order to learn the qualities of good citizens. Though camp graduates might make Zanzibar Town their permanent home afterward, they were supposed to merely live in the city and not be of the city. Since all camp youth equally shared conditions of privation, ethnic chauvinism or urban conceit would theoretically have no place in the postcolony. By delivering camp youth at least temporarily from the materialism of city life, the regime would create a new kind of citizen with which to staff its expanding security and bureaucratic apparatus. As camp youth set aside desires for personal gratification and the comforts of home they would, after weeks of deprivation, grasp higher revolutionary truths and knowledge.[17]

Though the camps were meant, at least on one level, for bourgeois urban youth, or young and underemployed transients attracted by the wages and amenities of Zanzibar Town, the Youth League did not initially recruit from either category to people its new labor camps. It selected instead youth activists known for their past sacrifices and behavior; it focused more on patrimonial objectives than the erasure of unemployment or urban chauvinism. Issa recalled: "[T]hey did not choose just anyone to go; the young person had to have stamina and the right party history. They did not just round up unemployed youth; these boys volunteered through the Youth League."[18]

In April 1965, a few dozen youth were first sent to Kama camp ten miles outside the capital. The government gave them a farm of four hundred acres; they cultivated a variety of crops on forty acres of their allotment. The second "youth brigade" was founded at Bambi the following month. A farm of four hundred acres was allotted to sixty-five youth, who grew millet and after two years were supposed to move into new "dormitories," which they constructed themselves.[19] A third camp was founded in Pemba, at Ngezi. In October 1966 there were three officers, two enlisted staff, and 167 males and 18 female youth in the three camps.[20] By 1968 three further camps had been established at Chechele, Selem, and Machui, bringing the total to six; by 1972 this had expanded to twelve.

Kweupe, the official government organ and the only newspaper published in the islands in the late 1960s, provided regular reports of camp activities, which constructed happy images of youth building the nation, and of the discipline, harmony, and self-reliance prevailing in daily camp routines. The regime produced official stamps showing male and female camp youth turning their backs on shriveled corn stalks, ramshackle homes, and darkness, and looking toward a bright future symbolized by a full ear of corn, a brick wall, and farms with neat, parallel furrows. Such images were at least partially for the benefit of several key foreign patrons. Ghana sent uniforms.[21] The Soviet Union sent a few agricultural experts. At least three teachers from the German Democratic Republic assisted in training about fifty camp youth as plumbers and electricians, who also learned how to play basketball, volleyball, and badminton.[22] The GDR also sent tractors.[23] In March 1967 twenty-one youth from the camps were receiving training overseas.[24] Four went to study in Cuba, and nine to Russia.[25] Upon their return, five of the nine assumed leadership or clerical positions in the camps. One became camp commandant; another, however, was accused of "putting on airs" since his return and refusing to take orders. He drove a tractor without authorization, and broke another youth's bed.[26]

Each youth received ten or twenty shillings allowance per month allowance per month and was supposed to be issued a bed, mattress, pillow, pillowcase, bedsheet, bedspring cover, towel, spoon, mug, plate, basin, blanket, and mosquito net.[27] Such supplies were often unavailable, however.[28] Arising at dawn, camp youth followed a routine of exercises and morning tea, served without bread or biscuits (*chai ya mkono moja tu*). Camp youth then went to chop wood or work in the fields, ate lunch, completed more fieldwork in the afternoon, and then perhaps played football until darkness enveloped the camp. After sunset they ate dinner and then sometimes sang songs.[29] The living conditions were generally poor; there was no electricity or running water. Camp youth cooked over open fires food that was usually of the lowest price and quality: porridge, bad rice ("with pebbles"), cassava, and beans.[30] In 1967 the water supply at Bambi was unclean; youth complained of pain in their stomachs after drinking.[31] For months Ngezi camp youth subsisted primarily on cassava.[32] Sent from Ghana to direct the youth camps, E. A. Hawkson reported in 1966 a need in all the camps for dining tables. The food supply at Ngezi was "pathetic," forcing camp youth to walk seven miles to collect food.[33] The following year the food served at Ngezi was still "shocking"; only rice was served for two months solid: "such is the life of Brigadiers, who are hard working."[34]

Political lectures formed an integral part of the camp routine. Initially the need for national security was emphasized, though over the years instruction grew more sophisticated and elaborate. In 1976 the program for daily instruction at camps in Unguja Ukuu and Pete extended to the following topics: The History of the ASP; The Problem of Inequality; Opposing Foreign Attacks and Subversion and How to Keep Party Secrets; The Politics of Capitalist Nations Towards Africa; First Aid; The Meaning of Leadership; The Discipline of a Leader; Guarding the Nation; The Importance of Living in a Socialist Way; Traditions and Customs; The Politics of Socialist Nations; The Difference Between the Thoughts of the Leaders of Socialist Nations and Capitalist Nations; Why the Zanzibari Revolution Took Place.[35]

Hawkson provided repetitive reports of the absence of any camp entertainment: no parties, no cinema, and no indoor games; sports activities often couldn't be organized due to lack of equipment. Radios were banned from the camps, and for reading material only *Kweupe* was available; even the political lectures were sometimes discontinued.[36] Issa recalled: "We did not just send them there and dump them. We built *mabanda makuti,* thatched shelters, and later they had tents. Later, we provided uniforms contributed by the East German youth organization, the Frei Deutsche Jugend. At first we did not have blankets, mosquito nets, or even pit latrines; but as we progressed, we became more organized."[37]

Agricultural work was at the heart of the regime. Beginning in early 1967 farmwork was conducted on individual plots. Each youth was supposed to complete work on a plot of one hundred feet square per week. Failure to complete such work resulted in the loss of one week's wages. At Bambi camp there were two sessions of work, from 7:30 a.m.. to 12:30 p.m., and from 2:00 p.m. to 5:00 p.m. Females reportedly conformed to the same work expectations as men.[38] By July 1967 another work plan had been devised, however. The Youth League ordered the demarcation of twenty-acre plots, each to be cultivated by six brigadiers working in two shifts, from 6:00 a.m. to 12 p.m., and from 2 p.m. to 6 p.m.[39]

Continual logistical problems obstructed agricultural work. Hawkson reported a lack of seeds and machinery.[40] In November 1966 he reported that the general progress of Kama camp was at a standstill due to lack of materials. At Bambi the harvesting of maize was not completed, and the stumping of four hundred acres had stopped due to a broken-down bulldozer. At Ngezi there had been no transport for six months, so that Hawkson was moved to remark "those boys are suffering a great deal."[41] The unwillingness of camp youth to conduct routine maintenance on bulldozers and other camp equipment compounded the problems. They reportedly drove tractors at top speeds, even while pulling plows, and used the tractors to drive into town for routine errands, compelling Hawkson to announce, "the tractors are not to be used to carry food to and from the town."[42]

Poor morale was another cause for work to come to a halt. Hawkson reported in 1967 that camp youth were increasingly disappointed "in view of the fact that they were promised to be given places in the Army and Police. Since this was not done, they feel reluctant to work with full zeal. . . . [T]hey feel that they are working for the Gov[ernment]t and as such, they need not waste extra time to complete a day's work."[43] "I still feel they must be educated to know their responsibility to the Nation as such."[44] A Youth League report from 1968, however, cited poor soil conditions at Kama, Bambi, and Ngezi camps as the reason for poor agricultural yields. The same report claimed that the three new camps established in 1968 would not face such difficulties, since their locations had been chosen only after careful study of local fertility.[45]

Despite continual problems, hopeful news was now and then received at government and party offices, particularly from Ngezi. In October 1967 "steady progress" was recorded at Kama and Bambi, but the report from Ngezi was more effusive: "[P]rogress has been excellent and members of this Camp are duty conscious."[46] Evidence of such progress had been accumulating over several months. Under the leadership of a Russian-trained camp commandant, their dormitories, camp store, kitchen, and clinic were all clean and in good order. Ngezi youth constructed their own camp office, without orders to do so; such volunteerism was "a model for others to follow." The forty-acre plot of maize they had recently harvested was, due to its high yield and layout, "the talk of the town." In sum, camp youth had "given themselves to make an ideal village of their own."[47] They were also operating their own school for ninety-four children from the local village, providing tuition and materials for free, and were preparing to launch evening adult literacy courses. Local villagers were pleased and volunteered to clear bush one day a week in the camp in order to compensate for the education of their children.[48] In summary, Hawkson remarked that the "boys at Ngezi Camp have developed a spirit of tolerance and sacrifice; they are cooperative, and respect their work, law and order. Though they face continual food and transport problems, they are cheerful and work hard. Great credit goes to the Camp Commandants who are themselves determined to work for their mother land." Hawkson recommended 'that Brigadiers from Kama and Bambi [be] sent to Ngezi to study the true spirit with which their counterparts take to work."[49]

Nevertheless, camp discipline was tough, and the daily routine of fieldwork and poor food took their toll. Each camp had at least one representative of the Youth League serving as discipline and provost brigadier. Youth were punished with extra work assignments if they caused conflict in the camp or failed to meet their labor quotas. In 1967 the Youth League executive committee expelled eight camp youth for bad behavior.[50] Usually the camp commandant simply imposed fines of several days labor without pay. Although camp youth were allowed on a rotational basis to return home on the weekends, many still ran away, often because of hunger.[51] Desertion was not a major problem, though, since those who left the camps were easily replaced by new inductees. Issa recalled: "On the whole, they observed the discipline. If they didn't like the camps, they could always leave, but I did not have a major problem with that."[52]

The focus of the camps was on instilling attitudes of mind more than developing specific skills. *Kweupe* claimed the camps instilled "the sense of the need for hard work in order that the nation which is young may forge ahead. . . . [I]t is clear that after a stay of two years in a camp the youth will no longer have personal or selfish ambitions and will only be concerned with the well-being of the cultivator and the worker."[53] Although a 1975 government report stated the youth camps needed to be "reformed" to provide practical training for youth beyond agriculture and cutting firewood, no successes in this direction ever appeared in the records.[54] The most common nonagricultural lessons camp youth received were in how to shoot a gun. Few other practical skills were ever imparted. Moreover, the low crop yields recorded by a 1976 inspection report suggested a "seriously low level of expertise." At Chambani camp, seventy-one acres devoted to corn production yielded only eleven sacks; at Ngezi camp 950 chickens gave only 250 eggs per day. The committee reported that camp youth, who in some camps in 1976 were still living in temporary shelters, had high "political awareness" but no leadership or planning from headquarters.[55] Even with such poor results the state continued to invest heavily in the camps, with little financial return. The camps were not self-sustaining state enterprises. In 1974 the state spent 4,314,043 shillings to support the camps, which produced only 673,237 shillings of revenue. The following year was not much better, the state investing 2,173,515 shillings in camps that only produced 787,455 shillings in revenue.[56] Issa remembered:

> Some camps were for rice cultivation and some for cassava, depending on local soil conditions. We had to heavily subsidize the ones producing cash crops because we were experimenting unsuccessfully with wheat,

> peanuts, and cotton, for example. The camps producing cassava, sweet potatoes, bananas, and rice took care of themselves in terms of food, but each youth also received a stipend from the government, and each camp required other assistance such as for transportation and camp infrastructure that their harvests could not support. So the camps were never self-reliant.[57]

Despite the drain on state resources, the camps kept youth off the streets and temporarily employed; they graduated youth who would potentially return to their villages as loyal party volunteers, or were considered morally qualified for recruitment into the army and police. In 1968 it became government policy to hire only camp graduates for the army and police, and to give them preferential treatment in civil service hirings.[58] From 1971 to 1973 1,159 camp graduates were reportedly sent to work in various government and party offices.[59] Officials granted government or party jobs only after consulting the applicant's home Youth League branch about the political credentials, personality, and family background of the applicant, making sure they hired people from families of proven party loyalties.[60] The camps thus represented one of a few institutionalized means in the 1970s to determine which products of the school system would receive government salaries. And yet still they were resisted. The Youth League reported that children who failed Form III did not like to go to the camps; they often ran away after arriving.[61] The Youth League nevertheless drew up plans in 1976, never fulfilled, to send *all* children and youth to the camps four times a year, where they would be "taught to live together in socialist relations."[62]

The mandate of the camps broadened in the early 1970s to include underemployed graduates of Zanzibar's rapidly expanding educational system. By then Zanzibar faced a school-leaver problem, especially among youth with a Standard X education, most of whom after graduation sought employment in a public sector too small to accommodate all applicants. The government required all graduates hoping to gain state employment to live in the camps for a period of two years. The only exceptions were those who went to the Nkrumah Teacher's Training College, who looked forward to a lifetime of public service at low pay.[63] Such policy changes were probably responsible for the rapid increase in 1973 in the numbers of youth in the camps. In 1972, 1,245 youth worked in twelve camps in Pemba and Unguja.[64] By the following year that number had increased to 2,735.[65] Without unemployment statistics, it is difficult to say if the extension of the camps' purview in the 1970s was a response to growing youth joblessness, or, as appears more likely, a measure of the regime's growing confidence in the youth camp as a disciplinary institution.

Camp conditions remain a contested memory. Camp leaders reportedly "took the youth as prisoners to be punished": "The government really didn't care about unemployment—they thought the camps were the way to control the youth, because they had led the 1964 Revolution—they had to be controlled. The youth camp was like a prison without facilities; it made you hate your country."[66]

A former government teacher in the 1960s and 1970s, remarked, "Youth camps? They were only popular because graduates would join the government service. They were chaotic, with no discipline, no food. . . . [Y]oung people roamed about the countryside like vermin destroying people's crops, picking fruit."[67] Issa remembered that for youth from rural areas, the camps were like "a picnic," for which they sometimes volunteered; but for young people from town, their experience in the camps usually embittered them toward the government.[68] One camp graduate of an elite ASP background remarked that generally youth didn't like the camps, whether they came from town or countryside, but they endured them anyway to obtain jobs. They worried that, despite the government's promises, they wouldn't receive a job afterward, perhaps as a result of their political ancestry and family's former support for the regime overthrown in the revolution.[69]

Certainly for young people from the countryside camp conditions were often no worse than the conditions they endured at home. The camps were furthermore an escape from subordination to their village seniors. The promise of social promotion and government employment was delivered often enough that many saw the camps as less punishment than as an opportunity for inclusion. Youth were in fact regularly turned away from the camps because of a lack of vacancies. They arrived in the camps as a result of coercion, but also as volunteers.[70] They endured such spartan conditions in the hopes of earning revolutionary merit and a government job after "graduation."

In revolutionary Zanzibar, enduring discipline was thus the equivalent of a school certificate. The labor camps were intended to function as finishing schools for socialist citizenship. Living an austere agrarian life was not meant to prepare youth to farm so much as to serve the regime. After two years in a labor camp, he or she was able to work in the fields, fire a gun, and sing nationalist songs. Every youth knew how to participate in national rituals, could recount the nationalist historical narrative, and identify not only the elders but the enemies of the revolution. Every youth knew his or her duty, whether it was to perform "voluntary" labor assignments, or to avoid "town luxuries." Youth labor camps were one of a series of institutional innovations introduced in the 1960s and 1970s to instill a new citizenship ethic among islanders. As Zanzibar's economy declined and then virtually collapsed in the early 1980s, however, the government confronted bankruptcy and was forced to discontinue, phase out, or radically downsize most such innovations. It dramatically reduced its support for the Young Pioneers, the Volunteers, and the Youth League itself. Yet youth labor camps lingered on and continue to this day as one of the few relics of what in the islands most islanders regard as a more disciplined time.

MICHEL FOUCAULT MIGHT have noted that the camps employed many classic disciplinary techniques, including ranks, exercises, and surveillance,—all of which contributed to the construction of a hegemonic power-knowledge complex in the islands after the revolution. James Scott might interpret the camps as evidence of a modernist regime's impulse toward miniaturization, or to build "model villages, model cities, military colonies, show projects, and demonstration farms" in order to create "sharply defined experimental terrain," a "self-contained, utopian space," and "small islands of order and modernity."[71] In Zanzibar, however, the forms and techniques employed in the camps were derivative of and less significant than the ideas that animated the early postcolonial era. Discipline, along with nation building and the promotion of the economic interests of the African majority in the islands, was paramount. One of those sensibilities notably absent in current writing on the postcolony, discipline, was not only part of the official imaginary in Zanzibar, it was the stated objective of a series of state interventions in Zanzibar in the 1960s and 1970s, including the establishment of the Young Pioneers and the Volunteers. Such interventions did not just apply to the young: the state imposed food rations and forced labor when, at the height of the clove boom in the early 1970s, Zanzibar's cash reserves were reaching an all-time high.[72] Discipline was not simply a means to produce power and get people to obey and carry out the will of the revolutionary regime; it was an end in itself. Youth labor camps were one example of several nationalist-era innovations in Zanzibar that produced at least the appearance of discipline, whether coerced or internalized.

The youth labor camps also constituted an essential part of the fabric of everyday life in the islands during the nationalist era, a topic that demands far more research than is presented here. Although I have emphasized the contours of nationalist thought and official perspectives on the camps, we know little of how hundreds of thousands of both the islands and mainland of Tanzania experienced national service, and how such an experience figured in the process of maturation, or the formation of identity. How did it shape public attitudes toward the state, and how did it integrate (or not) youth of diverse ethnicities and backgrounds? What knowledge and understandings did it produce? Youth who matured during the nationalist age were exposed to a range of experiences unique for their time, which fundamentally influenced the narratives of their lives. They were hailed as the vanguard of a new order—and potentially also its saboteurs.

Notes

1. J.-F. Bayart, *The State in Africa: The Politics of the Belly*, trans. M. Harper (London: Longman, 1993).

2. A. Mbembe, *On the Postcolony* (Berkeley: University of California Press, 2001), 110, 238–39.

3. See, for example, P. H. Gulliver, *Social Control in an African Society* (Boston: Boston University Press, 1963).

4. T. Burgess, *Race, Revolution, and the Struggle for Human Rights in Zanzibar: The Memoirs of Ali Sultan Issa and Seif Sharif Hamad* (Athens: Ohio University Press, 2009), 38–41, 176–80.

5. For early colonial attempts to impose time and work discipline in Zanzibar through the criminalization of vagrancy and underemployment among former slaves, see F. Cooper, *From Slaves to Squatters* (New Haven: Yale University Press, 1987).

6. Nor did Zanzibar Town experience postwar rates of rapid urbanization anywhere near those of emerging cities on the mainland such as Dar es Salaam and Nairobi, a fact noted by colonial officers.

7. Symposium on Unemployed Youth, 1962, Zanzibar National Archives, Zanzibar Town, Tanzania (hereafter ZNA), BA 108/10.

8. T. Burgess, "Mobility and Discipline: Colonial Age Discourse in Tanzania," in *Rethinking Age in Africa: Colonial, Post-colonial and Contemporary Interpretations of Cultural Representations*, ed. M. Aguilar (Trenton: Africa World Press, 2006). See also A. Burton, *African Underclass: Urbanisation, Crime and Colonial Order in Dar es Salaam* (Oxford: James Currey, 2005).

9. Symposium on Unemployed Youth, ZNA.

10. See James R. Brennan, "Youth, the TANU Youth League, and Managed Vigilantism in Dar es Salaam, Tanzania, 1925–73," chapter 8 in this volume.

11. A. Mazrui, *Cultural Engineering and Nation-Building in East Africa* (Evanston, IL: Northwestern University Press, 1972), 220.

12. A. Ivaska, "Of Students, 'Nizers,' and a Struggle over Youth: Tanzania's 1966 National Service Crisis," *Africa Today* 51, no. 3 (2005): 83–107; Brennan, "Youth, the TANU Youth League, and Managed Vigilantism."

13. T. Burgess, "An Imagined Generation: Umma Youth in Nationalist Zanzibar," in *In Search of a Nation: Histories of Authority and Dissidence from Tanzania: Essays in Honor of I. M. Kimambo*, ed. G. Maddox, J. Giblin, and Y. Q. Lawi (London: James Currey, 2005).

14. Youth Training—Workers' Brigade, Zanzibar, 1966–68; #304–5, ZNA AD 5/65.

15. Burgess, *Race, Revolution, and the Struggle for Human Rights in Zanzibar*, 114–15.

16. Interview, Ali Sultan Issa, Zanzibar Town, 21 August 1996; also Enzi Talib, Zanzibar Town, 5 August 1997.

17. The nongendered employment of the term "youth" is a reflection of what was available for study in the postcolonial archive. Official observers of the young were primarily interested in issues of resources, productivity, morale, citizenship, and discipline. The scope of my oral history research was, perhaps unfortunately, also limited to such questions. A gendered analysis of youth camps in revolutionary Zanzibar would likely yield interesting insights, particularly concerning the construction of masculinity, since males made up the vast majority of early camp youth. Female youth were more commonly restricted by their parents from long-term residence in the camps. More girls and young women went to the camps when, as discussed below, it became compulsory in the 1970s for most secondary school students. Anecdotal evidence suggests the female students from town disliked the camps as much as the males.

18. Burgess, *Race, Revolution, and the Struggle for Human Rights in Zanzibar*, 116.

19. *Kweupe*, 11 December 1965, 447. As late as October 1966 no action had been taken on constructing huts for the brigadiers (monthly progress report for the month of October 1966, #278, Youth Training—Workers' Brigade, Zanzibar, 1966–68, ZNA AD 5/6).

20. Monthly progress report for the month of October 1966 for camps Kama/Bambi/Ngezi in Pemba, #9, Youth Training—Workers' Brigade, Zanzibar, 1966–68, ZNA AD 5/65.

21. Mipango ya Kambi za Vijana; #58, Katibu Mkuu, Wizara ya Elimu na Mila to Katibu Mkuu, Wizara ya Fedha, 12 August 1966, ZNA AD 5/6.

22. Mipango ya Kambi za Vijana; #63, Ripoti juu ya mitihani ya skuli ya ufundi huko Kupaz, ZNA AD 5/66.

23. Monthly progress report for the month of October 1966 for camps Kama/Bambi/Ngezi in Pemba, #8, Youth Training—Workers' Brigade, Zanzibar, 1966–68, ZNA AD 5/65.

24. Monthly progress report for the month of March 1967, #327, Youth Training—Workers' Brigade, Zanzibar, 1966–68, ZNA AD 5/65.

25. E. A. Hawkson, national organizer, youth brigade, 1 October 1966, #1, Youth Training—Workers' Brigade, Zanzibar, 1966–68, ZNA AD 5/65.

26. National organizer, youth brigade, to Ministry of Education and Culture, 10 August 1967, #412, Youth Training—Workers' Brigade, Zanzibar, 1966–68, ZNA AD 5/65.

27. Mipango ya Kambi za Vijana, #108, "Kambi ya Vijana," 19 December 1967, ZNA AD 5/66.

28. Mipango ya Kambi za Vijana, #124, Skuli ya Uhunzi, Kambi ya Vijana Ujenzi na Skuli ya Ushoni, approved estimates, 1967–68, ZNA AD 5/66.

29. Interviews, Waziri Mbwana, Zanzibar Town, 26 August 1997; Mshindo Makame Vuai, Zanzibar Town, 21 August 1999.

30. Interview, Mshindo Makame Vuai, Zanzibar Town, 21 August 1999.

31. Monthly progress report for the month of July 1967, #455–56, Youth Training—Workers' Brigade, Zanzibar, 1966–68, ZNA AD 5/65.

32. Inspection Notes, Ngezi Camp, October 1966, #23, Ministry of Education and National Culture, Youth Training—Workers' Brigade, Zanzibar, 1966–68, ZNA AD 5/65.

33. Monthly progress report for the month of November 1966, Part E, #290, Youth Training—Workers' Brigade, Zanzibar, 1966–68, ZNA AD 5/65.

34. Camp inspection report on Ngezi Camp from 11 to 17 July 1967, #406–12, Youth Training—Workers' Brigade, Zanzibar, 1966–68, ZNA AD 5/65.

35. YL Headquarters to Ministry of Education, 11 December 1976, #321, Umoja wa Vijana, 1974–77, ZNA AD 5/53.

36. Monthly progress report for the month of October 1966 for camps Kama/Bambi/Ngezi in Pemba, #9, Youth Training—Workers' Brigade, Zanzibar, 1966–68, ZNA AD 5/65.

37. Burgess, *Race, Revolution, and the Struggle for Human Rights in Zanzibar*, 115–16.

38. Part Two Orders, 3 April 1967, #324, Youth Training—Workers' Brigade, Zanzibar, 1966–68, ZNA AD 5/65.

39. Camp inspection report on Ngezi Camp from 11 to 17 July 1967, #406–12, Youth Training—Workers' Brigade, Zanzibar, 1966–68, ZNA AD 5/65.

40. Hawkson, "Visit by 2nd Vice President and Discussion," 16 September 1966, #3, Youth Training—Workers' Brigade, Zanzibar, 1966–68, ZNA AD 5/65.

41. Monthly progress report for the month of November 1966, #286, Youth Training—Workers' Brigade, Zanzibar, 1966–68, ZNA AD 5/65.

42. "Movement and Maintenance of Tractors," 21 April 1967, #339, Youth Training—Workers' Brigade, Zanzibar, 1966–68, ZNA AD 5/65.

43. Monthly progress report for the month of June 1967, #400–404, Youth Training—Workers' Brigade, Zanzibar, 1966–68, ZNA AD 5/65.

44. Youth Training—Workers' Brigade, Zanzibar, 1966–68; Monthly Progress Report, no date, #194, ZNA AD 5/65.

45. Maendeleo ya Umoja wa Vijana wa ASP 1964–68, ZNA AK 34/5.

46. Monthly progress report for the month of October 1967, #221, Youth Training—Workers' Brigade, Zanzibar, 1966–68, ZNA AD 5/65.

47. Camp inspection report on Ngezi Camp from 11 to 17 July 1967, #406–12, Youth Training—Workers' Brigade, Zanzibar, 1966–68, ZNA AD 5/65.

48. Camp inspection report on Ngezi Camp from 4 to 9 September 1967, #181–82, Youth Training—Workers' Brigade, Zanzibar, 1966–68, ZNA AD 5/65.

49. Camp inspection report on Ngezi Camp From 11–17 July 1967, #406–12, Youth Training—Workers' Brigade, Zanzibar, 1966–68, ZNA AD 5/65.

50. Katibu Mkuu, ASPYL, to Katibu Mkuu Wizara ya Elimu na Mila, #250, Youth Training—Workers' Brigade, Zanzibar, 1966–68, ZNA AD 5/65.

51. Interview, Mshindo Makame Vuai, Zanzibar Town, 21 August 1999.

52. Burgess, *Race, Race, Revolution, and the Struggle for Human Rights in Zanzibar,* 116.

53. *Truth Prevails,* 1 February 1972, 20 January 1972.

54. Report of Young Pioneers at 4th meeting of the ASPYL, 1975, uncollected files of the Afro-Shirazi Party Youth League (hereafter ASPYL HQ), Zanzibar Town, Tanzania.

55. Report of JKT touring group, 21 September 1976, ASPYL HQ.

56. Four-month volunteer report, 1975, ASPYL/2/1, File Zanzibar Region, ASPYL HQ.

57. Burgess, *Race, Revolution, and the Struggle for Human Rights in Zanzibar,* 116.

58. Interviews, Muhammed Ali Khatib, Makunduchi, 18 August 1999; Mshindo Makame Vuai, Zanzibar Town, 21 August 1999.

59. Three-year report on Youth League activities, 1973, ASPYL HQ.

60. Ibid. In practice this meant scrutiny of an applicant's racial/ethnic identity and prerevolutionary party affiliation.

61. "Mkutano wa kamati ya mapinduzi ya mkoa kaskazini," meeting minutes, 18 July 1977, #343, Umoja wa Vijana, 1974–77, ZNA AD 5/53.

62. Activities of ASPYL, 1976–1978, ASPYL/1/63, ASPYL HQ.

63. Interview, Muhammed Ali Khatib, Makunduchi, 18 August 1999.

64. *The Nationalist,* 2 February 1972; *Truth Prevails,* 10 November 1972.

65. Three-year report on Youth League activities, 1973, ASPYL HQ.

66. Interviews, Rashid Khamis Rashid, Zanzibar Town, 12 July 1996; also, anonymous, Zanzibar Town, 22 July 1996; anonymous, Zanzibar Town, 17 August 1996; Faridi Suleiman Abdallah, Zanzibar Town, 12 July 1996.

67. Interview, anonymous, Zanzibar Town, 19 August 1996.

68. Interviews, Ali Sultan Issa, Zanzibar Town, 4 July 1996, 13 July 1996, 21 August 1996.

69. Interview, Mshindo Makame Vuai, Zanzibar Town, 21 August 1999.

70. Interviews, anonymous, Zanzibar Town, 22 July 1996; Enzi Talib, Zanzibar Town, 5 August 1997; Waziri Mbwana, Zanzibar Town, 26 August 1997; Abdul Shakur Talib Ali, Kizimkazi, 22 February 1999; Seleman Pingo, Jambiani, 18 February 1999.

71. J. Scott, *Seeing Like a State: How Certain Schemes to Improve the Human Condition Have Failed* (New Haven: Yale University Press, 1998), 257–58.

72. Esmond Martin, *Zanzibar: Tradition and Revolution* (Zanzibar: Gallery Publication, 2007), 63 ff.

10

Premarital Sexuality in Great Lakes Africa, 1900–1980

SHANE DOYLE

THE DEFINITION OF youth is problematic. A liminal state, it is perhaps best understood by being contrasted with the life stage that follows it, adulthood. Adulthood itself, though, is not a concept with the same meaning in all places and at all times. And within any particular historical context, the process of social recognition of maturity might not occur at the same time as the key event that accords the legal status of adulthood. Adolescence has been viewed by some scholars as an essentially Western, modern phenomenon, as the gap between childhood and adulthood lengthened in the context of industrialization, education, and urbanization.[1] But Margaret Mead's work demonstrated that adolescence was an experience that existed across cultures, albeit with local variations, and that the influences of Westernization have generally been synthesized with local cultural attitudes toward the achievement of adulthood.[2] Although in most modern societies adulthood automatically and universally accompanies the survival of usually eighteen years, historically becoming an adult usually involved the drama of ceremony: initiation, the burial of a father, the acquisition of property, or marriage. Marriage is the most significant marker of the end of youth because it demonstrates humanity's unique distinction between physical maturity and adulthood. The biological capability for reproduction does not necessarily equate with social maturity.

There has been some debate about whether this fundamental distinction applies to sub-Saharan African societies. The demographer Jack Caldwell, adapting the anthropologist Jack Goody's theories, has argued that African societies, unlike those in Europe and Asia, have not historically been characterized by settled agriculture, the production of large surpluses, major social differentiation, or monotheistic religion. Consequently African social life was not dominated by the need to guarantee the safe transfer of property, especially land, within the family by ensuring marital stability. Thus the requirement to restrict premarital and extramarital sexuality, especially for females, did not apply to Africa. Instead, Caldwell argues that African family life focused on the extension and multiplication of the lineage, which consequently encouraged the maximizing of fertility, and the condoning of pre- and extramarital sex.[3] This theory has been so controversial because it states that an ancient African sexual system has survived to the present day essentially intact and that this explains the rapidity of the spread of HIV across modern Africa. This hypothesis has been criticized by several scholars, mainly because it appears to reinforce old assumptions about African promiscuity.[4] Caldwell's basic thesis, though, may also underestimate the diversity of sexual behavior across precolonial Africa,[5] and it seems to ignore the evidence for the existence of heritable landed property in many East African societies.[6] Certainly in Great Lakes societies, although extramarital affairs may have been tolerated in the past, it does not appear that premarital sexual activity, particularly among girls, was condoned.

This essay focuses on the history of the institution of marriage in four Great Lakes societies in southern Uganda and northwest Tanzania, between 1900 and 1980. It will suggest that the sexual behavior of the young at the time of HIV's emergence was largely a product of modern developments, most importantly a decline in the correlation between sexual activity and marital status. In 1900 adults were differentiated from youths by both formal marriage and sexual freedom. By 1980 these distinctions had broken down. What changed was not so much that the age of sexual debut declined dramatically,[7] but rather that the age of formal marriage increased.

Youth and AIDS

Any discussion of evolving youthful sexuality in Africa must be set in the context of AIDS. When the AIDS pandemic emerged in East Africa, it was not initially linked primarily to youthful sexuality. Epidemiologists' early concern was with the key high-risk groups, such as commercial sex workers, soldiers, and truck drivers, who made the disease appear an essentially urban phenomenon. But as the epidemic in the Great Lakes matured and spread from the towns and trading centers into the rural hinterland, it quickly became obvious that young adults, and especially adolescent girls, were also particularly vulnerable to infection (see also Nyairo and Kamaara's chapter, this volume). A survey of fifteen- to nineteen-year-olds in Rakai in 1990–92 found that 19 percent of females were HIV positive, compared to 1.8 percent of males.[8] A female who had not fully matured was more likely to experience genital trauma during intercourse, and her cervix was more vulnerable to infection than that of an older woman.[9] These physiological facts made little impact on early official statements and press coverage, which frequently condemned young women for being "loose" or tempting men into errors of judgment and had a tendency to associate all single, urban women with commercial sex workers.[10] By the late 1980s, however, the accumulation of evidence that young women were if anything the chief victims of HIV began to change first the rhetoric and then policy regarding AIDS. A series of reports revealed that males had far more lifetime sexual partners than females.[11] Rape and the deliberate seduction of underage girls were especially emotive issues that pressed home the need to protect young females. Denunciations of sexually exploitative sugar daddies and schoolmasters regularly featured in newspapers across the region from the mid-1990s.[12] HIV-prevention policy also increasingly focused on the young, believing that their sexual behavior would be easier to mold or change than that of the older generation. Sex education was introduced in primary schools, and intensive community programs ensured that the youth of Uganda and Buhaya were some of the most sensitized and mobilized in Africa. These policies were remarkably successful in the 1990s and early 2000s, with HIV prevalence among pregnant women in Uganda falling from a peak in 1991 of 21.1 percent to 6 percent in 2000. The rapid decline in HIV infection rates was spearheaded by a rise of several years in the average age of sexual debut and both high condom usage and a reduction in casual sex among adolescents and young adults.[13] The experience of AIDS, then, has resulted in dramatic change in the sexual behavior and attitudes of the young in this region, but these developments have not yet altered the perception of most elders in Great Lakes societies that youthful sexual morality is in terminal decline. To a large extent, the persistence of this critical commentary is due to the weakening of prohibitions against premarital sex.

The Case Study Areas

Ankole,[14] Buganda, Buhaya, and Bunyoro were chosen as case study sites for research into the history of population and sexual behavioral change for several reasons. The four societies are culturally very similar, sharing many customs and beliefs, speaking languages that are to some extent mutually intelligible, and possessing a tradition of monarchical government. Yet they are divided by their demographic and sexual histories. Buganda, Buhaya, and Bunyoro were unusual for East Africa in experiencing population decline or stagnation well into the twentieth century. Ankole by contrast experienced extremely rapid population growth from the 1920s.[15] The former three societies were all condemned by colonial commentators for their high rates of sexually transmitted diseases (STDs), and in the 1980s it was the Buganda-Buhaya borderland that experienced the world's first rural HIV epidemic.[16] Before 1980, by contrast, Ankole largely escaped such moral criticisms and was of interest to medical researchers because of its low rates of gonorrhea.[17]

Buhaya was divided from the other societies by the international boundary between Uganda and Tanganyika/Tanzania, but was, with Buganda, one of the wealthiest cash-cropping societies in East Africa. Bunyoro followed the same pattern of development from the 1930s, whereas Ankole depended more on pastoralism and labor migrants' remittances than cash-crop income until the 1950s. Ankole, Buhaya, and Bunyoro all belonged to the family of interlacustrine cattle kingdoms that included Rwanda and Burundi, whereas Buganda has been characterized as a banana economy. In Bunyoro, and later Buhaya, however, the power of the pastoralists, who were variously known as Bahima or Bahuma, was in decline from the late nineteenth century, as raiding and disease reduced livestock numbers.

These societies possessed political systems that were unusually hierarchical and centralized by East African standards, so that to some extent chiefly power, often channeled through the aggression of young men, limited the authority of elders. Yet these were still gerontocratic societies, and although politics may have been characterized by recurrent generational conflict, particularly around the time of the installation of a new king, within rural communities status was associated with the accumulation over time of wealth, experience, and specialist knowledge, both secular and spiritual. Adulthood here was not marked by dramatic ritual, but involved both biological maturity and the gradual achievement of several categories of status. For men, full adulthood required the establishment of an autonomous home, with independent possession of property in land or livestock, and both males and females were not considered fully adult until they had been married and had children, in theory at least. But there were degrees of adulthood, and the physically mature who were unmarried or childless would not be treated in the same way as children, although real autonomy was acquired through the successful negotiation of dependence.[18] Nonetheless, marriage, which signified the establishment of a socially recognized new household, was the most significant stage in the transition from childhood to adulthood.

Precolonial Marriage

Few contemporary sources on precolonial marriage exist. Early explorers made only passing references to the institution, and the missionaries who arrived in Buganda from the 1870s focused their attention on the often problematic marital status of converts. Early mission writings on marriage therefore are skewed toward issues of polygamy and slave concubinage.[19] The early colonial period saw the beginning of formal anthropological research, conducted initially by Christian missionaries,[20] and the emergence of the first generation of indigenous historians, usually members of the political elite, such as Apolo Kaggwa, John Nyakatura, and Francis Lwamgira.[21] These early works gave an excessively homogeneous and male-centered view of past societies, and wrote about "traditional" marriage and morality explicitly in order to highlight the misbehavior of the early colonial youth. These normative tendencies are also prominent in oral testimonies collected in the present day, but, by focusing interviews on informants' family histories, stereotypical accounts of past norms can be tempered with the complex diversity of individual experience.

In all four societies marriage arrangements were classically negotiated by the bride and groom's parents or guardians. Bridewealth payments by the groom's family would vary according to the wealth, status, and relationship of the negotiating parties, and the attractiveness of the bride. In Bunyoro, for example, officially bridewealth or *mukaaga* should total six cows ("*mukaaga*" means "six" in Runyoro), but in practice agriculturalists would pay five to twenty-five goats (the equivalent of one to five cows), whereas wealthy pastoralists might have to pay much more.

In rare situations marriage payment would not be made because the rights it implied would not be appropriate or necessary. Bridewealth might be waived where the parents were already tied by bonds of friendship or clientage; would not be required when a man took a slave as a concubine; and would not be considered when marrying a princess. Ideally, marriage would occur once physical maturity had been reached, but in reality the age of marriage, particularly for men, was mainly determined by economic factors. Marriage was not just the establishment of a close relationship between two individuals and their clans. It was also an avenue for the redistribution of wealth, and an opportunity for the old and wealthy to extend their control over the young and poor. Men from poor families had to find much of their own marriage fee, being unable to rely entirely on their fathers' help. Clientage, borrowing, and hard work were usually the only routes to marriage for such individuals. Sometimes the parents of the bride would allow the groom to marry before he had collected his bridewealth, in order to gain rights over his labor and earnings, and to earn interest on the debt he incurred. In Bunyoro, each child born before the bridewealth was paid off should officially be redeemed by the payment of a cow. Marriage then often involved the young in a network of debt, both moral and material. It was in its essence a formal, social institution, usually arranged by a couple's parents, facilitated by loans, gifts, and obligations, and sustained by family mediation.[22]

Great emphasis was placed on female virginity at marriage, because it brought honor to the bride's family and was rewarded with a supplement to the marriage payment. Evidence of the bride's condition was made public the morning after the marriage ceremony was completed.[23] Young girls would be closely supervised and threatened with punishment if they had sex before marriage. The scale of punishments, though, differed from one society to another, suggesting that the significance of female chastity might also have varied. It was common in Buhaya and Ankole for informants to report that in former times girls who got pregnant before marriage would be ritually killed by drowning or having a metal spike hammered into their skulls. Some claimed to have witnessed such murders or to have lost relatives in this way. The concern with premarital abstinence was very clearly greater in these societies than in Bunyoro and especially Buganda. Here an unmarried pregnant girl would typically be punished by being sent away to live with a relative, or by being banished to live alone on the margins of the family banana garden for some months.[24] In both Buganda and Bunyoro, although elderly informants claimed that girls were of course virgins at marriage in the old days, they did also admit that mothers would arrange for abortions for their adolescent daughters who had gotten pregnant by a man of whom the mother disapproved. These reports describe the experience of the early colonial rather than the precolonial period, but it is likely that the control of premarital pregnancy where the monitoring of premarital sex had failed was a long-established second best. The methods of abortion employed do not seem to have been colonial innovations.[25]

Greater tolerance was shown toward young men's sexuality. In many agricultural clans unmarried men had theoretically uncontested sexual access to their older brothers' wives, whereas a Hima pastoralist's cousins or even visitors could expect to sleep with his wife.[26] Male promiscuity was condemned everywhere but there was a sense that young men's desires were difficult to control and that a sexually inexperienced bridegroom risked dishonor. The likelihood of premarital sexual activity was in any case greater for males than females simply because men married a few years later than women on average, and they had more freedom of movement. Herding, war, and visiting all presented young men with sexual opportunities, though more with their peers and married women than with unmarried girls.[27] Chiefly and especially royal courts, meanwhile, possessed sexual cultures that were quite different from those of the village. Pages at Buganda's capital added to their already considerable vulnerability by conducting illicit affairs with the wives of powerful men. In addition, kings and chiefs acquired young women as servants whose duties might involve sleeping with their masters, and perhaps their masters' guests and dependents.[28] Once married, external regulation of sexual behavior was significantly weaker, for men at least, largely it seems because male infidelity was not regarded as grounds for divorce in these societies. Overall, though, the sense that comes through the accounts of precolonial sexuality is one of controls and limits, of relatively closed sexual networks. All this would change under colonial rule.

Colonial Change

Missionization

Age at first marriage is one of the most important demographic indicators in societies where premarital sex and contraception are uncommon. Because fertility declines with age and typically ends for women around the age of forty-five, the age at which people and especially women first become sexually active is crucial for measurements of the potential reproductive ability of any society. Unfortunately censuses in East Africa did not attempt to collect such information during the colonial period, and indeed relatively few people knew their precise ages until recent decades. A typical response to being questioned about age at marriage was "Do you think I can remember? But I was a grown-up." One interviewee might emphasize that she had been "an adult"; another would state that she had been "very young"; and a third that she married within a year of starting to menstruate—but these conceptions of life stages could refer to precisely the same chronological age. Only half of my 240 elderly informants provided a precise age of marriage, ranging for females from fourteen to twenty-eight, and for males a few years later. Formal education was a key means of transmitting the significance of age but, given the gendered nature of schooling in Uganda and Tanganyika before the late 1940s, men were more likely than women to be in a position to report how old they were. However, churches in this region were particularly interested in recording female age because of their objection to child marriage, a concern which would over time contribute to a changing perception in wider society about the right time to marry.[29] Missionaries therefore referred to their registers of baptism in order to calculate and record the bride and groom's age in the marriage register.

Consequently church registers should enable changes in the average age at first marriage to be traced. But the nature of evangelization in this area means that the marriage registers are a problematic source.

One of the many distinctive features of Great Lakes history is the rapidity with which these societies adopted the world religions that were introduced in the middle decades of the nineteenth century. The early success of evangelization followed on from another unusual feature of this area's religious history, which was that the first converts tended not to be orphans, widows, disabled, and other outcasts. Instead Islam and Christianity were initially religions of the court, attracting especially ambitious pages and younger chiefs. Martyrdoms in the 1870s and 1880s, followed by religious wars between 1888 and 1892, dispersed the new faiths from Buganda's capital across the region and culminated in young Christian chiefs coming to power. Colonial and missionary expansion then proceeded hand in hand, but the early development of a church of the masses was led by the first generation of militant, crusading chiefs, who demanded conversion of their followers.[30] By the 1930s Christians already made up a majority of the population of Buganda, Bunyoro, and Buhaya, a position they would achieve in Ankole a decade or so later.[31]

The depth of this rapid, massive conversion though has been debated,[32] due to many new believers' reluctance to abandon particular indigenous beliefs and practices which conflicted with Christian orthodoxy. Of special concern for clergy was the persistence of polygamy, the relative rarity of church marriage, and the frequency with which the sacrament of marriage, when it was entered into, was merely the formalization of a preexisting traditional union. To some extent these problems were interrelated. Known polygamists would not attempt to marry in church unless they were extremely well connected, whereas one of the most common situations which led to the church merely blessing a traditional marriage occurred when a polygamist decided to dispose of "surplus" wives.

We are left then with the paradox that in these largely Christian societies Christian marriage was the exception rather than the rule. In 1950s Buganda, for example, only one in four Anglicans had been married in church.[33] Missionaries reported that many parishioners avoided a church marriage because, depending on their attitude to divorce, they feared either being tied into a marriage which might not work out, or making vows that they would not necessarily wish to keep. Church marriage registers therefore recorded only a sample of all the marriages conducted by practicing Christians, a sample that may not have been representative of parish communities as a whole. It is possible that over time church marriage increasingly became a marker of prosperity, as it invariably involved the payment of bridewealth and was the form of marriage that carried the highest status. Another problem with the registers is that it is difficult to be sure whether a marriage conducted in church was indeed the first union ever entered into by the individuals involved. Although some marriages were marked *benediction nuptiale* in the registers to indicate that an existing union was being formalized in church, the frequency with which couples aged in their thirties and forties got married, apparently for the first time, suggests that missionaries did not always identify and record such situations. It is also difficult to know how accurate the recording of widowhood would have been.

The age at first marriage, then, as recorded in church registers should be treated with some caution. The following data come from old, mostly rural Roman Catholic parishes from the center of each of the four societies in the case studies. Roman Catholicism was the largest denomination in these societies, and Catholics were typically poorer than Protestants but wealthier than people from other religious groupings. Catholics in these parishes may have been representative of wider society, but Catholics who married in church were possibly not. Nonetheless, there is no obvious large-scale alternative to church records as a source for age at marriage before 1960, so despite their weaknesses these results are important. What they indicate is that between 1905 and 1969 the average male marriage age in Bunyoro was 27.7, and in Buganda it was similar at 26, whereas Ankole's was much lower at 23.9, and Buhaya's lower still at 22 years. The registers show that by contrast female age at marriage was not dramatically different across the four societies. In Bunyoro it was 22.3, in Buganda 21.5, Buhaya 21.4, and in Ankole it was lowest at 21.

These mean ages of marriage in church are almost certainly inflated, because of the problems outlined above, but it is likely that the degree of inflation was reasonably consistent across the four different communities. The results are interesting in several ways. First, it is significant that many women appear to have married for the first time at a relatively advanced age. This finding is supported by oral evidence and by contemporary village surveys, one of which in Bunyoro found that no woman had married before the age of twenty.[34] Many women, then, in these societies were not marrying for some years after reaching physical maturity. Second, it is surprising that the average male age at marriage was higher in some of the more economically developed societies than in Ankole. According to Marxist demographic historians, colonial capitalism should have resulted in a decline in the average male age at first marriage, as young men could now accumulate bridewealth relatively quickly and independently of their older relatives.[35] Yet in all four societies the male marriage age actually rose with time, despite the post-1945 boom in cash crops and employment that these societies enjoyed, to a greater or lesser extent. One explanation for this outcome is that the new wealth of the colonial economy was distributed extremely unequally, so that some young men benefited little from the postwar bonanza. It is surely significant that the age at marriage fluctuated in line with economic change to a greater extent in the heavily monetized societies than in less commercialized Ankole.[36] Another reason for the rising male marital age though is that many of the young men who did achieve early financial independence did not rush straight into marriage, but, as will be discussed below, instead enjoyed other adult pleasures.[37]

What is most interesting of all about the church marriage registers is that, when compared with hospital maternity registers, they indicate that premarital sex was relatively common by the end of the colonial period, assuming that Catholics were representative of the larger population. Some hospitals began routinely recording expectant mother's ages in the 1960s, and although hospital registers in the region have survived patchily, the data which exist show that the female average age at first marriage in church was significantly higher than the overall female average age of first sexual encounter. To give the example of Bunyoro, in 1961 the average age of women attending Masindi hospital's maternity ward who were pregnant for the first time (primigravidae) was 19.38, whereas the average age at first marriage in nearby Hoima parish was 23.67. By 1979 the average age of primigravidae giving birth in Masindi had fallen to 17.8, in which year Hoima's brides were 26.4 on average. Between 1996 and 1998 over 90 percent of first pregnancies at Hoima's antenatal clinic were among women under 20, indicating a huge change in sexual behavior in the second half of the twentieth century.[38] So what caused this apparent increase in premarital sex, which contributed to a growing distinction between a concept of adulthood defined by socially legitimized marriage and one characterized by more individualistic sexuality and reproduction?[39]

Colonial Marriage

> Q. Did you ever marry?
>
> A1. I cannot recall. It is difficult, how can you recall? Some were *malaya.*[40] But there was only one woman I married and stayed with. The one I have at the moment is also *malaya.*
>
> A2. I have only one, the mother of my children. Of course I used to go with *malaya* but I cannot recall how many they were. . . .
>
> A3. Both parents would agree among themselves that their children would marry. But if you wanted a *malaya* you had to look for her on your own. . . . It was not easy for you to separate from that woman because you were known by her parents. It is not like when you would get a *malaya;* for a *malaya* even if you had children you could easily separate.[41]

A crisis of marriage destabilized colonial societies across Africa, as elders fought a rearguard action to preserve their control over wealth and the reproductive power of young women, now threatened by young men's education, experience of the outside world, and paid employment. The frustration of young males propelled colonial change across the continent,[42] but nowhere more than in central Kenya. Here population growth and rigid settler boundaries caused such severe land shortages that by the 1940s many young men found it impossible to secure property and so were unable to marry. John Lonsdale has argued that the Mau Mau uprising was fueled by a generational crisis, with young men unable to foresee a future where they could progress to the status of a household head and thus achieve full adulthood and manhood. Young men's enemies were not only the white settlers but also the clan heads who had begun to redefine the rules of who was entitled to land and the status of a full member of male society. Mau Mau then was provoked by a crisis of frustrated masculinity as well as by generational conflict over the correct definition of adult rights and duties.[43] In most of Africa, though, the bitterness of the young was salved more by evasion than direct conflict.

Fears of a crisis in marriage came early to colonial Uganda. Young men were believed to have been deterred from establishing independent households by the realization that they would then become liable for forced labor and payment of hut tax, while the extra burden faced by wives as a result of cash cropping made marriage a less attractive prospect for young women.[44] The colonial government responded to the hut tax problem by shifting to a poll tax system, but this universalization of nongraduated taxation hit young, resource-poor men hard. Soon missionaries were complaining that the young in Buganda and Bunyoro could not afford to marry and were instead choosing a life of sin. The churches focused their condemnation on the colonial state's inadequate response to the reported rapid inflation in bridewealth in the early decades of the twentieth century. There are four possible reasons why bridewealth appears to have increased. First, the value of livestock, and especially cattle, had increased dramatically as stock levels had fallen due to a series of epizootics. Second, members of the older generation, threatened with the loss of their sons' labor through the development of a colonial economy, seem to have demanded higher bridewealth because they wanted to reassert control over young men, in this case sons-in-law, through debt. Third, the introduction of cash crops had caused the economic value of wives and daughters to rise, since it was through their labor that the early profits of cash cropping were made. And fourth, some local councils added to the problem, as chiefs imposed a 10 percent tax on marriage payments.[45] Uganda's colonial government's initial response, which was to impose a cap of fifteen shillings on bridewealth payments in 1911, proved unpopular and was not enforced. Young women reportedly felt "insulted and demeaned" by so limited a payment, and their parents evaded the law by demanding extra gifts to accompany the formal bridewealth.[46]

A range of colonial sources reported a common perception among Europeans that bridewealth in Bunyoro, Buhaya, and Buganda was excessive. It is true that bridewealth in Buhaya was exceptionally high during the coffee boom of the 1920s (peaking in real terms in 1924 at four hundred to six hundred shillings, around eighty times the prewar average), but such levels proved unsustainable.[47] In Buganda and Bunyoro, meanwhile, bridewealth was never remarkably high by East African standards, but here, as in Buhaya, it was unusual in being monetized, and thus individualized, so early. Poor young men were even less likely than their predecessors in earlier generations to obtain contributions to their bridewealth payments from family and clan now that the payment was to be made in cash rather than livestock.[48] The Ugandan historian Nyangabyaki Bazaara was told by his oral informants that in the 1930s it would take a laborer eight years to accumulate enough money to pay bridewealth.[49] The outcome was that many adult Banyoro and Baganda were forced to marry late. According to census data, the proportion of men and women in Bunyoro who were married fell from 86.2 and 89.6 percent in 1911 to only 71 percent each in 1931, which is an exceptionally low rate, particularly for women.[50] The inequality of marital opportunity created a strong sense of resentment among young men.[51] In 1961 Archie Dunbar, an agricultural officer, recorded various forms of social and economic differentiation in Kisonga, a parish in Bunyoro's cash-cropping heartland. Dunbar found that 42.1 percent of all adult men were unmarried. Most of these men were either still living as dependents, or lived alone, with little land or livestock. The 10.3 percent of adult men who were polygamous, and typically very wealthy, meanwhile had married 27.6 percent of the parish's women.[52] It was the perceived injustice of the bridewealth system that began to undermine both it and formal marriage more generally.

Bridewealth began to be rejected by some of Buganda's young soon after the First World War, and by the 1930s missionaries were complaining that the trend was being exported, with some young Banyoro copying the Baganda by engaging in free, trial relationships, which required neither bridewealth payment nor formal approval from the couple's parents, community, or church. The young, in other words, were declaring their own maturity.[53] As anthropologists such as John Beattie observed, the monetization of bridewealth devalued the institution of marriage. Bridewealth that was paid in livestock had remained and reproduced in the community as a collective asset, to be eaten during feasts or redirected to enable another marriage, thus helping maintain communal solidarity. Livestock bridewealth was typically dispersed through clan and patronage networks, reinforcing the claim that marriage was a contract between two families, not two individuals. A cash bridewealth, however, was quickly spent by the father of the bride, in the form of personal investment or consumption. Formal marriage thus became more like a commercial transaction.[54] A family that had already spent a cash bridewealth was unlikely to defend their married kinswoman's rights because they feared the material consequences of divorce. As marriage became more personalized, meanwhile, the function of clan elders as arbiters of marital disputes became obsolete. This decline of traditional forms of mediation contributed to the extreme instability of Ganda and Nyoro marriages, as women became much more likely to abandon their husbands permanently. Parental disapproval of their daughters separating reduced in significance as the new commercial economy provided opportunities for women to repay their bridewealth and live autonomously if they wished.[55] These problems with bridewealth and the breakdown of clan arbitration of spousal disputes were the main factors that pushed so many Baganda and Banyoro to live together without a formal marriage ceremony. Village surveys in the 1950s and early 1960s seem to show a gradual decline in the formalization of marriage. The proportion of relationships that were free according to surveys in Bunyoro increased from 25 percent in 1953 to 43 percent in 1966.[56]

These trial relationships, where individuals chose partners on the basis of personal attraction, were extremely unstable. Some of the experiments were successful and resulted after time in formal marriage ceremonies involving the payment of bridewealth. But most failed. The 1966 survey found that 96 percent of trial relationships had ended in separation. As the anthropologist Peter Gutkind observed, even where a relationship that had produced children dissolved, "the questions of sanctions and their enforcement or litigation" in court did not arise.[57] In fact this demi-legal status came to be regarded by the young as a positive advantage, given the frequency with which relationships of various degrees of formality broke up in this period, and the incomprehensibility of the colonial divorce laws that applied to formal marriage in church or the registry office. Young women, moreover, came to appreciate the much greater financial independence that came with trial relationships, where male partners had no formal rights to appropriate the profits made from a woman's commercial endeavors. This new pattern of sexual behavior among the young caused outrage among the elders of Buganda and Bunyoro. One of the factors stimulating the flowering of indigenous historical writing under colonial rule was a desire to remind the young of the values of the past. Thus John Nyakatura felt obliged in his *Customs of the Banyoro* to emphasize traditional virtues and deplore the fact that "the present-day attitude to sex has become so lax."[58] John Beattie was told that Europeans and their notions of individual choice were partly to blame for the decline in moral standards among the young, as they had encouraged girls to "find husbands for themselves; this has led many of them into unsuitable marriages or into informal liaisons, leading to promiscuity and disease." Male elders were shocked by some women deciding not to marry: "[T]hey like to live as prostitutes which means that young men . . . have to remain" bachelors, and "people play with one another in the fields and on the paths like animals."[59] In the early 1950s male parish councilors in rural Bunyoro passed a number of recommendations for the kingdom government's consideration such as "rules should be made against prostitution," and "a girl who is impregnated by a man should be made to marry him, . . . because parents are eating a lot of money on account of their daughters just selling themselves but not marrying."[60] The royal administration took such demands seriously, in 1951, for example, passing a law that a man who tempted a girl into prostitution or impregnated her would have to compensate her father, whereas impregnating an unmarried nurse or midwife would be punished by a fine of one thousand shillings. But the colonial records contain little evidence that such laws were widely enforced, perhaps because chiefs themselves recognized that they were in a difficult moral position, as their combination of power and wealth, and willingness to offer sanctuary to single women, gave them unrivaled opportunities for multiple sexual relationships.[61]

Youthful Sexuality in the Colonial Period

Trial relationships constituted only one of a range of new forms of sexual activity in late colonial East Africa. Informants state that premarital sex in Buhaya and Buganda became much more common toward the end of the colonial period because of a variety of legal, cultural, and economic changes. The availability of older women for affairs with younger, unmarried men first increased because of the rising incidence of divorce. A 1952 survey found that 60 percent of Bahaya women in their thirties had been divorced at least once.[62] Overall the most common cause of marital breakdown was husbands' habitual retention of the profits made on the sale of cash crops grown by their wives and the resentment this engendered. But divorce was already on the increase before the cash-crop economy had time to stimulate marital antagonism. Ironically Christian conversion was often associated with divorce, because missionaries pressed polygamous neophytes to choose one of their wives as a "ring" wife, and send the rest away. Polygamists were instructed by the church to make provision for their discarded wives, but according to colonial officials this was rarely done, and the subsequent sexual availability of these divorcees was held up as one of the many causes of the epidemic of immorality which was believed to be sweeping Buganda in the early twentieth century.[63] European concerns about forced marriages, meanwhile, combined with autonomous women's ready access to migrant labor transformed the situation faced by widows on the death of their husbands. By the later colonial period widows enjoyed sufficient legal protection and economic independence to often be able to hold onto their late husbands' land while their children grew up, while also resisting the pressure from their in-laws to marry one of their late husband's brothers. Oral information from Buhaya indicated that in the 1950s the typical village would contain two or three widows who lived independently and conducted secret love affairs with adolescents.[64]

Young men's sexual freedom and attractiveness were both on the rise after the Second World War. The economic diversification and administrative expansion of the 1940s and 1950s greatly increased the ability of male youths to secure wealth outside of their family's household. New employment opportunities in trade and the state made many sons economically independent of their parents. Yet they frequently chose to continue living at home, rejecting the possibility of early marriage. Instead, it seems that young men often preferred to use their wealth to secure lovers.[65] Formal marriage then was being delayed not only because poor young men could not afford to pay bridewealth, but also because many affluent young men chose to postpone it.

The growing prosperity of the rural economy in postwar Buganda and Buhaya brought about another significant development: a major change in the nature of commercial sex work. Baganda and especially Bahaya women were very prominent in East Africa's sex industry before the Second World War, but they mostly worked in the large cities of Kampala, Dar es Salaam, and Nairobi.[66] As the cities grew rapidly after the war, again due to commercial and administrative expansion, so did the scale of urban sex work greatly increase. By the 1970s one survey reported that up to 8 percent of Haya women were sex workers in the cities. Most of these women were divorcees who saw sex work as an opportunity to repay the bridewealth that had enabled their unhappy marriages. But after 1945 there was also a growing trend for young, unmarried women to be recruited from Buhaya by successful sex workers with the promise of wealth and autonomy as an alternative to marriage. More important for the epidemiology of STDs in the region was that from the 1940s significant numbers of sex workers began to return home from the cities to rural Buhaya, where they continued to exchange sex for money. Informants stated that in the 1950s in their home villages, whose populations averaged about a thousand people, there were two to six sex workers active at any one time.[67] The definition of a sex worker is problematic, as people throughout East Africa commonly label any woman who received gifts, such as a cigarette, for sex as *malaya*, but informants did distinguish between women who had several boyfriends who gave them frequent presents and women whose profession and major source of income was sex work. These were separate but related categories, and in any case, both groups of women were sexually available for young, unmarried men.[68]

Finally, young unmarried women who remained at home also experienced new levels of legal protection and sexual opportunity. From the midcolonial period courts across the region grew less tolerant of parents' physical punishment of their daughters for becoming pregnant before marriage. Meanwhile the late 1940s saw a shift toward gender equality in education, which resulted in a sharp rise in the numbers of young girls who went to school in Buganda, Buhaya and Bunyoro, though not yet in more traditionalist and impoverished Ankole.[69] School tended to delay marriage, thus increasing female adolescents' exposure to the risk of premarital sex and conception, and inevitably presented girls with the possibility of meeting boys free from parental supervision. Odaybea Morrow's interviews with Ganda elders revealed an interesting shift over the course of the colonial period in the nature of youthful sexual encounters. Before the 1950s most sexual encounters with other adolescents were opportunistic, discreet, and sporadic, arising from chance meetings while grazing or fetching water. Toward the end of the colonial era, by contrast, early sexual relationships "were the culmination of an intensive courtship with a girl," often at school, in which mutual interest was established through females accepting gifts. Elderly Baganda had much more romantic memories of adolescent sexuality than the more materialistic middle-aged Baganda, who had grown up in the late colonial period and whose experiences were distinctly similar to those reported in later decades.[70] Those of the older generation were also more likely to marry girls whom they impregnated. According to Obbo, "since the 1950s, school boys or migrant laborers who made girls pregnant during vacation increasingly denied paternity because they could not afford to pay the fines demanded by the fathers or male guardians."[71]

Sexual Change in the 1960s and 1970s

These late colonial developments then laid the foundations for a rural, village-level sexual culture that was characterized by the commoditization of sexual relationships, the informalization of marriage, and a significant reduction in elders' control of the sexuality of the young. The 1960s and 1970s saw a deepening and widening of these sexual patterns, and also an increasing integration between rural and urban sexual culture. By 1969, 50 percent of female fifteen- to nineteen-year-old Ugandans and 92 percent of males in the same age group had not yet married. These decades also saw an acceleration in population growth across the region, so that the young made up an ever-increasing proportion of the societies under discussion. In Ankole in 1969, for example, children from birth to fourteen years of age constituted 51.8 percent of the total population, with another 15.4 percent belonging to the fifteen-twenty-four age group. In other words, the young accounted for more than two-thirds of the entire population. Ankole was exceptional in its high fertility, but even in Buhaya, whose rate of demographic increase was one of the lowest in East Africa, 54.7 percent of the population was under twenty-five in 1967. This swelling of the lower levels of the region's age pyramid put immense pressure on newly independent governments, which struggled to meet the ever-growing demand for education, health care, and job creation. The deepening antagonism between the generations in this period must be understood as, in part, arising from youthful frustration with their unequal share of the fruits of independence, as well as from elders' fear of the underemployed young. These tensions were most visible in the towns, whose educational facilities and formal employment opportunities drew in adolescents from across the region. In 1969, 27 percent of Kampala's population were aged fifteen to twenty-four.[72] Although many of these would be temporary residents, they would return to their villages and local trading centers with an infectious taste for urban culture (see Burton's chapter, this volume, for a wider discussion of aspirational urban culture).

One of the striking changes of the postcolonial period in this region is the homogenization of sexual behavior. All of the developments that occurred in late colonial Buhaya, Buganda, and Bunyoro spread out across the Great Lakes area in the 1960s and 1970s. Banyankole informants described the sexual history of their villages in almost exactly the same way as Banyoro, Baganda, and Bahaya, but with a time lag of fifteen to twenty years.[73] Partly this was due to Ankole's commercial awakening in the 1950s and 1960s, with the rise of coffee, dairy and *matoke* (plantain) production. But it was also due to the growing social integration of the postwar world, with informants reporting an increase in interethnic sex, the imitation of other ethnic groups' sexual techniques, and a growing awareness among the youth of Ankole of different gender and generational relationships in the more commercialized societies. Whereas the oldest informants in Ankole spoke of their fear of Baganda women, whom they regarded as difficult to manage and sexually immoral, those who worked as labor migrants in the 1960s were more adventurous. Female Baganda too grew less disdainful of foreign laborers over time.[74] The postcolonial expansion of rural primary and especially secondary education, meanwhile, changed sexual behavior right across Uganda. Throughout the country parents worried that young girls and boys would be able to get to know each other and arrange assignations unsupervised. The rise of the school was popularly associated with the increase of premarital pregnancy throughout postcolonial Uganda. It also created a new venue for the development of gangs, as groups of age-mates traveled to school and studied together. Accounts of individuals' early sexual lives detail the increased generational autonomy particularly of the male young, whose social lives increasingly revolved more around friends than family. Adolescents were more likely to be allowed to walk to markets and water sources unaccompanied by adults and attend social functions such as weddings than in the past. Opportunities for sexual assignations, often encouraged and facilitated by groups of friends, expanded.[75] The sexuality of the young is always competitive and emulative, but these characteristics were heightened when children gained new freedom of association.

Another major development of the postcolonial world was rapid urbanization. The population of Bukoba, the main town of Buhaya, grew from 3,760 in 1957 to 8,141 ten years later. To the north, Uganda's urban population increased equally dramatically by 137 percent between 1959 and 1969. By the end of the 1960s Kampala had been transformed into a city of 330,000 people, and glorified villages like Mbarara had become small towns with a distinctly urban culture. Urbanization then slowed significantly, increasing by just 47 percent between 1969 and 1980, as the economic collapse and violence of the Amin years diminished the attractions of the major cities like Kampala and Jinja. Towns such as Masindi, which housed large numbers of government and military personnel, actually declined in size during the 1970s, but small trading centers, particularly those located near borders and major routes, mushroomed. So by 1980 the relative decline of Uganda's major urban centers was countered by the eruption of new towns such as Kyotera, which fed off the *magendo* black market economy. The social memory of urban sexual culture in the 1970s is dominated by the activities of the security services and the *mafutamingi* ("a lot of fat") businesspeople who "fell into things." Although Amin's regime acted against immorality on the rhetorical and symbolic level (the presidential decree against hot pants and miniskirts was very popular among traditionalists), the beneficiaries of Amin's asset-stripping were notorious for coercive and commodified sex.[76]

In general, the urban family was marked by severe instability and the weak supervision of adolescents when both parents worked away from home. This phenomenon caused the same concern about social breakdown right across postcolonial Uganda and Buhaya as had been expressed in the 1950s by observers of Kampala, such as Peter Gutkind: "Older children are expected to provide their own amusement. . . . [T]he free play of sexual activity is a pleasant and satisfying pastime. Parents seem generally to take little notice of these activities and when children are discovered to be 'playing with each other' they are as likely to be joked about as pulled apart. Of course the lack of privacy [due to cramped town housing] among the members of the family makes children aware of the sexual activity of their parents and older siblings."[77] As Davis has noted, public discourse in the years after independence often blamed single mothers in particular for producing this new category of dangerous adolescent, the "wild children," or *bayaye*.[78] Elderly informants described how by the end of the 1970s their local towns and trading centers had witnessed a proliferation of bars, an increase in public drunkenness, the arrival of the nightclub, and commercial sex workers becoming a familiar sight. Some of the earliest investigations by HIV researchers into rural sexual networks in southwest Uganda found that 61 percent of young male hospital outpatients surveyed had had commercial sex. But the key role played by young male temporary migrants and visitors to towns in the diffusion of sexually transmitted infections among rural communities was identified long before the age of AIDS.[79]

THIS ESSAY HAS focused on constructing a narrative of change over time, because much writing on the emergence of HIV in this region tends to look no further back than the 1970s. Those who peer deeper into the past have often become wrapped up in the disputes about the problematic diagnosis of STDs before the Second World War and the unmistakable racism and sexism of early colonial discourse. Previous historical research has focused on early colonial European and chiefly concerns about female sexuality being unleashed by the unexpected consequences of Christianity, the commercial economy, or new legal protections.[80] But in fact this essay would suggest that the most dramatic changes in sexual behavior occurred in the late colonial period, a time that has been largely neglected by writers on the sexual history of Great Lakes societies. Tabitha Kanogo's recent work on Kenyan women is unusual in taking the story of East African female colonial sexuality through to the postwar era, tracking the emergence by the 1950s of a more individualistic, autonomous, and assertive sexuality among young women by exploring issues such as rape, clitoridectomy, bridewealth, and underage marriage.[81] Yet, European discussions of sexuality in the Great Lakes, looking at the sources for the colonial period as a whole, were in fact more concerned with male than female sexuality.[82] Within this male-focused discourse, though, there was a marked change in generational focus after the Second World War. Pre-1945 European commentators were as likely to blame male elders as youths for high rates of STDs. Older men were regarded as being sexually predatory and excessively acquisitive. They were aggressively seeking to acquire young girls, in a way which most European observers considered improper, or they were deliberately inflating bridewealth, which made it increasingly difficult for young people to marry each other, or they were delaying passing on their wealth to their sons, which encouraged young men to live a life of dissipation.[83]

Post-1945, however, although Europeans' underlying concern remained focused on the difficulty in effecting real progress in these societies, the blame shifted toward young males, who were seen more and more as a socially disruptive influence and as wasting the new economic opportunities available to them. In Buhaya, for example, young men were described as suffering from education and easy money—both being wasted on alcohol and sex workers. Within African chiefly hierarchies as well, the discourse was not purely misogynistic. Certainly laws were introduced that aimed to stop women from traveling without a male escort or living alone in towns. But at the same time local governments were also introducing bylaws in order to punish men who got unmarried women pregnant.[84]

Most interesting of all is elderly local informants' tendency to instinctively blame the rise of HIV on the changes of the 1970s, when a younger generation had engaged in what they perceived to be new, urban forms of socializing and alcohol consumption (compare Willis's chapter, this volume). But as interviewees continued to discuss these issues, they acknowledged that in fact these changes had started before the 1970s, that rural behavioral patterns had also changed, and that their own sexual conduct was perhaps no purer than that of the following generation that was wiped out by AIDS. For example, one elderly informant stated early in an interview: "You know children start playing sex at an early age today, so the uterus gets prepared and you end up going into menstruation at an early age. But for us we used to fear our parents so we would take long before doing these things." "The girl would only go to the man after marriage. Children were not allowed to have sex before marriage like it is today." Yet this woman, now in her seventies, became pregnant while a fifteen-year-old schoolgirl, never married, but had four more children, all while living with her parents.[85] Today one of the great obstacles to achieving greater control of the spread of STDs in this region is the lack of cross-generational discussion of sexual issues, and the assumption of the old that the youth of today are much less sexually moral than they had been themselves.[86] In fact such assertions of moral displeasure and superiority have been made by elders in these societies for at least four generations, with no great effect, and today with little justification.

Since the early 1990s there have been dramatic increases in the average age of first sexual encounter, a decline in the number of sexual partners, and other indications of sexual responsibility among the young adults of Buganda and Buhaya in particular. One of the more interesting, and still understudied, responses to the crisis of HIV in this region has been the growing social and financial investment by members of the middle classes in their mid-twenties in formal marriage. There are many fascinating aspects to this revival in marriage: the frequency with which HIV tests are required; the persistence of preliminary traditional marriages, usually referred to as introductions, among this highly Christianized, modern elite; the sense that a marriage in church is an opportunity to demonstrate one's material success; the extent to which the older generation have reconciled themselves to the dangers of premarital sex by a recognition of the importance of investing in education, which by delaying marriage has done most to create a recognizable state of adolescence; and by the belief that more mature, better educated women will be better wives, mothers, and perhaps breadwinners.[87] Most significant of all, though, is the scale of the social networks on which engaged couples depend in order to gather the resources necessary for the lavish weddings they desire. The actual bridewealth is a very minor element today in the overall budget for an elite wedding. What matters are the gifts that are exchanged and the size of the celebration. But these material displays are supported now by a modification of the old concept of marriage as a communal, collective institution. The engaged couple pays the costs of marriage by raising cash only partly from family and clan, but especially among friends and colleagues, who then expect reciprocal support when it is their turn to marry. The revival of marriage seems to exemplify the way in which people in Buganda and Buhaya have rebuilt their societies in response to the catastrophe that is AIDS with a combination of social networking and a new, hard-headed materialism.

Notes

This research was funded by the British Academy, the British Institute in Eastern Africa, and the Economic and Social Research Council. The cooperation of the Uganda National Council for Science and Technology, the Tanzanian Council for Science and Technology, Bujumbura (Hoima), Bukoba, Kisubi, and Nyamitanga Roman Catholic parishes, local and national archivists in Uganda and Tanzania, and participants in interviews and group discussions is gratefully acknowledged. The paper benefited from questions asked at seminars at the universities of Cambridge, Durham, Leeds, Oxford, School of Oriental and African Studies, and University College London, and at the Youth Conference in Nyeri. Thanks also to Asiimwe Godfrey, Benedict Bigirwamungu, Emma Coombs, Ros Davies, John Iliffe, Jesse Karugaba, John Lonsdale, Lubega Gerald, Mbatya Phillip, Musinguzi Mark, Ninsiima Christine, Jim Oeppen, Otim Charles, Richard Smith, and Yvonne Swai.

1. See, for example, J. Kett, *Rite of Passage: Adolescence in America 1790 to the Present* (New York: Basic Books, 1977); C. Nathanson, *Dangerous Passage: The Social Control of Sexuality in Women's Adolescence* (Philadelphia: Temple University Press, 1991).

2. M. Mead, *Growing Up in New Guinea* (New York: Mentor, 1953).

3. J. Caldwell, P. Caldwell, and P. Quiggin, "The Social Context of AIDS in Sub-Saharan Africa," *Population and Development Review* 15, no. 2 (1989): 185–234; J. Goody, *Production and Reproduction: A Comparative Study of the Domestic Domain* (Cambridge: Cambridge University Press, 1976).

4. M.-N. Le Blanc, D. Meintel, and V. Piché, "The African Sexual System: Comment on Caldwell et al.," *Population and Development Review* 17, no. 3 (1991): 497–505; B. Ahlberg, "Is There a Distinct African Sexuality? A Critical Response to Caldwell's 'African Sexuality' Thesis," *Africa* 64, no. 2 (1994): 220–42; S. Heald, "The Power of Sex: Some Reflections on the Caldwells' 'African Sexuality' Thesis," *Africa* 65, no. 4 (1995): 489–505.

5. Caldwell does display an awareness of variation and change in sexual norms across Africa in later work, such as J. Caldwell et al., "The Construction of Adolescence in a Changing World: Implications for Sexuality, Reproduction and Marriage," *Studies in Family Planning* 29, no. 2 (1998): 137–53.

6. See, for example, P. Reining, "Haya Land Tenure: Landholding and Tenancy," *Anthropological Quarterly* 35, no. 2 (1962): 58–73; H. Cory and M. Hartnoll, *The Customary Law of the Haya Tribe, Tanganyika Territory* (1945; London: Frank Cass, 1971), 20.

7. The decline in the age of puberty from the mid-twentieth century, which was linked to improving diet, also contributed to the lengthening of adolescence by bringing forward the potential age of first sexual activity.

8. J. Konde-Lule et al., "Adolescents, Sexual Behaviour and HIV-1 in Rural Rakai District," *AIDS* 3, no. 8 (1997): 791–99.

9. M. Laga et al., "To Stem HIV in Africa, Prevent Transmission to Young Women," *AIDS* 15, no. 7 (2001): 931–34.

10. For example, *Weekend Magazine* (Tanzania), 3 August 1990.

11. For example, E. Konings et al., "Sexual Behaviour Survey in a Rural Area of Northwest Tanzania," *AIDS* 8, no. 7 (1994): 987–93; Konde-Lule et al., "Adolescents, Sexual Behaviour and HIV-1 in Rural Rakai District."

12. For example, *Daily News* (Tanzania), 16 December 1993; *Business Times* (Tanzania), 31 January 1997.

13. R. Stoneburner and D. Low-Beer, "Population-Level HIV Declines and Behavioural Risk Avoidance in Uganda," *Science* 304, no. 5671 (2004): 714–18.

14. Ankole in its modern form was created at the start of the colonial period by the amalgamation of a number of small principalities with the large kingdom of Nkore. Although Nkore was dominated by pastoralist Bahima, the population of the newly subjugated principalities was predominantly made up of cultivators, referred to by the pastoralists as Bairu.

15. O. Dak, *A Geographical Analysis of the Distribution of Migrants in Uganda* (Kampala: Makerere University, 1968); P. Reining, "The Haya: The Agrarian System of a Sedentary People" (PhD diss., University of Chicago, 1967).

16. P. Reining, "The Haya"; M. Vaughan, *Curing Their Ills: Colonial Power and African Illness* (Stanford: Stanford University Press, 1991).

17. O. Arya, H. Nsanzumuhire, and S. Taber, "Clinical, Cultural and Demographic Aspects of Gonorrhoea in a Community in Uganda," *Bulletin of the World Health Organisation* 49, no. 6 (1973): 587–95.

18. 2004 Bunyoro Int. 2 (transcript in author's possession); P. Kilbride and J. Kilbride, *Changing Family Life in East Africa: Women and Children at Risk* (Philadelphia: University Park Press, 1990), 64; J. Roscoe, *The Baganda: An Account of Their Native Customs and Beliefs* (London: Macmillan, 1911), 81; O. Morrow, "Sexual Cultures and Vulnerability to HIV Infection among Baganda Youth in Mpigi, Uganda" (PhD diss., Johns Hopkins University, 2000), 68–69. In Buganda menarche was ritualized to the extent that it should be marked with a feast. In Bunyoro, John Beattie found that a childless man could be highly respected if he possessed other qualities, particularly politeness, a key marker of social maturity (J. Beattie, "The Nyoro of Western Uganda," in *Cultural Source Materials for Population Planning in East Africa,* ed. A. Molnos [Nairobi: East Africa Publishing House, 1972], 3:192–93).

19. Cf. M. Tuck, "Women's Experiences of Enslavement and Slavery in Late Nineteenth- and Early Twentieth-Century Uganda," in *Slavery in the Great Lakes Region of East Africa,* ed. H. Médard and S. Doyle (Oxford: James Currey, 2007), 174–88.

20. For example, Roscoe, *The Baganda.*

21. A. Kagwa, *Customs of the Baganda,* ed. M. M. Edel, trans. E. B. Kalibala (New York: Columbia University Press, 1934); J. Nyakatura, *Anatomy of an African Kingdom: A History of Bunyoro-Kitara,* ed. G. N. Uzoigwe (New York: Anchor Press, 1973); Francis X. Lwamgira, *Amakuru ga Kiziba n'Abakama bamu: The History of Kiziba and Its Kings,* 2d ed., trans. Ephraim Kamuhangire (Kampala: Makerere University, 1969); see also A. G. Katate and L. Kamugungunu, *Abagabe b'Ankole (History of the Kings of Ankole, Books 1–2),* 2 vols. (Kampala: Eagle Press, 1953).

22. J. Roscoe, *The Bakitara or Banyoro: The First Part of the Report of the Mackie Ethnological Expedition to Central Africa* (Cambridge: Cambridge University Press, 1923), 261–76; Achte to Livinhac, 16 July 1894, *Chronique de la Société des Missionaires d'Afrique, Nyanza Sept.,* IV, de 1895–1903, 111–12; J. Gorju, *Entre le Victoria, l'Albert, et l'Edouard* (Rennes: Oberthüss, 1920), 288; J. Roscoe, *The Soul of Central Africa: A General Account of the Mackie Ethnological Expedition* (London: Cassell, 1922), 183; J. Beattie, *The Nyoro State* (Oxford: Clarendon Press, 1971), 248; J. Nyakatura, *Aspects of Bunyoro Customs and Traditions* (Nairobi: East African Literature Bureau, 1970), 20; G. Schweinfurth et al., *Emin Pasha in Central Africa* (London: George Philip, 1888), 16, 85–86; S. Baker, *Ismailia: A Narrative of the Expedition to Central Africa for the Suppression of the Slave Trade* (London: Macmillan, 1874), 2:212.

23. Beattie, "Nyoro of Western Uganda," 189; J. Roscoe, "Further Notes on the Manners and Customs of the Baganda," *Journal of the Royal Anthropological Institute* 32 (1902): 38.

24. Buhaya 2000 Interviews (Ints.) W.R.; 2004 Ankole and Buganda Ints. 37, 46, 84 and 85. Cf. J. Roscoe, "Uganda and Some of Its Problems, Part I," *Journal of the Royal African Society* 22, no. 86 (1923): 106–7.

25. 2004 Bunyoro Ints. B.K.; Buganda Male Focus Group Discussion (FGD), Kiwulwe, 4 September 2004. The abortifacients used were herbal medicines.

26. 2004 Ankole and Buganda Ints. 20, 37, 5 and 6; "Lambkin, Mission to the Uganda Protectorate on the Prevalence of Venereal Diseases. Summary of Evidence," December 1907, Public Record Office, London (PRO), CO/536/15.

27. J. Willis Interviews, 28b, 35c and 36c, University of Essex Data Archive; M. Kisekka, "Heterosexual Relationships in Uganda" (PhD diss., University of Missouri, 1973), 159.

28. See, for example, N. B. Musisi, "Women, 'Elite Polygyny,' and Buganda State Formation," *Signs* 16, no. 4 (1991): 778.

29. A. Fisher, "Diaries," 16 November 1907, Acc. 84. Church Missionary Society Archive (CMSA), Birmingham. The best account of changing marriage age in colonial Africa is in M. Wilson, "Zig-zag Change," *Africa* 46, no. 4 (1976): 399–409.

30. J. Iliffe, *Honour in African History* (Cambridge: Cambridge University Press, 2005), 171–80. As early as 1911 Christians made up 46 percent of Buganda's population.

31. Uganda Protectorate, *Census Returns, 1931* (Entebbe: Government Printer, 1933).

32. J. Taylor, *The Growth of the Church in Buganda* (London: SCM, 1958), 176; J. Peel, "Conversion and Tradition in Two African Societies: Ijebu and Buganda," *Past and Present* 77, no. 1 (1977): 133; H. Hansen, *Mission, Church and State in a Colonial Setting: Uganda 1890–1925* (London: Heinemann, 1984), 294.

33. Taylor, *Growth of the Church in Buganda,* 176.

34. For example, Bunyoro 1996 Int. 44 (women typically did not marry until "eighteen or twenty"); J. McFie, c. 1956. "Nutrition Surveys" (unpublished typescript in Makerere University Kampala [MUK]), 18.

35. G. Kitching, "Proto-Industrialisation and Demographic Change: A Thesis and Some Possible African Implications," *Journal of African History* 24, no. 2 (1983): 229–30; D. Cordell and J. Gregory, *African Population and Capitalism: Historical Perspectives* (London: Westview Press, 1987). The theory is adapted from A. Wrigley and R. Schofield, *The Population History of England, 1541–1871: A Reconstruction* (Cambridge: Cambridge University Press, 1981).

36. S. Doyle, *Crisis and Decline in Bunyoro: Population and Environment in Western Uganda 1860–1955* (Oxford: James Currey, 2006), 239–40.

37. Bukoba District Annual Report, 1951, Tanzania National Archives, Dar es Salaam (TNA), 215/2510.

38. R. Ndyomugyenyi and P. Magnussen, "Anaemia in Pregnancy: *Plasmodium Falciparum* Infection Is an Important Cause in *Primigravidae* in Hoima District, Western Uganda," *Annals of Tropical Medicine and Parasitology* 93, no. 5 (1999): 459. The age at which Catholic women married in church may have been higher than the average female marriage age for society as a whole, but it is unlikely that the difference would have been as much as four years.

39. Cf. P. Gutkind, "Some Problems of African Urban Family Life: An Example from Kampala, Uganda, British East Africa," *Diogenes* 37 (1962): 102–3. For comparable

situations elsewhere in Africa see Caldwell, "Construction of Adolescence in a Changing World," 141–42, 150–51: "[T]he boundary between the single and married state is becoming less clear, and many couples in first unions have either taken no steps or not taken all the steps necessary for acceptance as a traditional, Christian or government-recognized marriage."

40. *Malaya* can refer to both sex workers and unmarried people, locally regarded as promiscuous.

41. Bunyoro Male Focus Group Discussion, 5 September 2004—five participants, aged 60+.

42. One of the richest studies is J. Peel, *Ijeshas and Nigerians: The Incorporation of a Yoruba Kingdom, 1890–1970s* (Cambridge: Cambridge University Press, 1983).

43. J. Lonsdale, "The Moral Economy of Mau Mau," in *Unhappy Valley, Book Two: Violence and Ethnicity*, ed. B. Berman and J. Lonsdale (Oxford: James Currey, 1992), 315–504.

44. Tucker to Boyle, 23 December 1909, G3/A7/0/1910/45, CMSA, Birmingham.

45. Report on Busindi district, January 1911, Entebbe Secretariat Archives (ESA), A46/126; Northern Province report, August 1911, ESA, A46/787; see also J. Iliffe, *A Modern History of Tanganyika* (Cambridge: Cambridge University Press, 1979), 124; G. Kitching, *Class and Economic Change in Kenya: The Making of an African Petite Bourgeoisie, 1905–1970* (Yale: Yale University Press, 1980), 221.

46. H. Ladbury, Journal (2 vols., MUK), I, 4 March 1904; Mrs. Ladbury, Journals (2 vols., MUK), I, 12 December 1907; Report on Busindi district, January 1911, ESA, A46/126; Northern Province report, August 1911, ESA, A46/787; R. Fisher, *Twilight Tales of the Black Baganda* (London: Marshall Brothers, 1911), 44.

47. Bukoba District Annual Report, 1924, Appendix 2, TNA 1733/33 (AB105); Digest of replies to questionnaire accompanying the chief secretary's circular, 19 April 1938, on the subject of native marriage (J. Willis papers, MUK).

48. Diaire Hoima, Rome, 23 June 1929, White Father Archive (WFA); W. Bazley, *Bunyoro, Tropical Paradox* (Durham: Pentland Press, 1993), 32; J. Beattie, "Nyoro Marriage and Affinity," *Africa* 28, no. 1 (1958): 4.

49. N. Bazaara, *The State and Social Differentiation in Kakindo Village, Masindi District, Uganda* (Kampala: Centre for Basic Research, 1991), 6.

50. Uganda Protectorate, *Report on the 1911 Census of the Population of Uganda* (Entebbe: Government Printer, 1911); Uganda, *1931 Census.*

51. Bunyoro 1996 Int. 45. See also Peel, *Ijeshas and Nigerians.*

52. A. Dunbar, "Mutala Survey of Bujenje Bunyoro District" (unpublished typescript in Haddon Library, Cambridge, n.d.), 18.

53. Diaire Hoima, Rome, 31 December 1934, WFA.

54. J. Beattie, "The Story of Mariya and Yozefu: A Case Study from Bunyoro, Uganda," *Africa* 34, no. 2 (1964): 114. Priscilla Reining was told in 1952, by contrast, that although bridewealth in Buhaya had been largely monetized, it was still distributed widely among the bride's kin, largely it seems because of a local belief that where this was not done, the marriage would be sterile. P. Reining and A. Richards, "Report on Fertility Survey in Buganda and Buhaya, 1952," in *Culture and Human Fertility*, ed. F. Lorimer (Paris: Unesco, 1954), 369–70.

55. For mediation see Beattie, "Story of Mariya and Yozefu," 105–15. Cf. Kitching, *Class and Economic Change in Kenya*, 231–32.

56. Beattie, "Nyoro Marriage and Affinity," 1–3; A. Dunbar, "Mutala Survey of Bujenje (Kisonga), Bunyoro," *Uganda Journal* 29, no. 1 (1965): 70; S. Charsley, "A Note on Marriage in Bunyoro," *Uganda Journal* 34 (1970): 196.

57. Charsley, "Note on Marriage in Bunyoro," 198; Gutkind, "Some Problems of African Urban Family Life," 102.

58. N. B. Musisi, "Morality as Identity: The Missionary Moral Agenda in Buganda, 1877–1945," *Journal of Religious History* 23, no. 1 (1999): 51–74; Nyakatura, *Aspects of Bunyoro Customs and Traditions,* 42, 13.

59. J. Beattie, "Bunyoro through the Looking Glass," *Journal of African Administration* 12, no. 2 (1960): 91.

60. Beattie, *Nyoro State,* 220, 228–29. It is unclear whether parents "eating a lot of money" referred to a girl's parents having to maintain her while losing potential bridewealth income or to the parents profiting by imposing heavy fines on the genitor.

61. Agenda for Rukurato October 1953 and 17 November 1954, ADM 20/2 District Council, Hoima District Archives (HDA); Minutes of Bunyoro-Kitara Rukurato General Purposes Committee, 22–23 May 1950 and 5–7 March 1951, HDA; e.g., 2000 Ints. S.K., 21 June 2000.

62. 2004 Ints. 40 and 84; East Africa High Commission, *East African Medical Survey Report* (Nairobi: Government Printer, 1952). By 1952, 28 percent of households in a Buganda parish surveyed by Audrey Richards were female-headed. Reining and Richards, "Report on Fertility Survey in Buganda and Buhaya, 1952," 359.

63. Digest of replies to questionnaire accompanying the chief secretary's circular, 19 April 1938, on the subject of native marriage (J. Willis papers, MUK).

64. For example, Buhaya 2000 Ints. W. Rugaimukamu.

65. Ibid.; V. Berry, ed., *The Culwick Papers, 1934–1944: Population, Food and Health in Colonial Tanganyika* (London: Academic Books, 1994).

66. L. White, *The Comforts of Home: Prostitution in Colonial Nairobi* (Chicago: University of Chicago Press, 1990); D. Parkin, "Types of Urban African Marriage in Kampala," *Africa* 36, no. 3 (1966): 274; C. Smith and L. Stevens, "Farming and Income-Generation in the Female-Headed Smallholder Household: The Case of a Haya Village in Tanzania," *Canadian Journal of African Studies* 22, no. 3 (1988): 552–66.

67. Buhaya 2000 Ints. V. Kyairuzi, W. Rugaimukamu, J. B. Kyembuga.

68. Buhaya 2000 Ints. W. Rugaimukamu and J. B. Kyembuga.

69. Beattie, *Nyoro State,* 17; Reining and Richards, "Report on Fertility Survey in Buganda and Buhaya, 1952," 356–60.

70. Uganda Census Office, *1969 Census Vol. III Additional Tables* (Kampala, 1972); Morrow, "Sexual Cultures and Vulnerability to HIV Infection," 280. Morrow's female informants described the beginnings of sexual relationships among schoolchildren in the 1940s and '50s in some detail. "Where boys had bicycles they would always want to give you a ride. . . . They would buy you soda, buns. That's how they used to start." "I used to see students starting that kind of relationship. . . . In primary I used to see children writing letters, some used to say that we saw somebody with so and so in the bush, that this and this happened." Cf. S. Nyanzi, R. Pool, and J. Kinsman, "The Negotiation of Sexual Relationships among School Pupils in South-western Uganda," *AIDS Care* 13, no. 1 (2001): 83–98.

71. C. Obbo, "HIV Transmission: Men Are the Solution," *Population and Environment* 14, no. 3 (1993): 225.

72. Uganda, *1969 Census,* 7; Tanzania Census Office, *1967 Population Census, Vol. III Demographic Statistics* (Dar es Salaam, 1971). Concern about population growth exceeding resources prompted Milton Obote's government to draw up a national plan for birth control in the late 1960s, which was abandoned following Idi Amin's coup. M. Okello, "Family Planning in Difficult Times," in *Crisis in Uganda: The*

Breakdown of Health Services, ed. C. Dodge and P. Wiebe (Oxford: Pergamon Press, 1985), 234–35.

73. 2004 Ankole FGDs 37, 39, 40 and 49; O. Arya and C. Bosa, "Treatment Of Gonorrhoea with Three Different Penicillin Schedules—A Preliminary Report" (unpublished paper presented to Uganda Medical Association Annual Conference, 19–20 February 1972, Uganda National Council for Science and Technology Library, Kampala, 1972).

74. Ankole male FGD, Kyangyenyi, 22 August 2004; Buganda male FGD, Kagezi, 25 August 2004; Buganda male FGD, Kiwulwe, 4 September 2004.

75. Obbo, "HIV Transmission," 223–24; Morrow, "Sexual Cultures and Vulnerability to HIV Infection," 309–10.

76. Tanzania, *1967 Census;* Uganda Census Office, *Report on the 1980 Uganda Census,* vol. 1 (Kampala, 1982), 244–47; H. Tadria, "Changing Economic and Gender Patterns among the Peasants of Ndejje and Ssegulu in Uganda" (PhD diss., University of Minnesota, 1985), 80. Similar sexual patterns associated with the smuggling economy also evolved in Buhaya in this period.

77. Gutkind, "Some Problems of African Urban Family Life," 95. Cf. C. Obbo, *African Women: Their Struggle for Independence* (London: Zed Press, 1980), 26–28; D. Parkin, *Neighbours and Nationals in an African City Ward* (London: Routledge and Kegan Paul, 1969), 95.

78. P. Davis, "On the Sexuality of 'Town Women' in Kampala," *Africa Today* 47, no. 3/4 (2000): 39–41.

79. Parkin, "Types of Urban African Marriage in Kampala," 269–85; 2004 Ankole Ints. A. Ndyaba; Bunyoro male FGD, 5 September 2004; O. Arya, "Attitudes of College Students in East Africa to Sexual Activity and Venereal Diseases," *British Journal of Venereal Diseases* 44 (1968): 160–66; C. Hudson et al., "Risk Factors for the Spread of AIDS in Rural Africa: Evidence from a Comparative Seroepidemiological Survey of AIDS, Hepatitis B and Syphilis in Southwestern Uganda," *AIDS* 2, no. 4 (1988): 255–60.

80. Vaughan, *Curing Their Ills;* M. Lyons, "Medicine and Morality: A Review of Responses to Sexually Transmitted Diseases in Uganda in the Twentieth Century," in *Histories of Sexually Transmitted Diseases and HIV/AIDS in Sub-Saharan Africa,* ed. M. Lyons, M. Lewis and P. Setel (London: Greenwood Press, 1999), 97.

81. T. Kanogo, *African Womanhood in Colonial Kenya, 1900–1950* (Oxford: James Currey, 2005), 4, 55, 120–23, 144–49

82. See, for example, Berry, *Culwick Papers;* Bukoba District Annual Report, 1947, TNA 215/2154; H. Cory, "The Haya Tribe and the Incidence of Venereal Disease," (unpublished typescript, University of Dar es Salaam Library, 1949).

83. For example, Berry, *Culwick Papers;* Dr. G. A. Macgregor and M. O. Bukoba, "The Incidence of Syphilis among Ante-Natal Women Attending Kagondo and Bukoba Hospitals' Maternity and Child Welfare Centres," March 1942, Bukoba District Book, TNA.

84. See, for example, Cory, "Haya Tribe and the Incidence of Venereal Disease"; W. Laurie and H. Trant, *East African Medical Survey, Monograph no. 2, A Health Survey in Bukoba District, Tanganyika* (Nairobi: Government Printer, 1954).

85. See, for example, 2000 Buhaya Ints. A. Kitanzi; 2004 Bunyoro Int. 84 and FGD 93; 2004 Buganda FGDs 79 and 53, and Ints. 41 and 46. Cf. K. Stewart, "Toward a Historical Perspective on Sexuality in Uganda: The Reproductive Lifeline

Technique for Grandmothers and Their Daughters," *Africa Today* 47, no. 3/4 (2000): 123–48. Kearsley Stewart's data show that the female age at sexual debut in Bunyoro was already low in the 1960s and 1970s at 16 years and declined only marginally to 15.4 years by the 1990s.

86. Stewart, "Toward a Historical Perspective," 129.

87. Cf. Caldwell, "Construction of Adolescence in a Changing World," 150; Davis, "On the Sexuality of 'Town Women' in Kampala," 39–41.

11 "Ruined Lives"

An Analysis of Gender Relations, Youth Sexual Behavior, and HIV and AIDS in Early Twenty-First-Century Kenya

JOYCE NYAIRO AND EUNICE KAMAARA

HIV AND AIDS remains one of the major challenges to human life in the world. Over the past twenty-two years HIV has infected more than 35 million people, killing millions and leaving 14 million children orphaned.[1] In spite of all efforts to control the epidemic, the situation has been worsening; the prevalence of HIV continues to increase at an alarming rate. Sub-Saharan Africa suffers the greatest toll, where HIV prevalence has shot up from less than 1 million people in 1985 to 27.9 million in 2003, with 2.3 million people having died of AIDS and 3.2 million newly infected with HIV in 2003.[2] Although the region has only 10 percent of the world's population, it contains over 75 percent of all people living with HIV and has over 10 million children orphaned by the scourge. Since 2005 some decline in HIV prevalence is being witnessed in some countries in the continent, but this is not significant.

Youth, especially female youth, suffer the brunt of the epidemic in the region. Speaking at an international AIDS conference in 2004, Peter Piot, the executive director of the joint United Nations program on HIV/AIDS (UNAIDS), described the "feminization of HIV/AIDS" and observed that the African woman is the "face of HIV/AIDS." Young women are particularly vulnerable. In sub-Saharan Africa "young girls and women 15–24 years of age have 2–8 times higher infection rates than men of the same age." Of the total 25.7 million people living with HIV/AIDS in Africa in 2001, 14.6 million were women within the fifteen to forty-nine age group.[3] Women in Africa are being infected at an earlier age and by older men. On average there are thirteen HIV positive women for every ten such men in sub-Saharan Africa. Besides the biological factors that make women and girls more vulnerable to HIV infection, sociocultural factors related to the low status of women account for this disparity.

In Kenya, statistics indicate that 1.1 million adults ages fifteen to forty-nine are living with HIV, with the rates of infection in women nearly double the rates in men.[4] Although new infections in young women are said to have significantly declined in the last five years according to data collected from pregnant women under the age of twenty-five, the Ministry of Health in Kenya notes: "HIV prevalence in girls 15 to 19 years old is 6 times higher than in boys in the same age group, despite lower levels of sexual activity, and the rate in pregnant teens is even higher. Protecting teenage girls and young women remains a great challenge for controlling HIV infection in Kenya."[5]

Although statistics provide a quantitatively measurable, easy, and important way of presenting situations, they are not accurate presentations of human situations, especially with regard to human attitudes and behavior. Hence having set out the above statistical data, in this chapter we go on to analyze qualitative data to propound and advance our argument that controlling HIV and AIDS among youth in Kenya will remain a great challenge if we continue to focus only on statistics rather than interpreting these statistics alongside sociocultural systems and structures. We concentrate on the sociocultural definitions and expectations of femininity and masculinity in contemporary Kenya in relation to youth sexuality and, more specifically, the vulnerability of female youth. Generally, unequal gender relations, characterized by male dominance and female subordination, continue to be manifested in Kenya in the last decade of the twentieth century and the first decade of the twenty-first century. Further we advance the argument that the continued presentation of the HIV and AIDS situation as hopeless and helpless in a context marked by unequal, complex, and inconsistent gender relations serves to worsen the situation rather than to address the challenge.

This chapter uses the idea of urban legends to decode Kenyan youth sexuality and gender relations in the context of HIV and AIDS. Such decoding of present realities necessarily involves a historical analysis of experiences of young people because of the influence of the past on the present. Hence the first section of this paper discusses precolonial gender relations and the impact of colonialism on institutions and processes of socialization that led to erosion of values in human relationships. The second section then seeks to decode contemporary gender relations among Kenyan youth in the context of HIV and AIDS.

Youth may be defined subjectively from different perspectives depending on the context in which it is discussed. Generally, however, youth is a period of physiological, mental, and spiritual transition in the process of human development from childhood to adulthood. Demographers agree that the period of youth ranges from eleven to twenty-four years of age, though puberty, the physical indication of onset of youth, is experienced at different ages in different parts of the world. In this context, we adopt the demographic definition of youth.

Gender Relations and Youth Sexuality in Kenya: A Historical Perspective

Traditional African societies had a clear process of socialization through which individual members learned of sociocultural expectations with regard to specific issues such as gender relations in sexual encounters.[6] This process, as all other processes, was a religious one in that the societies believed in divine presence, guidance, and support through its implementation.[7] The socialization process was marked by initiation rites that marked graduation from one stage in life to the next—from birth to childhood to adulthood to elderhood and to ancestorhood. This process of socialization provided lifetime education. As individuals graduated from one stage to another, their knowledge and application of sociocultural values widened and intensified. Although inculcation of expected gender relations in sexual behavior was a lifelong education process, initiation from childhood to adulthood marked the specific moment in which gender awareness was intensified and emphasized especially in relation to sexual life. Indeed, the fact that initiation typically occurs at the critical psychosexual stage of human development dramatizes and makes explicit the difference between male and female social and sexual roles as well as the expected relations between the two sexes. Moreover, in most traditional African societies, initiation involves modification of sexual organs, an act that clearly indicates the sexual significance of this process.

Commenting on the relevance of the initiation process in traditional African societies, John S. Mbiti observes that it is only after initiation that individuals are allowed to share in the full privileges and duties of their people; it is only after initiation that individuals enter into a state of responsibility where they have rights and obligations as men and women.

> The initiation rites prepare young people in matters of sexual life, marriage, procreation and family responsibilities. . . . Initiation rites have a great educational purpose. The occasion often marks the beginning of acquiring knowledge, which is otherwise not accessible to those who have not been initiated. It is a period of awakening to many things, a period of dawn for the young. They learn to endure hardships, they learn to live with one another, they learn to obey, they learn the secrets and mysteries of man/woman relationships.[8]

Judith Bahemuka Mbula concurs with Mbiti when she affirms that in traditional African societies, it is not birth, but socialization and initiation that make a person a member of his /her community.[9] Karen Erickson Paige and Jeffrey M. Paige note that the initiation rite in Africa provides the critical moment of becoming male or female, the moment when female power is diminished and male power is enhanced and validated.[10] Margarethe Silberschmidt, in reference to the Kisii of Kenya, observes that female initiation involves excising a girl's masculine element to remove female aggression and to control her sexual excitement whereas the male initiation, on the contrary, is believed to be the removal of fear to enable the man to gain control, especially over women.[11]

There are variations in the initiation process from one ethnic group to the other. Nevertheless, the meaning and significance of these varied practices in instilling manhood (and the attendant masculinity) and womanhood (and the attendant femininity) are similar. Initiation from childhood to adulthood, highlighted by circumcision of boys and clitoridectomy for girls in many African societies, served the same purpose of attaining maturity and belonging. It is:

public confirmation of the rights of the individual to become an adult person. Thus initiation moves each gender into a new social world, and childhood comes to an end . . . serves to underpin not only the making of male and female identities—but in particular the difference between these identities. Through the rituals, the moral code for each gender is taught and new restraints are imposed on individuals—to replace an immediate source of authority embodied in the parent with the simultaneously remote and internal one of social obligation.[12]

In terms of social value system, what is expected of males is opposed to what is expected of females. Silberschmidt notes, "What is appropriate behaviour and gives social value to a man is certainly not appropriate for a woman and vice-versa. It is morality in which—when speaking in sexual terms—virtue is at stake. Not men's virtue but that of young girls and in particular a wife's virtue."[13]

The instructions that girls received during initiation on marital relations included how to treat their husbands in bed, how to be attractive, and how to raise children, all feminine roles which calls for subordination to the man. In contrast, boys received instruction on how to command authority and respect from their wives as husbands.

On initiation, girls and boys assumed labels as members of certain age-groups, age-sets, and generation. It was prestigious to acquire such identities, and the initiation rite was largely desired by the youth. This system of socialization of boys and girls into responsible adulthood, though lacking in gender justice, served the community well, especially in terms of marriage and family stability. It would probably be in place in Kenya today had British colonization not caused its disruption. Clitoridectomy was condemned outright by the colonizers, and the entire initiation process eroded as a new system of formal education was introduced. Unfortunately, the new system did not address gender and sexual education, thus leaving young people neglected, ignorant, and vulnerable to rapid uncoordinated social change.

The socialization process in traditional African societies was holistic and extended into all areas of life. Initiation from childhood to adulthood was not just about gender relations and sexuality but also about instilling self-esteem in young people and training them for responsible adulthood. Traditionally, for example, over the period of seclusion after circumcision young men received instructions on the value and ethics of work and the defense of their societies in case of war. Erosion of traditional forms of socialization has therefore left young people neglected, ignorant, and vulnerable not only in the area of gender relations but in many other areas. Through the colonial period traditional societies struggled to retain the socialization process, though this was often internally contested (see, for example, Richard Waller's discussion of Maasai murranhood in chapter 6). However, the demands of modern life, notably formal education and employment, have taken their toll on traditional methods of socialization. In postcolonial Kenya, socioeconomic and cultural change has created the uncoordinated and haphazard adoption of new thinking and values, which have only served to complicate the situation. For example, the development and popularization of gender empowerment programs which antagonize men and women in the name of gender equality has adversely shaken the foundation on which the African family. The bottom line is that whole societies suffer the consequences of not preparing young people for adult life. The advent of HIV and AIDS has served to worsen the implications of neglecting sexual and gender education for youth. Attempts by individual young men and women not just to cope but to survive in a situation of confusion and ignorance have unfolded in various tragedies, many of them translating into hopelessness. In the following section we present such tragedies as we seek to decode youth sexuality and gender relations among the youth in Kenya today in the context of HIV and AIDS.

Decoding Youth Sexuality and Gender Relations among Kenyan Youth in the Context of HIV and AIDS

Two narratives, the first a confessional letter that was purportedly posted on a university notice board by "N.P.," a student, and the second the title story by Macharia Mwangi in the collection *Reversed Dreams* (1998), provide the data for this section. N.P. titled "her" confession "Ruined Lives." We retain the title "Ruined Lives" in quotation marks in part because this is not our description or understanding of youth lives. Indeed, the argument consistently propounded in this chapter is that there is hope for justice and life for the human race, for the African people and even more specifically for Kenyan youth in spite of HIV and AIDS.

The Narrative
"RUINED LIVES"

> *When I joined Moi University in September 2001, I promised myself "that it's in Moi University I got it and it's here I will leave." I have indeed lived to keep my promise.*
>
> *I was in Form Three when a student on his attachment in our school proposed for a relationship. He had all the qualities a woman would want in a man so I gave in. He told me all a form three girl would want to hear. In my innocence and naivety, I succumbed to his pressure to have sex with him; consequently, I lost my virginity to him.*
>
> *After his placement, he reported to college for his final year and we still had contacts. I visited him on a number of occasions (I've even lost count the number of times I visited him). He was my first and only love and therefore I hung on every word he told me.*
>
> *My boyfriend later graduated and we lost contact until last month (March) when his sister told me about his whereabouts (details of this later). Before registration in the Faculty of Law, in PSSP, I went for medical tests as is the requirement. I then opted for an HIV test, which unfortunately turned out to be +ve. It then dawned on me that I had traded the rest of my life for a university student who had deliberately and intentionally preyed on my innocence.*

My first impulse was to take away my life, counselling sessions did not mean much to me and I quickly walked out of the session. I however did not confide my status to anyone until today.

The following day I went to a different Health facility and the results were still +ve. Therefore there was no doubt that I had been infected by this teacher-student. Since as the sister said, he had passed away after 6 months of being bed-ridden, besides, I had never had any other sexual relationship with anybody, no blood transfusion and the last time I used a syringe was in 1989.

Now, since whoever infected me did not mind about my life, I will also infect as many as possible as long as they are university guys oblivious of my status. So guys, anyone of you out there who may have crossed my "path" should count himself unlucky and should quickly place an order for ARTs supply before it's too late!

I decided to spread the virus indiscriminately in the Campus, (and have no apologies), because it's here I got and I intend to leave it here.

I've a well-documented report of all those guys who "crossed my path" since I joined this college. I will be posting their full names and registration numbers on the Students' Notice Board after the end of Sem. II Exams (August).

So far, I've had 124 students, yes one hundred and twenty four. Out of these, only 6, yes six used a condom. I still reiterate the fact that I owe nobody an apology and am still on a spreading spree till August.

Otherwise, I wish you success in your end of First Semester exams as you wait for your slow and sure DEATH.

N.P.

Silence and Denial

In April 2005 a person identifying "herself" only as "N.P." and claiming to be a student of Moi University in Eldoret, Kenya, posted this confessional letter on a notice board at the Eldoret West Campus. Its revelations of a deliberate campaign to infect as many Moi University males as possible with HIV sent ripples of shock far and wide, particularly once the local press and modern information technology widely circulated the legend. The anxiety was further heightened by the anonymity of the author, and calls for investigations into the real identity of the author were heard everywhere. The university administration oscillated between, first, denial and, later, claims that "a suspect ha[d] been arrested and [wa]s helping police with investigations." It is interesting to note that at the time, there was no law in Kenya to deal with people who deliberately infect others with HIV. One might even speculate that it is revelations such as those of N.P. that have drawn the attention of the authorities to the need for this kind of legal provision. As behind-the-scenes investigations to reveal the author of "Ruined Lives" progressed, word on the grapevine had it that in fact N.P. was not a female but a male student. We shall return to the gendered politics triggering this "sex change" later on in this essay.

The discourses informing the pseudo-legal reactions of the university administration are worthy of interrogation. They are reactions clearly driven by two related concerns. First, the panic over a possible HIV and AIDS epidemic on their campuses and, second, a sense of shame and fear of public indictment of an administration that has lost control and which might therefore be seen to be abetting public ills and chaos. These anxieties about degenerating social order that the legend of "Ruined Lives" generated echo the reasons behind the official sentiments of silence and denial that prevailed in Kenya on the outbreak of HIV and AIDS in the early 1980s. When the first case of the disease was diagnosed in Nairobi in 1984 the government maintained that the patient, who was then admitted at Kenyatta National Hospital, was a Ugandan national. This couched denial played on the stereotyped discourse of the sexual deviance and promiscuity of Ugandans that had circulated in Kenya since the late 1960s when Ugandans, fleeing the political troubles of their home, flooded Kenya and brought with them a lifestyle hitherto unknown by Kenyans.[14] This reaction of national distance and implicit denial that the Kenya government adopted from 1984 was to have far-reaching effects on both the spread of the virus and campaigns, largely by nongovernmental organizations (NGOs) and the churches, to educate the public on the facts surrounding HIV and AIDS. It was not until November 1999 that former President Moi declared HIV and AIDS a national disaster.[15]

In the early years, ignorance about the disease led to many extreme measures like isolating patients in special wards and wrapping up corpses in plastic bags before speedy burial. At the time NGO initiatives to break the silence on HIV and AIDS encountered many challenges, not least that of effective and compassionate communication about the nature and outcome of the disease. Invariably the messages dwelled on heterosexual intercourse as the key factor behind the transmission of the virus, and their attempts at maintaining order worked through frightening messages that dwelled on prolonged suffering and premature death as the result of sexual promiscuity. The reactions of Moi University administration to "Ruined Lives" are precisely rooted in this 1980s mind-set of official denial and the inelegant messages of NGOs and churches.

The Game of Numbers: Rumor, Shock, and Humor

Long after official attention to "Ruined Lives" had faded, reactions to its fear-inducing message continued to circulate in those realms that often fall below the radar of institutionalized officialdom. The forums for these public debates ranged from court corridors (N.P. had stated she was a law student on the Privately Sponsored Student Programme) to banking halls and pubs, and ultimately crossed national boundaries through email, blogs, and chat rooms on the Internet. Indeed, it is on the Internet that the moral and health implications of "Ruined Lives" have been interrogated over the longest period. As recently as 19 January 2006 the confessional letter surfaced on the website http://www.kimanzichana.jubiiblog.co.uk under the title *Mkenya Aliyeuwa Watu* (the Kenyan who killed people). The narrative was preceded by a photograph of a dead body at the mortuary.

This photograph—whatever its source may have been—not only spread the impression that N.P. had finally succumbed to the virus, it also lent visual amplification to the images of corrupted bodies that the resigned title of her confession suggests. The shock tactics employed by the hosts of this website are reminiscent of the methods of preaching the HIV and AIDS message that NGOs and Church initiatives originally adopted. In her study of sexuality in Nairobi, R. Spronk recalls an early 1990s Red Cross and Ministry of Health poster: "[It] depicts a man following a shapely figure clad in a red mini dress and high heels. Against a backdrop of a city at night, we can see the frontal view of the skeletal figure, which is a mask of death. The caption reads: 'WHAT YOU CAN SEE IS NOT WHAT YOU GET—AIDS KILLS.'"[16]

One can see the extent to which N.P.'s story amplifies this position. Inasmuch as she makes mention of her victims needing to "quickly place an order for ARTs [antiretroviral therapy] supply before it's too late!" her title, tone, and parting shot indicate that for her HIV/AIDS is a death sentence and the question of "people LIVING with HIV and with AIDS" is a mission impossible. Again, N.P. is clearly embittered by the fact that she could not detect the presence of HIV in the man she says infected her. Ironically, she exploits the fact of the concealed presence of the virus, which allows her to maliciously spread it to any "university guys oblivious of [her] status."

Although the photograph depicts the fate of the infected persons, the heading *Mkenya Aliyeuwa Watu* that flags the photograph not only signals the malice aforethought that guided the spread campaign by N.P., but also reverberates with the drama of affected numbers. N.P.'s sinister announcement of the sheer number of men she succeeded in enticing to have sexual relations with her invites a gendered analysis of sexual relations in Kenya, a point we shall come to later on in the chapter. For now we argue that the focus on numbers in a sense stems from and also reinforces the current campaign strategies of governmental and nongovernmental bodies working in the area of HIV and AIDS education. It is thought that the endless repetition of these alarming numbers will serve to prevent people from engaging in "risky behavior," that is, illicit sex or sex outside the socially approved institution of marriage. The numbers themselves have come to live a life of their own, in their sweeping and frightening statements of death. The repeated recitals that indicate thousands and even millions of "HIV cases" or "death cases," or, in the common phrase in town, "Every one out of seven Kenyans has it," create an uncanny atmosphere marked by implicit and sometimes explicit accusations.[17]

N.P. had had sex with 124 males from the Moi University community of whom only 6 wore condoms. Therefore the number that N.P. presumably succeeded in infecting with HIV was 118. Like the posters of decayed bodies and worm-infected fruit that were earlier used by campaigners for behavioral change, the strategy of reverberating statistics is a fear-inducing one. It therefore runs the risk of either being dismissed as alarming exaggeration or, conversely, as painting a picture of a world so grim and doomed that people simply abandon all hope and plunge headlong into "risky behavior." In all probability reactions oscillating between these two positions were behind the "118" label that was variously applied to the "Ruined Lives" episode. *Matatu*[18] touts gleefully called out "stage 118" to passengers wishing to alight at the Eldoret West Campus where the confessional letter was posted. In other instances the whole legend of the mysterious author, her letter, and arrests by the police was referred to as the "118" scandal. The coining, varied application, and mobility of this label "118" are clear evidence of the appropriation, circulation, and editing of popular culture texts in(to) new contexts.[19] Indeed, here we have the unlikely shift of emotional contexts from moments of deep fear and anxiety to ones of flippant jocularity and gallows humor. In this bleak humor we find new evidence about what HIV and AIDS have meant to Kenyan populations and the various ways in which they live with the pandemic. The coining of new idioms such as "118" in this instance, or "slim" and "slow puncture" in earlier moments, speak not only to the dominant mental images of the disease but also to the terms within which people grapple for hope and squeeze life, humor, and relief, however fleeting, out of seemingly interminably bleak moments. Indeed these "light-hearted" idioms demonstrate that the impulse to fight for life is intrinsic to humanity.

By promising to provide a list of the many men she deliberately tried to infect with the HIV, N.P. projects her ingrained belief that AIDS as a disease is a punishment for immorality—hers and that of the men who cross her path. This moralistic reading of the disease does not deal with either the sociocultural functions of sex among youth or the biological impulses triggering it. It adopts as a priori the Christian view of sex as the just province of monogamous marriage. Thus N.P. implicitly regrets giving in to the pressure to have premarital sex, and once she receives the news of her HIV positive status, she no longer sees a purpose or value for her own life. The sense of chaos that echoes in her mind is played out in her deliberate smear campaign. The certainty with which she sees death—which is to her the climax of individual destruction—is imposed on the world around her in ways that suggest an apocalyptic vision. This gloomy projection subverts every aspect of the "ABC" (Abstain, Be faithful, Condomise) campaign.[20] The fact that only 4.8 percent of her target group paid heed to the idea of condom use as part of the practice of safer sex—which includes preventing the spread of the HIV and AIDS—demonstrates the very marginal success of that particular strategy of education among the youth.

But what if the narrative contained in "Ruined Lives" is not factual but is indeed an urban legend? What if, as the Moi University administration claimed, it was to emerge that "Ruined Lives" was no more than the product of a fertile imagination? Would that make the story any less indicative of the sociocultural basis and impact of HIV and AIDS in Kenya? The idea that "Ruined Lives" may have been the product of a person's (whether male or female) imagination rather than a factual account leads us to consider the importance of literary fiction as illustration as well as product and definition of individual and societal identity. In this particular instance, literary discourse would help to outline perceptions and reactions to the HIV and AIDS pandemic in Kenya. We will not belabor the point that literary fiction mirrors, indeed, is inspired by and in turn echoes social reality.[21] Equally worthy of note is the fact that specific genres of fiction are framed to serve and communicate particular ideals about the world we live in. Like parables, legends are essentially cautionary tales whose chief characteristic is the mapping of extreme circumstances of destruction and suffering, which are alleviated or overcome by the timely and moral actions of a selfless hero. In postcolonial Africa, urban narratives often take on these qualities of the legend. They are infused with depictions of the urban space as a morally corrupting and ethically vile environment in which ethnic mores compete hopelessly against an alienating and dehumanizing global culture of capitalism, which has in particular long claimed the women who cavort recklessly with modernity and its things of glamour.[22] Urban legends then—written and unwritten—emerge as those condensed moral tales of the city as the place where African social and cultural values have been corrupted and where people search in confusion for moral anchors that will stem their glide into debased modernity.[23]

Signifying Death: "Reversed Dreams"

As with "Ruined Lives," the title of Macharia Mwangi's short story "Reversed Dreams"[24] graphically captures the sense of finality that dominates perceptions and reactions to HIV and AIDS in our society. "Reversed Dreams" is the story of the emotional turmoil that a young man, Munga, suffers when a doctor pronounces him HIV positive. With a haunting empathy it describes the treacherous ways of romance in this era of HIV and AIDS and gives us compassionate insights into the forces that compel the victim to run the risk of infecting his unknowing girlfriend. In this regard, "Reversed Dreams" might very well have been the flip side of "Ruined Lives," that is, the story of N.P.'s much demonized boyfriend who infected her with the virus. Mwangi's story is told in the first person by Munga. N.P.'s tone moves from vicious revenge to regret and finally to sardonic glee in the statement, "I wish you success in your end of First Semester exams as you wait for your slow and sure DEATH." By contrast, Munga maintains a tempo of a deeply felt despair and dread expressed in intricate flashbacks that lend urgency to the hopeless present.

The language of "Reversed Dreams" dwells on images of destruction and metaphors of fear. As he sits in the reception of the office where his girlfriend, Salome, works, Munga lapses into a nightmarish daydream in which he sees his life choked by "scorching flames" as an unrelenting "seven-horned demon" approaches him (1). He contemplates the certainty of the social stigma and discrimination that his HIV-positive status will invite. He worries about the hurt his condition will cause those closest to him, his mother, "father, his brothers, his sisters, his good friends and oh . . . Salome" (1–2). Munga resolves to inform his girlfriend Salome of his status because he cannot bear the guilt of deceiving her about something so important. But Munga's thoughts are constantly on his impending death. At the time he discovered his status the poster in the doctor's office screamed "HELP CRUSH A.I.D.S.," but Munga distrusts its message and focuses instead on the finality that has put paid to his best-laid plans. The narrative's sustained refusal to name either HIV or AIDS, save the brief reference to the message on the poster at the doctor's office, signifies the extent of the dread that Munga feels. The unmentionable—distant and improbable as he may have thought it—has happened to him and there is no way of confronting it. Munga variously thinks of HIV as a "monster" (1), "the dreaded thing" (3), "this beast" (4).

"Reversed Dreams" gives us a glimpse into the changing face of romance in this era of HIV and AIDS. Rather than being a site of expectant planning and jubilation romance is now a minefield laden with apprehensions and suspicions. At thirty-two Munga has not yet settled down to marriage and now in all likelihood he never will for "he knows now that he will soon be gone. He will soon be extinct, out of this world forever, shamefully" (5). Munga goes in search of his girlfriend, Salome. Oblivious of Munga's troubles (nor indeed of her own impending ones) Salome bubbles on excitedly as soon as they meet. Munga answers her distractedly, speaking at cross-purposes and totally consumed by the need to confess his status to her. He fears the revelation will destroy her and wonders whether she shouldn't just "follow him to the grave" (5). Outside, the impending darkness symbolizes the gloom surrounding this meeting between Munga and Salome. His tongue-tied attempts at confessing end when he succumbs to the pressure of his physical desire, which Salome both incites and echoes. Even through this act, it is difficult to think of Munga as a vicious murderer in the way N.P of "Ruined Lives" so easily emerges. Rather, Munga comes off as a terrified coward who chooses momentary comfort in the wake of haunted nightmares, guilt, and fear.

Gender, Youth Sexuality, and HIV and AIDS

In many ways, postcolonial Kenya is precisely defined by its lack of an agreed-on or coherent value system for sexuality. Although some people, especially in rural Kenya, still uphold traditional ethnic cultural value systems, others uphold Christian value systems, and yet others espouse a "modern" value system largely borrowed from the West.[25] The majority, however, are at a crossroads. They are cultural mulattoes who hold a bricolage value system that bears a mixture of traditional ethnic culture, Christian culture, and a host of other value systems resulting from modernization and secularization. Suffice it to note that this complex value system does not always have consistent or readily recognizable values even within one individual. Depending on the specific situation, every individual chooses what values to adhere to. In the absence of systematic sex education, most young people in Kenya are left to seek answers to questions of their sexuality from their peers and the media. In so doing most end up adhering to inconsistent and complex value systems.

Although there have been a lot of changes with regard to sexual values and the consequent behavior due to modernization and the attendant cultural globalization, gender relations with specific reference to sexuality have not changed much. Writing on the construction of gender, specifically of womanhood in colonial Kenya (within the first half of the twentieth century), Tabitha Kanogo presents a situation that could be compared to that of Kenya today where women are subordinate to male authority embodied in their fathers, elders, and missionaries.[26] A study by R. L. Munroe and R. H. Munroe on the Maragoli in Western Kenya on cultural reproduction and differentiation of sex within the last ten years of the twentieth century suggests that social change has had little impact on cultural reproduction of gender differentiation.[27]

Gender relations continue to be characterized by male dominance and female subordination. Theoretically, but not practically as we will discuss later, this implies that men make decisions on when, where, with whom, and how sex takes place. This model of sexual relations is based on a negative view of female sexuality that presents women as sexually evil and that therefore their sexuality has to be controlled by men if humanity is to escape doom. Consequently, male sexual morality is rarely under scrutiny. It is female sexual morality that has to be monitored and controlled by the "moral" sector of humanity—men. This view has been inherited from both traditional African and Christian cultures and is perpetuated in modern cultural settings. It is a model of gender relations that unconsciously encourages and pressures young people into premarital sex even in this era of the caution demanded by HIV and AIDS.

The representations of HIV and AIDS that we have read in "Ruined Lives" and "Reversed Dreams" find another point of convergence in their (sub)conscious projection of gendered youth sexuality in Kenya. In both narratives women emerge as "AIDS-givers" and men as "passive victims."[28] The first few paragraphs of "Ruined Lives" appear to indicate that the man who infected N.P is the guilty person in the story, but this impression fades as one reads on. As the narrative unfolds the man's guilt melts away and his behavior becomes inconsequential as N.P. fits into the stereotypical sexually uncontrolled and evil woman who tempts men into sexual disaster, thereby putting a whole community at threat. And whether "Ruined Lives" is fact or fiction, its interpretation does not change much in so far as gender relations and sexuality are concerned. Critical reading of the text of "Ruined Lives" reveals no knowledge of how the man got infected with HIV and whether he was aware of it when he infected N.P, if indeed he is the one who infected her. It appears the man's behavior is of no consequence and is therefore not under scrutiny; indeed, it is not really the focus of the confessional.

In "Reversed Dreams," although we are told nothing of Munga's previous sexual relationships, Salome's promiscuity is suggested by her portrayal as a single mother whose son, Babito, was the outcome of a "treacherous love" with Meshack, the man who "vanished" after he impregnated her. To add to the power of Salome's depiction as a temptress (5), it is she who makes sexual overtures to Munga at a time when his mind is resolved on confessing to her his HIV positive status. The implicit suggestion is that Salome must bear the brunt of the consequences of her seduction since traditional and contemporary views of women's sexuality cast them in the light of sexual aggressors every time sexual activity has an unwanted outcome.

In *Youth, Gender and HIV/AIDS: A Kenyan Experience,* Eunice Kamaara contends that gender relations are positively related to youth sexual activity and the consequent possible HIV infection.[29] Her argument is that sociocultural definitions and expectations of masculinity and femininity dictate gender relations that are primarily characterized by male dominance and female subordination. As young people conform to these definitions and expectations, they engage in sexual relations, and many are infected with HIV in the process. Nothing illustrates this argument better that "Ruined Lives." The narrator in the story describes "herself" as a powerless and naive victim of a beast that "deliberately and intentionally preyed on my innocence." The student-teacher took advantage of her inferior position as a form three secondary school student as against his position as an older, more mature, and more educated student at a public university. The female "succumbed" to the sexual advances of the male not because she wanted sex but because he put "pressure" on her to meet his needs. Notice that the male initiated the female into sexual experience.

This experience is typical of theoretical explanations and popular understandings of male-female relations in sexual encounters. Beatrice Paola in an article titled "Turning Down Sex" accurately observes: "[M]ost women are brought up with the mentality that their job is to make men happy. They attach this belief to their roles as wives, girlfriends and even to shallow friendship like flings."[30] Yet, the practical situation (implicit) is that N.P. is no less responsible for what befell her than the man. There is no indication that the man coerced N.P. to have sex, and therefore N.P. should take responsibility for her choices and actions. Moreover, according to the text, N.P. visited the man in his university hostels on so many occasions that in her own words: "I've even lost count the number of times I visited him." N.P. readily fits into the stereotypical representation of women as objects that exist for the pleasure of men, a role they play until tragic results occur.

James N. Henslin, a professor of human sexuality, argues: "Women often try to be unselfish, giving and accommodating men's desires and needs, so that when men express a desire to have sex, it is difficult for some women to reject it thinking that they may lose the relationship if they do."[31] Having studied macho men, David Lewis, a British psychologist, argues that male chauvinism (characterized by dominance especially in sexual encounters) exists in every man in the world but the level to which each displays it differs due to sociocultural factors.[32] Both Henslin and Lewis capture the Kenyan context accurately. Male dominance and female subordination characterize sexual encounters: men largely determine when, how, where, and with whom sex takes place while women are passive participants. The reversal of this scenario is the fodder of tragic urban legends in which men become helpless victims of the treachery of heartless modern women.

Even then, the circumstances of N.P.'s campaign to spread HIV as presented in "Ruined Lives" leave one curious about the pattern of men's sexual relations. N.P. must have noticeably changed partners often; so why did men continually give in to her advances? Were these men completely unaware of her mobility, or did the bug of male dominance extend to a rivalry that saw every man struggle to equal the sexual exploits of his peers? It seems that an uncanny capacity for emulating the behavior of other men and a general tendency to want what every other man has are part of the psyche and performance of male dominance. In other words, once there is a "popular" girl on campus, every man wants to be seen with her. The social definitions of manhood—indeed the performance of masculinity in our society— seem precisely hinged on dominating and being noticed.

But is it practically the case that men always determine when, where, how, and with whom sex takes place? Did N.P. not determine whether sex took place with her teacher? Did she not, out of her own volition, visit the student teacher on campus? Dominant cultural practices shape her perception of herself as a victim even when she has willfully reversed the norm and become, however maliciously, proactive. In "Reversed Dreams" Salome initiates the sexual act with Munga, and Munga fails ethnic and Christian convention by being unable to contain female sexual desire. Does the story portray the expectation that Salome should have played the role of steadfast Mother Africa and controlled the situation? Hardly, because she is a fallen woman, an unmarried mother tainted in the eyes of both ethnic tradition and Christian morality. Inverted gender roles are seen to result in aborted futures, thereby further complicating the antinomies and contradictions that attend to the sexuality and gender identities of postcolonial youth.

Clearly, contemporary value systems in Kenya especially with regard to gender and sexuality in youth are contradictory or, as earlier expressed, complex and inconsistent. Against such a cultural background, it would seem not just irrational but impractical to expect youth to behave in a responsible way just because we provide information on how HIV is transmitted and how many people are dying every day. Statistics make little sense and therefore do not influence behavior especially when they perennially depict a "hopeless" situation. Statistics on human subjects must be presented alongside shrewd interrogation of social and cultural value systems and structures with emphasis on justice and life rather than on injustice and death if any positive change is to be realized.

The predicament of N.P. is indicative of the fact that there has been little if any behavior change among the youth, not even in a university population that represents our most educated youth, and for whose consumption 75 percent of HIV and AIDS messages are now tailored. For if only 4.8 percent of N.P.'s target group bothered with condom use, it means that the ABC campaign has largely failed. True, we have no way of knowing how many men N.P. propositioned in total, and what percentage of these the 124 "victims" represent. But seemingly, it is a dismal number if we consider that she managed her 124 in under 4 years! That gives us a rate of 2.5 men per month, and if we consider that she was not on campus 365 days a year, the figure may be that much more alarming, say 10 sexual encounters per month!

Our argument remains that continued assumption that knowledge about HIV and AIDS alone will translate to positive behavior change needs to be challenged because sociocultural systems and structures play a major role in determining human behavior. In this case, empowering men and women to critique and transgress the limits set by the sociocultural definitions and expectations of femininity and masculinity is central to winning the fight against HIV and AIDS.

THE BASIC ARGUMENT propounded here is that whereas gender relations in many aspects of life, such as in division of labor in professions, may have radically changed, in the area of sexuality, they have not changed much in Kenya at the dawn of the twenty-first century. This is in spite of many years of gender empowerment programs in Kenya. There is still a general tendency to present and understand women as sexually dangerous for the community, thereby creating a need to control female sexuality. Consequently, gender relations are basically characterized by male dominance and female subordination in sexual encounters, so that men are continually presented as the ones who must make decisions of when, where, how, and with whom sex takes place. Yet, should the result of the sexual act be undesirable, as in instances of unwanted pregnancy or HIV infection, women are presented as being entirely responsible for both the deed and the outcome.

Typical of many real-life situations, this chapter seems to present a contradiction that gender relations in Kenya have changed even as they remain the same. But there is no contradiction.

Although the process of socialization in traditional Kenyan societies, specifically initiation from childhood to adulthood, served to equip young people with necessary knowledge and life skills, the continued hangover of male dominance and female subordination in the context of rapid uncoordinated change creates a situation of extreme negligence, ignorance, and vulnerability for young people. As deeper analysis of contemporary literary texts selected for this chapter indicates, men do not necessarily make decisions on sex. Covertly, women have some level of control, but it is one that society does not want to admit to or endorse as either practical or desirable. Therefore both young men and women fall back on societal expectations of male dominance and female subordination, thereby blaming society for their woes.

In the texts we have used to arrive at these conclusions, one a confessional letter that quickly grew into an urban legend and the other an award-winning work of fiction, we have argued that embedded gender relations are positively related to irresponsible sexual behavior in young people and consequently to the spread of HIV. There is therefore a need to confront this structural aspect of culture and society. Further, we argue that in this context, representations of the nature and outcome of HIV and AIDS seem to have been focused on destruction and death for far too long. It therefore seems that, its prohibitive cost implications aside, it will take time for the antiretroviral therapy gospel of "living positively with HIV and AIDS"—which has only gained volume and visibility in the millennium—to erase these images of doom from public discourse on the pandemic. Indeed, unless advocacy campaigns are pegged to a dismantling of sociocultural gender imbalances as well as promoting resilience and hope, the war against HIV and AIDS will never be meaningfully won. Instead notions of "ruined lives" and "reversed dreams" will continue to dominate perceptions of youth and their futures in the context of HIV and AIDS.

Notes

1. UNAIDS, *Report on Global HIV/AIDS Epidemic* (Geneva, 2007), http://data.unaids.org/pub/EPISlides/2007/2007_epiupdate_en.pdf.

2. S. Weinreich and Ch. Benn, *AIDS: Meeting the Challenge: Data, Facts, Background* (Geneva: WCC Publications, 2004), 5.

3. UNAIDS, *Report on Global HIV/AIDS Epidemic,* 8.

4. National AIDS and STI Control Programme (NASCOP), Kenya Ministry of Health, *AIDS in Kenya: Trends, Interventions and Impact,* 7th ed. (Nairobi, 2005), 8.

5. Ibid.

6. Our use past tense here should not be misconstrued to mean that this process of socialization is completely absent in contemporary Africa. The cultural practices mentioned in this section are described as they are (were) in traditional setting with the understanding that some of the practices have remained intact, whereas others have been discarded or modified. Both past and present tense will be used to indicate this reality.

7. As John S. Mbiti observes of African societies: "Religion permeates all departments of life so fully that it is not easy or possible to isolate it. A study of the religious systems is, therefore, ultimately a study of the people themselves in all complexities of both traditional and modern life" (J. S. Mbiti, *African Religions and Philosophy* [Nairobi: East African Publishing House, 1969], 1).

8. Mbiti, *African Religions and Philosophy,* 121–22.

9. Judith Bahemuka Mbula, *Our Religious Heritage* (Edinburgh: Thomas Nelson and Sons, 1983), 71

10. Karen Erickson Paige and Jeffrey M. Paige, *The Politics of Reproductive Ritual* (Berkeley: University of California Press, 1981).

11. M. Silberschmidt, *Women Forget That Men Are Masters: Gender Antagonism and Socio-economic Change in Kisii District* (Stockholm: Stata Corps, 1999), 62.

12. J. G. Peristiany, *The Social Institutions of the Kipsigis* (London: Routledge and Kegan Paul, 1964), 73.

13. Silberschmidt, *Women Forget That Men Are Masters, 72.*

14. See, for example, the testimony of Selina Onyango at the Ouko Commission of Inquiry in which she referred to Nicholas Biwott's preference for Ugandan women. The proceedings and report of the Ouko Commission were carried in all the Kenyan public press through 1991/1992.

15. R. Spronk, "Ambiguous Pleasures: Sexuality and New Self-Definitions in Nairobi" (PhD thesis, University of Amsterdam, 2006).

16. Ibid., 101.

17. Ibid., 90.

18. *Matatu* refers to a ten-seater minibus public transport vehicle common in Kenya.

19. K. Barber and C. Waterman, "Traversing the Global and the Local: Fuji Music and Praise Poetry in the Production of Contemporary Yoruba Popular Culture," in *Worlds Apart: Modernity through the Prism of the Local,* ed. D. Miller (London: Routledge, 1995); I. Hofmeyr, J. Nyairo, and J. Ogude "Who Can Bwogo Me? Popular Culture in Kenya," *Social Identities* 9, no. 3 (2003): 373–82.

20. The ABC campaign has been propagated as a strategy to control the spread of HIV and AIDS in spite of its limitations and clear indications that it does not work even among young people: All research on the sexual behavior of the young concurs

that the majority of young people are sexually active, most of them with many sexual partners, and yet they rarely use condoms. Lately, the strategy has been queried as ineffective even among married people. See, for example, G. Byamugisha, *What Can I Do?* (St. Albans, UK: TALC, 2004).

21. Ngugi wa Thiong'o, *Homecoming* (London: Heinemann, 1972); David Lodge, *The Art of Fiction* (London: Penguin Books, 1992); Cyprian Ekwensi, *Jagua Nana* (Oxford: Hutchinson, 1961).

22. See particularly Mwangi Ruheni, *What a Life* (Nairobi: East African Publishing House, 1972); Meja Mwangi, *Kill Me Quick* (Nairobi: Heinemann, 1973), *Going Down River Road* (Nairobi: Heinemann, 1976), and *The Cockroach Dance* (Nairobi: Longman, 1979). In Ngugi wa Thion'go's *Petals of Blood* (Nairobi: Heinemann, 1977) Nairobi is a treacherous den of immorality, and, in Manichean terms, what was once the idyllic rural Illmorog is seen to be hopelessly corrupted once the transnational highway connects it to other urban centers, rapidly urbanizing it, to its detriment. Without exception, these writers depict unmarried women in the city as an amoral lot whose greed for material well-being turns them into ruthless prostitutes.

23. For historical work that examines discourses connecting urbanization and demoralization in neighboring Tanzania, see A. Burton, *African Underclass: Urbanisation, Crime and Colonial Order* (Oxford: James Currey, 2005); and, for the manner in which gender is connected to these discourses, see the work of Andrew Ivaska, including the forthcoming monograph "Cultured States: Youth, Gender and Modern Style in 1960s Dar es Salaam" (from Duke University Press), adapted from his PhD dissertation "Negotiating 'Culture' in a Cosmopolitan Capital: Urban Style and the Tanzanian State in Colonial and Post-colonial Dar es Salaam," University of Michigan (2003).

24. Macharia Mwangi, "Reversed Dreams," in *Reversed Dreams and Other Stories,* ed. Nana-Wilson Tagoe and Wanjira Muthoni (Nairobi: Writers Association of Kenya, 1998). Page references in parentheses in the text refer to this edition.

25. See, for example, V. Lema, "The Determinants of Sexuality among Adolescent School Girls in Kenya," *East African Medical Journal* 67, no. 3 (1990): 191–200; Silberschmidt, *Women Forget That Men Are Masters;* Spronk, "Ambiguous Pleasures"; Th. Weisner et al., eds., *African Families and the Crisis of Social Change* (Westport, CT: Greenwood Press, 1997).

26. T. Kanogo, *African Womanhood in Colonial Kenya 1900–1950* (Nairobi: East African Educational Publishers, 2005).

27. R. L. Munroe and R. H. Munroe, "Logoli Childhood and the Cultural Reproduction of Sex Differentiation," in *African Families and the Crisis of Social Change,* ed. Th. Weisner et al., 299–314; see also Lema, "Determinants of Sexuality among Adolescent School Girls in Kenya," and E. Kamaara, *Youth, Gender and HIV/AIDS: A Kenyan Experience* (Eldoret, Kenya: AMECEA Gaba Publications, 2005).

28. C. Nzioka, "AIDS Policies in Kenya: A Critical Perspective on Prevention," in *AIDS: Foundations for the Future,* ed. P. Aggleton, P. Davies, and G. Hart (London: Taylor and Francis, 1994), 169.

29. Kamaara, *Youth, Gender and HIV/AIDS.*

30. B. Paola, "Turning Down Sex," *East African Standard,* 23 April 2005, 15.

31. Cited ibid.

32. Cited by Florence Machio, in "Male Chauvinism," *East African Standard,* 18 June 1997.

12 Protecting Young People

Alcohol, Advertising, and Youth in Kenya

JUSTIN WILLIS

IN JUNE 2005 the government of Kenya announced that it intended to ban alcohol advertising from television and billboards. The announcement was explicitly linked to the dangers that such advertising posed to young people: the ban was intended to "protect young people from becoming hooked."[1] The decision, which had been under consideration since the previous year, came some months after a decision to ban alcohol advertisements on billboards from the vicinity of schools.[2]

The announcement was greeted with enthusiasm by some commentators, who immediately located it in the context of anxieties over the vulnerability of the young to the wiles of advertisers: "Adverts lure, especially youth, to start drinking early. We cannot do away with alcohol but unless the consumption levels are checked, our country will be doomed," opined one correspondent in the *Daily Nation.* Another observer emphasized the extraordinary power of television: "[T]he constant association of alcohol use with glamour on TV has the great potential for conditioning young people into imagining that alcohol consumption always goes together with success. . . . This conditioning leaves many people completely powerless over alcohol, the victims of their circumstances."[3] Another correspondent noted the success of the beer industry, but argued "Let us not think only about profit. Let us also consider the health and the future of Kenyans, especially the young. Let us support the ban."[4]

Others were much less enthusiastic. The formal liquor industry in Kenya is dominated by various corporate manifestations of a single company, East African Breweries Limited (EABL), which merely announced that it was "consulting with the Government"; but the newspapers recorded much protest from the advertising industry, and (apparently) from ordinary people.[5] "[T]his will lead to many people losing their jobs," wrote one; "there are people who never watch or listen to the adverts, who are serious drinkers," noted another.[6] In a public opinion survey, 50 percent favored the ban while 49 percent opposed it.[7] The chair of the Marketing Society of Kenya (a Muslim woman, incidentally) demanded that the government convene a "stakeholders' meeting" to discuss the ban: "We do not want to believe that this Government, which was elected on a platform of change, will renege on its pre-election pledge of creating employment."[8]

The sense of outrage on behalf of industry was predictable. The formal liquor industry in Kenya has enjoyed a generally very close relationship with the state since the 1950s; and although this has been somewhat strained in the early 1990s, the election victory at the end of 2002 of the National Rainbow Coalition had apparently restored the earlier coziness.[9] EABL, as it never lost an opportunity to remind anyone who would listen, was a very substantial and reliable contributor of revenue to the Kenyan treasury, through a range of taxes; and it had continued a well-established pattern of advertising that associated its products with success and—on the whole—with the aspirations of good citizenship. That the government was nonetheless willing to ban advertising must have come as a significant shock.

As it turned out, both the celebrations of the temperance lobby and the protests of the advertisers were premature. A week after announcing the imminent ban, the government spokesman, Alfred Mutua, appeared to temporize on the subject, saying that "We will give a balance between economic benefits and the social impact when we come to a decision." Having said that the ban would be imposed within weeks, the government soon announced that the ban would be postponed for six months, and there were reports of "high-level consultations" with the industry.[10] The six months has somehow not yet quite passed, and debate over the issue has apparently faded. In January 2009, television advertisements for alcohol were still appearing, and giant billboards along the roadside still proclaimed the virtues of Smirnoff vodka and Tusker beer.

The "ban" and its quiet demise each raise questions, which this essay will explore. In considering how it was that the government came to publicly announce a ban, the essay will explore the evidence for problem drinking by youth in Kenya; it will suggest that this evidence is questionable but that a new line in advertising catalyzed wider concerns about youth behavior to produce a brief explosion of concern over youth drinking. The ban, then, was the consequence not of clear evidence of a youth drinking crisis, but of wide anxiety about youth, through which the debate over alcohol advertising was drawn into discursive efforts to create an authentic morality. Recent scholarship has highlighted the ease with which youth behavior could become the focus for "moral panics" in colonial Africa that drew both colonial officials and older African men into advocating dramatic forms of state intervention that showed a certain blindness to empirical data.[11] Debates over the consumption of alcohol were often drawn into these panics because of alcohol's particularly ambiguous role in the construction of everyday authority; in many societies in precolonial East Africa, too, young people's access to alcohol had been restricted and contested as part of the quotidian practices that constantly asserted the authority of older men.[12] In one way, this case simply offers a modern example of such shared societal panic, which subsided, not as a result of any clear reappraisal of the situation, but rather because the substantial influence and economic importance of the liquor industry secured a quiet forgetting of the ban in return for some adjustments to its advertising practice.

But these events also invite reconsideration of the relationships between young people's agency, international commercial culture, and the very idea of "youth." Some Kenyan commentators were quick to see young people as vulnerable victims of advertising, spoiled children whose dress, language, and behavior were simply local imitations of global trends. But it can also be argued that some younger Kenyans—by no means all of them wealthy—have appropriated the material forms of an international youth culture to challenge the political and cultural dominance of an older generation who, young at independence, have grown old in power and now routinely deploy a language of authenticity and patriarchy to justify their positions. Unlike the young men who challenged elders' claims to a monopoly of alcohol in many nineteenth-century Kenyan societies, these drinkers are not trying to gain early entry to the drinking culture of their seniors. To be a "youth" is not simply to be an elder-in-waiting; it is to challenge the very idea of "elders." Kenyan society has been profoundly affected by the way that young people's developing self-consciousness as "youth" has been encouraged by an awareness of the commercial possibilities of that self-consciousness and by an increasingly active advertising industry: the effects are apparent in the way that people dress and talk, in their leisure choices, and in the open discussion of sex in newspapers and on FM radio. Both the ads for alcohol themselves and the reaction to them suggest the growing importance, in conflicts over culture and proper behavior in Kenya, of the idea of youth as a distinct category that implies a distinct set of values and kinds of behavior.

The story of the "ban," then, is partly one of continuity—the latest round in a long cultural argument over age and authority. But although disputes over the access of young people to alcohol are by no means novel, the innovative aspect of the ads, and of the "youth" culture that they sought to exploit and encourage, was the idea that young people could consume in a distinctive way—not just aspiring to drink alcohol, but aspiring to be drunk in ways that were different—that is, to be "youth." Andrew Ivaska has explored the intense and sometimes violent debates in 1960s Tanzania over young people's involvement in an "international culture of self-fashioning through bodily adornment and consumption"; the debate over drinking advertising offers a window on similar debates in Kenya.[13] It was this idea that young people did not just wish to claim the privileges of adults, but saw themselves as culturally different, that made these advertisements so controversial.

Youth in Peril?

In 2001, a new body had been created by the Kenyan government—still, at that time, under the control of the long-standing president, Daniel arap Moi. The National Agency for the Control of Alcohol and Drug Abuse (NACADA), formally a public corporation, was itself a response to an earlier political furor, over the emergence in the 1990s of what had become known as the "New Generation" drinks. Of varying recipe, these had mostly shared two features: they were compounded from a spirit base, and they operated on the fringe of the law in terms of both packaging and the payment of tax. There was widespread suspicion that President Moi's administration had in some way connived at the spread of these drinks, as a way of punishing particular areas of the country that were deemed opposition strongholds. Official rhetoric, in contrast, located the perceived problem not as a governmental conspiracy but rather as a mark of the disobedience of a populace who were failing to commit themselves wholeheartedly to the project of national development, which lies at the center of Kenya's public political culture. A number of serious poisoning incidents occurred, apparently in consequence of the production of some alcoholic beverages with methanol. Whether or not these were actually connected to "New Generation" drinks, a public outcry led to some attempts to control these beverages, and to the creation of NACADA, under the leadership of Joseph Kaguthi, a former provincial commissioner.[14]

NACADA's focus was, from the first, on youth; rather than condemning the public as a whole for lack of devotion to development, the organization argued that the real problem lay in the collapse of moral standards among young people. It immediately commissioned what it described as a baseline survey—a sociological report on the extent of substance abuse among youth in Kenya. The report was rather long in coming; it was apparently completed in 2002, but it was not until the beginning of 2004 that an abridged form was released to the public, after what Kaguthi described as some "panel-beating" to make it more "user friendly and readable."[15] In the meantime, however, it had been extensively leaked to the press, encouraging some strident headlines on "rampant drug abuse" and "how drugs find their way into schools." The release of the report itself produced further headlines. According to the report, it was said that "alcohol consumption is the highest form of drug abuse among the youth"; and there were some alarming-sounding figures: "in Western Province, 43.3% of students abuse alcohol, while in Nairobi 40% have abused drugs."[16] Some reports drew conclusions on the relationship between alcohol and sexual health: "Reckless sexual unions, most likely inspired by alcohol, are responsible for spiralling AIDS cases."[17] In May and June 2004, newspaper comment suggested that blame for all this lay principally with the plastic tot sachets (packets containing small measures or "tots" of spirits)—mostly of 30 or 50 milliliters—in which cheap spirits were sold. These were believed to be particularly attractive to youth because of their "affordability and portability," and they were a "cause of rising indiscipline."[18] In June 2004 the government announced restrictions on the sale of these, to applause from the press: "By limiting the minimum package to 200 millilitres, it will now be out of the reach of those young Kenyans on whom the future of the country depends."[19]

The newspaper coverage very much reflected the tone of the abridged report itself. The report identified alcohol as the main substance abused in Kenya and suggested that the problem was particularly intense among "youth" (who were, for this purpose, defined as those aged ten to twenty-four). A substantial proportion of youth were alcohol abusers, according to the survey, with certain provinces seeing particularly high levels of use. The report ended with a clarion warning.

Substance abuse, it said, could lead to a "national disaster." The danger lay especially in youthful abuse, as substance abuse "predisposes the youth to diseases and poor health, conflict with the law, poor academic performance. . . . [S]ubstance use and substance abuse distort the national political economy and subvert political order."[20]

Looked at more carefully, the baseline survey provided slightly less evidence for alarm than first appeared. There were, for instance, certain methodological problems with the collection and analysis of data. There was no indication of the number of respondents surveyed, or how the individual respondents were chosen, though the report explained that the sample was drawn from university and school students, on the one hand, and from certain other groups, on the other. NACADA's survey reported a very low response rate among the university students; some of the other selected groups seem by their very nature to be likely to report a high rate of substance abuse since they comprised, among others, those "operating as prostitutes, brewing illegal alcoholic drinks, peddling drugs and living on the street."[21] More seriously than that, however, was the definition of abuse that was offered—or rather, the lack of a definition. The whole report was apparently predicated on the assumption that any use of alcohol (or any other drug) would automatically lead to abuse, and neither the text nor the tables offer any indication of frequency or volume of consumption. Apparently, to report any use of alcohol in this survey was to be characterized as an abuser. In contrast to the alarmist tone of this report, a consumer survey of 1,755 youths in 2004 reported, rather modestly, that 19 percent drank beer at least once a month, with 2 percent drinking it daily.[22] The baseline survey really did nothing to address the well-known "paucity of data" on drinking in Africa, and it certainly offered no conclusive evidence of a drinking crisis.[23]

NACADA's success in persuading the government to act did not, then, derive from the reliability or clarity of its statistics, although newspapers continued to proclaim that "the reality is stark and the statistics alarming."[24] It was rather the very idea that drink was a youth problem that proved so persuasive, for it successfully tapped into a much wider set of concerns about youth. The report itself made this explicit: "The rapid spread of substance abuse can be traced to the breakdown of the indigenous society and to the introduction of foreign influences. . . . [S]ubstance use by the youth implies a breakdown of family values evident in the indigenous society. As a result, several parents have lost control over their children."[25]

Alcohol abuse, it was implied, was directly associated with "the introduction of foreign ways of life that have been undermining the cultures of the indigenous society"; it brought unruliness and disobedience among youth, and the prevalence of violence. The wealthy, as well as the poor, were prone to such problems, for their households were corrupted by modern influences.[26] The abuse of substances was both a cause and consequence of cultural inauthenticity; for in indigenous society, the use of alcohol (and of cannabis and *miraa*) would be restricted to those who could manage it—that is, older men, or as the report put it, "senior age-groups and . . . special occasions."[27] The vigor of this rhetoric recalls the campaigns against certain styles of youthful dress and behavior that characterized Tanzania in the 1960s and 1970s; there too, "foreign" cultural influences were identified as the root case of youthful misbehavior, and official condemnation drew strength from the anxiety of older men.[28]

The report identified new communications technologies as particularly malign cultural forces: "The abundance of television programmes, video shows and internet services in urban areas exposes young people to a global pop culture that links substance abuse to popularity, success, sophistication, sex appeal, good times, growing up and independence."[29]

This concern with the role of advertising on youthful drinking was not in itself unique; international commentators had already drawn attention to a general trend in the alcohol industry to target "youth" audiences through a sort of globalized marketing strategy that plays on youth "subculture" as an international phenomenon.[30] What was distinctive about the NACADA report was the emphasis on this as a process that undermined Kenyan cultural authenticity. Kaguthi called publicly for a ban on alcohol advertising, in order to counter the "drinking culture that has taken root, especially among the youth,"[31] and he reiterated the message in a newspaper interview late in 2004, saying that "some of our cultural foundations have been eroded to the extent that we have tended to lose our feet as a community." He explicitly linked this problem to advertisements, which led to the "destruction of children through substance abuse."[32]

The enthusiasm with which newspapers took up this theme suggests that, in identifying "foreign influences" on youth as the real problem, NACADA had offered a means to express a widespread concern over the nature of culture and over intergenerational relations in Kenya. That youth represented a social and political problem seemed widely agreed; that this was the consequence of foreign culture was readily accepted, as was evidenced by parental irritation at the 2004 hit song "Keroro" (by Hubert Nakitare, aka Nonini) which celebrated the singer's drunkenness.[33] As the popularity of that song very clearly showed, young Kenyans were happy to flaunt the idea of a distinctive "youth" culture as a challenge to an older generation. The dress and musical styles of an international youth culture were taken up not only by the children of a wealthy urban elite but also by relatively poor young people in towns and in rural areas—appropriately enough, since many of these cultural forms were themselves evocations of economic and cultural marginality. This appropriation of youth culture was in turn condemned with a language of African authenticity; as one letter to a newspaper in 2003 had put it, "I would advise young people to shun the culture of whites. Instead they should dig out what is truly Kenyan and emulate it."[34]

The debate over alcohol advertising was part of a public discourse that linked youthful disobedience and disorder with the general influence of "foreign" culture on youth—it was the power of this discursive link that encouraged the government to act. NACADA did not create this linkage: as "Keroro" showed, young people themselves saw the celebration of alcohol as a defiant assertion of a commercially derived freedom, and the alcohol industry had been very ready to encourage this with its advertising. Even before the NACADA report began to be leaked, complaints had appeared in the press about liquor ads in which "the youth are the key targets," and particularly over ads for Smirnoff (and its alcopop offspring, Smirnoff Ice), which challenged established ideas of decency in advertising and played very much to a youthful audience.[35] The challenge posed by the prominence of young people in these ads was compounded by their gender; young women were very visible in this campaign, and the clothing—or rather the lack of clothing—of women in some billboard advertisements had excited particular outrage and calls for direct action to impose modesty on the images: "Let us, the residents of Funguo and Nyayo-Highrise Estates, well-wishers and others who are upset like myself, get together, climb up and cover the girl's nakedness."[36]

The Smirnoff Experience

Ironically, the advertisements that had excited this attention were the consequence of a demonstrable decline in the consumption of some "foreign-derived alcoholic drinks." For years, EABL had built its commercial success around bottled beer, and its advertising centered on the association between bottled beer, respectability, and adulthood. But bottled beer consumption in Kenya fell substantially after a peak in 1990; the figures released by EABL for 2001/2 varied slightly, but they suggested a drop of around 30 percent over ten years from 1992/3.[37] Some of this consumption was transferred first to "new generation" drinks and then to the tot sachets, a market segment initially dominated by small distillers and/or compounders who produced "an avalanche of new whiskies, vodkas, brandies and rums."[38]

Part of EABL's response to this was to extend its involvement in the spirits market, taking complete control in 2002 of a local distilling company in which it had long been involved.[39] From this base, EABL launched its own venture into the sachet market, though its product cost around twice as much as other sachets.[40] More visibly the company began to use in Kenya the same sort of marketing strategies used for spirits in other parts of the world, identifying them both with sporting events and with a particular vision of youth culture in which drinking and partying appeared prominently.[41] Smirnoff and Smirnoff Ice featured conspicuously in advertisements and promotions as part of this strategy. Basketball tournaments were sponsored under the slogan "Smirnoff Ice—Smart Stuff."[42] The "Smirnoff Experience" included musical events that linked Smirnoff drinking and youth music. These events were a central part of Smirnoff's promotions three accidental deaths until occurred at an event in December 2004; for some time thereafter press ads and billboards were the mainstays of the campaign.[43]

In some ways the marketing emphasis of Smirnoff seem to be a curious strategy—given their price, premium spirits comprised only a very small part of the overall market. Smirnoff Ice, for example, cost more than three times as much as a whisky sachet in terms of absolute alcohol content.[44] But the ads reflected the emergence in Kenya of a self-conscious "youth" market, who defined themselves partly through consumption and whose aspirations both drove and were driven by advertising. At the same time, Diageo, the international drink company that had effectively taken control of EABL in 2001, was concentrating on these brands in its international campaign, and so it was easy to follow suit with a campaign closely modeled on the global marketing strategy. The success of the campaign in terms of sales is hard to estimate: EABL reported that their sales of spirits actually fell by 6 percent (in volume) in 2004, perhaps partly as a consequence of the ban on sachets, but in subsequent years Smirnoff sales improved. And overall EABL continued to return impressive profits, partly because the company was remarkably successful in controlling costs, and partly because it had in 2002 reestablished an effective monopoly in the shrunken, but still dominant, bottled beer market.[45] The introduction in 2004 of a new low-cost keg beer, Senator, attracted rather less publicity and criticism than did the Smirnoff advertisements but may have had rather more market impact: EABL claimed that it was providing 10 percent of total sales volume by May 2005.[46]

The advertisements that provoked the most debate were, then, for products that were too expensive to command a substantial market. But the reaction to them was cultural, rather than a response to their effect on drinking. The Smirnoff campaign—the most obvious example of a new advertising focus on youth, on female drinking, and fun—evoked and encouraged the multiple challenges to authority and the established order that "youth" culture offered; and it was this which made alcohol advertising so controversial.

Lethal Brews?

Meanwhile, as some commentators noted at the height of the debate in 2005, alcohol advertising had little to do with another drinking "problem": "[T]he largest quantity of alcohol consumed by Kenyans is not that advertised in the media. It is illegal brews."[47] While sachets and Smirnoff occupied the attention of NACADA, many Kenyan drinkers busied themselves with other beverages, belonging to the increasingly broad category of "new generation" drinks, which had one shared characteristic—they were produced from spirit that had been distilled on an industrial scale largely for nonbeverage purposes. There were a very substantial range of producers involved: from the larger operators, such as the maker of "Kenya Kingi," who was cleared of various charges brought against him, to the former civic dignitary in Nyeri charged with bottling and selling a drink called "Budget," to the woman whose inexpert cocktail of industrial alcohol killed fifty drinkers near Machakos.[48]

The precise size of this market remains unclear. EABL suggests that the illegal and informal sector accounts for 60 percent of alcohol consumption in Kenya, which seems generally plausible; estimates have been made especially problematic since the government decision in the late 1970s to make all such production illegal.[49] How much of that 60 percent is composed of "traditional" fermented drinks (which were particularly affected by that decision), how much is composed of artisanal distillation, and how much takes the form of these "new generation" drinks is impossible to say, though clearly the availability of the "new generation" drinks has increased since their introduction in the 1990s. There has, so far as I know, been no attempt to systematically compile information on those killed and injured in these events, but such detail as is revealed by the press does not suggest that this is a youth problem, still less that it is a disease of affluence. The reported victims of "poison brews" do not appear to be predominantly "youth," although they are overwhelmingly men in rural areas or low-income urban areas. Quite how many such victims there are, however, it is impossible to say, since it is quite likely that only the most dramatic cases reach the press: in 2005, apart from the widely reported Machakos case, a dozen died in two incidents in December.[50] In May 2004, three died in one incident; in November of the same year, another thirteen.[51]

In the light of these events, one is tempted to agree with the letter writer who argued that banning ads was "a right effort in the wrong direction." The real problem, suggested the writer, was the "lethal ingredients" being used in "illicit brews." Taking up the theme of authenticity, he suggested that "traditional brewing" had been distorted by chemical innovation.[52] A few months later, Joseph Kaguthi himself called for legalization of "traditional" brews in order to "deter poisoning by additives such as methanol and industrial alcohol."[53] This casts the drinking "problem" in different terms, though there is a logical link in the argument: the danger still lies in the subversion of wholesome tradition.[54]

IN THE END, EABL—which in 2005 was awarded a prize as Kenya's best taxpayer—did not suffer significantly in consequence of the NACADA report and the brief, intense debate that followed it.[55] Advertisements for alcoholic beverages continued to appear on billboards and in the media. But the EABL marketing campaign has continued to reflect some of the societal tensions and uncertainties that cluster around the idea of "youth." Smirnoff was "relaunched" in March 2006, and the pictures of partying young women were briefly eclipsed in an advertising campaign that played on the adventurous life story of the eponymous Vladimir Smirnoff, in line with a wider international campaign with no particular "youth" content.[56] EABL has—with considerable publicity—played a leading role in organizing a voluntary code of standards for alcoholic beverage advertising that includes a commitment to eschew ads that link drinks to "social and sexual success" (though this does not apparently preclude promotions that offer spot cash prizes or hold out the possibility of winning a "souped-up" car[57]). EABL, like other companies controlled by Diageo around the globe, lays public stress in its promotional material—and in workshops and seminars—on the need to "drink responsibly" and the importance of observing legal age restrictions on alcohol sales; the company has in effect developed a new line of advertising that revolves around its commitment to "social responsibility."[58]

But despite all this, the presentation of a distinctive and international youth culture has become ever more important in EABL's advertising. EABL has begun again to sponsor music events, the advertising for which routinely bundles up alcohol with the images and language of a distinctive youth culture. By late 2006 Smirnoff was again sponsoring events that emphasized youth and a party culture; one of these, an "Eviction Party," was linked to EABL's new "Project Fame" venture, which was in itself a venture into reworking Tusker—formerly the respectable national drink—as part of an international youth culture.[59] By 2008 Tusker and Guinness were being advertised alongside Smirnoff as part of the same party culture.[60] As the crossover with Project Fame showed, the "youth" focus with Smirnoff led the way in an attempt to reposition EABL's other brands as less staid and more attractive to "youth." For those interested in selling drink, the idea of this distinctive youth market seems to exercise an irresistible allure; and in seeking to cultivate this market they are both appropriating youth culture and making it available as a cultural tool to young people in Kenya. This growing interest in the advertising of "youth" is not incompatible with refusing to supply alcohol to under-eighteens (for "youth" embraces many above the age of eighteen) but it provokes a continuous rumble of criticism from those who see the very idea of a distinctive youth culture of consumption as problematic.

Notes

1. Samuel Siringi, "Alcohol Adverts to Be Banned on Television," *Daily Nation,* 10 June 2005.

2. "State Considers Banning Alcohol Adverts," *Standard,* 7 October 2004; "Outcry on Tobacco and Alcohol Ads," *Daily Nation,* 7 January 2005; Lucas Barasa, "New Liquor and Tobacco Rules to Protect Schools," *Daily Nation,* 12 February 2005.

3. "Here's the Middle Ground on Alcohol Adverts," *Daily Nation,* 28 June 2005; see also Joshua Araka, letter, *Standard,* 15 June 2005.

4. Daniel M. Mbugua, letter, *Daily Nation,* 12 July 2005.

5. "Adverts Ban on Alcohol and Beer to Stay," *Daily Nation,* 16 June 2005.

6. Lorrine Awuor, letter: "Alcohol Adverts Won't Deter Drinkers," *Daily Nation,* 20 June 2005; see also letters from Ivy Keitany and Gladys Njeri in *Daily Nation,* 3 August 2005; "Cutting Edge," *Daily Nation,* 17 June 2005; see also "Advertisers' Lobby Group Says Embargo Is Punitive," *Daily Nation,* 10 June 2005

7. "Great Divide on Alcohol Promotion," *Daily Nation,* 30 July 2005.

8. "Plan to Ban Beer Adverts Met by Stiff Opposition," *Daily Nation,* 11 June 2005.

9. J. Willis, *Potent Brews: A Social History of Alcohol in East Africa, 1850–1999* (Nairobi and Oxford: James Currey, 2002), 181–96, 246–48.

10. "Adverts Ban on Alcohol and Beer to Stay," *Daily Nation,* 16 June 2005; "Fair Play Pledge on Alcohol Adverts," *Daily Nation,* 17 June 2005; "Agencies Want Order on Beer and Alcohol Ads Lifted," *Daily Nation,* 12 July 2005.

11. R. Waller, "Rebellious Youth in Colonial Africa," *Journal of African History* 47, no. 1 (2006): 77–92; A. Burton, *African Underclass: Urbanisation, Crime and Colonial Order in Dar es Salaam* (Oxford: James Currey, 2005), 6–10, 71–72, 75.

12. Willis, *Potent Brews,* 12–14, 118–40; for the ambiguous relationship of alcohol and power in West Africa, see E. Akyeampong, *Drink, Power and Cultural Change: A Social History of Alcohol in Ghana, c. 1800 to Recent Times* (Portsmouth, NH: Heinemann, 1996), 8.

13. A. Ivaska, "'Anti-Mini Militants Meet Modern Misses': Urban Style, Gender and the Politics of 'National Culture' in 1960s Dar es Salaam, Tanzania," *Gender and History* 14, no. 3 (2002): 584–607.

14. J. Willis, "New Generation Drinking: The Uncertain Boundaries of Criminal Enterprise in Modern Kenya," *African Affairs* 102, no. 407 (2003): 241–60.

15. Samuel Siringi, "Nacada Cites Rampant Drug Abuse in Schools and Universities," *Daily Nation,* 27 October 2003.

16. Liz Gitonga, "How Drugs Find Their Way into Schools," *Daily Nation,* 28 March 2004; Mike Mwaniki, "Packaging of Cheap Alcohol in Satchets [*sic*] to Be Banned," *Daily Nation,* 25 May 2004.

17. Mr. Gichuru, commentary, "Alcohol, Sex and Abortion Out of Control," *Daily Nation,* 2 June 2004

18. Editorial. "Yes, Ban This Cheap Alcohol," *Daily Nation,* 26 May 2004

19. Editorial, "Ban on Drinks Was Overdue," *Daily Nation,* 12 June 2004

20. NACADA, *Youth in Peril: Alcohol and Drug Abuse in Kenya* (Nairobi, 2004), 3, 36–37.

21. Ibid., 26, 40.

22. Clay Muganda, "Kenyan Youngsters Calling the Shots," *Daily Nation,* 12 May 2004. For the tentative results of another survey, from 1996, see Amayo, cited in D. Jernigan, *Global Status Report: Alcohol and Young People* (Geneva: WHO, 2001), 16.

23. For comment on this paucity, see World Health Organization, *Global Status Report on Alcohol* (Geneva: WHO, 1999), 21.

24. Mildred Ngesa, "Is Drinking Now the Curse of Kenyans?" *Daily Nation,* 18 March 2005.

25. NACADA, *Youth in Peril,* 1.

26. Ibid., 33.

27. Ibid., 3, 34.

28. T. Burgess, "Cinema, Bell-Bottoms and Miniskirts: Struggles over Youth and Citizenship in Revolutionary Zanzibar," *International Journal of African Historical Studies* 35, no. 2/3 (2002): 287–313; Ivaska, "Anti-Mini Militants Meet Modern Misses."

29. NACADA, *Youth in Peril,* 34.

30. Jernigan, *Global Status Report: Alcohol and Young People,* 10–13.

31. Mike Mwaniki, "Alcoholism Rising among the Youth," *Daily Nation,* 12 November 2004.

32. "My Take—Joseph Kaguthi," *Daily Nation,* 31 December 2004.

33. Philip Mwaniki, "The Big Songs of the Year and the Colourful Artistes," *Daily Nation,* 2 January 2005.

34. David Ochomo, letter, *Daily Nation,* 16 September 2003.

35. Stephen Sosio, letter, *Daily Nation,* 14 March 2003.

36. Summaries of these letters appeared in the Watchman column of the *Daily Nation* on 29 September 2001 and 1 November 2001.

37. Variant figures, all supplied by EABL, are reported in Clay Muganda, "Raising a Generation of Drunkards," *Daily Nation,* 31 March 2004, and "Is There an End to EABL's Deal-Making," *Daily Nation,* 29 March 2005.

38. Editorial, "Brews a Potential Disaster," *Daily* Nation, 11 June 2002; S. Kimanga, "No Money? Forget about Beer, Get a Sachet of Whisky," *Daily Nation,* 24 March 2004.

39. Chris Mburu, "EABL to Buy Distillers in Kenya, Uganda," *Daily Nation,* 24 June 2002.

40. Washington Akumu, "Spirits Firm Out to Increase Market Share," *Daily Nation,* 11 May 2004.

41. Kenyan Cane retailed at 30 shillings for 60 milliliters, compared to 10 shillings for a 30–50 milliliter minipack from other producers (Kimanga, "No Money? Forget about Beer, Get a Sachet of Whisky").

42. Advertisement, *Daily Nation,* 17 December 2003.

43. "Disco Deaths: Scene from Hell," *Standard,* 5 December 2004.

44. Taking a 2004 retail price of 60 shillings for a 330 milliliter bottle of Smirnoff Ice; and 10 shillings for a 30 milliliter sachet of whisky. See also Muganda, "Kenyan Youngsters Calling the Shots."

45. Nick Wachira, "EABL's Supercharged Profit Machine," *Daily Nation,* 13 September 2005.

46. Isaiah Andebe, "'Obama' Offers Serious Challenge to Informal Brews," *Daily* Nation, 12 May 2005; Wachira, "EABL's Supercharged Profit Machine"; Wachira King'aru, "Brewer's Upgrade to Cost Sh 2.5 bn," *Daily Nation,* 25 October 2005.

47. Emmanuel Wetang'ula, "Banning Alcohol Ads Not Enough," *Daily Nation,* 20 June 2005.

48. "Former Mayor Faces Bootleg Brew Charge," *Daily Nation,* 17 July 2002; Silvia Njeri, "Suit over Drinks Sale Dismissed," *East African Standard,* 18 July 2003; "I'm Innocent, Says Woman in Brew Case," *Daily Nation,* 27 July 2005.

49. Willis, *Potent Brews,* 213–14.

50. "Brew Death Toll Increases to Six," *Daily Nation,* 3 December 2005; "Death Toll from Illicit Beverage Rises to Six," *Daily Nation,* 14 December 2005.

51. "DC Warns Chiefs on Brewing of Liquor," *Standard,* 11 November 2004.

52. Daniel Kimani, letter, *Daily Nation,* 30 June 2005.

53. Mburu Mwangi, "Compelling Case Made to Legalise Traditional Brews," *Daily Nation,* 29 September 2005.

54. Simbi Kusimba, "Legalise Local Liquors, Urges Drugs Boss," *Daily Nation,* 28 September 2005.

55. Muna Wahome, "KRA Fetes Top Tax Contributors," *Daily Nation,* 3 November 2005.

56. "EABL Gets into High Spirits," *Daily Nation,* 28 March 2006; see, for example, the Smirnoff ad, *Daily Nation,* 10 December 2007.

57. "Brewers Form Lobby to Stop Alcohol Abuse," *Daily Nation,* 16 March 2007; advertisement in the *Daily Nation,* 17 July 2007. The "tusker na chapaa" campaign was a particularly egregious violation of this self-imposed "code"; see, for example, the ad in the *Daily Nation,* 29 June 2007.

58. John Oyuke, "Government Urged to Act on Underage Drinking," *Standard,* 12 December 2005; the most recent manifestation of the EABL campaign against underage drinking is the "We ID" campaign: see advertisement in the *Daily Nation,* 23 October 2007.

59. See Smirnoff ad in *Daily Nation,* 24 November 2006, and the "Raev It Up" poster and media campaign of 2006–7. For Tusker Project Fame, see, for example, the ad in the *Daily Nation,* 6 October 2006. A rather different reading of Project Fame—as a site for discourses on ethnicity—can be found in Mbugua wa Mungai, "Tusker Project Fame: Ethnic States, Popular Flows," *Journal of Eastern African Studies* 1, no. 3 (2007): 338–58.

60. "Here Come da Cans," ad in the *Daily Nation,* 23 April 2008.

Contributors

James R. Brennan is Assistant Professor of History at the University of Illinois. He received his PhD in African History from Northwestern University in 2002. He has published a number of articles and book chapters on nationalism and urbanization in Tanzania, and is currently researching the historical role of radio and other mass media in Eastern Africa's political culture. His publications include the coedited (with Andrew Burton and Yusuf Lawi) collection *Dar es Salaam: Histories from an Emerging African Metropolis.*

G. Thomas Burgess is Assistant Professor of African History at the U.S. Naval Academy. His research interests include generation, nationalism, and African intellectual history. Aside from numerous essays, his most recent book is *Race, Revolution, and the Struggle for Human Rights in Zanzibar.*

Andrew Burton is Honorary Research Associate of the British Institute in Eastern Africa, currently based in Addis Ababa. He has published widely on East African urban history. His publications include *African Underclass: Urbanisation, Crime and Colonial Order in Dar es Salaam* (Oxford, 2005), and (as editor) *The Urban Experience in Eastern Africa, ca. 1750–2000* (Nairobi, 2002), and (with James Brennan and Yusuf Lawi) *Dar es Salaam: Histories from an Emerging African Metropolis.*

Hélène Charton-Bigot is a CNRS researcher at the CEAN (Centre d'étude de l'Afrique noire) at the University of Bordeaux. She is a former assistant director of the Institut français de recherche en Afrique in Nairobi. Her main area of research is the history of education and elites in East Africa. She is currently working on a monograph on the making of the Kenyan elite after World War II. She coedited *Nairobi Contemporain, les paradoxes d'une ville fragmentée* with D. Rodriguez-Torres, and *L'Annuaire de l'Afrique de l'Est,* 2004 and 2005 with Claire Médard.

Shane Doyle is Senior Lecturer in African History at the University of Leeds, and has previously worked at the British Institute in Eastern Africa and the Cambridge Group for the History of Population and Social Structure. He is the author of a number of articles on Ugandan history and has recently published *Crisis and Decline in Bunyoro: Population and Environment in Western Uganda, 1860–1955* and, with Henri Médard, *Slavery in the Great Lakes Region of East Africa.* He is currently completing a project on the history of sexuality and demographic change in Great Lakes Africa.

Dave Eaton teaches African history at Albion College, Michigan. He received his PhD from Dalhousie University in 2008. He has published a number of articles and book chapters on pastoralism and conflict in Kenya and Uganda.

James L. Giblin is Professor of History at the University of Iowa. He is the author of two books, *A History of the Excluded: Making Family and Memory a Refuge from State in Twentieth-Century Tanzania* and *The Politics of Environmental Control in Northeastern Tanzania, 1840–1940.*

Eunice Kamaara is Associate Professor of Religious Studies at Moi University, Kenya. She has research interests in youth sexual and reproductive health from socioanthropological, ethical, and gender perspectives. Her publications include *Youth, Gender and HIV/AIDS: A Kenyan Experience.*

Joyce Nyairo is Senior Lecturer in the Department of Literature, Theatre and Film Studies at Moi University. She coedited *Urban Legends, Colonial Myths: Popular Culture & Literature in East Africa* and has published numerous articles on Kenyan popular music in a variety of journals such as *African Affairs, Journal of African Cultural Studies, Social Identities, Social Dynamics,* and *Scrutiny2.*

Richard Reid is Lecturer in the History of Africa at the School of Oriental and African Studies, University of London. He has previously taught at the University of Asmara in Eritrea and at Durham University. He is the author of *Political Power in Pre-Colonial Buganda, War in Pre-Colonial Eastern Africa, A History of Modern Africa: 1800 to the Present,* and a number of articles on various aspects of interstate conflict and liberation struggle in nineteenth- and twentieth-century northeast Africa. He is the editor of *Eritrea's External Relations: Understanding Its Regional Role and Foreign Policy* and is currently working on a history of conflict in northeast Africa.

Carol Summers is Professor of History at the University of Richmond in Richmond, Virginia. She is the author of *Colonial Lessons: Africans' Education in Southern Rhodesia, 1918–1940, From Civilization to Segregation,* and articles on both Zimbabwean and Ugandan history. Her current work on late colonial Uganda examines the development of mass politics, civil society, and political radicalism in Buganda from 1939 to 1956.

Richard Waller teaches in the history department at Bucknell University, Lewisburg, Pennsylvania. He has researched and written extensively on Maasai history and, more recently, on aspects of crime and the law in colonial Kenya.

Justin Willis is Reader in History at the University of Durham; from 2006 to 2009 he was seconded as Director of the British Institute in Eastern Africa. He is the author of *Potent Brews: A Social History of Alcohol in East Africa, c. 1850–1999.* Alongside other interests, he continues to research and teach on the social and cultural aspects of drinking in East Africa.

Index